LETTERS TO BELLE

Camp near Louisville Ky
Sept 29th 1862.

My Darling wife!

Yours of the 22d reached me yesterday on my return from "picket duty" with the regiment. How glad I was to hear from home you can scarcely appreciate. We went out on Saturday in a hard rain staid all night and the only effect it had on me was to make me as hungry as a bear. My Company was one of three in the extreme advance in the post of danger. 1st Lieutenant Abe Longworth of the 36th step son of Aunt Julia at Morris was also with us. I have been so busy in Camp I have had no time to do any thing in the way of writing home or to any one else. Last Friday was the first day I was out of Camp, in town to see about the "soldiers bounty

Letters to Belle

Civil War Letters and Life of Chicago Lawyer and Volunteer Colonel John A. Bross, 29TH U.S. Colored Infantry

John A. Bross
Justine Bross Yildiz

First published by John A. Bross and Justine Bross Yildiz in 2018

ISBN: 9781983368905

Cover image: Detail, Frederic Edwin Church, *Our Banner in the Sky* (1861); portraits (Private Collection).

For the descendants, physical and spiritual, of Colonel John A. Bross and the men who fought beside him

CONTENTS

PREFACE

The letters written by John Armstrong Bross between September 1862 and July 1864 were preserved by his widow, Belle, who gave them to their son, Mason. After Mason's death, they belonged to his widow, Isabel, and after her death, they belonged to her son, John Adams Bross, of McLean, Virginia, who gave them to his daughter, Justine Bross Yildiz, of Cambridge, Massachusetts. Justine personally transcribed the letters in 1996 and some twenty years later, in 2015, decided to work with her brother John Adams Bross, Jr., of Chicago, in publishing them. This volume is the result.

Justine and John engaged the expert staff of the Imaging Services of Harvard Library at the University's Widener Library to have the letters scanned, and the transcripts have been proofread from scanned images of the original letters, a procedure that is, of course, safer for the manuscripts and also easier to use, since texts can be magnified to help decipher passages that are difficult to read.

In transcribing the letters, we have been guided by an underlying principle of authenticity, keeping original spellings and punctuation where they would not be misunderstood or pose obstacles to a reasonable flow of legibility. For example, in the manuscripts the word "today" is shown as two words, and the word "stayed" is spelled "staid," and we have kept the original spacing and spelling because the meaning would be immediately understood. Where the word "battalion" was spelled by John as "battallion," we have dropped the extra "l" as a needless distraction, whether or not that was a permissible use in his day. Often there is a mark that might be a comma or might be a period; in such a case, an editorial choice has been made as to whether the writer intended one or two sentences.

The punctuation ". - -" has been used to indicate the beginning of a new thought that was denoted by a space between sentences; the writer's wish to save space on the rather small letter paper may have kept sentences together when they would otherwise have been put into separate paragraphs. New paragraphs in the transcriptions reflect those in the original text. A few words have been left marked as "illegible" after an earnest effort to decipher them. In one or two passages, portions of the original text have apparently been erased by Belle, such as a mildly critical remark about William, which she must have wished to prevent others from seeing. This suggests that she expected the letters to be read by others; perhaps our great-grandmother would have approved their eventual publication.

Needless to say, the handwriting of these 19th century letters is excellent, putting to shame the current state of penmanship in our era of typing and email. The condition of the paper is remarkably good after a century and a half. It is said that the paper used at the time of the First World War was considerably more acidic; letters and documents from that period are often in a more fragile state than those from the earlier Civil War period.

INTRODUCTION

"We marched down Pennsylvania Avenue in grand style and then to this point. I was pleased with the regt and the occasion. Little did I think three years ago when I sat on the steps of the Treasury building and looked down the Avenue to the Capitol and cried with indignation over the affairs of the country, that I should at this day march a regt of Colored Troops down that same avenue." – *Letter of May 1, 1864*

"I shall never forget my enthusiasm or the sublime scene as we retreated through a cedar forest, came out into the open field in front of our left, with the enemies left just behind us and their right wing coming forward over a large open field in splendid array advancing to the charge. Their two wings might be compared to a huge vise that was about to close up & crush our army and the Union at one turn of the rebel screw. The scene is engraven on the tablets of my memory & will ever be as vivid as the noon day sun." – *Letter of January 11, 1863, describing the Battle of Stones River*

"To day everything speaks and sings of thee. If I should have a skirmish I know I would go at it with blessings upon your name. Happy in our wedding, happy in seven years of wedded life, I feel a glow of pride and joy and intense devotion that I trust will increase while mortal life shall last, and 'Spread undivided operate unspent' through the countless ages of eternity. Oh! tongue cannot tell nor pen describe how much I should enjoy being with you to day! How gladly would I comply with your request to come home soon and fold you to my breast my own darling wife!" – *Letter of June 5, 1863, their seventh anniversary*

John Armstrong Bross (1826–1864) was a married, politically active, Chicago lawyer who at the age of 36 volunteered to join the Union Army during the Civil War. He raised two companies of infantry in the summer of 1862 and served as captain of one of them in Kentucky and Tennessee in the 88th Illinois Regiment during the remainder of 1862 and most of 1863, his regiment having been assigned to the Army of the Ohio, subsequently renamed the Army of the Cumberland. He saw action in October 1862 at the battle of Perryville, southeast of Louisville in Kentucky; at the end of December 1862 at the Battle of Murfreesboro, southeast of Nashville in Tennessee; and in September 1863 at the Battle of Chickamauga, a few miles south of Chattanooga, Tennessee, in Northern Georgia.

In late 1863 he returned to Illinois to raise and lead an African American regiment, the 29th Infantry, United States Colored Troops, the only black regiment from Illinois, which in April 1864 was transferred to the Army of the Potomac in Virginia and beginning in June 1864 took part in the siege of Petersburg, Virginia. On July 30, 1864, he was killed leading his troops into action at the Battle of the Crater, an innovative assault operation involving a tunnel and buried explosives to open a breach in the enemy line, which could have led to the capture of Petersburg and the fall of Richmond and shortened the war by eight months. But it was mismanaged and resulted in a disastrous defeat that General Grant called "the saddest affair I have witnessed in the war." John was survived by his widow, Belle Mason Bross, and one child, his son, Mason, who was two years old when his father went off to war and almost four at the time of his father's death.

While serving in the field after he left Chicago, John, like many other soldiers and officers serving on both sides of the conflict, continually engaged in correspondence, mostly with his wife, Belle; occasionally with his older brother William, who lived in Chicago; and with his father, Moses Bross, who lived in Morris, Illinois, with John's mother, Jane. Eighty-seven of his letters were preserved by his widow and are now in the possession of his great-granddaughter, Justine Bross Yildiz, of Cambridge, Massachusetts. The publication of these letters, together with several of his poems, is intended to make them available to his descendants because it offers them a more vivid understanding of their country's history as a part of their own family history, and to anyone who may find them of general or scholarly interest as a contribution to the existing literature of Civil War letters and diaries.

John's letters present the wartime experience and opinions of a volunteer Civil War officer who had been a well-educated lawyer with a 19th century fondness for poetry, who lived with his wife and family in the new and rapidly growing western frontier city of Chicago, and who, like virtually all inhabitants of that city, had moved to it from another part of the country. He began the war devoted to the Union but opposed to the abolition of slavery, yet ended by raising and leading an African American regiment that included many freed slaves. John grew up in the Delaware River Valley, where New York, New Jersey, and Pennsylvania come together, as one of twelve children in a family descended from Dutch settlers who had moved west from New Amsterdam in the late seventeenth century. He came to Chicago in 1848 at the age of 22 as a young law student, following his energetic older brother William, who had been his teacher and who had decided to begin a new career in the West, in a small town on Lake Michigan that seemed to him to have good potential for commercial growth.

The most important source of information about the life of Col. John A. Bross is a small book called *Memorial of Colonel John A. Bross, By A Friend,* published in 1865 in Chicago. This book contains a brief summary of his early years, an account of his service in the 88th Illinois Regiment in the Army of the Cumberland, his decision to lead an African American regiment in Illinois, the assignment of that regiment to the Army of the Potomac, and a detailed account of his death at the Battle of the Crater. It also includes several letters to his widow from soldiers and officers of the regiment and others who knew him, and several memorial resolutions and speeches about him made at a special proceeding of the Chicago Bar, of which he had been a member, as well as a memorial sermon by Arthur Swazey, the pastor of the Third Presbyterian Church in Chicago. The author of the book is unknown, but according to family tradition, it was written by his widow, Belle, who had literary talent.

In addition to the *Memorial,* there are thirteen letters, preserved at the Chicago History Museum, written by John's father, Moses Bross, to John's older brother William while he was a student at Williams College in

Williamstown, Massachusetts. These letters send William news of the family, including occasional items about his younger brother John, who was 12 years old when William graduated from college in 1838.

There are also several letters composed by William, some written while he was a student at Williams College, some written soon after he had graduated, and some written after he and his family moved to Chicago in 1848.

In addition, there are occasional references to John's activities in newspaper articles, especially in the *Chicago Tribune*, one of the last of these being a lengthy front-page memorial printed four days after his death.

In order to give an account of John's life, attention has to be given to the career and writings of John's 13-year-older brother, William, because William, about whom a much greater amount of published information is available, was a mentor for John throughout his life. John studied at Chester Academy, in Orange County, New York, where William was the principal and his teacher, graduating as the valedictorian of his class; his valedictorian address was directed to William as his instructor. John began studying law in Goshen, New York, but soon followed William to Chicago, continuing his law studies there and living with William and his family for the first two or three years after 1848. In Chicago during the 1850s, William became a prominent journalist and newspaper owner, and as he grew active in the new Republican Party after 1854, John also became politically involved. William's influence was probably decisive in securing John's commission in 1863 to raise the only African American regiment in Illinois and to serve as its commanding officer. Finally, the front-page memorial article about John in the *Chicago Tribune* was probably written by William. William's diaries would have been an invaluable source of information about John's life, but they were destroyed, along with many other irreplaceable records, in the Chicago Fire of 1871.

From one point of view, the story of John A. Bross is that of an average, though educated and socially prominent, citizen of mid-nineteenth century America in the new and rapidly growing Northern city of Chicago, who gradually became caught up in the unfolding story of racism as a major element in the political history and social fabric of the United States. He supported the new Republican Party, which wished to limit the spread of racial slavery but not abolish it, and he took an active role in the presidential campaign of Abraham Lincoln. When the Southern slave states acted to secede and dismantle the Union in order to preserve their "peculiar institution" of slavery based on race, John, like most Northerners, understood the rebellion as a mortal challenge to their cherished Union, which they believed had brought a new life of freedom and equality for its citizens and which they considered a beacon of hope to the world. Being married with a child, John did not at first volunteer for the Union Army, but in the second year of the war, when things were going badly for the Union cause, he did enlist, believing that it was his duty to take a leave of absence from his family and to risk his life in battle for the "old flag," to save the Union.

Abolition of black slavery was no more the goal for him than it was for most Northerners. But the Confederate challenge to the Union was based on racial slavery, and the underlying racial nature of the conflict inevitably came to the surface when Lincoln decided that in order to save the Union it was necessary to strike at slavery with the Emancipation Proclamation and soon thereafter concluded that blacks should serve as soldiers, which implied eventual citizenship and equal rights. These things were abhorrent to the South and by no means fully accepted in the North. Illinois, for example, had a code of black laws that forbade blacks even the legal right to live in the state; these laws were mostly ignored, especially in the northern part of the state around Chicago, but they were legally in effect until they were abolished shortly after the Civil War. John, in sympathy from the start with the Lincoln administration, became personally caught up in these questions of slavery and race when he accepted a commission to become the commander of a black regiment in Illinois. His regiment was sent into battle before it had attained the fully required number of enlistments, so that at the time of his death he remained a lieutenant colonel rather than a full colonel.

Racial prejudice was the primary reason for John's death, since it was General Meade's general disapproval of blacks as soldiers that caused him at the last minute to remove specially trained black regiments from leading the assault that followed the explosion of the mine at Petersburg. And racial prejudice was responsible for the murder of President Lincoln after he had succeeded in abolishing slavery but before he had time to move American society away from the racism that had been used to justify it. We cannot know how much Lincoln might have accomplished, but it is clear that after his death the federal government lost interest in questions of racial inequality. For the next hundred years, official racial oppression of blacks persisted, not in the form of legal slavery but in the system known as Jim Crow, a network of state laws, mostly in the former slave states, that deprived blacks of the basic rights of citizenship, especially the right to vote. These laws were ideologically based, as slavery itself had been, on the theory of white supremacy. The cause for racial equality in American society was greatly strengthened by the work of Martin Luther King and the civil rights movement of the 1960s, but it is clear that racism was still powerfully present in American society as this was written in 2017.

Chicago lawyer and volunteer Lieutenant Colonel John A. Bross willingly offered his life to defend the Union, a Union whose meaning was changing and which would now include what he approved of as the "new birth of freedom" proclaimed by Lincoln. The Union was saved and slavery was abolished. The new birth of freedom, which Lincoln probably understood as including racial equality, has not been fully achieved to this day, but John's able and sympathetic leadership of his black regiment helped lay the foundation for full equality, including racial equality, even if that was to be postponed to future years. He wrote in a letter to Belle shortly before his death, "Whatever be my fate, I know I can give to my child this one thing: 'his father fought for the Union and the old flag.'"

PART ONE

The Life and Death of Colonel John A. Bross

Colonel John A. Bross (Private Collection).

CHAPTER 1

Growing Up in the Delaware Valley 1826–1848

John Armstrong Bross was born in 1826 into a large and active family of farmers and tradesmen in the town of Milford, in Pike County in eastern Pennsylvania, among the tall forests and rolling hills of the Delaware River Valley. John was the seventh child in a family of nine sons and three daughters, of whom only one daughter died in infancy.[1] The father of the family, Moses Bross, was born in 1795 and in 1812 was married to their mother, Jane Winfield, who was born in 1798. Their oldest child, William, was born in 1813, when Jane was 15 years old, and their youngest child was born 25 years later in 1838. Large families were not unusual in early nineteenth century America.

Moses and Jane began their marriage living with Jane's widowed mother, Margaret Winfield, in an old log house on the east bank of the Delaware River situated near a point where the Neversink River runs into the Delaware. They lived in what is now the town of Montague in the northwestern corner of New Jersey, just south of the New York state border. Moses had grown up in this neighborhood, two or three miles from Port Jervis, in Orange County, New York. In this area three states come together, New York and New Jersey on the east side of the Delaware River and Pennsylvania on the west side. The river was the highway; commercial traffic and social life were more focused on the Delaware River than on the state lines.

1817 map of New York state by Amos Lay, showing the Delaware River Valley region where John grew up (Library of Congress).

After the birth of William, Moses built his family a new house on a nearby 57-acre piece of land that Moses bought just west of the house of his father, Peter Bross. There Moses established a tanning and shoemaking business. One of William's earliest memories was that he and his younger brother Stephen fell into one of the tanning vats and nearly drowned "before rescued by some kindly hand."[2]

In 1822 Moses and his family moved across the river to Milford, on the Pennsylvania side, where he began a business to supply lumber for the new

Delaware and Hudson Canal. There John was born, their seventh child, on February 21, 1826. Their new house stood on a hill just north of the mouth of the Vandemark Creek. William described their Milford home in an unpublished recollection of his family and childhood:

> It was a romantic, beautiful spot. A spur of the Blue Mountains bounded the eastern view; while another ran parallel to it in Pennsylvania (Pike Co.) to the west and the beautiful rich Delaware valley lies nestled between them as far as the eye can reach to the south. The valley north of Port Jervis is shut in by the Shawangunk Mountains. The Delaware River for months in the summer was placid and most beautiful. In winter it afforded fine skating & in the spring the breaking of the ice & the floods that followed filled my boyish mind with the most sublime & thrilling emotions. I attribute my strong love for natural scenery and my disposition to travel to the early teachings of my boyhood's home.[3]

The family's Bross ancestors were Dutch settlers in what had been the colony of New Netherlands until the English captured the city of New Amsterdam in 1664 and changed the name of the city and the colony to New York. New Netherlands, founded by Dutch traders in 1624, had extended its claims from the Connecticut River on the east to the Delaware River on the west, which ran south to Delaware Bay.[4] The colony was centered on the growing city of New Amsterdam on the island of Manhattan at the mouth of the Hudson River and extended north along the Hudson to Fort Orange, whose name the English later changed to Albany, where the Mohawk River meets the Hudson River. During the forty years of Dutch rule under the Dutch West India Company, the colony's settlers had moved north up the Hudson River Valley, east to Long Island, and west some fifty miles across what became New Jersey to the Delaware River Valley, clearing fields for farms and building settlements. As their settlements grew, they interacted, often peaceably and often not, with the Native American tribes who lived in those areas.[5]

By the time John was born, the former Dutch colony had been English for over a century and then, some fifty years before, had become part of a new independent nation, the United States of America. John's grandfather, Abraham Winfield, had been a lieutenant in the American Revolutionary Army. But the Dutch heritage was not forgotten: New York localities often retained Dutch names such as Renssaeler, or Dutch words, such as *Plattkill*, combining the word *platt* for flat and an old Dutch word *kill*, meaning "stream" or "clove," from an old Dutch word meaning "ravine or valley," which William used to refer to the valley where he was born. New Amsterdam, like the new Dutch nation from which it came, was a place where tolerance and relative freedom of thought had from the beginning encouraged the settlement of immigrants from diverse places; the language and the culture were Dutch, but many or most of the population came from other places.[6] The well-known characterization of New York as a melting pot in a nation of immigrants came from its Dutch heritage: both before and after the English takeover, Dutch settlers had intermarried with English, Scottish, French Huguenot, and other groups.[7]

There are proud references in William's letters to the family's Dutch heritage: in an 1837 letter to a college classmate, William promises to correspond "after the manner of a <u>Dutchman</u>," and in a letter from Chicago to his sister written the day after New Year's, 1852, he tells her that "we kept the day after the good old Knickerbocker style." His wife, he said, was honored with many calls: "She was (in the eyes of <u>her husband at least</u>) a fine example of what a '<u>gude vrow</u>' is & should be." *Gude vrow* was Dutch for "good wife."

The family was also aware of other ancestral traditions. In his memoir, William speculated that his name might be a shortened form of the Huguenot French name "de la Brosse." William, like most Americans of his time, admired French culture. He also wondered whether Bross might be a German name and wrote that his mother's name, Winfield, could signify a Welsh tradition of military courage. Scottish culture had also come to be admired and John was proud of his wife's Scottish ancestry: in a letter of 1864, written to John's widow soon after his death, his friend Dr. Mackay said, "The bond of union which existed between us I owe principally to my being a Scot. Among the first things he told me was, that his wife was Scotch, and often he said he hoped to introduce me to his father-in-law, at Sterling."[8]

As in almost every area of North America, the settlers of the Delaware Valley collided culturally and often quarreled with existing Native American populations, especially as they and the settlers became involved in wars between the European powers. William Bross's book, *Legend of the Delaware*, written during his retirement, furnishes an unhappy but fairly typical illustration of the hostility that arose between the Native Americans and the European descendants, often based on completely different cultural views of land ownership.[9] The book contains, among other things, a short novella about a man named Tom Quick "the Indian Slayer," whom we now recognize to have been emotionally unhinged. His father had been killed and scalped by Delaware Indians who had once been family friends, and Tom spent the rest of his life murdering Native Americans of all ages and both sexes, long after peace had been made.[10] The novella is really a piece of family history, since Tom Quick was the uncle of William and John's grandmother, Jane Winfield, and it contains long, loving descriptions of the scenery of the Delaware River Valley where William and John had grown up. It ends with the happy engagement of Jane to the handsome Revolutionary War officer Abraham Winfield, their grandfather.[11]

The *Legend of the Delaware* claims, in the introduction, to be the translation of a manuscript in Old Dutch, found in an attic near Port Jervis, New York, translated by the fictitious Jacobus Van Wyck and sent to the editor of Port Jervis, New York's *Evening Gazette*. This is another reference to the Bross family's Dutch ancestry as well as a light-hearted tribute to Washington Irving, referring to Irving's *Legends of the Alhambra*, and even more to Irving's *History of New York*, which began as a series of newspaper articles about the history of New Amsterdam, purportedly translated from an old Dutch manuscript written by the fictitious Diderich Knickerbocker and sent to the *New York Evening Post*.

As might have been expected of descendants of Dutch settlers, Moses's family belonged to the Dutch Reformed Church near Port Jervis. In his unpublished memoir, William recounts the religious conversion of the family during his early childhood:

> But to return to my Father's early history. He was a pretty wild boy & gay young man. In 1816 Rev. Phineas Camp, just licensed to preach by the

> Hudson Presbytery, held a series of meetings in the old Mahackemack church. The church was a quaint old affair and stood directly opposite the cemetery on the west side of the Neversink river, near where the Erie Ry. crosses over it. In this church I first heard the gospel preached by Rev. C. C. Elting. I might write many paragraphs about the impressions the services made on my boyish mind. Under the preaching of Mr. Camp my Father and Mother united with the church in 1817. In 1818 or about that time, my father was elected deacon (Elder) in the Dutch church near the Brick House. This church and the Mahackemack were both under the pastoral care of Rev. C. C. Elting.
>
> My father's labors in the church and in prayer meetings were incessant and effective. He also was largely influential in building school houses, one near John Nearpa's, one near Jas. R Cole's and one near Peter Van Noy's all in the Clove and all of which I attended.
>
> [I]n 1822 father moved from his home in Red Brook near my grand father's to Milford. It was then & still is the shire town of Pike Co. The only public buildings then in the place were an old dilapidated school house and the court house, with a fish for a weather-cock. Not a church organization of any kind then existed in the place. Sabbath was given up to drinking and horse racing and gambling & all kinds of wickedness stalked abroad at noon-day. Occasionally a missionary like Rev Wm Jainlow came along and held a service or two, but it seemed to have little or no effect upon the habits and morals of the place. This state of things my father in the strength of his Divine Master set himself diligently at work to correct.[12]

When he crossed the river to Milford in 1822, Moses became one of three founders of the First Presbyterian Church of Milford, which initially met in a local office but soon built a wooden church. The move from a Dutch Reformed to a Presbyterian church was not a major theological step, since both churches were in the Calvinist tradition, but it represented a positive decision by Moses to take seriously his Christian faith.[13]

As Presbyterians, Moses and his family were deeply committed to education. Some education was obviously necessary for everyone for the general business of life, but it was especially important for Protestants because reading and understanding the Bible, believed to be the word of God, was essential for salvation. Study of the Bible, preaching, and teaching, grounded in sound scholarship, based, for Presbyterians at least, on the writings of John Calvin, made the difference between successful lives in fulfillment of the word of God and failed lives of sin and despair, of which there were numerous examples in every community. Children were usually taught to read from the family Bible.

Because of their respect for education and because they probably hoped that their son would become an influential Presbyterian minister, it is not surprising that William attended Williams College in Williamstown, Massachusetts. He prepared for college by studying for two years at Milford Academy, which was run by The Rev. Edward Allen, who had come to Milford in connection with the new Presbyterian Church of which Moses had been a founder.[14] According to one account, William walked from Milford to Williamstown. Money was often scarce for the family, but it was evidently worth considerable sacrifice to Moses to have his oldest son educated at Williams College, which he considered to be an institution of great spiritual authority. Their second son, Stephen, two years younger than William, also began studying at Williams but left without graduating. William was 21 years old when he entered Williams College and 25 when he graduated.

The importance for the Bross family of biblical scripture and education, and of Christian faith as the high purpose of education, is amply demonstrated in thirteen surviving letters by Moses written to William while he was attending college between 1834 and 1838.[15]

In an insert to Moses's letter of January 31, 1836, to William and Stephen, in which he reports the birth three days earlier of a new baby boy, their sister Margaret writes that she will soon be going to the Troy Female Seminary:

> My dear Brothers.... How much cause have I to praise God for his goodness in thus providing a way for me to complete my education. Surely are we not favoured much more than some of our near relatives who are as good by nature as we? When I reflect on what privileges we

> enjoy and have enjoyed, I am constrained to say that if any who live in this enlightened land live in ignorance and go down to Hell it will be a Hell indeed.

In the same letter there is also a short insert from John, then aged 10:

> Dear Brothers i have quit goin to school for this winter and I have to make shoes all the time and i like the business. Edward [a younger brother born in 1833] begins to talk quite a good deal ... he is all the time teasing mother to call the babe Stephen, I dont know how Edward come to call Stephen such a name but he has his own name for every thing.
>
> your affectionate Brother
> John A. Bross

Probably John had objected to further schooling, and his parents had wisely put him to work at a useful task that his father knew well from his former business. However, John was evidently persuaded to go on with his studies, since in a letter of February 14, 1837, when John was 11, Moses reports:

> Peter, Josiah & John go to school to Cousin Ira, they are to use John's expression roaring it out in the Old Academy in their weekly speeches, and Cousin is striving to teach the young idea how to shoot.[16] Phinney goes to C. Young's and Jane Ann to Miss E. Benton and now you are ready to ask, how can you get along and send all your help to school. I answer it is hard making both ends meet, our fare is of the humblest kind—my eye is on the end of the race.

There are other references to lack of funds. In a letter of March 11, 1835, Moses informs William that a letter from William enclosing a ten-dollar note was a timely arrival:

> It may not be amiss to acknowledge the hand of God in this event. We were out of bread and I had been hunting for money to buy with and got none, next I endeavored to borrow of those that had and they said

> we cannot help you (be fed and clothed) and arriving at the post office they gave me the letter as above stated. I felt somewhat distressed in mind but not cast down believing that God would provide although night began to spread her sable curtain around me and my little ones had no bread for supper or Sabbath. You can faintly imagine the feeling of gratitude was felt by all of us.

In the same letter there is an insert by Margaret that refers to William's lack of good clothes: "How do I long for the time when you shall come home. You cannot imagine my feelings when you wrote home you was ragged. I thought William would be looked down upon as a little inferior to those whose clothes were of the finest textures."

But apparently it was well worth financial hardship for Moses and Jane to have their son at an educational institution of such spiritual excellence. In his letter of February 14, 1837, Moses wrote: "Your notice of college refreshes my soul and my prayer shall be Lord through thy work make my favorite college the scene of a glorious refreshing from thy presence—may the Holy Ghost rest on Williams, such influence be felt within her walls that shall bring down at the foot of the Cross the tallest sinners and make them ambassadors for Jesus."

John evidently loved music; his musical education would have come from singing hymns in church rather than from any study in school. In a letter of November 2, 1834, when John was 8 years old Moses remarks, "And while I am writing you this Epistle little John is singing Bishop Hebert's beautiful missionary hymn From Greenland's Icy Mountains etc. with a voice all most angelical." Music continued to be an important part of his life: in Chicago he would be put in charge of the choir and the children's music at the Third Presbyterian Church; the *Memorial* relates that as the commander of his regiment, he would often improve morale by leading his men in song.

Moses's plan that his sons should be educated for church leadership didn't work out quite as he had hoped, since neither William nor Stephen nor John became an ordained minister of the Gospel, but it did bear fruit in other ways. William and John both became strong supporters of the Presbyterian Church in Chicago, William like his father serving as a Deacon and being afterwards often referred to in public as "Deacon Bross." William became a successful and influential journalist, founding first a religious newspaper and then a political newspaper, which after a few years merged with the *Chicago Tribune.* Through his journalism and his political activism, William worked to achieve social and political goals that reflected his father's Presbyterian vision for a just society, including a flourishing Presbyterian presence in Chicago, the energetic development of commerce and communications, the election of Abraham Lincoln, and unwavering support for the Lincoln administration in its struggle to preserve the Union and abolish slavery. John began a successful career as a lawyer in Chicago, where he also actively supported the Presbyterian Church and pursued similar progressive social and political ideals. After John's death in 1864, the speeches and resolutions in his memory included numerous references to his Christian faith and his participation in the Church.

Moses and Jane lived to see all this. In 1863 they moved to Morris in Grundy County, Illinois, a busy transportation center on the Michigan and Illinois Canal, the waterway that linked Lake Michigan to the Mississippi River by way of the Illinois River. There William bought them land and a house. During the war, Moses and Jane corresponded with John; John's letters reflect his ongoing respect for his parents.

William graduated from Williams College in 1838, in debt by the then-considerable sum of $600. He considered making a career of lecturing on natural philosophy in Milford, but his father diplomatically reminded him, in a letter of April 24, 1837, that he could earn more money in Milford by cutting timber than he could by giving lectures: "You have no apparatus and without it you could not make your illustrations interesting to the Vulgus Populi of this place. You must not forget that I should be pleased to hear you exert yourself for the good of your native place but I remember that a prophet is not without honor save in his own country and in his own house." William evidently agreed and decided that teaching would be a more dependable way of earning his living. He accepted a position as principal of Ridgebury Academy, a school in the town of Ridgebury in Orange County, New York, just a few miles from the place of his birth. Five years later he moved to Chester Academy in the town of Chester, also in Orange County, and led the academy there for another five years. One of the students at Chester Academy was his thirteen-year-younger brother, John.

John was twelve years old when William graduated from Williams College in 1838. John lived with the family at Milford and apparently pursued studies in some fashion while probably also doing useful work. In his letter of April 24, 1837, Moses reports that he had been in "tight times this winter to get bread and meat but times are easier now" and that "the boys say they would like to study Latin and if I was ever at a loss what would be duty it is at this time—do you ask me which I answer—all of them—and John is the most anxious." Although the family was never far from financial hardship, the boys wanted to study Latin and Moses felt a serious obligation to find a way for them to do so. John was apparently the most eager student.

In 1843, when William became the head of Chester Academy, John was 17 years old, and it was probably then that he began his studies there under William's direction. John may have received a family discount for tuition, and it might have been William's suggestion for a favorite and promising younger brother. In any case, John seems to have been a good student. He was the valedictorian when he graduated, evidently in 1846. His valedictorian speech was a lengthy and well-crafted discourse on the theme of change in human life, ornamented with rhetorical flourishes suitable for the nineteenth century and for his age. The last two paragraphs are the Valedictory, in which he addresses William as his instructor:

> My instructor and brother and fellow students of Chester Academy:
>
> The present occasion is one of peculiar interest to us all. It brings home to our minds in living reality the constancy of change. You as instructors have spent five years in this institution exerting yourself for the good of your fellow beings. You have stamped your influence upon hundreds who have gone forth upon the wide world to seek fame, fortune, and renown. The close of every term has seen them bidding farewell to these halls and tomorrow you finish your own course, and as a teacher leave its precincts forever. The relation in which we stand prevents my

saying in behalf of myself and fellow students what might otherwise be proper. Be it our care never to forget your instruction and advice.

Schoolmates! What shall I say to you? What can I say? If you have never felt that time is change, feel it now. During the last time we have shared together the troubles and pleasures of the recitation hour. The joyous laugh has echoed and reechoed through these halls. Nothing has occurred to mar those better feelings existing in our hearts. The exercises of this evening close up our connexion as a body and tomorrow's sun goes down beholding the separation of teacher and pupil, friend and schoolmate, as such to meet no more forever. When next the sound of the morning bell shall ring along these hills and vales, these halls shall echo with the footsteps and voice of strangers, science shall be taught by other tongues and the goddess of eloquence wooed by other votaries. Schoolmates! This is change. May heaven shower his richest blessings upon each and all of you, may you keep in mind the truth that time is change and knowing this may you continually change for the better, so that eternal happiness shall be your lot. With a heart full of friendship and love for you all, I can only bid you

"Farewell! A word that hath been and must be
A sound that makes us linger yet, Farewell."[17]

The members of the Bross family, whom William good-naturedly referred to in his letter to his sister Margaret as "the tribe of Jane and Moses," clearly felt close to each other, but the relationship between William and John must have been especially close, since William had been in actual charge of John's high school education.[18]

The *Memorial* says that John had entertained plans for a collegiate course and "had fitted himself for that purpose; but circumstances prevented the prosecution of his designs." John may have wished to follow William and Stephen in studying at Williams College, but Moses and Jane probably decided that they didn't have the resources to support another child at college and possibly that such an effort was unlikely to achieve their objective of raising up a leader in the church, since neither William nor Stephen had become ministers of the Gospel. Stephen had, in fact, dropped out of college and gone to New York City, losing all contact with his family. Whatever the reason, the *Memorial* states of John that "making choice of the profession of the law, he commenced the study of that science in Goshen, New York." In those days one studied law, not by attending law school but by reading law and helping out for several years at the offices of a practicing lawyer; it was in the nature of a professional apprenticeship. William evidently had a hand in this decision, as John became a student in the Goshen law firm of Booth & Jansen, Jansen probably the brother of William's wife, Mary Jane Jansen.

By 1846 John was twenty years old and a successful graduate of Chester Academy, beginning his studies for a legal career in the state of New York, not far from the corner of New Jersey where his ancestors had lived for generations. Later that year when William made a visit to the West and began thinking about a new life for himself and his family, he probably had it in mind to suggest that his former student and favorite younger brother should come along with him to the western frontier.

NOTES

1. The eleven children of Moses and Jane Bross who survived infancy and their years of birth: William (1813), Stephen Decatur (1815), Margaret (1819), Peter (1821), Josiah H. F. (1823), John Armstrong (1826), Phineas Camp (1828), Jane Ann (1830), Edward Allen (1833), Ira B. Newman (1836), and Charles Edmonston (1838).
2. William Bross, *William Bross Papers*, Chicago History Museum.
3. Ibid., Jan 5, 1874.
4. Russell Shorto, *The Island at the Center of the World: The Epic Story of Dutch Manhattan and the Forgotten Colony That Shaped America* (New York: Vintage Books, 2005), 43.
5. Ibid., 50.
6. Ibid., 95.
7. Ibid., 270–272, 317–18.
8. *Memorial of Colonel John A. Bross, Twenty-Ninth U. S. Colored Troops, By A Friend* (Chicago: Tribune Book and Job Office, 1865), 78.
9. Both Russell Shorto's *Island at the Center of the World* and William Cronon's *Nature's Metropolis; Chicago and the Great West* provide useful and detailed accounts of early American and colonial land ownership histories and contracts.

10. William Bross, *Legend of the Delaware: An Historical Sketch of Tom Quick. To which is Added the Winfield Family*, Chicago, 1893 (Nabu Public Domain Reprints).
11. The novella centers on the story of Tom Quick told from an unapologetically Eurocentric point of view, using language which would be unacceptable today but which reflects the generally accepted opinions of dominant European-descent society in the nineteenth century: "Then and there, over the dead savage, Tom made a solemn vow of eternal enmity to the whole Indian race, and that he would kill them wherever he could find them; and most faithfully, thus far, has he kept that vow. Aside from the precepts of the Holy Book, who can blame him? ... It is related in the traditions that ninety-nine Indians were killed by Tom as a sacrifice to the manes of his father; and that he regretted, most deeply, that he had not made it an even hundred. The facts in relation thereto would make this history too horribly monotonous for this age. He gloried in the name of the 'Avenger of the Delaware'" (*Legend*, 85). In the 1880s William paid for the erection of a large, obelisk- shaped monument in Milford inscribed "Tom Quick 'The Indian Slayer' or 'Avenger of the Delaware,'" with a plaque explaining that the monument was erected by a fifth-generation descendant of Thomas Quick Sr., who had become Lieutenant Governor of Illinois (he did not name himself). By the late twentieth century, the monument was attracting unfavorable attention, perhaps because Tom Quick was in fact a psychopathic racist serial killer; it was damaged by unknown persons and although subsequently repaired, has wisely been kept in undisclosed storage by the Pike County Historical Society.
12. William Bross, *Papers*, 13–15.
13. In the 1870s the wooden church was replaced by a handsome brick structure to which William contributed the bell and the clock in the tower, although by that time Moses and Jane had also moved to Illinois.
14. *Biographical Sketches of the Leading Men of Chicago; Written by the Best Talent of the Northwest* (Chicago: Wilson & St. Clair, 1868), 36.
15. The letters, which include information about John as he was growing up, are preserved at the Chicago History Museum. They are large folded sheets, written by Moses and often signed "Moses and Jane Bross," suggesting that Jane shared in their composition. Occasionally they contain written messages, letters within letters, from Margaret, their first daughter and third child, and one from John. They display a fairly high level of literary ability; the handwriting of both Moses and Margaret is well formed and legible, comparing favorably to most handwriting in the present age of computers and text messages.

16. "Delightful task! To rear the tender thought,/ To teach the young idea how to shoot." James Thomson, *The Seasons* "Spring," 1728, lines 1149–1150.
17. Transcription of the speech by Justine Yildiz; the handwritten original has disappeared.
18. William Bross, *Papers*, January 2, 1851.

CHAPTER 2

Building a Career and a Family in Chicago, 1848 to 1862

In October 1846 William started on his tour of observation, visiting Chicago, St. Louis, and other western cities. A chapter on William in *Biographical Sketches of the Leading Men of Chicago,* "Written by the Best Talent of the Northwest" and published in Chicago in 1868, relates that "He found at the head of Lake Michigan a little town, and recognized it as the future focus of the commerce of the great Northwest, when the West should be settled and its vast resources developed. He had faith in Chicago, and showed his faith by his works. He decided to make it his home. He closed his school and moved hither, arriving in the Garden City on the 12th of May, 1848."[1]

William's wife and children arrived in Chicago three months later in August. John left his legal studies in Orange County and arrived four months later in December, probably convinced by his older brother to join him in seeking their fortune in the West. Two of the eleven children of Moses and Jane Bross were now established in Chicago, and others would follow them to Illinois, finally including Moses and Jane themselves.

In 1848 the city of Chicago was beginning an era of rapid growth that astonished the world. In 1812 Chicago had consisted of one small fort, Fort Dearborn, and five houses of trading families outside the fort.[2] In August

1812, as a result of the war with Britain and some poor judgment by its commander, who carried out an evacuation under unnecessarily risky conditions, the better part of the garrison of some 60 men, along with two of nine women and most of the 19 children, were slaughtered and the rest taken prisoner by Potawatomie Indians who sided with the British. After this notorious "Fort Dearborn Massacre," the fort was rebuilt in 1817, and traders again settled around it.[3] By 1830 the population of Chicago was estimated at only 250 people, but there were distinct possibilities.[4] The little community was situated at the western end of the Great Lakes navigation system with a good prospect of connection to the Mississippi River if a short canal were constructed. In addition, it could become the natural commercial and transportation center for vast areas of unsettled but fertile land that lay west and north of Lake Michigan, but only if the title of the Indian tribes to those lands could be extinguished.

The next step, therefore, was to remove the Indian population of Illinois and Wisconsin to lands west of the Mississippi. In September 1833 a grand council of tribal chiefs was held for several days in Chicago and when it ended, a treaty was signed with the United Nation of Chippewa, Ottawa, and Pottawatomie tribes, by which the Native Americans ceded to the United States their title to the greater part of northeastern Illinois and southern Wisconsin. It was clear to the weakened tribes that they had no alternative: "The result of the treaty was what might have been expected. The Indians gave up their land and agreed for certain considerations, the most of which did not redound to their profit, to cede all their lands to the Government, and to leave forever their homes and the graves of their fathers for a land far toward the setting sun, which they had never seen and of which they knew nothing."[5]

Almost immediately settlers began to flow into the lands just acquired from the Pottawatomies and into all the western territory of Illinois, which had earlier been ceded to the United States but which had been blocked from settlement by the Indian territory around Chicago. Chicago was the logical portal to this territory and to distant new territories opening up in California and the Pacific Northwest. In August 1833 Chicago was legally organized as a town with an estimated population of 250. Three and a half years later, in March 1837, Chicago was incorporated as a city; its first census, taken in July, showed a grand total of 4,170 people.[6]

In 1834 the price of land in Chicago had become the subject of frenzied speculation, and prices had rapidly climbed to dizzying heights before the bubble burst in May 1837, leaving widespread ruin. This was followed by a depression that lasted until business began to recover slowly after 1840; in that year the population stood at 4,500. By 1845 the population reached 12,100 and by 1850, it more than doubled to 28,000, making the Chicago the 24th ranking city in the United States. Within the next decade, the city's population quadrupled and by 1860, at the eve of the Civil War, less than 25 years after its incorporation as a city, Chicago's population stood at 112,200, making it the ninth largest of the nation's cities.[7]

Two major events in 1848, the year of William and John's arrival, contributed to the growth of Chicago's importance and prosperity. The first was the opening of the Illinois and Michigan Canal from Chicago to LaSalle, Illinois, where it joined the Illinois River, which runs into the Mississippi River, so that shipping could now go from Chicago to the Mississippi and down to New Orleans and the Gulf of Mexico. Such a canal had been envisioned as early as 1673 by the French explorer Louis Joliet, but no action was taken until 1822, after Illinois became a state and requested and received from Congress permission to cut a canal through those public lands, along with a grant of ninety feet on each side of it. Construction did not commence until 1836 and soon was halted by the economic depression that lasted for several years and brought the state to the brink of bankruptcy. The project was reorganized in 1845 and on April 10, 1848, the *General Fry*, the first boat to make the journey on the new canal, arrived in Chicago, greeted by Mayor Woodworth and a cheering crowd.[8]

One unforeseen consequence of the Illinois and Michigan Canal was to keep Chicago in Illinois rather than having it become part of Wisconsin. The Ordinance of 1787 had authorized the organization of three states south of a line running east and west from the most southerly point of Lake Michigan; Chicago lay north of that line. John Wentworth, who was then a congressman from the Chicago area, recalled later that allegiance to Wisconsin had a lot of support from local residents and that Wisconsin might well have been successful in claiming all the land north of the Ordinance line "but for the embarrassment that would be caused by having the Illinois & Michigan canal owned by two states... and Illinois [had] been cut off from the lakes and her Legislature saved from the annoyance of Chicago lobbyists."[9]

The year's other major event occurred at 4:00 pm on November 20, 1848, when a retrofitted 11-year-old wood-burning locomotive called *The Pioneer* pulled away from Chicago with about 100 stockholders and editors seated in two baggage wagons to open Chicago's first railroad, the Galena & Chicago Union, which at that time ran just ten miles west from the city to the Des Plaines River. On the return trip, a farmer's wagon load of grain was transferred onto one of the cars, and this was the first shipment of grain by rail to Chicago.[10]

Chicago's position as a railroad center in the 1850s was more than anything else what made possible the city's extraordinary growth. The advantage to farmers of shipping by rail was immediately obvious: a report to Congress in 1852 stated that railroads could move wheat and corn at a tenth of the cost of transportation by ordinary road.[11] Farmers immediately began shipping their grain on the new Galena & Chicago Union road, which quickly became profitable. A Chicago merchants' pamphlet of 1856 noted that the Galena railroad had demonstrated that "owing to the cheapness with which railroads could be built... and the further fact that the resources of the country would at once furnish them with an immense business, railroads in Illinois would pay a large profit to the stockholders, and hence Eastern capitalists were willing to invest their means in these public improvements."[12] By 1852 there were five railroads in Chicago: two running to the west, the Galena & Chicago Union and the Chicago & Rock Island; two running to the east, the Michigan Southern & Northern Indiana and the Michigan Central; and one running to the south, the Illinois Central.[13] By 1856 Chicago was the focus of ten trunk lines, with 58 passenger trains and 38 freight trains arriving daily.[14]

With the new canal, and with the coming of the railroads in the 1850s, the whole territory to the west began to look to Chicago as the center of its trade and transportation. This shifted trade away from the river towns, especially St. Louis, Chicago's early rival for leadership of the Middle West.

"The river towns had, since the first settlement, enjoyed a monopoly of the public favor, and even for some time after a few railroads had been chartered, these proposed highways seemed to push towards the river and to promise most of their benefits to the river sections. St. Louis, especially, which had for many years enjoyed a large river trade, was looking for still greater commercial supremacy.... The Illinois Central Railroad may be called the first great 'St. Louis cut-off,' and as such placed Chicago firmly upon her throne as the magnificent Queen of the West."[15]

One important effect of the railroads, in addition to superseding rivers and canals, was to contribute to a change in the general direction of trade

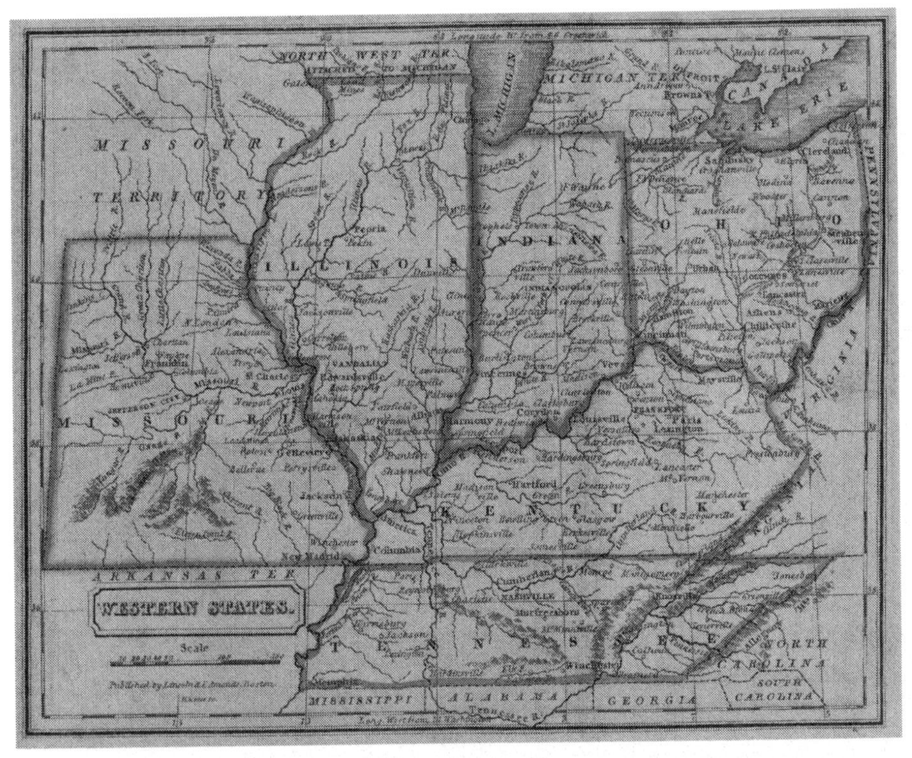

"Western States," 1832, by Daniel Adams (David Rumsey Map Collection).

Note the position of Illinois as part of what is now the called the Midwest and the Great Lakes region, connecting it with commercial interests on the East Coast.

from north-south, the direction of steamboats on major rivers, to east-west, the direction of most railroads.[16] This became a significant political factor in 1861, when the Civil War broke out. Southern Illinois was dominated by river communities, which were bound to New Orleans and the seceding Southern states by commerce on the Mississippi and consequently were sympathetic to the Confederacy. But the coming of the railroads in the 1850s had swiftly increased the population of Chicago and northern Illinois, binding the farmers and merchants of northern Illinois to the business and culture of New England and the Mid-Atlantic states. At the beginning of the war, the people of northern and eastern Illinois were solidly for the Union, while the people of southern Illinois around Cairo, where the Ohio River meets the Mississippi, were mostly in favor of the Confederacy.

In 1848, before the railroads had been built, a trip west to Chicago was no bed of roses. In his *History of Chicago*, written in 1876, William gave the following account of his journey:

> As a specimen of traveling, in 1848, I mention that it took us nearly a week to come from New York to Chicago. Our trip was made by steamer to Albany; railway cars at a slow pace to Buffalo; by the steamer Canada thence to Detroit; and by the Michigan Central Railway, most of the way on strap rail, to Kalamazoo; here the line ended, and, arriving about 8 o'clock in the evening, after a good supper, we started about 10 in a sort of a cross between a coach and a lumber box-wagon for St. Joseph. The road was exceedingly rough, and, with bangs and bruises all over our bodies, towards morning several of us left the coach and walked on, very easily keeping ahead.... The steamer Sam Ward, with Captain Clement first officer, and jolly Dick Somers as steward, afterwards Alderman, brought us to the city on the evening of the 12th of May, 1848.[17]

Once you had arrived, it wasn't always easy to get around in the city. In his *History*, William reports:

> I said we had no pavements in 1848. The streets were simply thrown up as country roads. In the spring for weeks portions of them would

> be impassable. I have at different times seen empty wagons and drays stuck on Lake and Water streets on every block between Wabash avenue and the river. Of course there was little or no business doing, for the people of the city could not get about much, and the people of the country could not get in to do it. As the clerks had nothing to do, they would exercise their wits by putting boards from dry goods boxes in the holes where the last dray was dug out, with significant signs, as "No Bottom Here" and "The Shortest Road to China."[18]

At night, getting around was even more difficult. William relates, "I said we had no gas when I first came to the city. It was first turned on and the town lighted in September, 1850. Till then we had to grope on in the dark, or use lanterns. Not till 1853 or '54 did the pipes reach my house, No. 202 Michigan avenue."[19]

The city's water supply, according to William, presented certain problems:

> But the more important element, water, and its supply to the city have a curious history. In 1848, Lake and Water, and perhaps Randolph streets, and the cross streets between them east of the river, were supplied from logs. James H. Woodworth ran a grist-mill on the north side of Lake street near the lake, the engine for which also pumped the water into a wooden cistern that supplied the logs. Whenever the lake was rough the water was excessively muddy; but in this, myself and the family had no personal interest, for we lived outside of the water supply. Wells were in most cases tabooed, for the water was bad, and we, in common with perhaps a majority of our fellow-citizens, were forced to buy our water by the bucket or the barrel from water-carts. This we did for six years and it was not till the early part of 1854 that water was supplied to the houses from the new works upon the North Side.
>
> But our troubles were by no means ended. The water was pumped from the lake shore the same as in the old works, and hence, in storms, it was still excessively muddy. In the spring and early summer it was impossible to keep the young fish out of the reservoir, and it was no uncommon thing to find the unwelcome fry sporting in one's wash-bowl,

> or dead and stuck in the faucets. And besides they would find their way into the hot-water reservoir, where they would get stewed up into a very nauseous fish chowder. The water at such times was not only the horror of all good housewives, but it was justly thought to be very unhealthy. And, worse than all this, while at ordinary times there is a slight current on the lake shore south, and the water, though often muddy and sometimes fishy, was comparatively good, when the wind blew strongly from the south, often for several days the current was changed, and the water from the river, made from the sewage mixed with it into an abominable filthy soup, was pumped up and distributed through the pipes alike to the poorest street gamin and to the nabobs of the city.... The Chicago river was the source of all the most detestably filthy smells that the breezes of heaven can possibly float to disgusted olfactories. Davis' filters had an active sale, and those of us who had cisterns betook ourselves to rain-water—when filtered, about the best water one can possibly get.[20]

William goes on to report that a two-mile tunnel into the lake was opened in 1867, pumping clean lake water into the city's water supply.[21] It should be remembered that the theories of Lister about the existence of bacteria did not begin to be taken seriously in the United States until the 1880s, so during the 1850s and throughout the war years, people drank water contaminated by animal or even human feces without realizing that this spread cholera and other fatal diseases. William and Jane had eight children, only one of whom, his daughter Jessie, survived to maturity; it seems probable that a contaminated water supply was the cause of death for at least some of his children.

In spite of the bad streets and bad water, Chicago was a busy city. William reports:

> It is a feature of our city, more noticed by strangers than by ourselves, who are accustomed to it, that we are a community of workers. Every man apparently has his head and hands full, and seems to be hurried along by an irresistible impulse that allows him neither rest nor leisure. An amusing evidence of this characteristic of Chicago occurs in connection with the first census of the city, taken July 1st, 1837, when the

> occupation, as well as names and residences of every citizen were duly entered. In the record of the population of four thousand one hundred and seventy, among the names of professors, mechanics, artisans and laborers, appears, in unenviable singularity, the entry, "Richard Harper, loafer" the only representative of the class at that time in the city. From this feeble ancestry the descendants have been few and unimportant; and we believe there is not a city in the Union where the proportion of vagabonds and loafers is so small as in Chicago.[22]

William adds in a footnote that he was pleased to learn later that Harper was very respectably connected in Baltimore, where he subsequently became the founder of an important temperance revival.

In later years the leading men of Chicago were justly proud of their accomplishments in building businesses in the city in the face of many difficulties both corporate and personal. After listing some of the "men who gave character to Chicago in 1848, and the years that followed," William notes, in 1876, that:

> Some of these gentlemen were not quite so full of purse when they came here as now. Standing in the parlor of the Merchants' Savings, Loan and Trust Company, five or six years ago, talking with the President, Sol. A. Smith, E.H. Haddock, Dr. Foster, and perhaps two or three others, in came Mr. Cobb, smiling and rubbing his hands in the greatest glee. "Well, what makes you so happy?" said one. "O," said Cobb, "this is the last day of June, the anniversary of my arrival in Chicago in 1833." "Yes," said Haddock, "the first time I saw you, Cobb, you were bossing a lot of Hoosiers weatherboarding a shanty-tavern for Jim Kinzie." "Well," Cobb retorted, in the best of humor, "you needn't put on any airs, for the first time I saw you, you were shingling an out-house."

William adds:

> Young men, the means by which they have achieved success are exceedingly simple. They have sternly avoided all mere speculation, they

> have attended closely to legitimate business and invested any accumulating surplus in real estate. Go ye and do likewise, and your success will be equally sure.[23]

A somewhat brash and outspoken stirring of Chicago pride seems to have taken hold early in the city's development. Newspaper articles and pamphlets of the period are full of exultations about the amazing growth of the city and its commerce, and equally full of confident predictions of future growth. By 1870 the city's population stood just under 300,000; William probably did not surprise fellow Chicagoans when, at the centennial of the United States in 1876, he predicted the city's population by the time of the next centennial in 1976: "With my eye upon the vast country tributary to the city, I estimate that Chicago will then contain at least 3,000,000 of people, and I would sooner say 4,000,000 than any less than 3,000,000.... And I also assume that the nation for the next hundred years will remain one united, free and happy people."[24] In fact, Chicago grew to over 3,000,000 people by the time of the census in 1930.

Politically, Chicago in 1848 reflected the growing national focus on the question of slavery. In the presidential election of that year, the Chicago followers of former president Martin Van Buren, whose increasing opposition

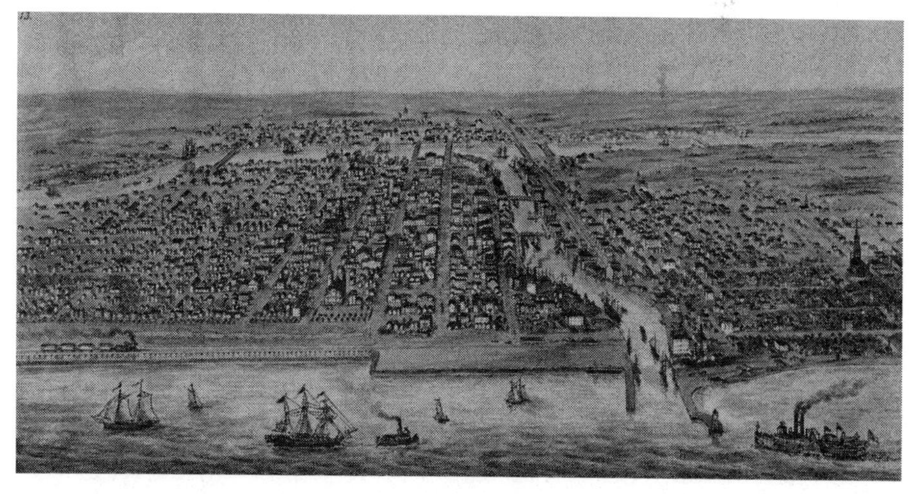

Bird's eye view of Chicago, 1853 (American Geographical Society Library).

to slavery and its extension had led to his nomination by the new Free Soil Party, conducted an energetic local campaign and the result in Chicago was 1,543 votes for Van Buren and Free Soil; 1,016 for the Democratic candidate Lewis Cass, who was considered friendly to slavery; and 1,283 for Zachary Taylor and the Whigs.[25] Anti-slavery feeling in Chicago that year was evidently stronger than in the rest of the country since the presidential election was won by the Whig candidate, General Zachary Taylor, hero of the Mexican War, partly because Martin Van Buren split the vote of the Democratic Party, which Van Buren himself had done more than anyone else to organize. But the slavery question was looming ever larger both nationally and locally.

In 1850 Congress passed a stringent new fugitive slave law, giving the federal government the novel power to pursue and recapture slaves who had made their way to free states. In Chicago sympathy for fugitive slaves was evident as early as 1846. A section of Andreas's history called "Annals of Chicago," recounting specific occurrences for the period from 1837 to 1858, reports among the events of 1846: "October 28, two runaway slaves were arrested and taken before justice Kercheval. While there the room became filled with excited negroes, who hustled the fugitives down the stairs and out of sight of Deputy Sheriffs Rhines and Daily forever."[26]

For 1850 the "Annals" reports: "During the year there was continued an increasingly anti-slavery excitement mainly centered in intense opposition to the fugitive slave law, which, during its discussion in Congress prior to its passage, was the absorbing theme. A convention was held by those who opposed it as early as February 21, and from then to the time of its passage, September 18, little else was talked of... October 11, a convention of colored citizens resolved to remain and defend themselves rather than to flee."[27]

This was the general state of things in Chicago when William Bross arrived to begin a new life in the West on May 12, 1848, a month after the opening of the Illinois and Michigan Canal and five months before the first official train ride on the Galena & Chicago Union Railroad. In August, three months later, William's family arrived. And, most probably in response to William's encouragement and arrangements, twenty-two-year-old John followed a few months later in December, terminating his legal studies in Goshen, New York, and continuing them in Chicago by reading law with Grant Goodrich, a Chicago attorney.

William came to Chicago as the only active partner in the book-selling firm of Griggs, Bross & Co. but finding the profits too small, joined with the Rev. J.A. Wright to start a religious newspaper called the *Herald of the Prairie*, "which was continued for about two years with moderate success."[28] In September 1850 he joined forces with John L. Scripps in founding another newspaper, the *Democratic Press,* which concentrated on commercial and financial news and statistics about Chicago but was also actively political, supporting a conservative Democrat point of view, opposing abolition but also bitterly opposing Senator Douglas and his Kansas Nebraska Act of 1854, which repealed the Missouri Compromise. After the Republican Party was formed in 1854, William's paper quickly began supporting Republican policies. As a result of the panic of 1857 and the ensuing depression, the *Democratic Press* joined forces with the *Chicago Tribune*. William became a 22% owner and president of the newly merged newspaper, which was renamed the *Chicago Daily Press and Tribune*, but two years later, in 1860, resumed the name of *Chicago Tribune.*

For the first two or three years, John lived with William and his family. William reports in his 1876 "Reminiscences" that for a week after arriving he had stayed at the City Hotel and then "was admitted to a most excellent home, that of the late Rev. Ira M. Weed, corner of Madison and State streets, where Buck & Rayner's drug store now is. This was considered far south. ... " William and his family and John must have stayed at Rev. Weed's house as paying guests until March of 1849, when "we commenced housekeeping on Wabash avenue between Adams and Jackson streets, in a cosy little house at the modest rent of $12 per month."[29] In May of that year, William bought a lot on Michigan Avenue, south of Van Buren, recalling, "In the fall of 1849 I bought a small wood house that I found moving along on Wabash avenue, and moved it on my lot. In this modest Home we spent some six very happy years."[30]

Small as the house may have been, John evidently lived there for several years along with William and his family, as Chicago city directories indicate that John boarded with William until 1853. William reported in his

William Bross (Chicago History Museum).

"Reminiscences" that "There were at first no sidewalks for a considerable distance north, and hence we were not troubled with promenaders on the avenue. The lake shore was perhaps a hundred feet east of the street. There my brother John and myself, rising early in the morning, bathed in summer for two or three years."[31]

The family must have had an adequate supply of milk since William wrote that, "We had an excellent cow—for we virtually lived in the country—that, contrary to all domestic propriety, would sometimes wander away, and I usually found her out on the prairie in the vicinity of Twelfth street. I saw a wolf run by my house as late as 1850."[32]

William and John seem to have enjoyed an active social life in their new frontier town. In a letter of January 2, 1851, William records that on the day before, New Year's Day, "We kept the day after the good old Knickerbocker style, viz. by calling upon the ladies. Br. John made some 40 calls and I made 30."[33] Apparently John, younger and still unmarried, was 30% more active. We may suppose that one could count all the ladies found at one gathering, rather than being obliged to visit 40 houses.

John spent the first two years reading law with Grant Goodrich, a lawyer who had been practicing in Illinois since 1834; a city directory of 1849 describes John as "student at Goodrich's."[34] When Goodrich spoke at the Proceedings of the Chicago Bar in memory of John after his death in 1864, he recalled that John had "entered his office as a student of law, and after years of close study, left it to commence the battles of life. His virtues were well known to all who were honored by his friendship. He was faithful as a student, and successful as a practitioner."[35]

After his apprenticeship was over, John was admitted to the Bar of the State of Illinois on March 1, 1850. By 1851 he is listed in a city directory as "attorney, Morris & Goodrich's," so he must have remained with Morris's firm for a time as an associate.[36] He must then have set up his own office or hung out his own shingle, as the saying went, because in a city directory published in 1852, he is listed as "attorney" at 127 South Water Street.[37] In commercial and professional advertising in the *Chicago Tribune*, his name appears in the late 1850s as an attorney and solicitor and a U.S. Commissioner at various addresses. In 1859 he is shown as being in a partnership, Jansen & Bross; this would have been a brother of William's wife, Jane Jansen Bross.[38] But by 1860 John is again listed only as "lawyer," so he must have resumed practice alone.[39]

John specialized in admiralty law. This branch of English law had been developed in medieval times and was conducted in special courts of Admiralty, which were not part of the common law court system. Maritime trade was naturally of great importance to the American colonies on the Atlantic coast, and it was also important to the new inland states because of river traffic, but especially to states bordering the Great Lakes, such as Illinois. The increasing commerce of Chicago on the lake as well as by rail offered a good professional future in admiralty to a young Chicago lawyer. Admiralty practice was entirely within the jurisdiction of the federal government and the federal courts, so professionally John would have been focused on the federal government; this might have strengthened his belief in the importance of the Union.

The *Memorial* reports that John was appointed a U.S. Commissioner during the administration of Franklin Pierce (1852–1856) and that he held the office until his death; that title appears in Chicago city directory listings for him and in his professional advertisements in the *Chicago Tribune*.[40] The office of U.S. Commissioner was developed in an effort to harmonize the conflicting jurisdictions of the existing state courts and the new federal court system; it was created by the earliest federal judicial statute, the Judiciary Act of 1789, to provide judicial officials of the Federal courts, comparable to justices of the peace in a state court system, with judicial authority to hear federal cases of lesser importance. Admiralty was one example of federal law where a minor case might come before a U.S. Commissioner. Being a U.S. Commissioner was at that time a source of fees and therefore a welcome addition to legal business. A U.S. Commissioner was appointed by the President, and since President Franklin Pierce, elected in 1852, was a Democrat, it is probable that John won the appointment with the help of William, whose newspaper, the *Democratic Press*, was at that time a strong supporter of the Democratic Party.

Contemporary news items in the *Chicago Tribune* contain reports of cases heard before John as Commissioner. For example, on June 20, 1860:

> **"Jack Tars in Trouble"** Five sailors were brought before United States Commissioner, John A. Bross, yesterday charged with being deserters and recusants from the Propeller Dacotah, on which vessel they shipped at Buffalo, and signed articles for the round trip. Saturday night the Captain gave each of them a small amount of money, and they

> went ashore upon a spree. Sunday morning found them half drunk, and they utterly refused to go on board to their duties. A Deputy U.S. Marshal served the process of Commissioner Bross, and arrested the five men.... Grippin, the moment he found himself under arrest, begged to be released, promising to go on board and behave himself, which he did. The others were ordered into the custody of the officers of the propeller, and they were taken on board.

The *Memorial* also reports that John served during the Pierce Administration as an assistant U.S. Marshal. Whereas a U.S. Commissioner was, in effect, a minor federal judicial official, the federal equivalent to a state justice of the peace, a U.S. Marshal was, and still is, a federal law enforcement agent and administrative official of the federal courts whose duties included serving federal arrest warrants, prisoner transport, keeping order in the courts, protection of officers of the court, and numerous other administrative matters necessary for the effective operation of the federal judiciary, such as renting courtrooms and making sure jurors and witnesses were on time. Federal Marshals served for a four-year term and were patronage jobs usually controlled by the District Judge. On the American frontier, U.S. Marshals were sometimes the only law enforcement officials in areas which had no local law enforcement structure; they were often seen as heroes in the fight against lawlessness, as when Deputy U.S. Marshal Virgil Earp and his brothers, Special Deputy U.S. Marshals Wyatt and Morgan Earp, and Special Deputy U.S. Marshal Doc Holliday shot it out with a desperado gang at the famous gunfight at the O.K. Corral in Tombstone, Arizona, in 1881. In a settled area such as Chicago, criminal justice was a matter of state law, and the work of an assistant U.S. Marshal would mostly have consisted of administrative matters. Under the Fugitive Slave Act of 1850, one of John's duties would have been to arrest fugitive slaves and return them to their Southern owners; as noted above, most Chicagoans were hostile to the recovery of fugitive slaves.

In addition to beginning a law practice, John evidently found time for other activities. He was naturally interested in the history of his new city and was ready and willing to supplement his income by writing about it, perhaps reflecting the influence of his brother William's journalistic talents. Danenhower's *Chicago City Directory* for 1851 includes a seven-page introductory "Historical Sketch" of Chicago written by John, dated December 1850. "It is not expected," his article states, "that a minute detail of local matters will interest any but those who have become Illinoisans, or those who expect to make this State their place of residence. But this local history is part of the material which is necessary to make up the general history of the State and Nation, and it is the duty of the citizens of each particular locality to see to it that no material for its own history be lost, or a page left unwritten." He describes the discovery of the Chicago location by Marquette and Joliet in 1637 and the subsequent establishment in Illinois of French settlements, some of which he lists as still remaining in Illinois, cultivating their fields in the old primitive style "while the Anglo-American race have been moving onward with rail road speed to a higher state of civilization. ... Formerly their [the French] settlements were the little oases in the desert waste of barbarism; now, all unchanged, they are barren spots in the garden of civilization." Such a glowing opinion about the higher railroad civilization of Anglo-Americans might not have been shared by the many Americans who in the mid-nineteenth century were visiting France and admiring French culture, but it does evidence the pride in their new American nation, which strengthened the resolve of Northerners such as John to risk their lives for the preservation of the Union when war came.

John's historical sketch continued, briefly describing the inclusion of Illinois in the U.S. Northwest Territory after the Revolution, the establishment of Fort Dearborn in 1804, a detailed account of the Fort Dearborn Massacre of 1812, the subsequent resettling of Americans in the area, and, after Illinois statehood in 1818, the planning of the Illinois and Michigan Canal, the progress of Chicago from village to town and finally to city in 1837, and the growth of population and commerce until 1850. It ends with a hopeful peroration on the future of Chicago:

> With the people of Chicago rests the duty, the responsibility of building up on the western shore of Lake Michigan a City whose influence

> shall be coextensive with the bounds of our vast Republic—an influence which like the Mississippi throwing its ten thousand arms over every portion of the Great Valley, shall reach in its ramifications the heart of every American. Our fervent aspirations are, that that influence shall ever be exerted in the cause of our Country, of Justice, of Religion and of Truth. May she do her part to hasten the "good time coming," when man shall rejoice in the existence of Universal Brotherhood, and then the "Garden City of the West" shall have fulfilled her destiny.

His prediction of Chicago's growing influence was accurate, but he failed to foresee that the contradiction between the ideal of Universal Brotherhood and the reality of slavery based on race would soon shatter that vast Republic, threatening to place most of the Great Valley of the Mississippi in one nation state and the Great Lakes in another.

William and John did not forget their parents. In a letter from William to his father dated November 2, 1852, and written on stationery of William's newspaper, the *Democratic Press*, he writes, "You will find by what accompanies this that your sons have not forgotten you. We bless God that you have been spared to complete your three score years.... I feel, and I trust your children will ever realize, that the moral and religious instruction we have received from our honored parents is of far more value than all the earthly riches you ever could have bestowed upon us." What accompanied the letter was a large, handsome, and obviously expensive illustrated edition of the Bible, published the year before. Inside the cover is a handwritten inscription: "This Bible is a birthday gift to our father on completing his Sixtieth Year; it is the richest boon he ever did or could give to his children, were his earthly treasures more precious than Gold of Ophir: all we are or ever hope to be is mainly due to the holy truths contained herein which our DEAR PARENTS through God's blessing impressed upon our youthful minds." The inscription is signed by William, John, and their brother Phineas, who had also moved to Chicago by then.

Phineas, two years younger than John, had followed William and John to Chicago and by 1852 was working as a bookkeeper at William's newspaper.

A city register printed in 1855 does not show Phineas but does show the name of Josiah, another brother 3 years older than John, working as a clerk at the Chicago Water Works. An 1858 directory shows Josiah living at 19 South May, evidently a neighbor of John, who was by that time married and living with his wife at 19 South May, in a fashionable residential area west of the South Branch of the Chicago River.[41]

As their parents would undoubtedly have wished, William and John became active in the Presbyterian Church in Chicago, both immediately becoming members of the Second Presbyterian Church. William had already made the acquaintance of the young Presbyterian minister, Dr. Patterson, when he visited Chicago in 1846 on his tour of the West to select the best place to live. In his 1876 "Reminiscences," he recalled their initial meeting:

> Soon after breakfast a tall young man, made apparently taller by a cloth cloak in which his gaunt figure seemed in danger of losing itself, and whose reserved, modest manners were the very reverse of what we had expected to find at the West, called on the clergy of our party and invited one of them to preach and the rest of us to attend service in the Second Presbyterian Church. That cloak would now be well filled by its owner, the Rev. Dr. Patterson, who has grown physically as well as intellectually and morally with the growth of the city, to whose moral welfare he has so largely contributed. Of course we all went to what by courtesy, as we thought, was called a church. It was a one-story balloon shanty-like structure that had been patched out at one end to meet the wants of the increasing congregation. It stood on Randolph street, south side, a little east of Clark. It certainly gave no promise of the antique but splendid church that before the fire stood on the corner of Washington street and Wabash avenue, or that still more elaborate and costly building, the Rev. Dr. Gibson's church, at the corner of Michigan avenue and Twentieth street.[42]

The Second Presbyterian Church, built in 1874 after the Chicago Fire, still stands in Chicago at the corner of Michigan Avenue and 20th Street, a remarkable example of Arts and Crafts architecture with nine magnificent

Tiffany stained glass windows; as this is written in 2017, it is undergoing a slow but steady process of restoration.

John's membership in the Presbyterian Church was not merely a civic activity. We know from William's recollections that their father, Moses, had been converted as a young man and from Moses's letters how seriously he and Jane took their religious commitment. The *Memorial* relates that when John was "but eight or ten years of age, in accompanying his father to a prayer meeting, while passing through a piece of woods, his father knelt, and prayed with an earnestness which made an impression upon his mind that was never effaced"[43] and that afterwards at his brother's academy:

> [W]hile studying Wayland's Elements of Moral Science, the truth as there laid down, as to man's moral obligations, fixed itself in his mind, and his sensibilities were much moved.... He deliberately made up his mind on the whole subject, and chose the fear of God.... He united with the Presbyterian Church at Chester, Orange county, New York, in the year 1847. Upon coming to Chicago, he connected himself, first with the Second Presbyterian, and afterwards cast in his lot with the Third Presbyterian Church, with which he continued his membership until the time of his death.[44]

John officially moved his membership from the Presbyterian Church in Chester, New York, to the Second Presbyterian Church of Chicago on February 26, 1849, a few months after William, who had joined the Chicago church in October 1848.[45] John and William both sang in the choir.[46] William was superintendent of the Sunday School beginning in 1852, and John was probably also active in the Sunday School, since he was later engaged with the Sabbath School at Third Presbyterian Church after he had transferred there.[47]

It appears to have been in 1851 that John became active in the Third Presbyterian Church, which stood in an increasingly fashionable residential neighborhood west of the downtown area, across the South Branch of the Chicago River, at the corner of Washington and Carpenter streets, although he did not officially become a member until 1856. Third Presbyterian had been founded in 1847 by a group of Presbyterians that included Nelson Mason and his wife Desire, the parents of John's future wife, Isabella.[48] We don't know why John would have moved to this church when he was still living on the east side of town with his brother and his family, who continued to attend the nearby Second Presbyterian Church. Possibly John, with William's approval, decided to join Third Presbyterian in order to give it his support because in 1851, it had been severely weakened by a quarrel that led a majority of the members of the church to leave and found the First Congregational Church of Chicago.

What happened at the Third Presbyterian Church in 1851 reflected the growing urgency of the slavery question as a religious, in addition to political, challenge. For some years, the so-called New School Presbyterians, like the Congregationalists, had been dissatisfied with what they regarded as toleration of American slavery by the national Presbyterian Church. In early 1850 the Presbyterian General Assembly met and, obviously attempting to hold together the Northern and Southern Presbyterian churches, adopted a resolution that seemed equivocal and disappointing to most members of Third Presbyterian, who had hoped for a ringing denunciation of slavery by the national church. A meeting was held at the First Presbyterian Church in Chicago to appoint delegates to a "Christian Anti-Slavery Convention" to be held in Cincinnati in April 1850 and resolutions were adopted, one of which stated, in part:

> [T]here is reason to fear that slavery, driven from favor in the State, may find apology and peace for its abominations in ecclesiastical judicatories and in the churches of Christ; and that in view of such indication every Christian should maintain firmly the ground assumed in the past progress of the anti-slavery reform, and continue to advance, trusting in Christ to the point where the demon of slavery shall be expelled from confidence and communion in our churches.[49]

At a time when leading opinion in the Southern states was more clearly concluding that slavery was a positive benefit to civilization and more forcefully demanding federal authority for its expansion, such a strong statement of opposition to slavery was clear evidence of the growing chasm in the early

1850s between public opinion in the Northern and Southern parts of the American Republic.

At the Christian Anti-Slavery Convention, which was in fact held that year in Cincinnati, a resolution was adopted in favor of separation from all churches "that are not fully divorced from the sin of slave holding" and in conformity with that sentiment a majority of the members of the Third Presbyterian Church in February 1851 approved a resolution that their church should "stand aloof from all meetings of Presbytery, Synod and Assembly." As a result, after some further negotiation, the Presbytery resolved that Session should strike the names of the supporters of the "stand aloof" resolution from the roll of the church.[50] A majority of members of the church then left to form the First Congregational Church; of 68 members at the beginning of the controversy, only 21 remained in late 1851, including Nelson and Desire Mason.[51]

Since John was at that time, according to the *Memorial*, firmly opposed to abolitionism, he would have been in sympathy with those members of Third Presbyterian who refused to turn their backs on the national church because it had declined to adapt an abolitionist stance. In moving his membership to Third Presbyterian, if in fact it was for that reason, he was continuing a pattern, since Second Presbyterian was said to have been founded in 1842 by members of First Presbyterian who left that church because they felt that it was too pro-abolitionist.[52] In this, John and the remaining members of Third Presbyterian were representative of general public opinion in the North that, even later at the beginning of the war, was strongly in favor of preserving the Union but not at all in favor of abolition.

The Third Presbyterian Church survived and attracted new members; in 1858 it moved to a splendid new church building located at Washington and Carpenter streets that had been completed in spite of a severe financial challenge posed by the panic and recession of 1857. "The church cost $50,000. It was built of Athens stone. The walls were rock-faced and the towers and trimmings of dressed stone. The main tower, steeple and spire were models of taste and symmetry. The audience-room was spacious, admirably arranged and neatly and comfortably furnished. A fine organ was put into the church and it had a superior choir."[53] John must have done his

Third Presbyterian Church of Chicago, c. 1860 (Chicago History Museum).

part to support the construction of the new building, which would have been a source of satisfaction not only to him but also to Belle, whom he had married in 1856, and to her parents, the Masons, who had been among the founders of the church and had remained with it when the majority abolitionist party seceded from the church.[54]

Whatever the reason for his joining Third Presbyterian, John became an active member. The *Memorial* reports that John was "a teacher in a remote Mission School, taking out a bevy of teachers upon Sabbath afternoons, during the entire summer of 1856." A September 1858 article in the *Tribune* reported:

> [T]he first annual celebration of the Sabbath School of the Third Presbyterian Church, and the Mission Schools connected therewith, under the management of the "Young Men's Christian Association." ... John A. Bross, Esq. President of the Association, and D. J. Lake, Esq. were Marshals of the day. The features of the day were a procession in which the several schools joined, the exercises at the Third Presbyterian Church, where the little folks were addressed by several speeches, united in singing, etc., the celebration concluding with a Pic-Nic which passed off delightfully.

While John had a successful relationship with Third Presbyterian Church that lasted for the rest of his life, the same could not be said for his younger brother Phineas Camp Bross, named for the evangelist Phineas Camp who had once converted Moses and Jane. The Session Register for the church shows that Phineas was received in May 1853 and dismissed in January 1854. The date of dismissal and "How Dismissed" is carefully shown for each member; the reason shown in "How Dismissed" is usually transfer to another church, death, or by order of Synod when a member has stopped attending for some reason. In the case of Phineas, the highly unusual reason given was "Excluded." Several pages of the beautifully handwritten Session Minutes for late 1853 report rumors that Phineas was leading an unchristian life and testimony about his alleged drunkenness (he said he used brandy for medicinal purposes) and gaming (he was seen playing checkers and chess with money lying beside the board). The minutes for January 21, 1854, state that in view of a recent letter of Phineas to the Clerk of Session "couched in offensive language and manifesting a most unchristian and vindictive spirit" he should "be excluded from the fellowship of the Church until he repents." There may have been a backstory, as there was reference to a lady whom he failed to take to a meeting, but it must have been with John's encouragement that he joined the church, and the affair must have been an embarrassment for John. Phineas seems to have left Chicago before 1855.

John continued for the rest of his life as an active member of Third Presbyterian Church. At the August 1864 memorial meeting of the Chicago Bar shortly after John's death, L. B. Taft, President of the Board of Education, recalled that he had come to know John twelve years before, when John was commencing the practice of his profession, and had since then been intimately acquainted with him:

> Connected with him in his church and social relations, I can speak with knowledge of his spotless life and eminent qualities. At the time of his death he was a member of the Third Presbyterian Church, with which he had been connected for many years. He was ever active and zealous in the work of his Divine Master. He was always prominent in the prayer and conference meetings of the church, always took an active part in the Sunday School, not alone in that connected with his church, but he followed the teachings of his Divine Master, and went into the streets, byways and alleys of the city, and gathered the children of the poor into the Mission Sunday Schools, and told them of the love of Jesus, to lead them to their Saviour.
>
> He loved this work. These children were dear to him, because he knew and felt that his Saviour loved them and had died for them. Colonel Bross is today enshrined in the hearts of these children. They will ever love and revere his memory. There are occasions when words utterly fail to express our feelings. There never was, nor, indeed, could be, a word or whisper against the daily life and Christian integrity of Colonel Bross. In all the relations of life, as a member of the church, as a member of the bar, as a citizen and neighbor, he did his whole duty. He was beloved by all with whom he was associated. He was ever affable, courteous and kind-hearted—in fine, a model Christian.[55]

On September 10, 1862, the *Chicago Tribune* reported "an impressive scene" at the Third Presbyterian Sabbath School where a sword, sash, and belt were presented to John, "who has been for years the leader of the musical exercises of the school and assistant superintendent for two years past." In a memorial sermon in 1864, Arthur Swazey, the pastor, stated that John had been a faithful and much loved member of the church, and added, "I have reason to know, that in the army he was constant in his religious duties, and in circumstances where it required no little degree of moral courage to acknowledge his convictions, and do his duty."[56]

It is not clear what John's religious duties might have been in the army, but in a letter of May 18, 1864 to Belle he reported:

> I hope you will not think that I wish to make a parade of my religious profession, when I tell you I commenced my "mess" in saying grace and I shall continue to do so. I did not do this in the 88th. The 5th Mass. Cavalry Colored were here some days last week. The first afternoon they came I entertained the officers at supper. They were hungry and pretty well exhausted. As they took their seats, one young officer partly in a half serious half comic mood asked me if I would say grace. I was standing at the head of the table at the time, having been engaged in seating them. I replied gravely that it was always my habit at home and should be pleased to do so here, and said it. There was a hushed set of officers for the time being and very respectful conduct through that meal, though the conversation on military matters towards the last took a lively turn.[57]

His letters make it clear that his Christian faith was never far from his thoughts. The *Memorial* indicates that he wrote dates of reading in the pocket edition of the Psalms, which he carried with him, and that in the margin of the 91st Psalm he had written the words: "Read at the battle of Chickamauga, during the heavy firing on our left, and before the action commenced in our front." "Sincerely could he feel," the *Memorial* observes, " 'I will say of the Lord, He is my refuge and my fortress: my God; in him will I trust.' "[58]

John shared his devotion, in particular, through song. The *Memorial* reports that at Third Presbyterian

> For many years he took charge of the choir and led the service of song. He was, also for a time, the Superintendent of its Sabbath School, and until entering the army, took charge of the children's music. ... A fine figure, a pleasant, commanding countenance, and strong musical voice, could not fail to aid him in his military duties ... He was gifted with fine musical taste, and possessed a sweet voice, well cultivated.[59]

In a letter of September 22, 1864, Dr. Mackay, the regimental surgeon, remembered spending the afternoon before the battle with him: "It was a very hot afternoon, and I had some iced lemonade, with what we in army parlance called, 'a brick in it.' We sang some hymns and a few Scottish songs. I can yet hear his rich bass voice joining in the refrain of 'my Nanni's awa.' Those few happy moments were too soon spent."[60] And another post-death letter to Mrs. Bross from Lieutenant Fred. A. Chapman of his regiment recalls, "How he enjoyed singing. At times when everything seemed dull and stupid, his clear voice would lead some well-known tune, in which he would have us all join. Soon stupidity would be changed to pleasure; and all gradually partaking of his spirit, would be merry and happy."[61]

In the early 1850s, as a young bachelor getting started in his professional career, John would have been paying some attention to the sentimental attractions of the opposite sex and thinking about the possibility of marriage, although marriage was out of the question for a young man until his income became large enough to support a wife and family. In 1854 John was beginning his law practice, and we know that he was not unready for a romantic attachment because there is in the collection of the Chicago History Museum a letter from him to his older sister Margaret dated March 31, 1854, explaining what had really happened between him and an unnamed young lady from Michigan. It is the letter of an earnest and articulate 28-year-old man responding to the ongoing concern of an older sister in a large and supportive family. John writes:

> Thanks for the overflowing fountains of sisterly affection with which you minister to a brother's feelings. It is a proof that the heart is right. Thanks also for the words of "gentle caution." A brother's ears are not shut when a sister speaks of a "woman's heart." Thoughts of her have more than once been the means of keeping the writer in the path of duty and of honor when the flashes of a meteor torch would have lured him to the chambers of death.

Apparently there was a mutual attraction between John and the unnamed young lady, but John was unable to propose marriage because he had not yet completed his legal studies. Nevertheless, he thought she had intimated that she loved him and hoped that they would later be engaged and was therefore devastated when she announced her engagement to their mutual friend, R. Three weeks later she broke off the engagement to R. because she realized she could not happily spend the rest of her life with him when her true feelings were for John. But John had in the meanwhile written her an angry letter, which devastated her and terminated the friendship. John wrote:

> [T]hen the conviction that she had played the fool with me and <u>lied</u> like the Devil himself to my face roused a storm in my heart the effects of which may last through life. But I <u>wronged</u> her. I sent her a letter which was gall itself. She was sick for a month and then she went to <u>Troy Female Seminary</u> and spent a year where you had finished your own education.... Subsequently I found out that interested friends had persuaded her into an engagement which upon sober thought she could not consummate and preserve her happiness and she upon her own responsibility broke off the engagement. She has told me that the influence of friends was the sole and only cause of her making the unfortunate agreement.... To condense it all in a sentence; she rejected R., I rejected her, or rather would have nothing more to do with her. This dear sister is the history of my disappointment. It made me feel like cursing womankind. The lady is now engaged to a third person & I sincerely hope she will be happy for now since I have got from her

> own lips the facts of the case corroborated as they are by circumstantial evidence she has my regard and respect for the course she took in the whole matter.

He adds:

> A word as to the lady, as you may be a little curious to know something of the lady that caused such confusion in the otherwise calm and unrippled surface of my existence. She is perhaps your height, light auburn hair, fair complexion, eyebrows slightly arched, great lustrous blue eyes that speak affection in every glance. And so Maggie "what could a poor man do" but fall in love? Thrown as I was into her society I would not have been a Bross had I not been affected by her charms. And now that my first and only dream of real love has been rudely changed from an ideal to a stern real and that by my own proud spirit and a determination to do justice though the Heavens fall, I look back with regret on some things and yet upon the whole with satisfaction. My heart is not scored, I have learned experience and am much better versed in the ways of the world.

Not long after the young lady from Michigan had left the scene, John evidently became close to another young lady, this time a member of a family in his own Third Presbyterian Church. The new young lady was Isabella Annetta Mason, called Belle, the oldest of three daughters of Nelson and Desire Mason, who, as mentioned above, had been among the founding members of the church in 1847 and who had remained loyal to its membership in the Presbytery when a majority of the members left the church in 1851 in support of a stronger abolitionist stance. Belle was 14 years old in 1851, when John began attending Third Presbyterian, and they were married on June 5, 1856, when Belle was 19 years old and John was 30.

Nelson Mason was born in Paisley, Scotland, in 1810 to a family of French Huguenots who had moved to Scotland after the French government in 1685 revoked the Edict of Nantes, which had decreed toleration for Protestants in France; his name was originally spelled Masson, but he changed it to conform to phonetic spelling. Ambitious and energetic, he emigrated to Vermont early in life in 1826, attended school there, and was married in 1835, in Barnett, Vermont, to Desire E. Barnett. Later that year they moved to Illinois, where the former Pottawatomie lands were now known to be available for settlement. He bought a claim in Whiteside County, opened with a partner the first general store in the county, which became the trading place for whites and Native Americans for many miles around, and among other commercial ventures, secured the first contract for carrying mail. He was one of four commissioners who negotiated the union of the rival towns of Harrisburg and Chatham and changed the name to Sterling. The Masons had three daughters: Belle, born in 1837, Emily, born in 1840, and Ann, born in 1842.[62]

In 1845 Nelson moved to the new and rapidly growing city of Chicago, which at that time was roughly twelve hours from Sterling over bumpy roads. He bought land in the Chicago suburbs, selling it profitably as the city grew. In 1855, when the railroad came through Sterling, he returned there and served as Mayor of Sterling in 1860, 1862, and 1865. Like William and John, Nelson was a strong Republican; political news articles reported him on the platform with William Bross at Republican political rallies, and a June 20, 1864, letter of John refers to Nelson furnishing political support for William's candidacy at the time for Lieutenant Governor of Illinois.

Belle was born in Sterling in 1837 and grew up there until they moved to Chicago when she was 8 years old in 1845. In Sterling she would have attended the local school founded in 1838 by the indomitable Sarah Worthington from Philadelphia who arrived with her husband and a baby in 1837 after a difficult journey of several months over canals, mountains, and rivers. Sarah was given a lot in the town, not yet called Sterling, on condition that she open a school in the house to be built there, which she did in April 1838, the first school in the county.[63]

The Mason family continued to be connected to both Sterling and Chicago. Belle and John lived in Chicago after their marriage in 1856, but Belle moved back to Sterling with their little son, Mason, to be with her family in 1863 after John had gone off to war. Emily married Zadok Galt (called Zad or Zed), a resident of Sterling, in December 1862; there are references to this wedding in John's letters of the period. Their younger sister Ann married Joseph Bullock; they lived in Chicago.

John must have met the Mason family no later than 1851, when he became a member of Third Presbyterian Church. Belle was 14 years old at the time and John was a handsome older man of 25, who became active in the education and music programs of the church. She would probably have noticed him. She might or might not have been aware of John's friendship with the unnamed young lady from Michigan; by 1854, when that friendship ended, she was 17 years old and probably thinking about her own future. Perhaps to John it appeared that a young Sabbath School student had rather suddenly turned into a charming young lady with whom he could imagine spending the rest of his life. We have no details of their growing friendship as it ripened into a courtship, but we do know that they were married on June 5, 1856, in Chicago, undoubtedly with the blessing of her parents, who by this time had moved back to Sterling. The marriage was performed by Asahel D. Brooks, who had just become the pastor of Third Presbyterian Church.

After their wedding, John and Belle lived in Chicago where he continued to build his legal practice. At Christmas they received a large and handsomely illustrated family bible, inscribed to "Mr. and Mrs. John A. Bross from their affectionate father Nelson Mason, Chicago, Dec. 25, 1856." The couple undoubtedly engaged in social activities, and they continued to attend Third Presbyterian Church. John also became increasingly interested in political activities, following the lead of his brother William, who became a strong voice for the new Republican Party both before and after he merged his newspaper, the *Democratic Press* with the *Chicago Tribune* in 1857. With the other owners of the *Tribune*, William actively worked for Abraham Lincoln in his 1858 race against Stephen Douglas for a U.S. Senate seat and then supported Lincoln's effort to secure the presidential nomination in 1860; John played a part in these political efforts.

Chicago city directories for 1858 and afterwards show John living at 21 South May Street, in the residential district across the South Branch of the Chicago River, not far from Third Presbyterian Church. The family lived there until John left for the war in the late summer of 1862. In early 1863

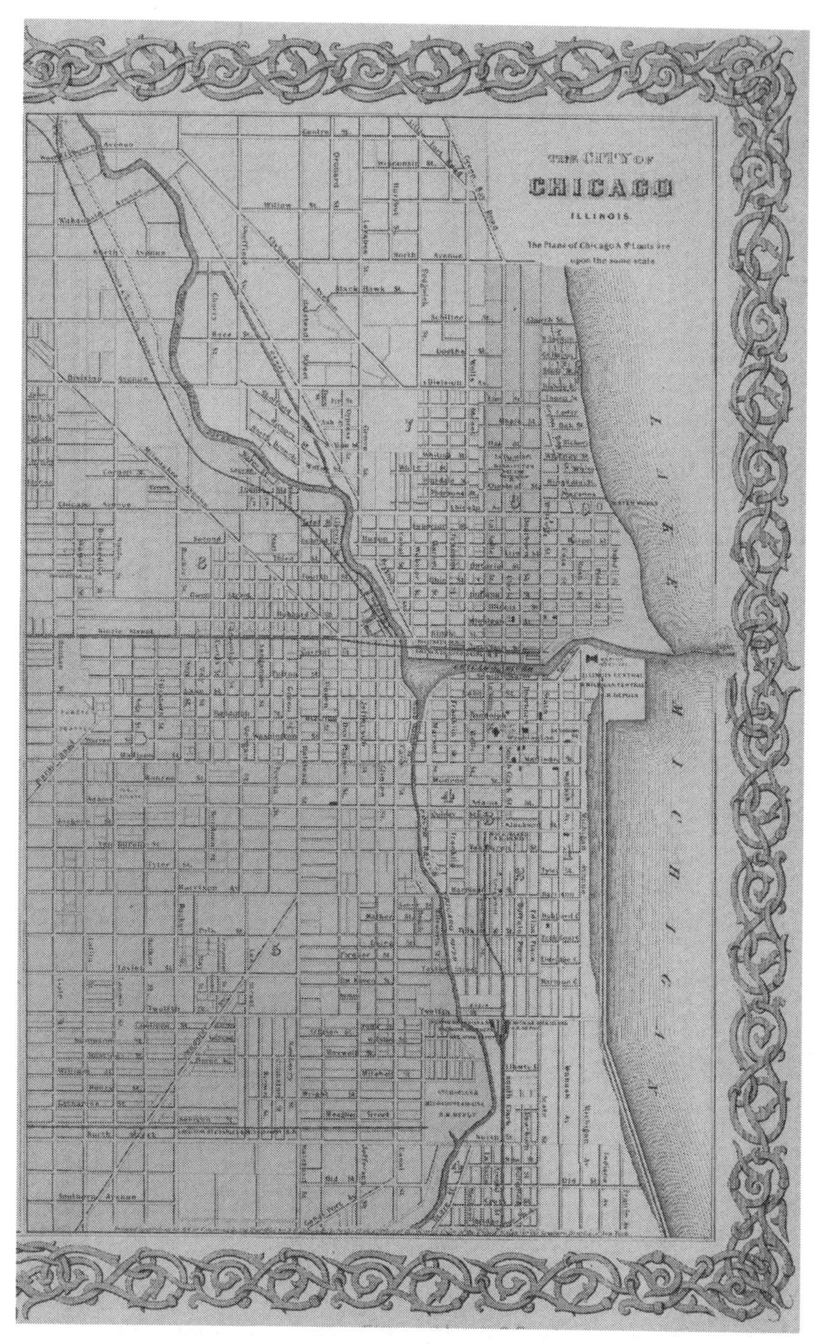

Street map of Chicago, 1855, J. H. Colton & Co. (The Newberry Library, Chicago).

Belle found a tenant for their Chicago house and moved back to Sterling to live with her family, probably intending to return to Chicago with John after he came back from the war.

The first child of John and Belle, a daughter named Cora, was born on December 2, 1858. She must have been a great joy to her parents, judging from the loving references to her in John's letters, but she died in 1861 at the age of two and a half years and was buried in the new Rose Hill Cemetery north of the city near Lake Michigan. Infant mortality in those days was high, probably related to the tainted water supply in Chicago as in most other cities. Her loss must have been hard to bear. A letter by John to his father-in-law in early 1863 after the battle of Murfreesboro describes how he thought about her during the battle: "Then again as shells, cannon balls and bullets of all kinds whistled and hurtled by in very dangerous proximity was it not peculiarly pleasant to think of a little angelic form whose mortal remains are sleeping on the shores of Lake Michigan hovering around and warding off the death-dealing instruments of the enemy?"[64]

Their second child, a son, was born on October 4, 1860. He was named Nelson Mason Bross, after Belle's father, but he was called Mason. He was less than a year old when his sister Cora died and less than two years old when his father volunteered for action in the Union Army and went off to war in September 1862. Virtually every letter to Belle from the campaign contains an affectionate greeting for his little boy. John would see Mason again only for a few weeks at the most when he returned to Chicago in October 1863 on his way to recruit the new Illinois black regiment in downstate Quincy and for the last time at the train station for an hour or so when he returned to Chicago in April 1864 on his way to Virginia with the new regiment.

From John's letters to Belle we may conclude that they had a successful marriage. The letters are full of references to their happy life together, to requests for various things he needed and his thanks for them when they came, and to his deep wish to be with her, weighed against his strong patriotic feeling of duty to protect and defend his country.

In June 1861, on their fifth wedding anniversary, John wrote a poem for Belle to mark the occasion. Appreciation and writing of poetry were far more widespread in Victorian America, both North and South, than they are today in the early twenty-first century, and John had an obvious love for poetry. At the end of his poem, which presents a glowing tribute to their happily married family life, he makes use of one Victorian theme that might not be understood so well in today's world: the reference, in the last stanza, to his wife growing older. This should be understood as an example of a common nineteenth century literary theme of love enduring into old age and true beauty shining through the physical changes wrought by time; these are found, for example, in such popular contemporary songs as "Silver Threads Among the Gold" or "When You and I Were Young, Maggie." The nineteenth century's embrace of poetry and its acceptance of aging among

Belle and Mason (Private Collection).

the deeper values of life may arguably have been wiser than the current popular quest for unchanging physical youth. The poem reads:

Five times hath June with beauty spread
The landscape o'er, since we were wed
Since hand in hand our vows for life
Were made and we were 'husband' 'wife.'
A year as happy lovers tied
And then I claimed my blushing bride
And wedded bliss we hoped for, prized,
Since then how richly realized.

Each circling year without alloy
Has brought its sound of purest joy.
And has with gentle hand revealed
Gems which your modest worth concealed.
Two little faces shining bright
With smiles and beams of Heavenly light
And eyes whose fond and speaking glance
Our hearts delight, our souls entrance,
And voices full of childish glee
In music's thrilling harmony
Bathe soul and sense in extacy.

Rich gifts of Heaven, sweet and rare
They lighten labor, sweeten care
Give sunshine to the sober face
Send pleasure's laughing form to chase
Dark clouds away, vexed care destroy
And wreathe our brows with heartfelt joy.
God help us guide their little feet
Along life's path toward Heaven & meet
Their savior by the way, & see
Them to his arms with gladness flee.

And now what though the lily grows
Upon your cheek where bloomed the rose
More sweet by far & dear to me
'Tis virtue's stamp of purity,
What though no maiden's blush I see
A maiden's charm still graces thee;
Thine eye a sparkling brightness gives,
And in the wife & mother lives.
Each little artless winning wile,
The graceful step, angelic smile
And beauty clustering round thy brow
All, crowned our wedding, charm me now.

John's poem, with its celebration of the lives of their two little children, was written for their anniversary, June 5, 1861. Just a month later, on July 6, 1861, little Cora died.

NOTES

1. *Biographical Sketches of the Leading Men of Chicago; Written by the Best Talent of the Northwest* (Chicago: Wilson & St. Clair, 1868), 37.
2. A.T. Andreas, *History of Chicago From The Earliest Period To The Present Time. [With Illustrations].* 2 Vols (A. T. Andreas, Publisher, 1884), vol. 1, 80.
3. John A. Bross, "Historical Sketch," *Danenhower's Chicago City Directory for 1851* (Chicago: 1851), 8–9; Andreas, *History of Chicago*, vol. 1, 80–82.
4. Andreas, *History of Chicago*, vol.1, 128.
5. Ibid., 123.
6. Ibid., 142.
7. Grossman, James R, Ann Durkin Keating, and Janice L. Reiff, *The Encyclopedia of Chicago.* (Chicago: University of Chicago Press, 2004), 233; Bross, William, *History of Chicago; Historical and Commercial Statistics, Sketches, Facts and Figures, Republished from the "Daily Democratic Press."; What I Remember of Early Chicago; A Lecture, Delivered in McCormick's Hall, January 23, 1876.* (Chicago: Jansen, McClurg & Co., 1876), 126.
8. Andreas, *History of Chicago*, vol. 1, 171.
9. Ibid., 171.

10. Ibid., 248.
11. Benjamin W. Dreyfus, *The City Transformed; Railroads and Their Influence on the Growth of Chicago in the 1850s* (1995), 3 http://www.hcs.harvard.edu/~dreyfus/history.html.
12. Ibid., 1.
13. Ibid., 2.
14. Harold M. Mayer and Richard C. Wade, *Chicago: Growth of a Metropolis* (Chicago: University of Chicago Press, 1969), 35.
15. Andreas, *History of Chicago*, vol. 1, 245.
16. Dreyfus, *The City Transformed*, 1.
17. William Bross, *History of Chicago*, 116.
18. Ibid., 119.
19. Ibid., 119.
20. Ibid., 120.
21. Ibid., 120.
22. Ibid., 35.
23. Ibid., 124.
24. Ibid., 125.
25. Andreas, *History of Chicago*, vol. 1, 154, 603.
26. Ibid., 154.
27. Ibid., 155.
28. *Biographical Sketches*, 38.
29. William Bross, *History of Chicago*, 118.
30. Ibid., 118.
31. Ibid., 118.
32. Ibid., 118.
33. William Bross, *William Bross Papers*, Chicago History Museum.
34. Hatheway, O.P., and J.H. Taylor, *Chicago City Directory and Annual Advertiser for 1849–50* (Chicago: Jas. J. Langdon, 1849), 85.
35. *Memorial*, 61.
36. *Danenhower's Chicago City Directory, for 1851; Containing an Alphabetical List of the Mechanics and Business Men with their several places of Residence; Also, Brief Notice of the Religious, Literary and Benevolent Associations of the City, Military, Fire Department, Etc., Etc., Etc., Etc.* (Chicago: W.W. Danenhower, 1851), 35.
37. *Udall & Hopkins Chicago City Directory For 1852 & 1853: Comprising an Alphabetical Directory of the City, Census of the Various Societies, Associations, and Institutions, Military and Fire Departments, Etc.* (Chicago: Udall & Hopkins, 1852), 31.

38. *Smith & DuMoulin's Chicago City Directory for the Year Ending May 1, 1860* (Chicago: Smith & DuMoulin, 1859), 59.
39. D.B. Cooke & Co., *D. B. Cooke & Co.'s Chicago City Directory for the year 1860–61* (Chicago: D.B. Cooke & Co, 1860), 51.
40. *Memorial*,. 4.
41. D.B. Cooke & Co, *D.B. Cooke & Co.'s City Directory for the Year 1858* (Chicago: D. B. Cooke & Co, 1858), 32.
42. John A. Bross, "Historical Sketch," *Danenhower's Chicago City Directory for 1851*. (Chicago: 1851), 5–11.
43. *Memorial*, 20.
44. *Memorial*, 21.
45. *The Second Presbyterian Church of Chicago, June 1st, 1842 to June 1st, 1892* (Chicago: Knight, Leonard & Co., 1892).
46. Ibid., 118–119.
47. Ibid., xvii.
48. Andreas, *History of Chicago*, vol. 1, 306.
49. Ibid., 307.
50. Ibid., 308.
51. Ibid., 309.
52. Tom Campbell, *Fighting Slavery in Chicago; Abolitionists, the Law of Slavery, and Lincoln* (Chicago: Ampersand, Inc., 2009), 51, 55.
53. Andreas, *History of Chicago*, vol. 1, 306.
54. By the late 1870s, Third Presbyterian was becoming the largest of the Chicago Presbyterian Churches; it outgrew the 1858 building and moved to a new building at Ashland and Ogden streets, where it became the largest Presbyterian Church in the United States, with over 12,000 members. In the late nineteenth century, the neighborhood became more commercial and membership in the church declined. Many of its members, including Belle and her parents in 1887, moved to the near north side of Chicago and joined the newer Fourth Presbyterian Church on North Michigan Avenue.
55. *Memorial*, 64.
56. *Memorial*, 53.
57. *Memorial*, 22.
58. *Memorial*, 8.
59. *Memorial*, 21, 24.
60. *Memorial*, 78.
61. *Memorial*, 33.

62. "Mason, Nelson," *History of Ryegate, Vermont Biographical Sketches and Family Records*, The Electric Scotland Classified Directory, *electricscotland.com* (n.p. n.d. 14 June 2017).
63. Sarah Worthington, "Retrospective," *Evening Gazette*, Sterling, Illinois: December 2, 1893 (Sterling-Rock Falls Historical Society, 2006).
64. January 11, 1863.

CHAPTER 3

Slavery, Politics, and the Coming of War

In May 1854 Illinois Senator Stephen A. Douglas pushed the Kansas-Nebraska Act through the U.S. Congress with Southern support and over bitter Northern opposition; it was approved by President Franklin Pierce. The Act changed everything and set in motion turbulent political currents that led with growing speed to the maelstrom of civil war. The central issue was slavery based on race.

From their beginnings in the early seventeenth century, the English colonies in North America, like the French, Spanish, and Portuguese colonies in the Caribbean and South America, had approved the importation, sale, and possession of African slaves, captured in Africa and sold to slave traders who brought them to the colonies stacked like livestock in specially designed ships to be sold, if they survived the filthy and appalling journey, at public auctions in slave markets. They and their progeny were legally considered personal property, like cattle or horses, to be bought and sold. At the time of the American Revolution, there were around 450,000 slaves in the English colonies, about a fifth of the total population.[1] Most of them in were in the Southern colonies, but slaves were also held in all of the Northern colonies, including Massachusetts, New York, and Pennsylvania. In the Northern colonies, though, slavery was just one form of labor among many, not the main model.[2]

It is important to emphasize that American slavery was based on race. There were many thousands of indentured white servants in the early days of the colonies, British people who were legally obliged to work for a number of years before gaining their freedom, but only blacks, Africans, and their descendants were held as permanent slaves and personal property. There had been slaves in ancient Greece and Rome, as well as in other cultures, and there are numerous references to slaves in the Bible, but those kinds of slavery were based on capture in war or debt, not on race. There was serfdom in Russia in the nineteenth century, where serfs could be bought and sold just as American slaves were, but the serfs were Russian, set apart by social class and economic status, not by race. In eighteenth and nineteenth century America, by contrast, all slaves were black and only blacks were slaves.

In the years immediately after the Revolution, sentiment in all parts of the country turned against slavery. The ideology of the American Revolution was based on French Enlightenment thinking, expressed perhaps most succinctly in Jefferson's famous phrase in the Declaration of Independence, which for Abraham Lincoln was central to what the American republic stood for: "all men are created equal." But right from the beginning of the revolutionary struggle, there was a conflict evident to everyone between the stated Enlightenment ideal of human equality and the existing social institution of slavery. When Washington defeated the British army at Yorktown, the American victory was not good news for the slaves, including several belonging to Washington, who had taken refuge with the British and were then returned to their owners. In England, Samuel Johnson famously remarked that the loudest yawps for liberty came from men who owned human slaves. The Marquis de Lafayette, after the war, said that he would never have drawn his sword in the cause of America had he conceived that he was thereby founding a land of slavery.[3]

The Northern states began abolishing slavery almost immediately after the Revolution, and leading opinion at that time in the Southern states held that the institution was headed for extinction. James Madison wrote that "Humanity & freedom" were "secretly undermining the institution," and George Washington said he wished the Virginia legislature would adopt legislation by which slavery would be "abolished by slow, sure & imperceptible degrees."[4] Thomas Jefferson in 1786 predicted "the gradual emancipation of slaves" through "the spread of light and liberality."[5] It was thought that the abolition of the slave trade, which a provision of the Constitution postponed until 1808, would inevitably lead to the disappearance of slavery.[6] By the early nineteenth century, all of the Northern states had provided for the ending of slavery and blacks in the North had become free.

But slavery did not die out in the South. The abolition of the slave trade in 1808 did not choke off American slavery as people had expected; for one thing, American slaves reproduced at about the same rate as whites, but it was also true that Southern staple crops, especially rice and indigo in the Low Country of South Carolina and sugar in the Orleans territory, continued to be more suitable for slave labor. Then the invention of the cotton gin in 1793 made possible a dramatic increase in cotton acreage in Southern states, increasing the demand for slave labor. South Carolina actually reopened its slave trade while it still could in the five years before 1808.

In addition, reports and fears of black slave uprisings cooled the enthusiasm of Southern whites for emancipation. In 1791 there was a black slave rebellion on the island of Hispaniola, which eventually led to the establishment of the Republic of Haiti, with many well-publicized reports of atrocities during the uprising. And in 1800 an elaborately planned slave insurrection, known as Gabriel's Conspiracy, was discovered in Virginia, leading frightened Virginians to turn away from ideas of liberalization and to reenact stringent measures to reinforce slavery.[7] Washington's vision of gradual emancipation never happened, either in Virginia or in any of the other Southern states. Washington, in his will, freed his slaves after his death, but Martha Washington did not, and none of the other founding fathers, including Jefferson, ever did so. By 1860, at the threshold of the Civil War, there were an estimated 4,000,000 slaves in the United States, most of them in the Deep South, with a market value estimated at $3 billion in 1860 dollars, making them the largest single financial asset in the country, worth more than the combined invested value of all manufacturing and railroads in the United States.[8]

It was never only a question of legally abolishing or retaining human slavery; the racial issue was always part of the question. Slavery and race are two distinct concepts, but they were conflated in the black slavery of the American South. Virginians and other Southerners were terrified of being slaughtered in an insurrection not just of slaves but of black slaves. In the aftermath of Gabriel's Conspiracy, Virginia and other Southern states moved not only to tighten regulation of black slaves but also to restrict the rights of free blacks, arguing that the presence of free blacks would be a corrosive influence on black slaves. In 1806 the Virginia legislature required free blacks to leave the state; other states prohibited them from settling within their limits. As time went on in the American South, all blacks, including free blacks, came to be considered as in some way intended for slavery. When General Lee's army invaded Pennsylvania in 1863 prior to the Battle of Gettysburg, his soldiers seized scores of black Pennsylvania citizens and sent them south to be sold as slaves.[9] It wouldn't have occurred to them to seize white citizens of Pennsylvania to be sold as slaves: black race and legal slavery went hand in hand in the American South.

There was a further question as to the definition of the black race. If a man had one white parent and one black parent, he was obviously a mixture of both; logically he might be considered to have the status of one or the other. In the South he was automatically assigned the lower legal status of a black person. Before the Civil War, he would have been a slave; after the Civil War, the institution of slavery was abolished, but the same man would be assigned to the successor form of second-class black citizenship known generally as Jim Crow. Well into the twentieth century, it was said by many that "one drop of Negro blood would make a person a Negro." It may seem absurd that a man with one black great-grandparent and seven white great-grandparents should be considered black, but there are photographs of slave children with fair complexions and nearly blond hair who were slaves because it was known or claimed that some ancestor of theirs was black.[10]

In the Northern states, the question of slavery had been settled with the legal abolition of that institution by the time William Bross was born in 1813; there were no longer slaves in New Jersey or Pennsylvania when William and John were growing up. But the question of racial prejudice, of racism, was by no means settled. Emancipation from slavery was one thing, but equal citizenship was another matter. In the first two decades of the nineteenth century, the liberal attitude of the post-revolutionary years tended to disappear in the North; black citizens there often found themselves facing a more hostile white attitude. Free blacks were in some cities confined to separate neighborhoods and segregated sections of theaters and churches. Ohio passed a law requiring incoming blacks to post a five hundred dollar bond (a very large sum) in guarantee of good behavior. Illinois had a law forbidding blacks to reside in the state; although largely ignored in the northern part of the state, this law was in effect until after the Civil War. Massachusetts passed laws prohibiting interracial marriage, and New York's legislature took away the franchise of free blacks, who had long had it.[11] Alexis de Tocqueville observed, in his *Democracy in America*, published in 1835, "Racial prejudice appears to me to be stronger in the states that have abolished slavery than in those where slavery exists."[12]

Most Northerners tended to agree with Jefferson, who wrote that blacks and whites could not live together without producing "convulsions which will probably never end but in the extermination of the one or the other race." As late as 1862, Lincoln said to a black delegation, "There is an unwillingness on the part of our people, harsh as it may be, for you free colored people to remain with us.... I do not propose to discuss this, but to present it as a fact with which we have to deal. I cannot alter it if I would.... It is better for us both, therefore, to be separated." James McPherson, citing James Oakes, argues that Lincoln did understand slavery and race as two separate concepts and skillfully used racism as a strategic diversion to help permit the abolition of slavery. "Extreme racism was at the core of the proslavery argument: If the slaves were freed, they would aspire to equality with whites; therefore slavery was the only bulwark of white supremacy and racial purity.... The most effective way to convert whites to an antislavery position, Lincoln believed, was to separate the issue of bondage from that of race" through a strategy of taking race off the table by agreeing that he also was opposed (at that time) to social equality.[13]

Perhaps the major factor in the growing conflation of race and slavery in America was the need to find a justification for slavery, as it was becoming clear that slavery would not be abolished because it was such an important part of the Southern economic system. The justification that emerged in the early nineteenth century was that blacks were racially inferior to whites. The argument was that blacks were inherently incapable of acting as free citizens, and therefore slaveholders had a Christian responsibility to keep them in bondage. Jefferson wrote that blacks were "inferior to the whites in endowments both of body and mind" and always expressed "great aversion" to racial mingling between blacks and whites (but not between whites and American Indians) even though, or possibly because, he himself was secretly living with a black slave woman who was his deceased wife's half-sister and, as is now known, had several children with her.[14] Under slavery, it was said, blacks had what amounted to a lifetime guarantee of social security: they would always be cared for, in contrast to Northern workers who were just left to fend for themselves when their employment ceased.

But of course the system of slavery rested on a foundation of violence and brutality, which hardly resembled the romantic vision of kind and paternalistic care advanced both before and after the Civil War by apologists for the Southern way of life. Masters branded and whipped their slaves, often proud to do it personally, often leaving brutal and sadistic punishments to overseers. Slave women were the property, including the sexual property, of their masters, and there was a lot of racial mixing; probably the interracial sexual connections were mostly understood as consensual, but in a system of slavery, there is really no such thing as meaningful consent. Families were routinely torn apart when parents and children were sold to different owners. A caring relationship between a family of slave owners and their slaves on a Virginia plantation was often ended when the chronic indebtedness of the Virginia planters required sale of the slaves, often at the death of the owner, and then the slaves from the enlightened family home would be separated from their spouses and children and sold down the river to a life of brutal suffering on the rice or sugar plantations of the Deep South. Northern public opinion, including the active intellectual and social life of Chicago, became increasingly aware of this with the publication of Harriet Beecher Stowe's enormously influential book, *Uncle Tom's Cabin*, in 1852.

As it became increasingly apparent that the institution of slavery was inconsistent with Jefferson's famous phrase in the Declaration of Independence that "all men are created equal," leading Southern thinkers became frankly willing to abandon the eighteenth century Enlightenment concept of equality, even though that concept agreed with the contemporary biblical understanding that God had created all men at one moment in time. Alexander Stephens, the newly elected vice president of the Confederacy, made this clear in his famous "cornerstone" speech delivered in March 1861. He said, "The prevailing ideas entertained by him [Jefferson] and most of the leading statesmen at the time of the formation of the old Constitution were, that the enslavement of the African was in violation of the laws of nature; that it was wrong in principle, socially, morally and politically.... Those ideas, however, were fundamentally wrong. They rested upon the assumption of the equality of races. This was an error.... Our new government is founded upon exactly the opposite ideas; its foundations are laid, its cornerstone rests, upon the great truth that the negro is not equal to the white man; that slavery, subornation to the superior race, is his natural and normal condition."

But for Northern political opinion the phrase "all men are created equal" remained valid; Lincoln included it verbatim in his Gettysburg Address as the essential concept of the American Republic. And if this concept was really valid, so valid that it could justify blacks fighting as soldiers in the Union Army, it must eventually lead to the concept of equal citizenship for blacks, as it was apparently doing for Lincoln at the end of his life. Lincoln's assassin thought so: on April 11, 1865, Lincoln told an interracial crowd on the White House lawn that he favored giving the vote to literate blacks and black Union military veterans. John Wilkes Booth was in the crowd and said, "That means nigger citizenship. Now, by God, I'll put him through. That is the last speech he will ever make."[15] Booth murdered the President three days later at the Ford Theater.

It might be thought that black slavery would have been popular among wealthy slave owners but not popular for the majority of Southern whites who owned no slaves. Northerners wondered why non-slave owners would fight for an aristocratic slave-owning minority, apparently against their own interests. A main reason, of course, was racism: no matter how poor or unsuccessful a white family might be, they were nevertheless guaranteed a higher status in society than their black neighbors. They might be poor, but at least they were of a superior race.

Religion was also harnessed to justify racial slavery. Numerous references to slavery in the Bible were cited, including those in which slavery seemed to be accepted by St. Paul, even though these did not refer to racial slavery. It was decided, on no particular authority, that the reference in Genesis to the "sons of Ham" who were to remain in bondage, referred to blacks. A telling example of the religious underpinning of racial slavery is furnished in an 1861 letter of Leonidas Polk, Episcopal Bishop of the Southwest, in New Orleans. When the war broke out, Polk resigned his Episcopal office and became a general in the Confederate Army. A fellow bishop wrote to say that he was already a general in another kind of army. Polk replied that he would be more faithful to the Church by winning the war and "above all, we fight for a race that has been by divine Providence entrusted to our most sacred keeping."[16]

Politically, slavery had presented one of the most difficult issues at the Constitutional Convention of 1787: how were slaves to be counted in tallying the population and therefore the number of representatives for each state? The Convention rejected a Northern proposal that slaves not be counted at all, and also a southern proposal that slaves be counted as full persons, settling on the compromise that slaves should be counted as three-fifths of a person for representation in the House of Representatives and in the Electoral College. This compromise was accepted by everyone, but by the 1820s, it was beginning to be viewed by Northern politicians as the basic cause of an unfair Southern domination of the federal government.

As slavery disappeared in the North but persisted and grew more central to Southern agricultural economy and society during the first decades of the nineteenth century, the two sections of the country had begun moving in fundamentally different economic and social directions. There were far fewer corporations and banks in the agricultural South than in the increasingly industrial North, fewer turnpikes and canals, and fewer factories and industrial plants. In the North labor was considered valuable and praiseworthy for all social classes, while in the South, labor came to be regarded as something fit only for slaves; what was valuable was the leisure that slavery provided, and that leisure was seen as the essential basis of civilized life.[17] The most common measure of a family's wealth in the Southern states became the number of slaves that it owned. Far from expecting slavery's eventual demise, Southern politicians and journalists now increasingly called for its extension, expressing indignation and anger at any suggestion of abolition as an insult to the honor of the South. Southern political leaders naturally favored the establishment of slavery in the new territories in the West, both those in the Louisiana Purchase and those farther west in Texas, California, and New Mexico. Later, in the 1850s, many, especially the "fire-eaters" in South Carolina, began calling for resumption of the slave trade and discussing the possible annexation of Cuba and portions of Central America in order to extend the area of their slave-based economy and increase the number of slave states. They now spoke openly of seceding from the existing United States government in order to establish a new and powerful independent Southern nation based on an agricultural slave economy.

By 1820 a corresponding political rivalry was developing between the Northern and Southern sections of the country for control of the federal government. By that year there was an equal number of free and slave states; neither side wanted the other to get control of the Senate by admitting an extra free or slave state. In March 1820, in what came to be known and revered as the Missouri Compromise, bills were passed admitting Maine as a free state and Missouri as a slave state, with the proviso that in the future slavery would be excluded from the Louisiana Territory north of the 36°30′ latitude, except for the new state of Missouri. Between 1820 and 1854, when William and John Bross were growing to maturity, the Missouri Compromise was accepted by everyone as almost on a level with the Constitution itself. There were increasing economic, political, and social differences between the two regions; there was growing disapproval of slavery in the North, although no majority opinion in favor of abolition, and growing approval of slavery in the South, but everyone agreed that the 36°30′ latitude line of the Missouri Compromise was the boundary between future slave states and future free states.

This, then, was the social and political background in which William and John grew up. In the Mid-Atlantic states, including New Jersey and

Pennsylvania where they lived, there was commercial, financial, and industrial growth in a society of free labor. There was also increasing opposition to slavery. There was an Anti-Slavery Society at Williams College when William was a student there in the early 1830s.[18] No evidence has been found that he joined, but his later opposition to slavery suggests that he was influenced by the group if not a member of it. By the time he arrived at Williams, the Anti-Slavery Society was split between those favoring abolition alone and those supporting "colonization," the idea that freed slaves should be shipped back to some colony in Africa, but both parties were opposed to slavery.[19]

In Chicago, after their arrival in 1848, William and John found increasing hostility to slavery, especially to the Fugitive Slave Law of 1850, but also some pro-slavery sentiment and varying shades of opinion within antislavery sentiment, ranging from outright abolitionism to a more moderate toleration of slavery where it existed but opposition to its extension. Chicago was a rapidly growing industrial and commercial center with a wide spectrum of social and political thought, but basically it was a Northern city, in sentiment not far removed from what William and John had experienced growing up in the Delaware Valley.

In 1850, two years after the Bross brothers arrived in Chicago, a tense national standoff between Northern anti-slavery and Southern pro-slavery interests had been resolved by several bills, together called the Compromise of 1850, conceived and eloquently supported by the aging political champions Henry Clay and Daniel Webster but chiefly achieved after lengthy negotiations by Illinois Senator Stephen A. Douglas, known as "the little giant" for the industry and forceful oratory that was in contrast to his short stature. California was admitted as a free state, balanced by the organization of Utah and New Mexico as territories without restriction on slavery. The slave trade, but not slavery itself, was prohibited in the District of Columbia. A strong Fugitive Slave Law was enacted, giving the federal government the role of pursuing and recapturing slaves who had made their way to free states. This was a novel expansion of federal power; the Southern states had generally favored states' rights in opposition to the central government, but they were quite prepared to favor stronger powers for the central government in support of slavery. It is generally agreed that the Compromise of 1850 succeeded in postponing the Civil War for a decade, but it also arguably made the war more inevitable because the Fugitive Slave Law outraged Northern opinion and crystallized Northern public opposition to slavery. Escaped slaves were arrested and forcibly shipped south, sometimes in the face of angry Northern mobs.

But the 36°30′ latitude line of the Missouri Compromise remained in effect, accepted by everyone as if it were part of the Constitution.

Then, in 1854, when William and John had been in Chicago for some 6 years, Senator Douglas secured passage of the Kansas-Nebraska Act, repealing the Missouri Compromise and substituting the theory of "popular sovereignty," the idea that the people of each territory could decide the issue for themselves; it explicitly permitted slavery north of the 36°30′ parallel if the people of a territory voted to have it. Douglas really had been interested in getting a railroad built through the Nebraska Territory and to get Southern support for that route, he eventually agreed to repeal the prohibition of slavery above the 36°30′ latitude within the Louisiana Purchase territory. Since the idea of popular sovereignty had already been relied on in 1850 for setting up the Utah and New Mexico territories further west, Douglas argued that the Kansas-Nebraska Act was just more of the same. But Northern public opinion was outraged and quickly began to harden against what was seen as an expansionist Southern slavery policy. What rapidly resulted for the Kansas Territory was a series of violent conflicts between pro-slavery and anti-slavery immigrants who moved into the territory in order win it for their side; people referred to "Bleeding Kansas."

Politically, the Kansas-Nebraska Act immediately brought various Northern anti-slavery and free-soil factions together, even before passage of the bill, to form the new Republican Party, which held its first national convention in Michigan in July 1854, two months after the bill was passed. Abraham Lincoln re-entered politics to register his opposition to Douglas and the theory of popular sovereignty, giving a widely noticed three-hour speech on the subject in October 1854 in Peoria and emerging as a significant political figure in Illinois.

In Chicago, William Bross was strongly opposed to the idea of popular sovereignty and became an early supporter of Republican principles opposing the extension of slavery. He quickly threw the support of his newspaper, the *Democratic Press*, behind the Republican Party and became a frequent public speaker on behalf of the cause. In 1856, when the party nominated John C. Fremont for President, William gave the first public endorsement for Fremont in Illinois, speaking at Dearborn Park on the night Fremont was nominated. He then went on a tour of southern Illinois, generally a pro-slavery area, courageously making speeches in support of Fremont.[20] At that time he became a political friend of Lincoln, often appearing with him on the same speaker's platform.

The panic of 1857 and the depression that followed brought hard times to Western businesses, including newspapers, and in July 1858, William and John Scripps and their newspaper, the *Democratic Press*, joined forces with the *Chicago Tribune*. When, in early 1861, the merged paper was incorporated as the Tribune Company with 2,000 shares, William and Joseph Medill each received 430 shares, Scripps and Charles Ray each received 420 shares, and Alfred Cowles received the remaining 300 shares. William became president of the Tribune Company.[21]

The *Chicago Tribune* had been founded in 1847. In its early years it had espoused the cause of anti-slavery, but its influence had been weakened by its hostility to the growing immigrant population, mainly Irish and German, by its warnings about Romanism and by its support of legislation prohibiting liquor. However, in the spring of 1855, control of the *Tribune* was bought by two young journalists, Joseph Medill of Cleveland, who had been active in the founding and naming of the national Republican Party, and Charles Ray, who had run a newspaper in Galena that opposed popular sovereignty. The two had been introduced by Horace Greeley of the *New York Tribune* who suggested that they start their own newspaper in Chicago, but they decided to buy the *Tribune*. Beginning in mid-1855 under the new leadership of Medill and Ray, the paper continued its anti-slavery policy but dropped its opposition to Catholic immigrants and its former devotion to the cause of prohibition. Its circulation soon began to increase and it rapidly became the most influential paper in the West after the 1858 merger with William's *Democratic Press*. The *Tribune* exercised a major influence on the election of 1860 and furnished unwavering political support for the Lincoln administration during the Civil War.

William and the *Chicago Tribune* had had contacts during former years. In 1849 the *Tribune* had lost many of its assets in a fire and was presented with a new dictionary by William's bookselling firm, Griggs, Bross & Co.[22] In 1850 and 1851 the paper was printed on an Adams Power Press owned by the firm of Wright and Bross, then proprietors of the religious newspaper *Herald of the Prairie*.[23] In 1853 the *Democratic Press* was defending Senator Douglas against the *Tribune* on a railroad issue, and the *Tribune* sourly noted that the editor of the *Press*, William Bross, who was also an alderman, had secured the coveted public printing job; this led to a feud between Bross's paper and the *Tribune* that went on for several years. John Scripps, William's partner in founding the *Democratic Press*, had been an owner and editor of the *Tribune* from 1848 until 1852, when he sold his interest and joined William to start their new paper.[24] So the parties knew each other fairly well when on July 1, 1858, the two papers, roughly equal in circulation, announced their consolidation. One of the stated reasons for the merger was "to put an end to the expensive rivalry which had been kept up," but it would hardly have happened had not the editors of both newspapers been solidly in agreement in favoring Republican principles. The announcement stated that the consolidated paper would give "steady, zealous and consistent support ... to the great cardinal doctrines of the Republican party."[25] In fact, the owners of the two papers had already begun cooperating in support of the Republican Party and of Lincoln as its candidate for the U.S. Senate.

For the next two years, the paper was called the *Chicago Daily Press and Tribune*, usually referred to as "the *Press and Tribune*," but on November 1, 1860, the words "Daily Press" were dropped from the name with an announcement that "The Tribune will be precisely what the Press and Tribune has been. ... Changed in nothing but omission of part of its name, it will continue to be a live newspaper."[26] In his 1876 *History of Chicago*, William wrote that "The course of the Tribune during and before the war was the result of the matured opinions of four independent thinkers," Scripps, Ray, Medill and "whatever I could contribute to the common stock". The *Tribune*, he said:

> [L]ed and guided public opinion in the Northwest; inspired confidence amid defeat and disaster; always advocated the most vigorous measures to put down the rebellion; drove the Copperheads to their holes, and to say the least it has probably done as much as any other journal or influence in the country to bring back the peace and the security which it now enjoys.[27]

There is an 1858 photograph purporting to show Abraham Lincoln holding a copy of the newspaper with its new consolidated name. This was, in reality, an earlier photograph of Lincoln holding a German language newspaper doctored in 1858 to read "the *Press and Tribune*," but there was a reason

Lincoln holding a copy of the *Press and Tribune* (Library of Congress).

This photograph, taken in 1854, originally showed Lincoln holding a German language newspaper. It was altered to show him holding the *Press and Tribune* and published in 1858.

for associating him with the *Press and Tribune*. Lincoln was one of the new subscribers to the *Tribune* in 1855 after Medill and Ray took control. That summer he had climbed the stairs to the *Tribune* office, introduced himself, and paid four dollars in advance for a six-month subscription. Lincoln said to Medill, "I like your paper; I didn't before you boys took hold of it. It was too much a Know-Nothing sheet." Lincoln soon became a frequent visitor to the *Tribune* office, using it as his headquarters for political or legal meetings when he was in Chicago.[28]

In the early months of 1858, the existing and incoming editors of the two soon-to-be-merged newspapers had begun working together for Lincoln's nomination as the Republican candidate to run for the U.S. Senate against Democratic Senator Stephen Douglas. Mayor John Wentworth also wanted the Republican nomination for Senator, and there was a meeting "in which Lincoln, Judd, and two members of the *Tribune* firm, Ray, and Bross, laid plans to thwart Mr. Wentworth."[29] The plans were successfully carried out, and Lincoln was nominated at the Republican State Convention held at Springfield on June 16, 1858. The next day Lincoln began his campaign in Springfield with a widely noted speech which, as he afterwards told Medill, revealed that he was even then thinking about his stand on slavery in light of a possible presidential campaign.[30] It began: "Mr. President, and Gentlemen of the Convention: If we could first know where we are, and whither we are tending, we could better judge what to do, and how to do it." The agitation about slavery "will not cease until a crisis shall have been reached and passed. 'A house divided against itself cannot stand.' I believe this government cannot endure permanently half slave and half free. I do not expect the Union to be dissolved—I do not expect the house to fall—but I do expect it will cease to be divided. It will become all one thing or all the other."

The editors of the *Tribune* helped Lincoln's team persuade Douglas to accept a series of seven debates in the doubtful central Illinois counties in August, September, and October. Each debate was begun by one of the two speaking for an hour, the other to reply for an hour and a half, and the first to reply for half an hour. Lincoln noted in his letter to Douglas that "Although, by the terms, as you propose, you take <u>four</u> openings and closes, to my three, I accede, and thus close the arrangement."[31] The *Tribune* engaged Robert R. Hitt to take down the debates in shorthand and printed a complete record of all of the speeches. This helped increase circulation and also helped bring Lincoln's name before a national public.

William traveled with Medill on a special train of seventeen cars that carried Lincoln and the Republicans to Freeport in Stephenson County for the second debate on August 27. During the trip Lincoln showed Medill a set of four questions he had prepared to put to Judge Douglas in his opening speech. The second one read, "Can the people of a United States Territory, in any lawful way, against the wish of any citizen of the United States, exclude slavery from its limits prior to the formation of a State Constitution?" Medill objected to this one because he thought Douglas would quickly answer in the affirmative in order to make himself more acceptable to the anti-slavery vote. Lincoln's team agreed and tried to talk him out of it before the speech, but Lincoln insisted on leaving it in. Douglas, as Medill expected, answered roundly in the affirmative in what became known as the "Freeport Doctrine," the idea that a territory could effectively exclude slavery by simply refusing to pass police laws for its protection.

Prior to Lincoln's Freeport speech, the *Chicago Tribune* history reports that William took the occasion to put in a plug for the paper of which he was now an owner:

> When Lincoln rose to speak in Freeport to the crowd of 15,000 there was an interruption. "Deacon" Bross called out from the back of the crowd:
>
> "Hold on, Lincoln, you can't speak yet. Hitt isn't here and there is no use of your speaking unless the *Tribune* has a report."
>
> "Ain't Hitt here?" asked Lincoln. "Where is he?"
>
> Bross called out: "If Hitt is in this crowd he will please come forward. Is Hitt in the crowd? If he is tell him Mr. Bross of the *Chicago Press and Tribune* wants him to come here on the stand and make a verbatim report for the only paper in the Northwest that has enterprise enough to publish speeches in full."

> The good deacon was getting in a little boosting for the paper of which he was now one of the editors and owners.
>
> Hitt finally called out from the rear that he could not get through the crowd and he was lifted over heads and passed to the platform. Then Lincoln began to speak.[32]

In the end Lincoln lost the election in the legislature, which in those days elected U.S. senators, but he won the popular vote and earned a national reputation that made it possible for him to be presented as a serious candidate for the presidency in 1860. And although Douglas won re-election to the Senate, Southern opinion noticed Douglas's Freeport Doctrine and began to turn against him, with the eventual result that the national Democratic Party split at their convention in Charleston in 1860, the Southern Democrats refusing to support Douglas and walking out to support Breckinridge in a splinter Southern Democrat Party. Lincoln had realized that Douglas was trying to appear to be pro-slavery in the South and anti-slavery in the North and had written before the campaign in May 1858: "Unless he plays his double game more successfully than we have ever seen done, he cannot carry many Republicans north without at the same time losing a larger number of his old friends south."[33] Years later Medill recalled that shortly after his election as President in 1860, Lincoln reminded him of the second question at Freeport and said, with a broad smile, "Now I have won the place that he was playing for."[34]

William was not as close to Lincoln as Medill was, but as a *Tribune* editor and political ally, he was certainly a friend of Lincoln. In May 1864 William and his daughter Jessie visited with John in Washington at his military camp. This may have been the occasion of an anecdote recalled at a memorial meeting of the Fortnightly Club in Chicago after Jessie's death in 1904:

> When a girl she once went with Governor Bross to Washington. It was during President Lincoln's administration, and one morning they called at the White House. The man at the door excused the President, saying he was too busy to see callers. Walking down the path, Governor

> Bross heard his name called, and turning, saw the President at one of the second-story windows. He called out, "Bross! Bross! Bring Jessie back; I want to talk to her!"[35]

Jessie was the only one of William and Jane's eight children to survive; when she grew older she served as hostess and companion to her father because her mother was often ill. She is referred to in John's letters and knew him as an uncle who was 13 years younger than her father and 18 years older than herself.

In the initial months after the senatorial election in November 1858, Lincoln did not appear to be an active candidate for President. Senator Seward of New York and Governor Chase of Ohio were thought to be the leading candidates for the Republican nomination. The *Tribune* declined to name a candidate, saying in March that "President-making is a dangerous and thankless business.... There is harm in premature discussion."[36] But in the fall of 1859, Lincoln began making political talks in other states as well as in Illinois. When he was invited to speak in Ohio in September, the *Tribune* said, "Well done, Cincinnati" and sent Mr. Hitt to Ohio to report the Lincoln speech, which it printed in six columns.[37] At that time the *Tribune* did not come out for Lincoln, and Lincoln himself had not announced as a candidate, but his political talks were making him better known, and Medill and the other editors were coming to the conclusion that Lincoln was the only man would could carry the essential states of New Jersey, Pennsylvania, Indiana, and Illinois. By December Medill was in Washington, talking up Lincoln to congressmen and preparing a series of pro-Lincoln letters. In late December Medill, as a member of the Republican National Committee meeting in New York, helped secure the choice of Chicago for the Republican nominating convention to be held the following spring.

In February 1860 the *Tribune* published an editorial endorsing Lincoln's nomination on the grounds that he was the candidate most likely to carry the four key states and the editorial was followed by a letter from Medill in Washington urging Lincoln as the man best suited to unite conservatives and radicals.[38] Medill later recalled that shortly afterwards, at a reception in Washington, Seward, who had been an old friend, told him, "I had always counted on you as one of my boys. Henceforth you and I are parted.... I shall never trust you again."[39] At the end of February, Lincoln delivered a long and careful speech at Cooper Union in New York City, laying out the constitutional case for limiting the spread of slavery. This was his first major appearance in the East, and his speech was received with enthusiasm.

Medill had secured the selection of Chicago as the location for the national convention before it was known that Lincoln would be a serious candidate; the reason for choosing Chicago was that Indianapolis had fewer hotels and St. Louis was in Missouri, which the party probably couldn't win anyway. The convention's location in Chicago turned out to be an important factor in Lincoln's nomination partly because the Lincoln team could strategically arrange the seating of delegates and partly because (it was alleged) they could issue tickets to pack the Wigwam, the giant auditorium built for the convention in Chicago, with Lincoln supporters. William and John were undoubtedly in the audience. No direct evidence is known that

The Republican National Convention at the Wigwam in Chicago, May 1860, published in *Harper's Weekly* (Chicago History Museum).

they were; this is one of many questions that would have been answered by William's diaries had they not been destroyed in the Chicago Fire of 1871.

At the convention there were 465 voting members; 233 votes were necessary to win the nomination. The result of the first ballot was 173 ½ for Seward and 102 for Lincoln. The result of the second ballot was 184 ½ votes for Seward and 181 for Lincoln. At this point Medill, seated with his old friends in the Ohio delegation, whispered to Cartter, Chairman of the Ohio delegation, that if Ohio went to Lincoln, Chase "can have anything he wants."

"How do you know?" asked Cartter.

"I know and you know I wouldn't promise if I didn't know," said Medill.[40]

On the third ballot, Lincoln's total reached 231 ½ votes, but before the result was announced, the following occurred:

The progress of the ballot was watched with most intense interest, especially toward the last, the crowd becoming silent as the contest narrowed down, when, before the result was announced,

MR. CARTTER, of Ohio, said—I arise, Mr. Chairman, to announce the change of four votes of Ohio from Mr. Chase to Abraham Lincoln.

This announcement, giving Mr. Lincoln a majority, was greeted by the audience with the most enthusiastic and thundering applause. The entire crowd rose to their feet, applauding rapturously, the ladies waving their handkerchiefs, the men waving and throwing up their hats by thousands, cheering again and again. The applause was renewed and repeated for many minutes. At last, partial silence having been restored, with many gentlemen striving to get the floor,

MR. EVARTS, of New York—Mr. Chairman, has the vote been declared?

The CHAIR—No, sir.

(Other delegations then announced shifts of votes to Lincoln)

MR. CARTTER, of Ohio.—I am requested by the delegation from Ohio to now present their unanimous vote for Abraham Lincoln; 46 votes. (Great applause.)

At this time there was great confusion. A salute was fired without, and responded to within the wigwam by vociferous cheers. A life size photograph of Mr. Lincoln was then brought upon the platform, and the audience greeted the sight with rapturous and long continued cheering.[41]

So Lincoln was nominated at a political moment when the Democrats were badly split and there was also an additional new party, making it likely that the Republican candidate this time could win. William and the *Tribune* began working hard for Lincoln's election, and so did John.

During the six years of mounting political crisis between the passage of the Kansas-Nebraska Act in 1854 and the election of 1860, John would not have been as involved in politics as William; he had been building a legal career and a personal and social life. He had been married to Belle in 1856; they had one child in 1858 and a second in late 1860. The *Memorial* does not mention any political activity of John during these years, but his close relationship with his brother William would have kept him well informed about the political situation, and he was in sympathy with his brother's enthusiasm for the principles of the new Republican Party. We know that he closely followed political news between 1858 and 1860 because in December 1860, he bound into a leather-backed two-and-a-half-inch volume the numerous pieces of campaign literature that he had been collecting, starting with a 268-page edition of the 1858 debates between Lincoln and Douglas, including several speeches given by both before the actual debates. On the top of each of these pages, John wrote in ink the name of the speaker, Lincoln or Douglas. Other items in the bound volume include a book of "Portraits and Sketches" of the four candidates for President and Vice President, a life of Abraham Lincoln published by the *Press and Tribune*, Lincoln's February 1860 address at the Cooper Institute in New York, the

Proceedings of the Republican convention in Chicago, and numerous tracts and speeches of influential political figures in the two years prior to the 1860 election, including several of Southern leaders such as Jefferson Davis and Judah Benjamin.

John, or possibly Belle, also glued into the volume several newspaper clippings about the Wide Awakes and Lincoln Rangers, some indicating that John served as Chief Marshal of the Chicago Wide Awakes in October 1860.

The Wide Awakes were a surprising and unprecedented national political phenomenon that sprang up in March 1860, first in Hartford, Connecticut, and rapidly spreading across New England, the Mid-Atlantic states, and what is now the Midwest. Republican supporters, mostly younger men, began organizing in marching groups, drilling in formation, wearing uniforms with

Parade of Wide Awakes in New York City, October 3, 1860, published in *Harper's Weekly* (Chicago History Museum).

black military style glazed hats and black shiny oilcloth capes, and holding six-foot staves carrying whale oil lamps. They engaged in torchlight parades, marching in silence except for the beating of a drum, and carrying flags bearing the symbol of the Wide Awakes: a single wide staring eye. They were not armed, but they were highly organized into companies and battalions, with sergeants, lieutenants, and captains, officers who were often Mexican War veterans and taught them military drill. For example, Ulysses S. Grant, who had resigned from the army and was then living in Galena, Illinois, met with the Wide Awakes during the campaign and "superintended their drill."[42] There were other named organizations, such as the mounted Lincoln Rangers in Chicago, but the Wide Awakes were the most numerous; estimates of their numbers range from 100,000 to 400,000.[43]

The excuse for a torchlight parade was often to "escort" a visiting Republican politician to the place of his speech. There was a Monster Torchlight Parade of twenty thousand Wide Awakes in New York City on October 4. In Chicago, John and three other members of the Wide Awake Invitation and Reception Committee issued a printed invitation dated September 17 addressed to Wide Awake clubs from far and near to come to Chicago on October 2 for a reception for William Seward, who was stumping for Lincoln. A gathering of fifteen thousand Wide Awakes was called for: "We want every county in Illinois and every state in the North West to be represented by a delegation of Wide Awakes," the Invitation said. It went on to report that "The ladies of Chicago will present a splendid banner to the largest Wide Awake company in proportion to the Republican vote of the town. The Chicago Clubs will not compete."[44] The *Tribune* reported on October 3 that after Seward's afternoon speech, practically the entire population turned out to line the marching route of the evening torchlight procession, which included by actual count 6,000 Wide Awakes, not counting many others who chose to be spectators. The "superb silk prize banner, costing $100," the *Tribune* reported, was presented to the Wide Awake club of Libertyville. "As the gathering of yesterday was the largest political rally that ever took place in the Northwest, so the torchlight procession of last evening that fittingly closed the same, was the largest ever known in the country." Some rivalry with New York might be detected here.

On October 24 there was a notice in the *Tribune* from John as Chief Marshal that the Wide Awakes and Lincoln Rangers were summoned that evening to escort the eloquent Ohio congressman Tom Corwin, known as "the wagon boy," to the Wigwam, and that the platform would be reserved exclusively for Wide Awakes. The next day the *Tribune* reported that "the Wide Awakes and Lincoln Rangers, under acting Chief Marshal John A. Bross, were out in full force, and with the finest display, as a whole, they have yet made. They were eight companies strong, and the torchlight procession extended four blocks, interspersed by fine bands, and presenting a most brilliant spectacle." Unfortunately, however, the Wide Awakes "reached the Wigwam to find nearly all the seats on the platform taken by those who would not vacate the same." The article expressed indignation that the Wide Awakes, who "have, throughout the campaign thus far, performed a most brilliant and efficient part in the labor," had been robbed of "a well earned and slight tribute to their usefulness and spirit.... [W]e are fully convinced that many were there whose conduct can only be characterized by the plain, simple old term of hoggish."

There was no national Wide Awake organization to speak of; the local clubs sprang up as word traveled rapidly throughout the Northern states. The paramilitary character of the clubs was not something entirely new, as there had been "militia fever" during the 1850s, probably as a result of the Mexican War, with men liking to dress in military attire and Militia Balls being popular, but there had not before been highly organized military-style groups for a specific political purpose and in such numbers. Some argue that the Wide Awakes were not a barometer of popular interest but instead were spectacles engineered by a few partisans to deceive the American voters; this seems to be related to the theory that the Civil War was unnecessary and would not have happened except for the clumsy maneuvers of a few politicians.[45] But the spontaneous and widespread appearance of these paramilitary groups in such enormous numbers could hardly have been produced by a few political agents, even had they been brilliant organizers.

It seems more plausible to view the appearance of the Wide Awakes as evidence of a widespread and growing feeling, especially among the young, that current political issues could be heading for a threat to the existence of the Republic and a military showdown. For decades, bellicose language had been used by Southern politicians and editors to describe a perceived Northern threat to their society. The appearance of the Wide Awakes was probably in part a reaction to the often violent Southern language, but it also played into Southern rhetoric. Texas Senator Wigfall blamed the Wide Awakes for a string of fires during an exceptionally hot and dry Texas summer, which were hysterically claimed to be part of an imaginary slave revolt plot, leading to the lynching of nearly 100 black and white people. In Virginia the *Richmond Enquirer* said of the Wide Awakes, "They parade at midnight, carry rails to break open our doors, torches to fire our dwellings, and beneath their long black capes the knife to cut our throats."[46] Still, the Wide Awakes should be understood more as a symptom of the situation than as a significant cause of the Civil War. For John, at least, his work with the Wide Awakes would have been an effort to win the 1860 election for Lincoln and the Republican Party, not to cause a Civil War.

Later, in April 1861, when the war broke out, there seems to have a suggestion that the Chicago Wide Awake companies should be turned into regular military companies, but the leadership rejected this as too political, feeling that enlistments in the new regiments should be free from any political affiliation. At a meeting of the Wide Awakes in Chicago, with John and William's brother Josiah H. Bross acting as Chair, "it was voted unanimously that the Companies composing said organization do now disband, and that when we adjourn we adjourn sine die" and that "Democrats, Republicans, and members of all parties be invited to enroll themselves as a band of brothers in defence of the Union and Constitution of their country."[47] A notice to the public signed by George W. Gage as Chief Marshal and John A. Bross of the Marshal's staff, as well as by several officers of individual companies, observed, "We have noticed with regret the call published for the formation of military companies from Company A, B, C and Excelsior Wide Awakes. Some time since, at a meeting of the officers of the Wide Awake organizations of this city, it was resolved unanimously that no steps should be taken to organize military companies from the Wide Awake organizations of this city.... [T]he present crisis of our national affairs demands that all political strife should be ignored. That Democrats and Republicans, without distinction of party, should rally to the support of our beloved Government."[48]

The election was held on November 6. The *Tribune* reported the next day that "At midnight the special despatches received at this office, and elsewhere given, told the story beyond peradventure that Abraham Lincoln had been elected by the people. The enthusiasm in our streets at the time was something tremendous. The air rang with jubilant shouts. The Wide Awakes were out, led off by a splendid band. All was rejoicing and jubilation." The November 8 *Tribune* reported that the next day orders were issued to the Wide Awakes by their officers for a general and final turn-out of the Wide Awakes "and their mounted brethren, the gallant Lincoln Rangers." They gathered on Michigan Avenue and marched to the Wigwam, where they heard several stirring but short speeches and then everyone went home. "So ends the Presidential election of 1860," the *Tribune* article stated. "Thus is peacefully inaugurated a change in our government. ... Peacefully, for not the most bitter Democrat in this city but laughs at the idea that the Southern States will not be able to 'hang their own traitors', and then in a better sense hereafter than for years past, 'keep step to the music of the Union.'"

But it was not to be. On December 20 a South Carolina convention voted unanimously to dissolve "the union now existing between South Carolina and other States." By February 1, 1861, South Carolina had been joined by the six other states of the Deep South: Mississippi, Florida, Alabama, Georgia, Louisiana, and Texas. Early in February delegates from those Southern states met in Montgomery, Alabama, where they rapidly turned themselves into a provisional Congress, elected Jefferson Davis provisional president, and started drafting a constitution that guaranteed the protection of slavery in any new territory it might acquire. The new federal administration would not take power until March 4; President Buchanan, a Pennsylvania Democrat, declared that no state had a right to secede but also said that the federal government had no power to coerce a state that tried to secede.[49] Many Northerners considered Buchanan's inaction treasonable; in Chicago the *Tribune* called for his impeachment.

In Chicago a large public meeting was held on January 5, 1861, in response to the secessionist activity. The meeting was described in the

Tribune on January 7 as a grand rally of citizens at Bryan Hall, which was reported to be "crowded to overflowing, by an assembly apparently without distinction of party, and representing Chicago in all the trades, professions and business interests, touched and influenced alike by the present imminently threatening condition of affairs." A "Board of officers of the evening" was appointed, including a president, 35 vice presidents representing distinguished citizens of Chicago, and 3 secretaries. After considerable discussion and several short speeches, including one of William Bross, resolutions were adopted in support of the Constitution and the Union. The lengthy resolutions stated, among other things, the following points: "The Union of these States under the Constitution framed by our fathers ... is the noblest form of government ever yet devised by man.... [T]o destroy it is to destroy the hopes of humanity ... THE UNION MUST AND IT SHALL BE PRESERVED." The Constitution was intended to be perpetual and no state could secede; secession is a usurpation of the powers of the general government. This nation has the mission of working out the "great idea of national self-government" and must "vindicate before the world its power to preserve our own harmony and integrity" and to suppress rebellion "without the aid of titled monarchs." All citizens should stand "shoulder to shoulder in defence of the Constitution, the Union and the laws":

> [T]here should be an exhaustion of peaceful measures before the sword shall be drawn; and therefore we are in favor of any just, honorable and constitutional settlement of the entire question of African slavery ... men of all political parties, in both sections of the country, should be ready to make great concessions to restore peace and harmony between the different regions of the country.

There was some objection to the phrase "great concessions," but it was retained in the resolutions as passed.

These arguments are probably typical of thinking at the time in all the Northern states. The Union formed under the Constitution was a new form of government, nobler than any yet seen in the history of the world; it was the hope of humanity and it must be preserved. Secession would destroy the Union and no "reckless political adventurers or fanatics" should be allowed to visit such a calamity on the nation. The Union must prove to the world that a nation built on self-government could defend itself against rebellion just as well as a monarchy could (decidedly not the opinion of most European powers who expected the collapse of the Union to vindicate older ideas of monarchy and absolutism). But war should be the last resort, and the reference to settlement of the question of African slavery seems to imply that while the question of the Union was not negotiable, the question of racial status was.

While the Committee on Resolutions was meeting to consider the proposed resolutions,

> [i]n response to calls all over the house, Mr. Bross of the *Tribune* came forward and responded in substance as follows:
>
> REMARKS OF WILLIAM BROSS
>
> This is a meeting of those who are determined to maintain the Union, the Constitution and the laws. We are not met as citizens of Illinois, of New York, or of Louisiana; we meet as citizens of the United States. ... Those who violate the protection of our flag, are traitors, whether they live at the South or the North. The supremacy of the constitution and the laws, and the Union as it is, must be maintained at all hazard and with the power of the Government.
>
> The Committee here came in and the Speaker at once closed his remarks.

Lincoln's inauguration took place on March 4, 1861. William and John probably attended the inauguration along with Joseph Medill and other Chicagoans, but the only reference we have to this is the remark in John's letter of May 1, 1864, that he had sat on the steps of the Treasury building three years before, looking up the avenue to the Capitol. William's lost diaries would have been the best source of detailed information about who traveled to Washington for the Inauguration. The diaries of Joseph Medill may also have been destroyed in the fire of 1871, as there are no known records of his participation in the inaugural activities. It seems probable that the senior editorial staff of the *Tribune* would have taken the train to Washington to attend the inauguration of the man whose candidacy they had done so much to promote and that John, who had been active in the campaign through the Wide Awakes, would have gone along with his brother, but the only evidence of this that has been found is the reference in John's letter.

It was on the morning after his inauguration that Lincoln, going to his office for the first time, found on his desk a report that Fort Sumter in Charleston Harbor, one of the only two forts in Confederate territory remaining in Federal hands, could only hold out for a few weeks if it did not receive provisions. After some careful and crucial maneuvering between the Lincoln and Confederate administrations about possible provisioning of the fort, Confederate forces opened fire on Fort Sumter on April 12, 1861, forcing it to surrender after two days of bombardment. Lincoln had probably come to think that war was inevitable, but he had skillfully managed the situation so that the war began with a Confederate attack on a Federal garrison flying the American flag.

The effect of the attack on Northern opinion was dramatic; great parades took place in all the large Northern cities in an outpouring of patriotic fervor. Northern politicians of all parties buried their differences in a common dedication to defending the Union. Stephen Douglas told a huge Chicago crowd, "There can be no neutrals in this war, only patriots—or traitors."[50] On April 15 Lincoln issued a proclamation calling 75,000 militiamen into federal military service to put down an insurrection "too powerful to be suppressed by the ordinary course of judicial proceedings."[51] Within days after Lincoln's proclamation, four more states—Virginia, Arkansas, North Carolina, and Tennessee—began taking action to secede and by the end of May, had officially voted to join the Confederacy, which now consisted of eleven states. The Confederate government agreed to make Richmond its permanent capital. The loss of Virginia was crucial because of its historic importance and location adjacent to the Federal capital, its large population, and its industrial capacity, greatly superior to that of the other Confederate states, and also because it was the home of some of the ablest military figures, including Robert E. Lee. And it was an open question whether the seceding states would be joined by the border states of Maryland, Kentucky, and Missouri, all of which were slave states and had strong secessionist as well as Union supporters. Lincoln was reported to have said that he would like to have God on his side, but he must have Kentucky.[52]

On April 19 the *Tribune* reported on the local situation in an article entitled "The War Spirit in Chicago!" Illinois Governor Yates had called for volunteers and the state's quota of six regiments had already been met, leaving only two companies to be received from Chicago. The railroads had offered to transport all military companies at no cost. There was a "look out for traitors": "all defamers of the government must be dumb. … Chicago has no provisions or breadstuffs to sell to a seceded South, and none will be sent thither"; a dealer in potatoes who had been sending large shipments of New Orleans was advised not to send any more.

The same article reported on a "Great Meeting at Bryan Hall last evening," committees having been appointed from the Board of Trade, the bench, the banks, the railroads, the citizens, the military, and the surgeons.

> As the evening set in, bonfires were lit at the corners of our principal streets, and our city was ablaze with enthusiasm. The business thoroughfares were thronged. Drums and fifes were playing at the different recruiting stations. At seven p.m. the procession left the Tremont House, headed by the Light Guard Band. … Entering the Hall it was found already densely filled save the platform, which was kept clear by the police. … Notwithstanding the crowd within, there was an even larger crowd without, which later formed a separate organization at Metropolitan Hall.

At the meeting, Judge Drummond was chosen as chairman and thirty-four leading citizens as vice presidents.

> Judge Drummond on taking the chair made an able and patriotic speech which was frequently interrupted by vociferous applause and cheering. He demolished the flimsy device of traitors, "No coercion,"

> and said there is now but one course, to sustain the Constitution and the law.... We have been electrified to-day by the tidings that within three days time of the President's call, the quota of Massachusetts were marching down Broadway. (Three rousing cheers were given for the noble old Bay State.)

The resolutions adopted by the meeting reflected the same themes as those of the January meeting, notably the sacred importance of the Union, both in itself and as a beacon of hope to the world, but with a more martial focus and an increased emphasis on the flag as the symbol of the nation:

> Resolved, that the armed Southern rebellion against our beloved and cherished Union is without excuse or patriotism, an outrage upon freedom and humanity, a most diabolical scheme to subserve selfish and ambitious ends, and that the traitors who have armed themselves and confederates together against our Government, shall be conquered, disarmed and crushed out, cost what blood, and treasures and time it may.
>
> Resolved, that the noble, firm and patriotic stand taken by National Administration to meet the most extraordinary crisis in the history of our country meets our heartfelt gratitude and cordial approval, and we hereby pledge our lives, our fortunes and our sacred honor to uphold our government in putting down rebellion and bringing the traitors to condign punishment.
>
> Resolved, that we are for our country—our whole country, first, last and forever, and that the Flag of the Republic, the Stars and Stripes, without a single star obliterated, shall continue to wave over the mountains, hills and valleys of our common country, and over every ocean and sea throughout both hemispheres, an emblem of freedom at home and a star of hope to all the oppressed peoples of the earth.
>
> Resolved, that we have borne with patience the gibes and sneers and insufferable insolence of Southern Secessionists until forbearance has ceased to be recommendable or politic, and now that they have dared, in the madness and folly and impudence of overweening pride and self-consequence, to attack the flag of our beloved country, it will be

made manifest to them that "those who sow the winds shall reap the whirlwinds."

Cash subscriptions were announced and "William Bross, Esq., of the Tribune, made a brief speech."

Illinois stayed strongly in the Union and was an important source of manpower and manufacturing support for the Union armies during the war. However, although the northern area of Illinois was strongly pro-Union and bound to the East Coast by the railroads that had proliferated during the 1850s, in its southern and western areas, Illinois was a river state bound to New Orleans by commercial traffic on the Mississippi River. Had the railroads not been built during the 1850s, feeding Chicago's rapidly

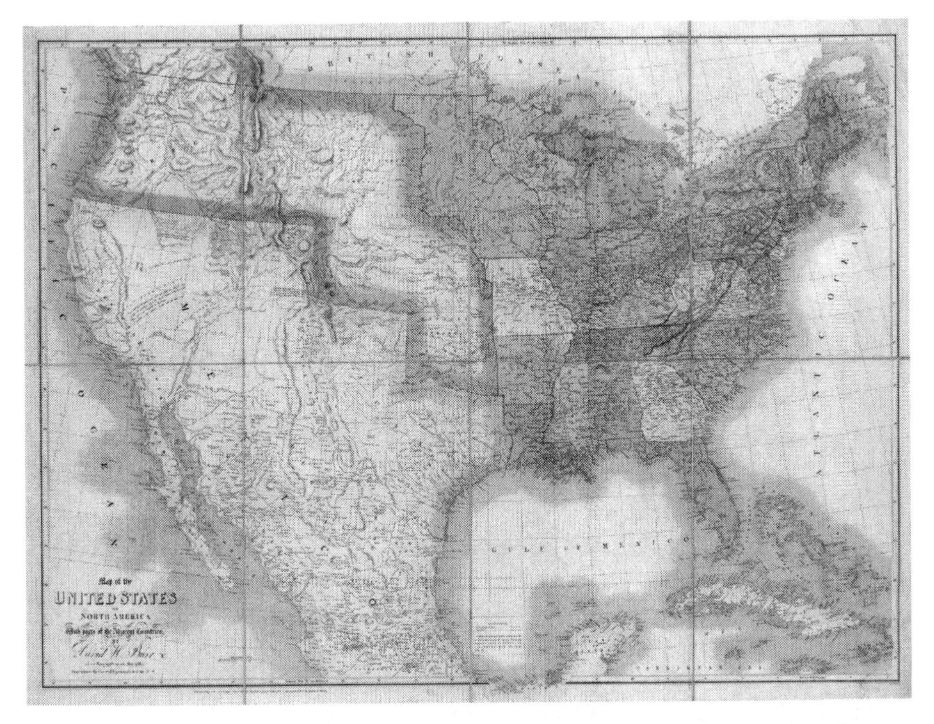

Map of the United States, 1839, David H. Burr (David Rumsey Map Collection).

This shows the United States prior to the Mexican War of 1846. Note the position of Illinois on the Mississippi River, connecting it with commercial traffic south to New Orleans.

growing population and industrial development in the northern part of the state, Illinois might have been in play to join the Confederacy. In April 1861 there was doubt about the loyalty of Cairo in southern Illinois and action was taken to secure it.

Within days of the fall of Fort Sumter, a Committee on the War had been created in Chicago. On April 19 Illinois Governor Yates sent a dispatch to General Swift, commander of the local military division, directing him: "As quick as possible have as strong a force as you can raised, armed and equipped... ready to march at a moment's notice."[53] On April 20 Swift raised a force of 400 volunteers "largely armed with squirrel rifles, shotguns, single barreled pistols, antique revolvers and anything that looked as if it would shoot that could be obtained from the gun stores, second-hand stores and pawnshops."[54] The armed group was secretly dispatched to Cairo on the night of April 21:

> At eleven o'clock at night, April 21st, p.m. the expedition started from the Illinois Central Railroad Station, amid the cheers of the people and the screaming of the steam-whistles.... [T]he railroad and telegraph companies' officers patriotically aided the authorities in every way, thus preventing any knowledge of the expedition being sent in advance. To this end, no telegrams were permitted to go over the lines, and the regular train on the Illinois Central Railroad was started at the usual hour, 7 p.m., but with orders to stop at a certain place until the military train had passed, giving to passengers, as an excuse for such delay, that some unavoidable accident, or other cause, prevented their going on. With this arrangement, the military train passed unheralded the length of the State, and rolled into Cairo to the astonishment of all, and rage of many of its citizens.[55]

It was believed that secessionist forces from Missouri were preparing within forty-eight hours to occupy Cairo, mostly Southern in sympathy and an important junction for railroads coming from the northwest. At the same time, Capt. James Stokes was sent on a secret mission from Springfield to the Jefferson Barracks arsenal in St. Louis, which was surrounded by thousands of rebel sympathizers, to rescue some 8,000 muskets and ammunition and ship them to Springfield. With the help of the commanding officer of the arsenal, the munitions were smuggled onto a waiting riverboat at 2 a.m. and brought safely to Alton, Illinois, from where they were shipped to Springfield for distribution to the new Union volunteers. It was thought that the removal of the arms from the St. Louis arsenal blocked rebel plans to take Missouri out of the Union and invade Illinois.[56] The war had begun.

In May 1861 Lincoln called for 75,000 additional troops to volunteer for three years, rather than the 90 days of the original 75,000 he had called for in April. In July Congress authorized another million three-year volunteers.[57] John, a married man of 35, was not among the Illinois volunteers; most were younger unmarried men under the spell of the initial enthusiasm for the war and under the illusion that it would be a short and glorious military parade.

The war began badly for the North in July when a relatively untrained Federal Army under General Irvin McDowell began an advance into Virginia, partly in response to political pressure from the Northern press, especially headlines in Horace Greeley's *New York Tribune* calling for an immediate advance "Forward to Richmond!" In spite of some initial success, the Union Army was defeated by General Pierre Beauregard's Confederate Army at the first Battle of Bull Run (or Manassas), and defeat turned into a rout. General George B. McClellan was immediately put in command to organize the new Army of the Potomac, and he did a brilliant job of organization and administration, but then as the autumn wore on, turned out to be incapable of risking the new army in an aggressive campaign against the enemy. A Union force in Missouri was defeated at Wilson's Creek, and the victorious Confederate Army then captured the large town of Lexington, Missouri. An expedition to dislodge a Confederate force in Leesburg, Virginia, 40 miles north of Washington, was humiliatingly crushed at the Battle of Ball's Bluff in November 1861.

During the first four months of 1862, however, the pendulum of success swung towards the Union. Nearly the whole of the Mississippi Valley was taken by Union forces, including the cities of New Orleans and Memphis.

In Tennessee in February, Fort Henry was taken, opening up the Tennessee River deep into Alabama, and soon afterwards, Fort Donelson fell, clearing the Cumberland River into mid-Tennessee and Nashville, which was evacuated by the Confederates and fell to Union forces in late February. All of Kentucky and most of Tennessee were now under Union military control. In southern Missouri a small Union army routed a larger Confederate force at the Battle of Pea Ridge. In early April in southwestern Tennessee, on the Tennessee River near a small church named Shiloh, there was a major two-day battle between a Confederate army commanded by Generals Sidney Johnston and Beauregard and a Union army commanded by General Ulysses S. Grant. The result was a Confederate retreat, but casualties of 20,000 killed and wounded, about equally divided between the two armies, made it a battle on a scale that had never been seen before but which would continue to occur in the remaining three years of the war. In Virginia it seemed only a matter of time before McClellan's large force closed in on Richmond.

In April 1862, Northern optimism about the war had resulted in the closing of recruiting offices throughout the North. But by early summer, the fortunes of war again turned against the North as McClellan's campaign against Richmond on the peninsula between the York and the James rivers ran out of steam in heavy fighting against the Confederate Army of Northern Virginia under General Robert E. Lee, who had been appointed to command that army on June 1. By July 1 McClellan had withdrawn his army from the peninsula. Lincoln recognized that it had been a mistake to cease recruiting in April. Seward arranged for northern governors to urge Lincoln to call on the states for new volunteers and on July 2, Lincoln called for 300,000 new volunteers for three years. This was the call for volunteers to which John decided that he ought to respond.

During the first year of the war, John had been carrying on as a private citizen. In January 1862 he served as secretary to a meeting of the Chicago Bar in honor of the recently deceased Judge Barron. On the Fourth of July, 1862, he delivered the oration at Blackberry, described as a thriving town on the Dixon Air Line Railroad in an article the next day in the *Tribune*:

> John A. Bross, Esq., of Chicago was then introduced to the audience. He paid a fitting tribute to the fathers of the revolution, the national holiday, and then addressed himself to the all-absorbing topic of the present day. This portion of his remarks was strongly in favor of supporting the government, not as partisans but as patriots, and in the use of all the means in our hands to put down the rebellion. He closed with an animated apostrophe to the ship of state. The enthusiastic approbation with which the address was received is the best praise of the speaker, and the soundness of the patriotic sentiments which he uttered. After the address the whole audience sat down to a basket picnic, and after enjoying the good things of this life, fathers, mothers, young men and maidens quietly returned to their homes.[58]

It is a scene worthy of Currier and Ives: a peaceful farming community at a patriotic festival, encouraged by an eloquent admiralty lawyer to take up arms to defend the ship of state.

Unlike the situation of a year before, volunteers did not rush forward in response to Lincoln's July 1862 call for volunteers. The war no longer seemed to offer a short and romantic opportunity for glory; news of terrible casualties in bloody battles had become well known. It was obvious that the war would go on for some time. Whereas, in 1861, the majority of volunteers had been younger, now more mature men such as John, often with wives and children, stepped forward in greater numbers. This argues for the ideological importance of the war to a broad spectrum of Northern society as a defense of the Union. The *Memorial* states:

> His decision in respect to entering the army, was no enthusiastic impulse, but the action of his judgment as well; which is shown by the fact that he did not join the first volunteers, deeming his family ties too dear to be severed, while men with less to bind them to their homes were offered in greater numbers than Government would accept. When, however, the progress of events made it necessary again to fill up the armies, the enthusiasm of multitudes had cooled, and exertion became necessary to secure recruits, he decided that duty called him to the field.

> Leaving the position he had attained in his profession and the home so fondly dear, he devoted himself thenceforth to his country.[59]

John was devoted to his wife and infant son and was building a successful legal career in Chicago. His age, 35 in 1861, was not considered too old to join but neither was it to be expected that a man of his age and marital status would volunteer. His feeling of duty to his country is reflected in passages from his letters from the field that weigh his obligation as a citizen against his love of home and family. For example, in a letter of January 1863, he wrote:

> I counted the cost at the beginning; I knew its dangers, and possible sacrifice; I am one of those who thoroughly believe that blood must be shed to bring this controversy to a close.... I do not know whether all can reconcile my position with the absorbing love of home which fills my soul. But it is that very love which urges me forward, that our boy may enjoy all the privileges of our noble, God-given republic. No other object could tempt me from a home so full of true enjoyment.[60]

Probably the family's connection to the *Tribune*, with its unwavering support of the Lincoln administration, was also a factor in persuading John to enlist.

On July 19, 1862, the *Tribune* announced a meeting that evening in Bryan Hall

> to put down armed rebellion at all hazards, and to maintain the supremacy of the Constitution and Laws, at whatever sacrifice of treasure and blood.... Distinguished gentlemen of well known patriotism will address the meeting, breathing the true spirit of self-sacrificing devotion to our common country, ignoring party questions and party ties, regarding the present as no time to indulge in party strife, or discussions, but to come one, come all! And send up our united voices for the support of the Government we love and cherish, in tones worthy of the great metropolis of the mighty Northwest.

John A. Bross is listed as a member of the Young Men's Delegation.

Subsequent articles in the *Tribune* show the progress of recruiting. On July 22 there is a report that the young men had held a war meeting the evening before in Bryan Hall:

> A large audience was in attendance, and much enthusiasm was manifested. John A. Bross called the meeting to order, and nominated John V. Farwell for Chairman.... Stirring speeches were made by John A. Bross, T. B. Bryan, D. W. Whittle, Col. W. S. Pope and others. A muster roll was opened and a respectable number of recruits enrolled their names.... This regiment presents unusual inducements. Let our young men come up. Chicago must furnish her quota.

On August 8 a *Tribune* article reported that 2,800 men had been enlisted in Chicago: "In Bryan Hall, which has been the headquarters of the Young Men's Christian Association, Capts. Holbrook, Whittle, Perkins, Brainard, Bross and Underwood are recruiting. Capt. Underwood has 80 men, Captains D. W. Whittle 62, Capt. Brainerd 60, and Capt. Bross probably about 80." An article of August 14 reports:

> Capt. John A. Bross' Company. The Invincible Guard, Capt. John A. Bross, one of the companies of the Young Men's Christian Association, in the Board of Trade Regiment, is now recruiting at Bryan Hall, and is nearly full. All who wish to enlist with an energetic and determined officer will do well to muster into the service under him. He is bound to have his company full tonight.

As he began raising the two companies, John also turned his attention and legal skill to learning about the art of war.[61]

In the Union Army, a company was normally composed of 100 men led by a captain. Theoretically, a regiment was composed of ten companies, a total of one thousand men, but most regiments averaged 300 to 400 men, due to attrition from disease, casualties, transfers, or desertion. The commanding officer of a regiment was a colonel. There could also be a lieutenant colonel, and there would be at least one major. Later, in 1864, John would be a lieutenant colonel in command of the 29th United States Colored Troops, rather than a full Colonel because his regiment was summoned to action before it had achieved the required number of full companies. In the center of a regiment was the color guard, 5 to 8 men assigned to protect the regimental or national colors, led by a color sergeant. Union regiments usually carried both regimental and national colors, whereas Confederate regiments usually carried only their national flag. Protecting the colors was considered essential to the honor of a regiment.

Three to five regiments made up a brigade, which became the main structure for battlefield maneuvers. A brigade was normally commanded by a brigadier general. Two to four brigades comprised a division, so that a typical division might include 10 to 15 regiments, perhaps 8,000 to 15,000 men, in theory commanded by a major general but often by a more junior officer. Several divisions constituted a corps, and multiple corps made up an army, often commanded by a major general.[62]

After raising two companies in August, John was mustered in on August 27, 1862, and on September 4 ranked as captain of one of them, which became Company A of the Eighty-eighth Infantry Illinois Volunteers Regiment.[63] John was designated senior captain of the 88th Illinois. The letters indicate that there was some disagreement about his rank as senior captain, but he was so designated in later articles in the *Tribune*.

The 88th Illinois, also known as the Second Board of Trade Regiment, was commanded by Col. Francis T. Sherman, who had served as an officer in an infantry regiment when the war began in 1861 and then as an officer in a cavalry regiment. Sherman's father was Francis C. Sherman, a Chicago hotel owner and politician who served as Mayor of Chicago in 1841 and again during the Civil War for two two-year terms beginning in 1862 and 1864. He was a moderate, taking a strong stand against the extension of slavery in the years before the war, but during the war becoming more tolerant of the "Peace Democrats," the faction of the Democratic Party who gradually turned against the war effort. These were regarded by Republicans as dangerous traitors and often reviled as "Copperheads" because they wore in their lapels liberty heads cut from large penny coins and in order to label them as poisonous serpents. They officially supported the Union but were firmly opposed to emancipation and in favor of a negotiated settlement to restore the Union as it had been, which Republicans, probably correctly, considered impossible, so they were suspected of disloyalty or at least of failing to support fully the war effort. This led to some political disagreement between Col. Sherman and his father, reflected in Sherman's letters, but it placed the Shermans in a different political camp than William and John Bross, who were, of course, enthusiastic Republicans and Lincoln supporters associated with the *Tribune*, which never wavered in its support of the Lincoln administration and the war effort.[64] This may explain several references in John's letters to his belief that he was being ignored for promotion because he didn't belong to the right clique. Had John been on the same political page as Colonel Sherman, it is possible that he would have been promoted in the 88th Illinois Regiment and remained there, instead of accepting a commission in late 1863 to raise a new black regiment in Illinois as its colonel.

By early September the 88th Illinois was organized. On September 4 it was mustered in and ordered to Louisville, Kentucky. It left Chicago on September 4 and went into camp at Jeffersonville, Indiana, across the Ohio River from Louisville.[65] The regiment received arms on September 11 and moved the next day to Covington, Kentucky, on the south side of the Ohio River, in support of Cincinnati on the north side, which appeared to be under threat from Confederate troops advancing across Kentucky. But the threat evaporated as the Confederates changed course and on September 21 the 88th was sent to Louisville on an Ohio River steamer, which ran aground, making it necessary to finish the trip on foot.[66]

A *Tribune* article dated September 10, 1862, reported on a ceremony held Sunday, September 7, 1862, at the Third Presbyterian Church:

> SWORD PRESENTATION
>
> An impressive scene occurred at the Third Presbyterian church on Sabbath afternoon last at the usual hour of the session of the Sabbath school. Capt. John A. Bross, of the 2d Board of Trade regiment, who has been for years the leader of the musical exercises of the school and

assistant superintendent for two years past, met with the school for the last time preparatory to joining his regiment. After the usual exercises, closing with singing, "My country 'tis of thee," a committee of three young ladies, Misses Helen W. Osborn, Hattie Fowler, Katie Willard and three children from the infant class came forward, bearing a beautiful sword, sash and belt. Miss Osborn, daughter of Elder William Osborn, one of our oldest citizens, made the following presentation address, which was delivered in admirable voice and manner:

Captain Bross: You are about to leave us—to change your position from an officer of the Sabbath School to that of an officer in the army. We as a school shall miss you and shall wish to be remembered by you in return. And in no way can we so appropriately express our thanks for your kind and pleasant labors among us, and your constant efforts for our welfare, than by connecting associations of the school with the badge of honor.

The advent of our Saviour, whose teachings it is for the Sabbath School to inculcate, was heralded by the angels' song—"Peace on earth, good will to men." And in ordinary times, this occasion would be in opposition to the precepts and spirit of the Gospel and ill befitting this holy day. But these are not ordinary times, nor is it any common call that has induced you to enter the army. We feel as if the cause in which you will bear this sword is truly the cause of God and the Prince of Peace.

On the Sabbath days to come, there will be no tolling bell to call you to a place of worship. May this, ever by your side, in danger and safety, lead your thoughts back to the happy hours spent with us here, and strengthen your heart in the duties of camp and field, by the assurance it bears of the loving memory and earnest trust of those you leave.

May God keep you from danger, and return you to us when this shall be no longer a token of coming struggle, but of complete and lasting victory.

Mr. Bross, having received the gift, replied substantially as follows:

Miss Osborn, young ladies, and friends: Language is a poor vehicle to convey the thoughts and emotions of my heart. Having been associated with this church and people for more than eleven years, I am about to separate from you, and try the realities of the tented field. No earthly consideration could induce me to leave a domestic circle replete with happiness—this church and all its sacred associations, but the single one of duty to my country in this her hour of trial. No man's life is his own when his country demands his services. I go hence to meet privations, trials, perchance disease, and death upon the field of battle. Sustained by an unfaltering trust in the Redeemer of mankind, why should I fear? The cause of our country is, as you have said, His cause, and I accept this beautiful present—the emblem of war—in this sacred place—in the spirit in which it is given. I accept it as a 'badge of honor,' radiant with sacred, golden-hued associations of this Sabbath School, and an ever-present memorial of this holy day. Wherever I go, it shall remind me of the dear friends I leave behind. I pledge you I shall keep this gift, and endeavor to bring it back with honor. May I never return if I shall bring disgrace upon it.

The pastor, Mr. Swazey, and Thomas Lord, superintendent, closed with appropriate remarks.

NOTES

1. Gordon S. Wood, *Empire of Liberty: A History of the Early Republic, 1789–1815* (Oxford University Press, 2009), 509.
2. Wood, *Empire of Liberty*, 517.
3. Ron Chernow, *Washington: A Life* (New York: Penguin, 2010), 485.
4. Wood, *Empire of Liberty*, 525.
5. Ibid., 519.
6. Ibid., 525.
7. Ibid., 533–535.
8. James McPherson, *This Mighty Scourge: Perspectives on the Civil War* (New York: Oxford University Press, 2007), 11.
9. James McPherson, *Battle Cry of Freedom* (New York: Oxford University Press, 1988), 649–650.
10. A well-known photograph of "Emancipated Slaves," showing several children with decidedly European-descent features, was on display at the Smithsonian's National Portrait Gallery in an exhibition entitled "Bound for Freedom's Light: African

Americans and the Civil War," which opened on February 1, 2013, organized by Ann M. Shumard, Senior Curator of Photographs at the museum.

11. Wood, *Empire of Liberty*, 541–2.
12. Cited in Tom Campbell, *Fighting Slavery in Chicago*, 56.
13. James McPherson, *For Cause and Comrades: Why Men Fought in the Civil War* (New York: Oxford University Press, 1997), 120.
14. Wood, *Empire of Liberty*, 539.
15. James McPherson, *For Cause and Comrades*, 115.
16. Glenn Tucker, *Chickamauga; Bloody Battle in the West* (Dayton, Ohio: Morningside Bookshop, 1984), 219.
17. Wood, *Empire of Liberty*, 530.
18. Selena Castro, "the mountains! the mountains!: Slavery in Williamstown, MA" (Undergraduate Paper for Dr. Dorothy Wang, Williams College, Fall 2015).
19. An ode sung at the second anniversary of the Williams College Anti-Slavery Society on July 4, 1827, ended with the lines: "And when on the soil of our sires we repose/ 'Neath the cocoa-tree lifting its voice to the wind,/ While we smile at the kindness that solac'd our woes,/ We will weep for the lov'd ones left groaning behind." "POEM," Spoken July 4, 1828, before the Anti-Slavery Society of Williams College, By William Pitt Palmer, Member of the Institution. Published by Request of the Society. Williamstown: Printed by Ridley Bannister. 1828.
20. *Biographical Sketches*, 39.
21. Megan McKinney, *The Magnificent Medills; America's Royal Family of Journalism During a Century of Turbulent Splendor* (New York: Harper, 2011), 27.
22. Philip Kinsley, *The Chicago Tribune; Its First Hundred Years*, 2 Vols (New York: Alfred A. Knopf, 1943), 13.
23. Ibid., 14.
24. Ibid., 10.
25. Ibid., 67.
26. Ibid., 76, 132.
27. William Bross, *History of Chicago; Historical and Commercial Statistics, Sketches, Facts and Figures, Republished from the "Daily Democratic Press."; What I Remember of Early Chicago; A Lecture, Delivered in McCormick's Hall, January 23, 1876* (Chicago: Jansen, McClurg & Co., 1876), 86.
28. McKinney, *The Magnificent Medills*, 21; Philip Kinsley, *The Chicago Tribune*, 47.
29. Philip Kinsley, *The Chicago Tribune*, 76.
30. Ibid., 181.

31. *Political Debates Between Hon. Abraham Lincoln and Hon. Stephen A. Douglas, in the Celebrated Campaign of 1858, in Illinois* (Columbus: Follett, Foster and Company, 1860), 66.
32. Philip Kinsley, *The Chicago Tribune*, 87.
33. Ibid., 75.
34. Ibid., 86.
35. *In Memoriam; Jessie Bross Lloyd, September 27, 1844–December 29, 1904* (Chicago: Press of the H. G. Adair Printing Co).
36. Philip Kinsley, *The Chicago Tribune*, 94.
37. Ibid., 97.
38. Ibid., 106.
39. Ibid., 107.
40. Ibid., 118.
41. *Proceedings of the National Republican Convention, Held at Chicago, May 16th, 17th & 18th, 1860.* Press & Tribune Documents for 1860, No. 3. (Chicago: Press & Tribune Office, 1860), 32.
42. Joan Waugh, *U. S. Grant; American Hero, American Myth* (Chapel Hill: University of North Carolina Press, 2009), 81.
43. Jon Grinspan, "'Young Men for War': The Wide Awakes and Lincoln's 1860 Presidential Campaign," *The Journal of American History* (96, no. 2, 2009), 357–378.
44. Announcement for Wide Awake Rally, October 1860. Private Collection.
45. Glenn C. Altschuler, and Stuart M. Blumin, *Rude Republic: Americans and Their Politics in the Nineteenth Century* (Princeton University Press, 2001), 5.
46. Jon Grinspan, "Young Men for War."
47. *Chicago Tribune*, April 19, 1861.
48. Ibid.
49. James McPherson, *Battle Cry of Freedom*, 248.
50. Ibid., 274.
51. Ibid., 274.
52. Benjamin P. Thomas, *Abraham Lincoln; A Biography*, (New York: Alfred A. Knopf, 1952).
53. Augustus Harris Burley, "The Cairo Expedition," *Reminiscences of Chicago During the Civil War* (Chicago: Lakeside Press, 1914), 54.
54. Ibid., 54.
55. Ibid., 56.
56. Ibid., 61–64.
57. James McPherson, *Battle Cry of Freedom*, 322.

58. *Chicago Tribune*, July 9, 1862.
59. *Memorial*, 5.
60. *Memorial*, 5–6
61. Several of the books John bought and studied are in the possession of his descendants. They are listed here to show what one Chicago lawyer studied in 1862 to prepare for an unexpected military career:

    Edouard La Barre Duparcq, Nicolas Édouard Delabarre-Duparcq, *Elements of Military Art and History: Comprising the History and Tactics of the Separate Arms; the Combination of the Arms; and the Minor Operations of War*, Translated by Brig. Gen. George W. Cullum, Chief of Staff of the General-in-Chief of the Armies of the United States (New York: D. Van Nostrand, 1863); Henry Wager Halleck, *Elements of Military Art and Science; Or, Course of Instruction in Strategy, Fortification, Tactics of Battles, &c., Embracing the Duties of Staff, Infantry, Cavalry, Artillery, and Engineers* (New York: D. Appleton & Company, 1859); *Revised Regulations for the Army of the United States, 1861, By authority of the War Department* (Philadelphia: J. B. Lippincott & Co., 1862); George Brinton McClellan, *Manual of Bayonet Exercise: Prepared for the Use of the Army of the United States* (Philadelphia: JB Lippincott, 1862); George Washington Cullum. *Systems of Military Bridges in Use by the United States Army: Those Adopted by the Great European Powers, and Such as are Employed in British India. With Directions for the Preservation, Destruction, and Re-establishment of Bridges* (New York: D. Van Nostrand, 1863); J.C. Duane, *Manual for Engineer Troops* (New York: D. Van Nostrand, 1862).

    Additionally, he would probably have had with him:

    William Price Craighill, *The Army Officer's Pocket Companion: Principally Designed for Staff Officers in the Field* (New York: D. Van Nostrand, 1862).
62. Garry E. Adelman, "Civil War Military Organization," *Essential Civil War Curriculum*, (2014) url:http://www.essentialcivilwarcurriculum.com/assets/files/pdf/ECWCTOPICOrganizationEssay.pdf.
63. *Report of the Adjutant General of the State of Illinois, Volume V; Containing Reports for the Years 1861–1866* (Springfield, IL: H. W. Rokker, State Printer and Binder, 1886), 242
64. C. Knight Aldrich, *Quest for a Star; The Civil War Letters and Diaries of Colonel Francis T. Sherman for the 88th Illinois* (Univ. of Tennessee Press, 1999), 9, 29.
65. *Report of the Adjutant General*, 260; *Memorial*, 7; Andreas, *History of Chicago*, vol.2, 236.
66. *Report of the Adjutant General*, 260; Aldrich, *Quest for a Star*, 11.

CHAPTER 4

1862: Kentucky, Battle of Perryville; Tennessee, Battle of Stones River

John's 88th Illinois Regiment had been sent on September 12 to Covington, Kentucky, to support the nearby city of Cincinnati, Ohio, against a Confederate threat from the forces of General Kirby Smith.[1] When Smith changed his objective and the threat receded, the 88th was moved on September 21 to Louisville, Kentucky, to bolster that city's defenses against what was thought to be an imminent attack by a Confederate army commanded by General Braxton Bragg, which had invaded Kentucky from Chattanooga in southeastern Tennessee.[2] In Louisville the 88th joined a growing Union force, now some 36,000 strong, under the command of General William Nelson, consisting of defeated remnants of the Army of Kentucky and new recruits arriving daily from Indiana, Ohio, Illinois, and Wisconsin. The city of Louisville was increasingly apprehensive about the approach of victorious Confederate forces and was waiting anxiously for the arrival of General Don Carlos Buell and his Union troops from western Tennessee.[3]

By September 1862 the Union position was looking bleak. In the Eastern Theater, Confederate General Robert E. Lee had moved the line of battle from within 20 miles of Richmond to within 20 miles of Washington, bringing panic to the residents of the Federal capital. The European powers were seriously considering intervention leading to recognition of the Confederacy; only the British government insisted on waiting for a decisive Confederate victory. Lee seemed about to produce one when, having shattered the Union forces at the second Battle of Bull Run at the end of August, he led his army across the Potomac on September 4 into Maryland, a border slave state, with the objectives of bringing Maryland into the Confederacy and burning the railroad bridge over the Susquehanna at Harrisburg, Pennsylvania, which would cut the main communication between Washington and the West.

In the Western Theater of the war, which in those days meant Kentucky, Tennessee, and Missouri, Confederate armies were also striking north into Union territory in the late summer of 1862. In mid-August Confederate General Bragg had moved his army from Tennessee north into Kentucky, heading towards the state capital of Frankfort and then Louisville, while Confederate General Kirby Smith invaded Kentucky from Tennessee on a parallel course to the east, planning to join up with Bragg. The Confederates hoped that the people of Kentucky, also a border slave state, would rise up in support of the Confederacy, and they did briefly install a pro-Confederate governor at Frankfort, the state capital.

But within a period of three weeks ending in mid-October, Lee's advance into Maryland was checked by Union forces under the reinstated General George B. McClellan at the Battle of Antietam on September 17, with Lee's army retreating back into Virginia, while Bragg's invasion of Kentucky was blocked by Buell at the Battle of Perryville on October 8, forcing Bragg to retreat from Kentucky south through the Cumberland Gap back into Tennessee. In neither battle did Union forces win a crushing victory over the opposing army; in both battles there was a high number of casualties on both sides. Lincoln was disappointed with both of his generals for missing what he and others thought had been a good opportunity to pursue and destroy the enemy force, which he correctly believed was the only sure way to victory. But Lincoln also appreciated that in both cases a Union force was left in possession of the field while the invading Confederate force retreated, so that both battles were counted as Union victories and both border states were secured for the Union. Antietam is better known and that battle gave Lincoln the support he felt he needed to issue the preliminary Emancipation Proclamation, which put a check to European intervention on the side of the Confederacy. But the Battle of Perryville was also of crucial importance because it kept Kentucky in the Union; Lincoln believed that the loss of Kentucky would probably have led to defeat for the Union cause.[4]

THE KENTUCKY CAMPAIGN, SEPTEMBER AND OCTOBER 1862

Bragg's plan of invading Kentucky had at first succeeded brilliantly. At the Battle of Richmond, Kentucky, on the way to Lexington on August 30, Kirby Smith's army completely routed a small Union army under General Nelson, who lost 75 percent of his force. On September 2 Smith entered Lexington without a fight and on September 3 occupied the capital city of Frankfort, hoisting a Confederate battle flag over the Kentucky Capitol amid cheers from Confederate sympathizers. On September 14 one of Bragg's brigades suffered a defeat at the Battle of Munfordville, but the small Union force there surrendered to Bragg's whole army three days later on September 17. Louisville, the largest city in Kentucky and mostly Union in sympathy, was in a panic. On September 22 all women and children were ordered to leave the city and the next day all hotels and bars were ordered to be closed; the *Louisville Daily Journal* reported that an attack on Louisville was expected that day or the next. General Nelson had put all his soldiers to work digging a chain of trenches around the southern rim of the city that were completed by September 28, planning to hold off Bragg's troops long enough for Buell's army to attack Bragg from the rear. If the defense failed, Nelson planned to burn the city and retreat across the Ohio River to Indiana.[5]

But Buell's army arrived in Louisville on September 26, and Bragg had halted, realizing that Buell would be there before he could attack the city. Buell immediately began reorganizing the Union forces in Louisville to go on the attack against the Confederate invaders, but Bragg thought it would take several weeks before Buell would be ready to engage him, and he left his army on September 28 to travel to Frankfort to attend the installation of the pro-Confederacy governor on October 4.[6] Although there was a good deal of sympathy for the Confederacy in Kentucky, it was not strong enough to bring anything like as many volunteers to the Confederate cause as had been hoped, even though Confederate armies had occupied most of the state. Bragg had announced to the citizens of Kentucky that his army would not stay unless it received popular support, but then he found himself obliged to engage with Union forces in Kentucky even without the local support he had counted on to raise a significant number of volunteer troops.[7]

General Buell had spent the summer moving the Army of the Ohio slowly east towards Chattanooga, Tennessee, from Corinth, Mississippi. Like McClellan, and unlike Generals Grant, Sheridan, or Sherman, who rose to leadership later in the war, Buell was politically moderate and thought that the war should result in the re-establishment of things as they had been; he also believed that property rights of Southerners, including slavery, should be respected. He was, in fact, himself a slave owner, having inherited several from his wife. For Buell and McClellan, it was impossible to move an army quickly because one had to respect the property rights of civilians and supply one's troops by railroad, although the railroads were an easy target for sabotage by a hostile population. For Grant and Sherman in later stages of the war, it, in fact, *was* possible to move an army quickly because they were prepared to send troops without back-up supplies to live off the land as they went, not respecting the property rights of civilians; this is what Sherman did on his march from Atlanta to the sea in late 1864. But for Buell in 1862, it took all summer to move his army from Corinth, Mississippi, to Tennessee and then to Kentucky, finally reaching Louisville in late September.[8]

Buell himself arrived in Louisville by Ohio River steamer on September 25 and the first soldiers of his army began to appear on September 26, receiving a joyful welcome. The *Louisville Daily Journal* reported, "The Cloud is Lifting."[9] In Louisville Buell's weary and ill-clothed veterans met the newly recruited regiments, including John's 88th Illinois Regiment, which had arrived five days earlier on September 21. In a letter of September 29, 1862, John wrote:

> Last Friday [September 26] was the first day I was out of camp, in town to see about the soldiers' bounty. I saw Buells army come in & it was a sight worth seeing—while one of the regiments was marching past all begrimed with dust & dirt, James Curtiss Jr. recognized me and was extremely glad to see me. It was the 15th regulars. We have moved our camp several times & are now located on the east side of the city near the river being the extreme left instead of the right as last week.

Buell immediately and efficiently set to work to reorganize the forces at Louisville, incorporating the newly levied troops, and within four days had his new Army of the Ohio, some 58,000 strong, ready to march against Bragg.[10] The new regiments were blended in with the veterans, most of the brigades being formed of one new regiment and three veteran ones. Buell divided his army into three corps, the First Corps under the command of Major General Alexander McCook, the Second Corps under Major General Thomas Crittenden, and the Third Corps, to which John's 88th Illinois Regiment was assigned, under Major General William Nelson.[11] In the Third Corps, the 88th Illinois Regiment, commanded by Colonel Francis T. Sherman, was one of six regiments assigned to the 37th Brigade under Colonel Nicholas Greusel. Greusel's was one of three brigades in the 11th Division, which was commanded by Brigadier General Philip Henry Sheridan, a West Point graduate who had been made a brigadier general less than a month before. General Nelson, commander of the Third Corps, was killed on September 29 in a personal quarrel, and Buell appointed General Charles Gilbert in his place as commanding general of the Third Corps. Gilbert had been appointed a major general after the defeat at Richmond, but his appointment had never been officially approved, a fact apparently unknown to Buell. Gilbert turned out to be out of touch with his men and dangerously aloof from participation when the battle took place.[12] General George H. Thomas was second in command of the Army of the Ohio.

On September 29, the same day as the death of his trusted subordinate General Nelson, Buell received an order from Washington removing him from command and replacing him with his second in command, General Thomas. Lincoln had concluded that Buell's tardiness in reaching Tennessee had allowed the Confederates to invade Kentucky. However, Thomas declined the appointment, requesting that Buell be retained in command, on the grounds that Buell had just completed his preparations for an attack and he, Thomas, was not fully informed about them. Washington acquiesced, but Buell knew that he had lost the confidence of the administration, and a resulting excess of caution may have impaired his confidence and flexibility during the battle. To make things worse, the day before the battle, Buell was thrown from his horse and received a thigh wound that kept him confined to his headquarters in a house two or three miles behind the action during the battle.[13]

On the evening of September 29, Buell met with his three corps commanders and outlined his plan for moving against Bragg, who was then at Bardstown. The three corps were to move by different routes from Louisville

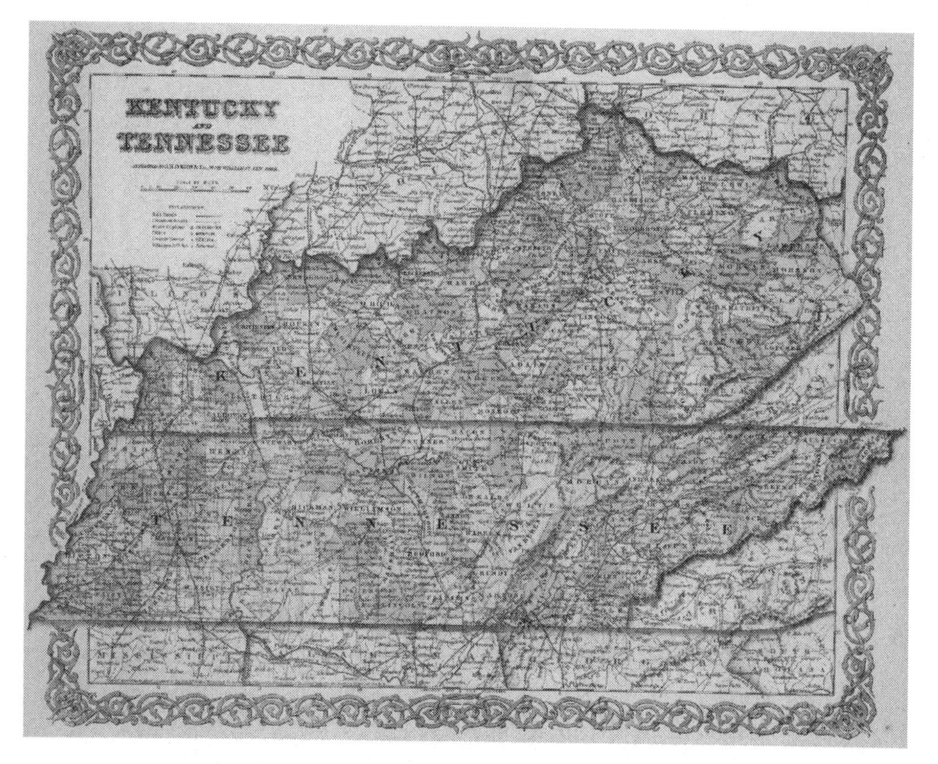

Map of Kentucky and Tennessee, 1856, J. H. Colton (David Rumsey Map Collection).

and converge on Bardstown, about thirty miles southeast, where Bragg's army was thought to be located. A detachment of the First Corps was sent west towards Frankfort to keep Kirby Smith's Confederate army occupied. Final orders were issued on the evening of September 30, and Buell's army marched out of Louisville on the morning of October 1. Gilbert's Third Corps, including the 88th Illinois, took the southern route through Shepherdsville.[14]

John was beginning to learn about a soldier's life. On September 30, the evening before the army's march began, he wrote, "Have been making ready for the march with 'light baggage' which means no tents & no baggage of any account. I will send my trunk home by express and key in this letter. We must 'rough it' and have the open sky for our tents. We have already had a taste of it, and I think we can stand it."

On October 2, the day afterward, he described his experience on the first day's march:

> Yesterday we took up the line of march from camp about 11 A.m. I rolled up my shawl, rubber blanket, a common soldiers overcoat, strapped them on my back & with my haversack filled with crackers, a piece of chicken, two lemons, a towel, a little soap, a toothbrush, a pair of stockings, a little tea sugar, a small bottle of that Bourbon that Bro Will give me, a pen & some ink, my sword & belt, you may imagine my appearance. Our march lay through a beautiful country & some fine old Kentucky homes made me feel like owning some of them.

Food gets prominent attention in John's letters. For example, "I assure you that the bacon, hard cracker and a cup of tea made in a tin cup was eaten with a relish unknown to dyspeptics."[15] Or:

> I awoke in the morning as bright as a new dollar, made me a cup of coffee, soaked some hard cracker & with a little sugar made what I thought a capital breakfast. It only whetted my appetite. I borrowed some bacon, broiled it over the fire with a stick & took course No. 2. After that, with expectations of being ordered off, I run the risk of cooking some rice,

> which I succeeded in doing admirably making course No. 3. With that I was satisfied.... The last thing I did when the regiment was moving out of Camp was to almost drink a splendid dish of beef soup enabling me to go into battle on a full stomach. Do not think I'm entirely given to eating. Yet it is one of the points in a soldiers life. I often wish that you & mother & the girls could see us cooking. I have made a reputation among the boys in this respect.[16]

The regimen seems to have agreed with him since by January 1863 he was reporting that he had gained twenty pounds and now weighed 161 pounds.[17]

Food was often obtained by foraging, although this was technically against the rules. John justified this because he thought the people of Kentucky had no real patriotism. "It is more fear of the north than anything else that keeps them in the Union. So I at least am ready to look after something to eat and not wait always the red tape of Uncle Sam or his 2M wagons."[18] On November 18 he wrote: "[W]e officers generally send a man who will bring us <u>under the hay</u> a leg of veal, mutton or chickens, potatoes or any other substantial, all this the lieutenant in command <u>never</u> sees although his eyes are wide open. Secesh are thus gulled but no union men. We would not hurt a hair of the Union men's heads."

Some of the senior officers shared this flexible view of foraging. On December 10 John described an incident in which a foraging party from his and another company was arrested and brought before Colonel Sherman, the regimental commander, who

> gave them a "particular cussing" & sent them over to Col. Greusel [the brigade commander]. <u>He</u> sent them back to quarters immediately, & all the punishment they got was to do a little policing of camp. <u>Moral</u>—I got the potatoes.... I suppose our dear mother may think this rather impinging on the moral law—I should myself if it were foraging on a true Unionist. But I am somewhat of the opinion of Old Brownlow—Secessionists have but two rights—to be hanged and be d----d.[19]

John learned to sleep in the open air: "I slept on the ground with nothing but the stars above me. It was a glorious nap."[20] And he came to like it. On December 10 he wrote: "Open air life is beneficial to my health provided I do not expose myself unnecessarily. I often think how I can stand it to go back to sleep in tight rooms." By late February 1863, he could write, "If I ever get through this war I do not wish to be confined in an office. I must have out door exercise. I do not like the thought of giving up my regular business, yet I never can be content to rust out in sedentary life."[21]

John's family and his deep wish to be with them are frequently mentioned in his letters, but the theme of absence from home and family often brings with it an expression of the patriotism that led to his enlistment and keeps him willing to fight. On October 2, 1862, he recalled a last rally of the Wide Awakes prior to the election of Lincoln two years before:

> I do not forget the scene two years ago this day in Chicago. Little did I then think at that immense gathering of Wide Awakes of the change so soon to come over our beloved land & that I should be fighting for the preservation of our government, that I should leave the sweetest wife and dearest friends & bear trials hardships & exposure that our son may enjoy the same privileges under a beneficent, God given Republic. I sometimes have an anxiety that you may think because I sought a position in the army, my love for you was not of that all absorbing engrossing nature which we expect from each other. And yet I am sure you appreciate my motives. Nothing could take me from you but my country.

The novel marching life of a soldier was about to lead to a major battle that would transform John from a relatively inexperienced volunteer to a veteran. On October 5 he described his feelings about a skirmish the day before on the road to Bardstown in which several companies of the 1st Ohio Cavalry were cut off by a large force of enemy cavalry but fought their way out, losing 40 men taken prisoner and taking 13 enemy prisoners:

> Our advance entered town from the north as the rebs left on the south. I have never realized until this morning that we were on the road to catch the enemy. It has seemed like parade more than anything else. I have seen a

> great many troops but this morning, the arrival of Divisions from various roads fills the mind with the power & resources of the Government.... We are now waiting in the centre of the town for the passage of another Division & hence I write. We passed over the scene of yesterday's skirmish & the first sign of battle was a dead horse in the road & that was all, as only one man was killed & five or six of the rebs wounded who were carried off. As we were passing the scene of the skirmish the 4th U.S. regular cavalry were ordered to the front and as they filed by us I began to feel that we were on the track of the rascals. I felt pleased and am now ready to "pitch in." To day is the Sabbath but the steady tramp of infantry & the passing of artillery at a gallop is indicative of anything else but "peace on earth."

Then, further down the page: "Oct 9th Dearest since the above we have overhauled the enemy and I have been in a 'fight.' I shall not claim anything more than that I did my duty. Dinsmoor, Willie Bross & myself are safe.... Will try & bring up as I have them the occurrences from Sunday. I am well & hearty. Yourself & Mason was in my mind more than ever yesterday. I thank God for his care of me."[22] The battle of Perryville had taken place the day before on Wednesday, October 8, 1862.

THE BATTLE OF PERRYVILLE, OCTOBER 8, 1862

Bragg, believing that Buell was still in Louisville, had joined Kirby Smith and his army in Frankfort on October 4 to attend the inauguration of the new Confederate Governor, Richard Hawes, but as the inauguration ceremony was ending, the sound of Union artillery was heard outside the town. By late that afternoon, Kirby Smith's divisions had left Frankfort along with the Confederate Governor; Federal troops entered the town the next day. The Confederate government of Kentucky had lasted less than eight hours.[23] The afternoon before, on October 3, the two corps commanders of Bragg's army to the south in Bardstown, General Polk and General Hardee, had independently decided that a strong Federal force was probably moving against them and that they should withdraw east towards Danville.

By the evening of October 7, Buell with one of his three corps had come within three miles to the west of Perryville and set up headquarters in a house there. Believing the combined armies of Bragg and Kirby Smith to be before him at Perryville, Buell planned to get his three corps into line before the town and then make a coordinated attack the next morning with all three corps on what he thought was the whole Confederate Army.

The battle began at 3:00 a.m. on October 8, when Colonel Daniel McCook's 36th Brigade of Sheridan's 11th Division, in Gilbert's Third Corps, moved forward across Doctor's Creek, thereby securing a water supply for the seriously thirsty Union troops, and occupied the heights of Peters Hill on the east side of the Creek. (Colonel Daniel McCook, Jr. was a brother of Major General Alexander McCook, commander of the First Corps; both were members of what was known as the Fighting McCook family of Ohio.) But Alexander McCook's First Corps on the left wing and Crittenden's Second Corps on the right wing did not arrive until later in the morning, and although his line was in place by noon, Buell decided that there was not enough time for an attack that day and that he should postpone the attack until the next morning. But the Confederate Army did not wait for Buell's intended crushing assault. Bragg and his staff had arrived in Perryville on the morning of October 8 to meet with Polk and Hardee. Bragg still did not believe that Buell's main army was arriving at Perryville and ordered Polk to prepare an assault at once, striking with his right to drive the Federal left back and then move against the flank of what he thought was a smaller Federal force, planning then to move north to join Kirby Smith's army. He kept only a small force on his left for a holding operation. In the early afternoon, Polk began the Confederate attack against Buell's left wing, McCook's Corps, and successfully drove back the Federal regiments. During the course of the afternoon, the Union left wing was driven almost to the point of collapse, but Buell, two miles back at his headquarters, was completely unaware of the battle and angrily sent orders to stop what he thought was a "useless waste of powder."[24] He did not authorize any reinforcement of McCook's First Corps from the Third Corps in the center until later in the afternoon, when it was almost too late.

John's 88th Illinois Regiment was located in the center on Peters Hill with the rest of Sheridan's division, in Gilbert's Third Corps. At around 4 p.m. a Confederate brigade was ordered to attack what Confederate General Anderson thought was a small Federal force holding Peters Hill. In fact, the Federal force there consisted of Sheridan's entire division and also two brigades of another division commanded by General Mitchell. The Confederate regiments came bravely up Peters Hill in the face of punishing fire and succeeded in crossing a cornfield and reaching a rail fence that bordered it, but fire from the 36th Illinois and the 88th Illinois stopped them at that point. When the 36th Illinois had fired its last round of ammunition, it was ordered to fall back, passing through the left part of the 88th Illinois line; some of the inexperienced soldiers of the 88th, believing the 36th to be retreating, broke and ran to the rear. However, Colonel Francis Sherman restored order and the 88th Illinois moved forward over the crest of the hill, delivering vigorous fire against the enemy in the cornfield.[25] General Anderson eventually realized that his brigade had been sent against a substantially larger Union force; he ordered a retreat and the Confederate regiments fell back across the cornfield. A short time later, Third Corps commander General Gilbert authorized reinforcements to be sent from the center to the First Corps on the Union left; they arrived just in time to prevent a collapse of Buell's whole left wing, but there were many casualties in the bitter fighting that ensued.

Darkness eventually brought an end to the battle. Buell did not realize until late at night what had happened to his left wing, and the Union forces expected another attack in the morning. At Confederate headquarters, however, Bragg had finally realized that the entire Union Army was arrayed against him and that the Second Corps of Buell's army was positioned to attack his weakened left wing. He made the decision to withdraw and when the morning of October 9 came, the Union forces found that the enemy had retreated during the night. Buell had ordered an attack at dawn by his right wing under Crittenden and had it taken place, Bragg might have been forced to renew the fight against overwhelming odds, but confusion over orders among the senior Union officers prevented anything from happening until 10:30 a.m., and then Union forces entered Perryville, finding it nearly empty except for numerous wounded Confederate soldiers.[26] Union casualties in the battle were about 4,200 and Confederate casualties were about 3,400.[27] In some cases, regiments lost up to 40% of their men. The 88th Illinois reported casualties of 5 killed and 38 wounded.[28]

The Battle of Perryville was characterized by major misconceptions and errors on both sides. On the Union side, Buell, immobilized at his headquarters and out of touch with the fighting, had initially decided to make a general assault on October 8, but when portions of his army were delayed in arriving, decided to postpone the attack until the next day without considering the possibility that the enemy might attack him. He was completely unaware during the afternoon that his entire left wing, McCook's First Corps, was under heavy assault and on the verge of collapse. One reason for the success of the Confederate assault was that Sheridan, in the center, allowed a Confederate brigade to pass unmolested right across his front on its way to assault the Union left wing. Sheridan was probably reluctant to engage without orders because he had been reprimanded earlier in the day for an unauthorized advance; Gilbert, the commander of the Third Corps who might have authorized such an attack, was dining with Buell at headquarters, equally unaware of the increasingly desperate situation of McCook's First Corps on the left. The right wing of the Union Army, Crittenden's Second Corps, which might have destroyed the Confederate center as it moved to attack the Federal left, stayed completely out of action. Finally, Buell expected the enemy to renew his attack the next morning, and Union troops were unprepared to pursue the defeated forces when they discovered that the Confederate Army had retreated during the night.

On the Confederate side, Bragg ordered his attack because he thought he was facing only a small part of the Union Army. General Anderson sent three regiments against Sheridan's forces, including the 88th Illinois, on Peters Hill because he thought that only a small Federal force was holding it, when, in fact, it was held by 14 Federal regiments, and the attack against them on high ground could have been suicidal. But misunderstanding by the Federal forces prevented them from taking advantage of the situation: in spite of his overwhelming superiority, Sheridan sent a message that he was hard pressed and needed help from the division on his right.

John described his experience in the Battle of Perryville in an excerpt from his letter of October 15, 1862, to Belle:

Camp near Lancaster, Ky
October 15, 1862

My Dear Sweet Wife!

... next day [Monday, October 6] we had a long and wearisome march as rear guard of the Division train of wagons, an endless string passing through Springfield & beyond about six miles eastward toward Perryville, reaching camp about midnight.... We lay there until afternoon when we took up the line of march & reached camp in the evening [Tuesday, October 7], where we remained until next day, Wednesday, the day of the battle [October 8] until about 11 A.m.... We marched from camp about two miles eastward on the Perryville road where it passes over a rise of ground between two hills. These hills to right & left of us were held by two batteries of artillery & we were their support. We were resting where we could see the battle raging on the left (our position was the centre) & it was grand beyond description.... While laying in the road our batteries kept up a continuous fire, between two & three P.m. we were ordered to form line of battle & advance over the hill on the right to repel a charge of a rebel brigade which was advancing to capture our battery. It was the key post of the centre. The enemy com[d] by Hardee were ordered to take it at all hazards. We marched over the hill & as quick as we appeared we were met by a shower of balls from the rebels hid in a cornfield in front of us & behind a rail fence. The hill between us fell away in a graceful slope about 50 rods with a few large oak trees growing on it. Down the hill we went about half way when we halted and poured in our fire the men laying down on the ground. We had not advanced a rod from the brow of the hill before one of my best dutchmen was shot down close by me in the eye the ball lodging in the brain. I thought he was dead but strange to say he revived a little after the battle & lived three days. I wish I could describe the sound of the balls as they passed by me. I was so anxious for my men & to keep them in line that I had no time to stop & think of the dangers of the situation. The regt held its position bravely, loading and firing at will until the enemy took to their heels & then such a shout you never heard. The regt was ordered up the hill, reformed & marched down to

> the rail fence where we lay on our arms all night. The first thing when we reached there was three cheers & a tiger for Capt Bross from my men.[29] It was praise which came to the heart. I had done my whole duty as far as I could & I lay down thankful to God for preserving me to you and friends. I ate a hearty supper & slept as if I never had been away from your sight. The boys however could not sleep until all the incidents of the battle had been told over. One instance of coolness of one of my corporals is related by Mr Rae. The corporal fired 4 times & now said he I will stop and take a drink, which he did with all the coolness of camp life. I have many things to say about my first experience in battle if I live to get home but cannot now. I had seven wounded out of 52 men in action.

As the Union Army entered Perryville on the morning of October 9, they found grim scenes of wounded and dying Confederate soldiers. Many houses had been turned into hospitals for the Confederate wounded, and the wounded Federal soldiers were now brought into the town. One Union soldier reported that they as they passed a house used for an amputating hospital they saw "a heap if bleeding limbs like a mound of clay as they were cut off and thrown from the window above."[30] The fields around the town were thickly strewn with corpses with a terrible stench and the sight of hogs eating the dead bodies.[31]

In the October 16 portion of the letter dated October 15, John wrote of his complex feelings at the sight of the wounded and dead:

> The 9th and 10 we camped near by the secesh Hospital and such a shocking sight I never saw or wish to again. With Longworth I visited the secesh line of battle the 3d day after the battle in a drenching rain. I cannot describe it. I was only affected to most indignant feelings as I saw piles of dead rebels. How vast the responsibility of the wicked leaders of this rebellion & I wished for the power of omnipotence to crush the satanic crew at a single blow. Never did I feel more like devoting our son body & soul to a life time of labor against this cursed pack of scoundrels who have spilled so much of brothers' blood. The heaps of dead showed the

> accuracy of our fire. In passing through the hospital I caught the eye of a wounded man who anxiously beckoned me to him. I stepped into the shed in which he lay. He asked me in a whisper to raise him up, he was shot through the lungs. He asked for a cup of water which I procured for him. He looked his thanks. I saw he was dying. I commended him to his maker told him to make his peace with God. I laid him gently down & in a moment he was in eternity. I cannot tell my feelings as we lay on that camp ground. I did not feel those solemn thoughts that would naturally arise. Rather was it a stern joy that we were victorious and that there lay all around us the evidence of justice asserting itself right through the heart & brain of rebeldom.

Bragg had concluded that since the Kentuckians had not risen to join his army and since he was faced by a superior force, his objective should be to save his army by retreating through the Cumberland Gap from Kentucky into Tennessee. Buell appreciated the importance of cutting off Bragg's retreat, but he proceeded deliberately because he wasn't certain of the location of the Confederate forces and didn't want to risk an attack on his flank. By October 15 Bragg had passed through the little town of Crab Orchard, where the good road turned into a narrow winding road up into the mountains, and Buell realized that he had lost the opportunity to stop him. Bragg had made good his escape.[32]

General-in-Chief Henry W. Halleck informed Buell from Washington that Lincoln wanted him to capture East Tennessee while the roads were still passable. The President, he said, "does not understand why we cannot march as the enemy marches, live as he lives, and fight as he fights, unless we admit the inferiority of our troops and of our generals."[33] Buell responded that he would need at least 80,000 men to take and hold East Tennessee and that securing Nashville and Middle Tennessee was more important; in defiance of administration directions, he ordered his men, including Gilbert's corps, back to Bowling Green in preparation for moving to Nashville. On October 24 Lincoln relieved Buell of command of the Army of the Ohio and replaced him with General William S. Rosecrans.[34]

Some historians think that a headlong pursuit with battle-weary troops might have put Buell's army in a dangerous position, but at the time it was generally thought that Buell had not pursued Bragg's army with sufficient vigor and determination.[35] One Union soldier heard that Bragg's army had resolved to "die in the last ditch" at a crossing of the Dicks River and remarked that "if any rebels died there, or anywhere else, it would be of old age, as there was little danger that General Buell's army would kill any of them."[36]

John agreed about Buell and also about his corps commander, General Gilbert. In a letter of November 14, 1862, to Belle's father he wrote:

> As to the generals we have been under little need be said. I have not spoken of them from the fact that in writing I have had so little time when I have sent you hasty letters. Our Division when we had left Louisville was part of Gen. Gilberts army corps, a special pet of Buell. Gilbert made himself thoroughly hated by officers & men. His regulations with regard to the movements of trains, baggage, supplies, officers baggage &c. were extremely hard on us all, while he had 21 wagons for his own personal convenience & his escort of cavalry must sleep on the ground. He was nowhere at Perryville as also Buell. The latter was miles in the rear & late in the afternoon wanted to know what those guns were firing for in the front. I saw his army come into Louisville & slept with a member of his signal corps. He told me how bitterly the officers & soldiers denounced him for his conduct. It was the same with us after the Battle of Perryville. We lay three days after the battle near the scene of action chafing like a spirited horse that wishes to dart off upon a gallop after the enemy. Our blood was all up, and our prestige gained in the recent battle would have impelled us like a whirlwind upon Bragg's retreating forces. But no, we must absolutely do nothing & not even crawl after the enemy. Curses loud & deep were muttered all through the army. It was a magnificent sight the morning after the battle as our Division formed in line & marched forward a short distance in the order of battle. A few guns about 7 A.m. to our right wrought up expectations to the highest pitch and the ball we thought was again open. We lay on our arms all day except towards night when we marched through

> cornfields. ... Here we lay two days and then started again after Bragg who had in the meantime got well off towards Crab Orchard with all his plunder. We followed him to that point, where the good roads stop & there we stopped & let him go. We retraced our steps to Lancaster thence to Danville, thence towards Lebanon. - - Within about six miles of that town the whole Division turned off into a by road to the left of that town where we got lost & Major Gen Gilbert besides. ... Such was Gen Gilbert who could issue a brutal order to prick up with the bayonet every soldier sick or shirker who should fall out of the ranks and get behind. It was at that camp on Rolling Fork of Salt Creek that we got word of Gilberts being superceded by McCook who now commands our Corps and that Rosecrans would probably be Buells successor. This was great news for us.

General William S. Rosecrans was considered by many to be the ablest strategist of the war. Gifted, intelligent, and industrious, by the age of 14 he had mastered retail skills and successfully liquidated a nearby store. Fascinated by science and mathematics, he applied to West Point without his family's knowledge and was admitted; he graduated fifth in his class. After graduation he served in the engineer corps, became an instructor in engineering and philosophy at West Point, and in 1854 resigned to begin a brilliant career in business as an architect, mining engineer, and founder of a business producing coal oil. In experimenting to develop a pure, odorless oil, he was severely burned in an explosion in his laboratory. Coming from a family of staunch Methodists, Rosecrans converted to Catholicism before his graduation from West Point, afterwards carrying a rosary in his pocket and enjoying theological discussions with his officers.[37] When the war broke out, he was pressed back into service, being appointed a brigadier general with unusual speed. In late October 1862, Rosecrans took command of the army, now renamed the Army of the Cumberland, at Nashville and began building supplies and reorganizing his troops.

One thing that occupies some space in John's letters of this period is the question of his rank. He had evidently been commissioned as captain of Company A and was senior captain of the regiment by order of the governor, but there was some mix-up about the actual commissions and when they came through, John's Company became Company D. John wrote that he did not care where his company was placed in line of battle but told the colonel that he would insist on his rank as senior captain.[38] John felt that he was discriminated against and denied promotion in the 88th Illinois regiment because Colonel Sherman and the others were Democrats and therefore political opponents. "Major Chandler is a Long John today and has no love for our name. I have not tried to make friends with either of them nor shall I. When the commissions come I shall demand my place and if I do not succeed I will resign. I will not serve under such men any longer than I can help."[39]

There is mention of other family matters. Belle had rented their Chicago house, having moved out with Mason to Sterling to live with her parents.[40] John's 13-year-old nephew, Willie Bross, son of his brother Josiah, had been detailed as a regimental drummer but had deserted at the time of the Battle of Perryville and walked to Louisville.[41] John had to write Josiah to explain what had happened and that he had had nothing to do with it.[42]

A happier family event was the marriage of Belle's sister Emily to Zadok Galt of Sterling, referred to in John's letters as "Zad" or "Zed." The wedding was set for Thursday, December 18 in Sterling, and John had hoped to get leave to be present, but it wasn't possible for him to get away. Instead, John organized his own parallel celebration in camp, as described in his letter of December 19:

> I was thinking of you all the whole day and imagining the little labors you were all performing in order that the affair might go off in good style. Mason chattering around, perhaps getting into places where he was not wanted. Then the dressing hour, then the hour of assembling, then the parlor filled with friends & then the ceremony. But I will not imagine any further but tell you what I did. In the afternoon I had some nice biscuit made or rather just before tea; these with butter beefsteaks, crackers, cheese, tea & sugar constituted our tea to which we sat down at 6 o'clock P.m.

After a time-out for a meeting in the colonel's tent:

> At 9 P.m. we sat down to an "oyster supper." This was the feature of the evening. To say that we enjoyed the oysters would but ill convey the sensations of pleasure which were derived from the bivalves.... Capt Bross as host & Chairman of the meeting rapped to order with his knuckles upon the mess chest and proposed as a toast "Our wives and children." ... It was drunk in silence as became the dignity and true hearted devotion, esteem & regard which Longworth & myself bear to the dear ones at home and the virtue and worth comprehended in the name of wife & mother. The young men honored you with the most evident respect.... The next was "sweethearts" drunk with all the honors. The next toast was given after I had stated that this occasion was in honor of the nuptials of my sister & I gave "Zad and Em: Long may they live to enjoy the sweets of wedded life and never regret the step which they this evening make and publish to all the world." This was received with demonstrations "long & loud" of mirth & jollity, so much so that we had a gentle reminder from the Col that what was passing in my tent could be heard outside. We came down of course to gentler language or rather our voices were pitched to a lower key & the hilarity of the occasion continued.... After a very pleasant evening spent in this manner, Lieut Longworth separated from us at 10 ½ P.m. just about the time you were eating your supper I presume, and we retired to our sleeping apartment which was simply to move our mess chest to one corner of the tent & lie down in our blankets.[43]

On December 10 John had written, "I hope we shall be permitted to go forward towards Murfreesboro, where the rebels are said to have been massing their forces for some weeks back. It is said that Rosecrans is actively engaged in making preparations to drive them out of that. I hope we shall." Within two weeks John would have his wish, as the Union Army of the Cumberland under General Rosecrans met the Confederate Army of Tennessee under General Bragg in the battle generally called Stones River by Union historians and Murfreesboro by Confederate historians.[44] Here John and Company A of the 88th Illinois were engaged in their second major battle.

After its withdrawal from Kentucky to Tennessee, Bragg's Confederate Army had been gathered at Murfreesboro, some 25 miles southeast of Nashville, to guard southeast Tennessee and possibly at some point to attack the Federal Army at Nashville. Confederate President Jefferson Davis visited Murfreesboro on December 13, 1862, to confer with General Bragg and after the meeting made the decision to detach Stevenson's division of 7,500 men from Bragg's army and send it to reinforce the Confederate presence in Mississippi.[45]

Rosecrans had been under pressure from Washington to advance into eastern Tennessee but waited because the Louisville & Nashville RR, one of his two major supply lines, needed some repair and some strengthening of its garrisons, and because dry weather had made the Cumberland River, the other major supply route for Nashville, too low for navigation. In late December the river began to rise to normal levels and the railroad looked more secure, and then Rosecrans received news of the detachment of an entire division from Bragg's army. He decided that the time had come to advance.[46]

On December 26 Rosecrans's army moved out, heading southeast towards Murfreesboro. The army was divided into three corps, each with about 15,000 men: McCook's corps, which now included the 88th Illinois in General Sheridan's Third Division, and two other corps led by Generals Crittenden and Thomas. The weather was terrible, cold with heavy rains, which turned the dusty Nashville pike into a sea of mud. Soldiers had to sleep on the muddy ground and weren't allowed to make fires. To make matters worse, Confederate cavalry, at that point far superior to Federal cavalry, starting on the night of December 29th, made a two-day ride around the whole Union Army, capturing weapons and prisoners and burning wagon trains.[47]

THE BATTLE OF STONES RIVER OR MURFREESBORO, DECEMBER 31, 1862

By December 30 Rosecrans's army was in place before Murfreesboro. The Union line of battle ran northeast-southwest, left to right, running across the Nashville & Chattanooga Railroad and the Nashville Turnpike, which ran east-west almost parallel to each other and, at that point, roughly parallel to Stones River. It would be the objective of the Confederate Army to attack and rout the Union right wing and come around to take the pike and the railroad, which were the supply lines in the Union rear, and then destroy the Union Army by attacking it from the rear. By coincidence, Rosecrans's plan was identical: to attack the Confederate right wing and wheel around to attack the enemy from the rear.[48] Rosecrans believed that his attack on the Confederate right wing would compel the Confederates to withdraw troops from their left so that his right wing should not come under severe pressure.

Crittenden's corps formed the left wing of Rosecrans's line, Thomas's corps formed the center, and McCook's corps, including the 88th Illinois, formed the right wing. Of the three divisions in McCook's corps, Sheridan's division was stationed at the left end of the corps, closest to Thomas's corps in the middle, with the other two divisions, those of Davis and Johnson, stretching out to his right, Johnson's division being at the right end of Rosecrans's line of battle. Within Sheridan's division, General Sill's brigade, including the 88th Illinois and three other regiments, was on the front line.[49]

McCook was prepared to rely on Rosecrans's assumption that the attack by his left wing would prevent an attack on his right wing. But General Sill, having noticed in the darkness significant numbers of enemy troops moving across his front to the right, informed Sheridan that he was concerned about a possible massive attack at dawn. Both Sheridan and Sill then visited McCook to personally tell him of their concern. McCook was not impressed, but Sheridan's apprehension persisted and he had his division assembled under arms long before daylight and personally visited each of his twelve regiments to see that his orders were executed. McCook did send a message to Davis and Johnson shortly before daylight on December 31 to be on the watch for an attack, but neither general did anything more than send a perfunctory message to their brigade commanders.[50]

As it turned out, Sheridan's apprehension and prudence probably saved the Federal Army from disaster. The Confederates struck first around 6:00 a.m. on December 31, attacking the right end of the Union line with irresistible force, achieving virtually complete surprise and overwhelming the unprepared regiments in Johnson's division and some of the regiments of Davis's division, some of the Union soldiers still making their breakfast.

These Federal troops fell back, attempting to form new lines of resistance but continued to retreat under Confederate pressure. Towards the Union center, however, Confederate attacks were repulsed by one brigade of Davis's division, commanded by General Woodruff—who, like Sill and Sheridan, had expected an attack and had ordered his men to sleep on their arms—and to Woodruff's left, by Sill's brigade, including the 88th Illinois. After repulsing an initial Confederate assault, Sill launched a counterattack but was instantly killed, and his men withdrew to their defensive position.[51] Under repeated Confederate assaults and finding their right flank exposed as the troops of Davis's and Johnson's divisions fell back, Sheridan's brigades remained in action, conducting a fighting retreat and forming new lines of defense, initially north of Wilkinson's Pike, which runs east and west a couple of miles south of the Nashville Pike.

Rosecrans initially believed that his plan was working and that his right wing was holding the enemy at bay as he prepared to attack with his left wing. He was reassured by a message from McCook that requested reinforcements but failed to mention the rout of several brigades. Eventually, realizing that his right wing was collapsing, he cancelled his own plan of attack and ordered troops from his left and center wings to reinforce his right wing. Colonel Parkhurst placed his entire 9th Michigan Regiment in line of battle along the Nashville Pike to stop the terrified fleeing Union soldiers. He wrote: "Cavalry, artillery, infantry, sutlers and camp followers came rushing with the force of a cyclone and the Ninth Michigan was ordered to fix bayonets and charge upon this panic-stricken mass of men."[52] This action, and similar action by other Union regiments, finally halted the fleeing Federal troops, who were re-formed into units along with fresh regiments from the left and center to reinforce a new last line of defense to defend the railroad and the Nashville Pike.

At this time General Rosecrans took personal charge of the battle, determined, confident, seeming to be everywhere, hurrying up ammunition, planting batteries, directing the formation of new lines and counterattacks, and exposing himself without fear in the thickest fighting. His presence and his example did much to strengthen the determination of the Union troops to hold the last line against the oncoming Confederate assaults. In the late afternoon, his assistant adjutant general and friend, Lieutenant Colonel Julius Garesché, riding beside him, was decapitated by a cannon ball; the headless body rode on for several paces before sliding off the horse. The blood spattered onto Rosecrans's coat, causing many to think he had been wounded, but he explained several times that "it was the blood of poor Garesché."[53]

At mid-morning the Union Army was desperately trying to establish its new defensive line in front of the Nashville Pike. Whether it would have time to do so largely depended on Sheridan's division, facing southeast, and Negley's division of Thomas's center corps, linked up at a right angle with Sheridan's left and facing northeast. Sheridan's troops did hold out against repeated assaults, in spite of a shortage of ammunition. The Union line at noon has been compared to a jack-knife bent in towards closing, the right wing having been driven back against the left wing into a v-shaped line.[54] John later described the posture of the Confederate Army as a "huge vise" about to close up and crush the Union Army.

The Union line held throughout the day, in spite of savage Confederate attacks especially at the point of the V, a four-acre piece of rocky land covered with cedars known as the Round Forest. Sheridan's division was no longer in action during the afternoon, having been stationed in the rear during the battle for the Round Forest. As the sun set, the Confederate command decided that their forces were too weak at that point for another assault, and the troops were ordered to go into bivouac for the night.

Bragg telegraphed Richmond that night that "God has granted us a Happy New Year" and that the Union Army had been "driven from every position except his extreme left."[55] He was convinced that Rosecrans would retreat to Nashville that night and telegraphed General Johnson that he would pursue the foe. But Rosecrans conferred with his generals and decided that his army would remain where it was, ready to fight. The next morning Bragg, to his surprise, found the enemy still in place and wasn't sure what to do. Neither general planned or attempted an attack. Early that morning, January 1, 1863, Union troops from the left wing crossed Stones River and occupied a hill on the east side of the river. There was no further action that day.

On January 2, in the afternoon, Bragg ordered General Breckenridge to mount an assault on the Union position on the hill they now occupied on the east side of Stones River, in spite of Breckenridge's objection that the position of his troops would be exposed to enfilading fire from Union artillery on the west bank of the river. Nevertheless, Bragg ordered the assault; as Breckenridge had predicted, the attacking Confederate troops were raked by Union artillery fire from across the river and the attack failed.[56]

The battle was over. On January 3 Bragg came to realize that the Union force was much larger than his and probably also about to be strengthened by reinforcements from Nashville. Shortly before midnight on that same day, the Confederate Army retreated. The Union Army made no serious effort to pursue. Both armies suffered casualties of over 30%, making this the most deadly battle of the war for the numbers engaged.[57]

The battle was considered a Union victory. Lincoln wired Rosecrans, "God bless you and all with you."[58] Later the President wrote Rosecrans: "I can never forget, whilst I remember anything, that... you gave us a hard earned victory which, had there been a defeat instead, the nation could hardly have lived over."[59] But the Army of the Cumberland was so crippled by the battle, victory though it was called, that Rosecrans was obliged to spend several months near Nashville rebuilding his army.

Probably no one on either side spent a lot of time considering that January 1, 1863, was the day on which President Lincoln's Emancipation Proclamation went into effect. It is often said that the announcement of the preliminary Emancipation Proclamation in September effectively foreclosed the British government from intervening on the side of the Confederacy. It has been argued, however, that a series of Confederate victories might still have brought about a British decision to intervene, and there had recently been a major Confederate victory on December 13 at Fredericksburg in Virginia. If, in fact, the British government was still undecided, the battle of Murfreesboro may have been decisive in forestalling intervention by the European powers.[60]

The defensive stand of Sheridan's division during the battle on the morning of December 31, 1862, has been described as a decisive fighting retreat that saved the Federal Army, one possibly never surpassed during the Civil War.[61] At the least, John's regiment was significantly engaged in the desperate fighting that arguably saved the Federal Army from defeat and contributed to a Federal victory that, as Lincoln wrote Rosecrans, may have saved the Union.

John's description of his part in the battle of Murfreesboro is contained in a letter to Belle's father dated January 11, 1863:

> We had the enemy beaten back near their left centre & if we had had proper support we should have broken their line in two parts. Mind you this was by the bravery of the 36 & 88, but just at that moment the two Divisions on our right had been driven back. Johnston's by his traitorous carelessness & Davis because he was outflanked & then ours had to give way in order to save themselves from being taken prisoners. It was too bad thus to have victory snatched from our grasp and so many of our two regiments killed & wounded. Our right wing being compelled to fall back swung round & over onto the left. Here as the broken right wing fell in behind the left the battle again became obstinate & bloody. It was a large open cornfield & cotton field in which our regiments were massed one behind the other & all laying down on their faces. To their rear on a slight elevation by the Rail Road our Batteries were placed in long lines which did terrible execution. I shall never forget my enthusiasm or the sublime scene as we retreated through a cedar forest came out into the open field in front of our left, with the enemies left just behind us and their right wing coming forward over a large open field in splendid array advancing to the charge. Their two wings might be compared to a huge vise that was about to close up & crush our army and the Union at one turn of the rebel screw. The scene is engraven on the tablets of my memory & will ever be as vivid as the noon day sun. We had just time to get out of the way of our own guns when the heavens were rent by the artillery of both sides & such horrid din never before met my ears. This was more on account of my being a witness than an actor perhaps. But the feeling uppermost in my mind was that of exultation as I saw such a mass of our own men ready to receive the advancing wave of rebeldom. Consider that our right was retreating, I was literally mad with indignation at the result thus far. [3]

> great Divisions giving way by reason of carelessness on the part of a Kentucky General & I felt just like invoking on the head of the criminal all the curses that had ever been uttered from Cain to Calhoun & if he had come within reach of our muskets that day he would have been shot like a dog. At that point "Old Rosey" exposed himself with perfect carelessness to the enemy's shots. His Chief of Staff was instantly killed by a cannon ball. The Gen. conversed with the common soldiers telling them what to do to give them a good volley, then the bayonet & they would never stand. His example was inspiriting & he saved the day but the struggle was awfully severe. Back & forth across that field went our forces at times driving the enemy clear into the cedar forest then they would rally & drive us again back towards the rail road, and so the fortunes of either side swung from side to side like a pendulum until night drew its veil over both armies and we slept exhausted.

He also describes his sensation, during the battle, of sharpened perception and enhanced consciousness:

> I wish you could have seen the activity of my mind in this battle; its grasping every little passing circumstance & taking note of every thing that occurred. The little rabbit that darted across the field, the birds that flew from tree to tree, the <u>porkers</u> that grunted around as if nothing could disturb them, nay every thing in animate nature within the scope of my vision I noticed. I have been amused frequently since then in recalling that <u>electric</u> state of my mind in contrast with "abstractions" out of which Belle has rallied me at times. It may be the shock of arms is the best and only thing that can bring <u>all</u> the dormant, latent, powers of my mind into play. I speak of these things for the <u>family</u>, it would have the appearance of egotism for strangers perhaps to see it. Even Bro Zad might misconstrue it. I can only say that with all this I never had better command of my company & myself, never <u>cooler</u> in the true sense of the term, & never in a better state of mind for the judgment to have its full sway. "Things present" were not the only things <u>present</u> to me; <u>you</u>, <u>Belle</u>, "Mason" all seemed <u>nearer</u> in my heart than ever before. My

> hands had not been washed for two or three days, very slovenly Mother would say, & so I thought how ridiculous it would look, & what Belle would think if I should be wounded and taken prisoner or if my corpse should be taken up with an awful pair of dirty hands. Then again, as shells, cannon balls and bullets of all kinds whistled & hurtled by in very dangerous proximity, was it not peculiarly pleasant to think of a little angelic form whose mortal remains are sleeping on the shores of Lake Michigan, hovering around and warding off the death dealing instruments of the enemy? And so the early morn passed.

The little angelic form he refers to was, of course, their beloved Cora, who had been buried at Rosehill Cemetery in Chicago a year and a half before, in July 1861.

NOTES

1. *Report of the Adjutant General*, 260; Andreas, *History of Chicago*, vol. 2, 236; Aldrich, *Quest for a Star*, 11.
2. *Report of the Adjutant General*, 260; Aldrich, *Quest for a Star*, 11; McPherson, *Battle Cry of Freedom*, 516; Kenneth A. Hafendorfer, *Perryville: Battle for Kentucky* (Louisville, Kentucky: K H Press, 1991), 59. The abbreviated narrative of the Battle of Perryville in this section relies mainly on the detailed and comprehensive account in Hafendorfer's work.
3. Hafendorfer, *Perryville*, 59.
4. McPherson, *Battle Cry of Freedom*, 284; Thomas, *Abraham Lincoln; A Biography*, 261.
5. Hafendorfer, *Perryville*, 59.
6. Hafendorfer, *Perryville*, 32ff.
7. McPherson, *Battle Cry of Freedom*, 517.
8. Ibid., 513, 517.
9. Hafendorfer, *Perryville*, 65.
10. Hafendorfer, *Perryville*, 67.
11. Ibid., 66.
12. Ibid., 68, 72.
13. Ibid., 118.
14. Ibid., 71.

15. October 2, 1862.
16. October 15, 1862.
17. January 22, 1863.
18. October 4, 1862.
19. William Gannaway Brownlow (1805–1877) had a colorful career as a Methodist minister, newspaper editor, and politician. A fiery and bitter opponent of secession in eastern Tennessee, he was quoted as saying, "I will fight secessionists until hell freezes over and then fight them on the ice."
20. October 2, 1862.
21. February 21, 1863, from portion of the letter written February 26th.
22. Willie Bross was the thirteen-year-old son of John's three-year-older brother, Josiah who was also living in Chicago. Willie served as a drummer in Company D, not John's Company; after the battle of Perryville, he deserted.
23. Hafendorfer, *Perryville*, 89, 91; McPherson, *Battle Cry of Freedom*, 518.
24. Ibid., 228.
25. Ibid., 295; Andreas, *History of Chicago*, vol. 2, 236.
26. Hafendorfer, *Perryville*, 400.
27. Ibid., 401.
28. Ibid., 452.
29. The phrase "three cheers and a tiger" is found in 19th century American literature, for example, in Mark Twain's *Roughing It*; it seems to have meant three hurrahs followed by a rising growl.
30. Hafendorfer, *Perryville*, 404.
31. Ibid., 405.
32. Ibid., 434.
33. Ibid., 437.
34. Ibid., 438.
35. Ibid., 439.
36. Ibid., 428.
37. James Lee McDonough, *Stones River, Bloody Winter in Tennessee* (Knoxville: University of Tennessee Press, 1980), 38; Tucker, *Chickamauga*, 32.
38. December 13, 1862.
39. December 8, 1862; Evidently a reference to "Long John" Wentworth, a larger-than-life journalist and politician who came from New Hampshire to Chicago in 1836 at the age of 21, ran newspapers, served as Mayor of Chicago twice, and also served as a congressman from Chicago. He was 6 feet 6 inches tall and weighed 300 pounds. The first steam fire engine in Chicago was named "Long John" in his honor while

he was serving as Mayor in 1857. The meaning of the reference in John's letter is not clear, since Wentworth became a Republican after 1854 and always opposed the extension of slavery; he, therefore, should have been in sympathy with the *Tribune* and the Brosses, rather than the Shermans, but there may have been some current political situation that put them at odds. See Andreas, *History of Chicago*, vol. 1, 622–628.

40. November 18, 1862.
41. November 14, 1862.
42. December 10, 1862
43. December 19, 1862.
44. Union historians generally named battles after a landmark, usually a river, while Confederate historians usually named them after the town that served as their base. Both are used for this battle. McPherson, *Battle Cry of Freedom*, 346.
45. McDonough, *Stones River*, 37. Our abbreviated narrative of the Battle of Stones River relies mainly on McDonough's detailed and readable one-volume history of the battle.
46. McDonough, *Stones River*, 65.
47. Ibid., 69–72; McPherson, *Battle Cry of Freedom*, 579.
48. McPherson, *Battle Cry of Freedom*, 850.
49. Andreas, *History of Chicago*, vol. 2, 236; "The Battle of Stones River: A Hard Earned Victory for Lincoln" by Jim Lewis, Ranger, Stones River National Battlefield, *Blue & Gray Magazine*, 28, no. 6 (2012): 14–15.
50. McDonough, *Stones River*, 82–83.
51. Ibid., 101.
52. Ibid., 112.
53. Ibid., 114–116.
54. McPherson, *Battle Cry of Freedom*, 580; McDonough, *Stones River*, 129.
55. McPherson, *Battle Cry of Freedom*, 582; McDonough, *Stones River*, 159.
56. McDonough, *Stones River*, 195, 200.
57. McPherson, *Battle Cry of Freedom*, 582.
58. McDonough, *Stones River*, 226.
59. Ibid., 231.
60. Ibid., 45.
61. Ibid., 118, 225; McPherson, *Battle Cry of Freedom*, 580.

CHAPTER 5

1863: Tennessee and Georgia, Battle of Chickamauga

After the devastating battle at Murfreesboro, General Rosecrans spent the winter and spring of 1863 in Nashville and Murfreesboro, restoring the Army of the Cumberland to strength. John remained there with the 88th Illinois. There were frequent messages to Rosecrans from General Halleck in Washington, urging him to advance against Bragg's army and Chattanooga, but Rosecrans would not advance until he was sure of his organization and his communications.

John's letters during this period report on the movements of his company and the important things of his soldier's life, one of the most important being food:

> Young Scudder, QM Sargeant & myself had bought some bread, sausages & head cheese & we had a grand supper of our own manufacture buttered with fathers & Mr D's present. While you & friends were enjoying yourselves at Uncle P I was luxuriating on buttered toast etc etc.... I buttered & toasted & toasted & buttered in true epicurean style oblivious of almost anything else, thanking my stars the while for such friends. I did think that I would never mention "appetite" or the "good things of life" again in my letters, but your oysters set my "mouth

> watering." ... At 4 A.m. the next morning I was up bright and cheery as the lark & among other things toasted a spare rib ("cramped" by my boys from a living animile the night before) on the clean side of a shovel before a rousing cedar fire. You must know that salt & pepper are a part of the "stores" in my haversack. With this I basted the "ration" and young "Scud" pronounced it some of the most delicate eating of his experience albeit he is very particular in his appetite. You see I am at it again. Well I will not quote scripture about it.[1]

The weather was bad in February: "Next day Feby 5th we started for the front a two days march. It was drizzly & sloppy & through it & over a horrible road we marched 15 miles, half way & reached our bivouac at Lavergne about 4 P.m. I expected to sleep on the wet ground but luckily we had a brick dwelling house to stay in."[2] But by March, spring weather had come to Tennessee: "It is a very pleasant evening the day has been hot especially in the forenoon. The peach blossoms are out & the foliage begins to come out & the grass looks so pleasant & the birds sing so gaily that I do wish you could enjoy it with me."[3] By April the weather was still better: "How beautiful all nature is this morning. Poets have sung of the attractions of the advancing sunlight as it throws its glad beams over hill & dale while they themselves are spending their time in bed. Nothing can be more grateful to the eye than the sight of day dawn and the cheerful flood of light that comes from the open gates of the East. I rejoice that 'Reveille' comes at day light."[4]

John had a high opinion of General Rosecrans, but worried a little about his being a Roman Catholic:

> You say well that we must admire Rosecrans. ... I felt in my bones as our right wing came out of the cedar woods into the open field in front of the long line of bristling cannon that we had a commanding general. ... I felt that that point was the key & there old "hold fast" was bound to stay. ... Rosecrans has a strong hold on the army & I admire his generalship but there is one thing that makes me fear sometimes when I think of what might happen should he eclipse every other general in military

> reputation. He is a Catholic of the Jesuit order & "Father Tracy" his confessor is one of the most bigoted as I understand of the same order. Suppose he should dazzle the country by his military genius so as to become a successful candidate for the presidency & be elected, I should have great misgivings on account of his religion. Not on account of himself perhaps, but of those who would be apt to control his councils. And does not the spirit of faction at home indicate that we may drift into military despotism.[5]

John's support for the Union and the war effort remained resolute and in this he reflected the mood of the army. In May his company gave an escort through the lines to Clement Vallandigham, the Copperhead Democratic gubernatorial candidate in Ohio whom Burnside had arrested and whose sentence Lincoln had decided to commute from imprisonment to banishment: "In the night I had the honor of passing out of our lines 'Vallandigham' and his escort. You should have heard some of the remarks of the 'boys' when they found out who it was. It would have made his ears tingle. They would have carried him out on the point of their bayonets if they could have had their way."[6]

John's Christian faith continued to support him and occupy his thoughts:

> I have a small pocket edition of the book of Psalms that I carry in my haversack. I lay down to rest soon after getting into camp and as I am reading the book in course, I read the 35th, 36th, & 37th. Oh how much comfort to me in these precious words and then to think that you & mother & father and all were at the same time worshipping at home in God's temple, and remembering me at the throne of grace.[7]

In his letters he thinks frequently of his family. "I am happy to hear that Mason is getting along so well. Tell him that 'John' will come & see him soon & bring along his sword too, & pa will teach him how to hold a little gun, & how to 'present arms.' "[8] Frequently the expressions of devotion to his family are accompanied by statements about the concern for duty and country that keep him away from his family. At dawn one day:

> I soon forgot all about secesh in watching the approach of the glorious old orb and wondering if my beloved wife & babe were enjoying a fairy, refreshing sleep, while husband & father was a small part of the periphery of the power of "Uncle Sam," watching on its utmost verge to defend the household of loved ones far away, and the inestimable birthright, the gift of our fathers, our free institutions. I trod the soil of Tennessee with the proud consciousness that this is my country, this my native land, that my love of country was not hemmed in by any narrow contracted views of imaginary straight lines, state boundaries, no "pent up Utica" but that I could exult in the glorious thought, the "whole boundless continent is ours," and for that I am willing to deprive myself for a season of that best of all, dearest of all spots on earth, the sacred little domestic circle.[9]

Family and patriotism were also the main themes of a few long poems that John wrote and sent home. Several of these are available in full in the *Memorial*, which has been reprinted several times. Here is an excerpt, addressed to little Mason, from "Lines written May 8th, 1863. Salem. On Picket":

> I pray that peace with gentle ray
> May soon throughout the land bear sway,
> And union, law, and liberty
> Be ours—a blood-bought legacy.
> But yet if this inhuman strife
> Shall last until thy young heart's life
> Shall grow to manhood—ever be
> Among the brave hearts true and free,
> Who give their lives to liberty—
> So shall the debt thou owest to man
> Be paid; with those who're in the van
> Of progress, with their flag unfurled,
> And giving freedom to the world.

Belle also wrote poetry. In a letter of July 3, 1864, John wrote that he was surprised and delighted that she had been chosen to be the poetess for an occasion at Sterling and insisted that she send him her poem. In an undated letter that we have placed after that of July 19, 1864, he expresses his pride in the poetry he had just received from her. To our knowledge, Belle's letters to John and her own poetry have not been preserved.

When Rosecrans did move, on June 24, 1863, his campaign was a brilliant success. In little more than a week, he had driven his adversary from a defensive position at Tullahoma some 80 miles back towards Chattanooga in southeast Tennessee with very few casualties. After his successful advance, Rosecrans stopped, ignoring further administration pleas to move forward, as he repaired the railroad in his rear and accumulated supplies.

The headings of John's letters during the summer of 1863 reflect the army's progress from Murfreesboro east through Tennessee and dipping south into Alabama and Georgia on the way to Chattanooga. On July 19 he wrote:

> Dearest! I am in a cotton state par excellence! Every step of the way from Louisville to this point I have footed it. Kentucky & Tennessee will ever be associated in my mind with the march, its fatigues, its dangers & its battles! I am grateful to my maker for sustaining me this far. ... This station is about 200 yards north of the Alabama Line. Yesterday P.m. I did not rest on arriving here until I had gratified my desire of "kicking up a dust" in the state that could hold such a man as Wm L. Yancey. So across the line I went echoing Alabama! Alabama! "Here we rest." I suggested to a brother officer whether it would not be best to put our ears to the ground to see if we could not hear the roll of the waves upon the shore of the gulf.

On August 16 Rosecrans moved forward again and by late August was nearing Chattanooga. Chattanooga, on the south bank of the Tennessee River just a few miles north of the Georgia border, was a key railroad hub for the southeastern Confederacy. It had been held by the Confederates since early 1861, although most of the population of eastern Tennessee was pro-Union.

The Confederate government considered Chattanooga of vital importance: to lose it would threaten to cut the Confederacy in half.

By making feints upstream to the northeast, including having campfires lit on the opposite bank of the river upstream from the city, Rosecrans managed to convince Bragg that he planned an upstream crossing, east of the city, but in early September two of his divisions crossed the river a few miles downstream and then approached to threaten the city from the southwest. Bragg concluded that it would be better not to be trapped in the city, and on September 8 the Confederate Army evacuated Chattanooga, retreating into Georgia, while Union forces entered the city. A few days before, on September 3, General Burnside's Union army had taken Knoxville. There was despair in the South.

As it approached Chattanooga, Rosecrans's army consisted of three corps, one commanded by General Thomas Crittenden, one by General George Thomas, and one by General Alexander McCook, plus a reserve corps commanded by General Gordon Granger. John's 88th Illinois Regiment was in the Third Division of McCook's corps, commanded by General Philip Sheridan. There were three brigades in Sheridan's division; the 88th Illinois was part of the First Brigade, headed by General William Lytle. Thomas recommended that the army should be halted at Chattanooga to reorganize, strengthen its line of communications, and consolidate forces with Burnsides's forces, which were expected to arrive soon from Knoxville. Then, reprovisioned, the Union Army could begin a well-organized advance south into Georgia.[10]

At this point Rosecrans's judgment seemed to fail him. He concluded that Bragg was in headlong flight southwards into Georgia and would offer no resistance. He therefore kept his army widely separated in three portions, sending Crittenden's corps along the south bank of the river to Chattanooga, Thomas's corps southeast to a pass through the mountains, called Stevens Gap, some twenty miles south of Crittenden, and McCook's corps, including the 88th Illinois, in the same direction to another mountain pass a further twenty miles south of Thomas. In fact, Bragg was not retreating; he had withdrawn some 25 miles southeast in Georgia to Lafayette, where he was consolidating his troops and awaiting the early arrival of reinforcements from General Longstreet, who had been detached from Lee's Army of Virginia and whose troops began arriving by train on September 18.[11] With the addition of Longstreet's troops, Bragg's army for once outnumbered that of Rosecrans; Bragg planned a counterattack to retake Chattanooga and drive the Federal Army back into Tennessee. Rosecrans's army was soon in a perilous position, its three corps many miles apart and in danger of being attacked separately. Crittenden's corps to the north was especially vulnerable, as he had further split his corps into three separated units, only a small force being left between Bragg and Chattanooga.[12]

Perhaps Rosecrans's brilliant and bloodless capture of Chattanooga had led to some kind of hubris, some belief in his own invincibility, but there were, in fact, some good reasons for the decisions he made. General Halleck assured Rosecrans from Washington that Bragg was fleeing south as the Confederacy disintegrated and urged him to follow in hot pursuit. Also, Bragg had sent scouts posing as deserters who told Union interrogators that the Confederate Army was in full retreat and could not offer any serious resistance this side of Rome, or even Atlanta.[13] Rosecrans was especially hampered by lack of adequate cavalry, which deprived him of adequate information about Bragg's whereabouts; Bragg's Confederate cavalry was far superior. Finally, news that Bragg was about to be reinforced by two divisions under General Longstreet had reached the Federal capital, yet Washington sent Rosecrans no information about it; in fact, as late as September 11, when Longstreet's forces were already under way towards Bragg, Halleck informed Rosecrans that Bragg was probably sending forces to help Lee.[14] Sheridan first heard about the Longstreet reinforcements on September 10, when a scout he sent out was captured but escaped and brought him that report. Sheridan immediately sent word to Rosecrans.[15]

John's letters at this time reflect his and the army's continuing confidence in Rosecrans and the general view that the road was open into Georgia. On September 10 he wrote from "On 'Look Out' mountain": "We are after Bragg once more & we are all full of ardor and cheerful over our success in climbing the second range of mountains on our march, & now the 'road to Rome' is open before us. ... We are about 35 or 40 miles south of the Tennessee line."

In the same letter he writes of meeting a local family, Mr. and Mrs. Wingfield, whose provisions had been taken by foraging Union soldiers:

> The soldiers had stolen three coffee pots from her, every article of the kind she had in the house & I had brought her one that day. She was more than grateful to me for this little act of kindness and I was amply repaid. She is a true lady without the hauteur and contempt which most of the f.f.! display for northern men. We talked of everything and I was very sorry that I had not my album with me to show her your phiz.

At the end of the letter John recalls that it is the anniversary of his departure from Chicago, now a full year since he has seen her:

> Well Dearest I have nearly filled a sheet and have not said a word of something in my heart! One year ago! Three words, and yet oh how much are crowded in them! Never shall I forget the last look the last kiss and the last pressure of your hand. It thrills me now by the lovely pine knot fire & I see your gentle, sad countenance as I convulsively rush from you to the cars. Through all the dangers, the lengthening absence, the long and fatiguing marches, this form moving further & further from you as each day succeeds to day yet oh yet "My heart untraveled fondly turns to thee." Let us have faith in the Lord who is our fortress, our refuge, and trust in him that he will grant us the happiness of each others society again. I lay down on a few oaken leaves blessing your name. Ever yours, John.

On September 9, Negley's division of Thomas's middle corps had marched into McLemore's Cove, a valley on the west side of the Chickamauga Creek, intending to pass through another mountain gap on the east side to occupy the town of Lafayette. Suddenly, the Union forces became aware that Bragg, far from retreating, had his forces concentrated at Lafayette and that Negley's division was almost surrounded. Negley immediately reformed his troops and called for reinforcements from Thomas's other divisions, which were still widely separated from his.[16] Bragg saw his opportunity and ordered an attack on September 10, but there was little cooperation between Bragg and his generals, and for various reasons the Confederate attack was not made on the 10th. Bragg therefore ordered an attack on the morning of the 11th, but again there was confusion and delay and Negley's division was able to withdraw that day through the same mountain gap by which it had entered McLemore's Cove. A great opportunity for the Confederate Army had been wasted.[17]

Rosecrans still thought Bragg was retreating and considered that the action at McLemore's Cove was probably only a show of force to check the Federal advance to Rome and Atlanta.[18] Thomas, however, had no such illusions and said to his staff, "Nothing but stupendous blunders on the part of Bragg can save our army from total defeat. I have ordered Negley to fall back from McLemore's cove and I believe we may be able to save this corps. But Bragg is also in a position to strike McCook and Crittenden before they have a chance to extricate themselves."[19] Bragg's united army could have crippled Thomas's corps and turned north to deal with the scattered units of Crittenden's corps and then McCook's position, isolated and cut off from the river, would have been perilous.

On the night of September 12, Rosecrans finally realized that he had been deceived, that the enemy was not in full flight but was concentrated not far from his center, and that his three widely separated corps were in acute danger of being gobbled up in separate attacks.[20] He immediately ordered his forces to concentrate on his center; McCook's corps was to move north to join Thomas and then both were to move north to join Crittenden near the villages of Crawfish Springs and Lee & Gordon's Mill, on the west side of Chickamauga Creek. This took five days of hard marching, but by the night of September 17, Rosecrans's three corps were in contact with each other west of the Chickamauga Creek and the acute danger to his army had passed.[21] On the way to the rendezvous, Lytle's brigade of Sheridan's division, in which the 88th Illinois was located, was assigned the work of moving the heavy baggage of McCook's corps over the mountains.[22]

On September 15, John wrote:

> The fact is our communication with the centre & left was endangered and we had to get out of the valley east of this mountain as quick as we could.

> It has been accomplished successfully trains & everything are up the mountain, but it was awful hard work. It seems Johnston is in command & there are reinforcements from Virginia & Rosecrans found out just in time that they were trying to get him into a trap. But he did not step in.

Bragg's basic plan was to move his troops northwards, downstream, on the east bank of the Chickamauga Creek, get north of the Union Army, then cross the creek at several points to the west side, getting between the Union Army and Chattanooga, and then head south to roll up the Union left flank. On September 18 he began these maneuvers, but a vigorous Union defense at two of the crossing points delayed his forward movement, and that afternoon Rosecrans had Thomas march his corps north to extend the Union left, so that when the Confederate forces crossed the creek they were no longer north of the Union Army facing south against its left flank, but facing west against Thomas's left wing of the Union line with their backs to Chickamauga Creek.[23]

THE BATTLE OF CHICKAMAUGA, SEPTEMBER 19, 1863

The battle of Chickamauga began on September 19 and lasted for two days; it was the bloodiest battle in the western theater of the war.[24] In the local Cherokee dialect, Chickamauga meant "River of Death," probably because it had played a part in transmitting the smallpox that decimated the tribe when the white men first arrived, and it was a fitting name for this battle.[25] It was fought in thickets of tangled brush and trees that made it hard for the troops to see the enemy or their own men; the position of the troops was constantly shifting back and forth as reinforcements and exhaustion on both sides changed the equation. It was called a soldier's battle because the generals had no clear view of the field and couldn't exercise effective control of troop movements.[26]

There was hard fighting on September 19th, and Thomas's line on the left wing was pushed back, but it remained unbroken. At a council of war that night at the Widow Glenn house, the headquarters of Rosecrans, Thomas

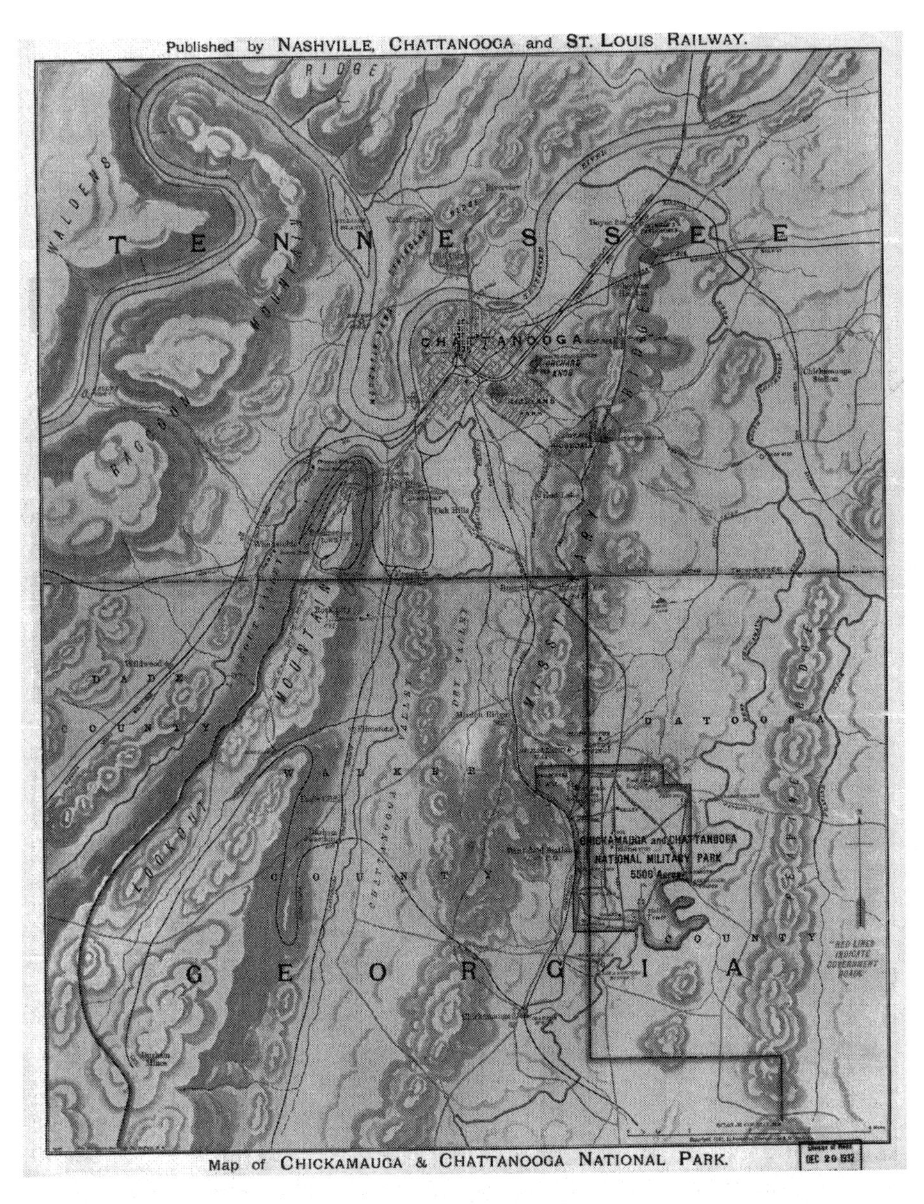

Map of Chickamauga and Chattanooga (1895), published by the Nashville, Chattanooga, and St. Louis Railway (Library of Congress).

This shows the battlefield some nine miles from Chattanooga, just beyond the Georgia state border.

recommended that the Federal right and center should be drawn back from along the north-south La Fayette road, where they were located, to a higher position on the lower slopes of Missionary Ridge, where they would be facing south with a strengthened line. But Rosecrans chose to leave the line as it was. During the night Thomas's men were working hard with axes to throw up defensive log fortifications to face the assaults they knew would come the next morning.[27]

On the morning of the 20th, Bragg had ordered Polk, commanding the Confederate right wing, to attack at dawn, but miscommunication and misunderstanding delayed the attack until about 10:00 a.m. Meanwhile, Thomas's men, on the other side of the line, had been strengthening their log fortifications. Repeated Confederate assaults failed to break their line. Bragg then ordered Longstreet, on his left, to attack. Longstreet did so and in an amazing piece of luck found that a gap had just opened in the Federal line in the exact place at which his attack was being made.

Rosecrans could be excitable and hot tempered, a serious flaw in a commanding general; that day it led to disastrous consequences. Early that morning he had publicly scolded General Wood for allegedly failing to follow an order quickly enough. Later, Rosecrans was erroneously informed that there was a gap on the left of Wood's division near the center of his line and sent an order to Wood to move to his left. The order was inappropriate to the circumstances and arguably self-contradictory, but Wood, having been publicly chastised by his commander scarcely an hour before, was in no mood to appear to disobey an order, so he moved his division to the left, thereby opening a real gap in the line.[28] This happened to be the very moment when General Longstreet launched his powerful and well-prepared assault column against that point in the Union line. The Confederate forces poured through the breach in the line and rolled up the Union forces on both sides of the breach.

Most of the Union right dissolved into a rout, soldiers and officers fleeing back towards Chattanooga in disorganized panic. Rosecrans, unnerved by what appeared to be a general disaster, rode back with his staff along with the fleeing troops. Being unsure whether Thomas's line had also been broken, Rosecrans sent General (later President) Garfield to consult with

Thomas while he went back to Chattanooga to organize a defense, since both agreed that his presence was needed there to direct the reorganization. When Rosecrans reached Chattanooga, he was apparently in a state of collapse; he had to be helped from his horse and was seen receiving spiritual comfort from a Catholic priest.[29]

Not all the Union right had given way. John's 88th Illinois Regiment was located in the brigade of General William Lytle, a Cincinnati lawyer, politician, Mexican War veteran, and nationally-known poet. Lytle's brigade, formerly commanded by Sill, who had been killed at Murfreesboro, was one of three brigades in Sheridan's division that had been stationed at the extreme right of the Union line at the Widow Glenn house. Just before Longstreet's massive attack, all three brigades of Sheridan's division had been ordered to the left of the Union line to support Thomas. Lytle's brigade was the last in line but had hardly begun to move when Lytle saw the onrushing Confederate troops approaching the Glenn house. He ordered his brigade into battle line, facing south. He immediately saw that he was surrounded and in a hopeless situation but gave no thought to retreat, deciding that a bold attack would offer the best chance of delaying the enemy in the hope of saving the right wing. Standing in front of the 88th Illinois, Lytle said to the men, "All right, men, we can die but once. This is the right time and place. Let us charge."[30] The brigade charged and fought with tenacity and courage, initially repulsing the enemy, but was then forced back by superior flanking forces, withdrawing under the command of Sheridan to Rossville, five miles to the north on the road to Chattanooga.

Lytle was shot three times; as he lay dying under a tree, he handed his sword to an orderly and motioned urgently for his officers to leave and save themselves. His body was treated with great respect by the Confederate officers, who knew about him because his poetry was well known to everyone in those days, especially a poem called "Antony and Cleopatra," whose first lines were:

I am dying, Egypt, dying,
Ebbs the crimson life-tide fast,
And the dark Plutonian shadows
Gather on the evening blast.[31]

In the pocket of Lytle's coat was found another poem called "Company K," possibly by him, which was moving to the army and to the public at home when they heard about it. The first stanza read:

> There's a cap in the closet;
> Old, tattered and blue;
> Of very slight value,
> It may be, to you;
> But a crown, jewel-studded,
> Could not buy it today
> With its letters of honor,
> Brave Company K.

Lytle's body was interred by Confederate officers with a funeral service in Crawfish Springs and later, during the siege of Chattanooga, a special truce was arranged to recover his body and send it back to Cincinnati, where it was greeted with public mourning and the largest funeral yet seen in that city.

In this action John evidently acted with courage and skill. In a brief history of the 88th Illinois Infantry contained in A.T. Andreas's *History of Chicago*, it is stated:

> The war correspondent of the *Chicago Tribune* wrote of this regiment as among the bravest, saying that if he were to particularize all who distinguished themselves, he would have to send almost the entire roster. He mentions, however, "the gallantry of Lieutenant Colonel Chadbourne ... Major Chandler ... Adjutant Orson C. Muller ... Captain George W. Smith ... and Captain John A. Bross, who, his company being on picket at the time of the enemy's attack not only extricated his men with consummate skill, but fought his way back, step by step, that his regiment might have more time to prepare for the shock."[32]

Another brigade on the Union right, that of Wilder, armed with Spencer repeating rifles, attacked the flank of one of the advancing Confederate columns, initially driving it back, and then moved west to mount another attack. This assault could have been decisive, but Wilder was dissuaded by hysterical orders from Charles A. Dana, who announced that he was Assistant Secretary of War and insisted that Wilder retreat.[33] Wilder did so, but the counterattack that he had already made probably gave Thomas just the amount of time he needed to draw a new line of defense running east and west along the crest of Snodgrass Hill, half a mile to the northwest on the battlefield.[34]

In the opinion of some historians, neither Sheridan nor Davis, commander of another division on the Union right, acted with the resolution and flexibility that they might have shown. Sheridan's division had not been much harmed in any action the day before and it is argued that Sheridan and Davis could have reorganized their commands and then sent them into action against the rear of Longstreet's forces as they moved north to attack Thomas, just as Wilder's brigade had counterattacked and driven back one of the attacking Confederate columns.[35]

In any case, Thomas had not been defeated. As the forces of the broken Union right were being pursued by Confederate forces, some groups and individual regiments rallied and turned to fight in holding engagements. Colonel Hunter of the 82nd Indiana fought a continuing rearguard action until his unit reached the high ground of Snodgrass Hill, where he said, "I will not retreat another inch" and gathered other retreating regiments into formation.[36] As more units coalesced with his, they became part of the right wing of the line that Thomas, with courage and steady judgment, had reorganized. The new line faced south along a crest that ran from a slope on the east to the crest of Snodgrass Hill on the west and Thomas's men held that line all afternoon against repeated Confederate assaults.[37]

But it was a close thing. At one dramatic moment, Thomas and his staff noticed a cloud of dust to the northeast; if it was Confederate cavalry, it meant certain defeat for his beleaguered force. A mounted Federal officer was sent out to determine the identity of the approaching troops and after a time was seen returning, emerging from a cloud of dust closely followed by a rider holding aloft the ensign of Steedman's Union brigade of infantry, and then Thomas knew that these were reinforcements from Granger's division, who had heard the guns and, on his own initiative, marched to support Thomas.[38]

During the battle General Garfield made a daring ride along the Confederate line to visit Thomas and bring him an order to withdraw immediately. Thomas, exercising the kind of battle judgment that Wood had not exercised, said that an immediate withdrawal would destroy the army; he therefore remained where he was until dark, repulsing the repeated confederate assaults. Garfield returned to a position halfway to Chattanooga and sent Rosecrans a telegram that included the words "Thomas is standing like a rock," which led to lasting national admiration of Thomas as "the Rock of Chickamauga."[39] Thomas's skill as a general was amply demonstrated in his afternoon defense of the line but perhaps even more so in organizing the withdrawal of his forces as darkness fell. Three regiments were taken, due to a mistaken order of Granger, but the rest of Thomas's forces withdrew safely towards Chattanooga.[40]

John described his part in the battle of Chickamauga in a letter to Belle of September 21, 1863:

Monday Sept 21st 1863

My own Darling Wife,

Again have we occasion to give thanks to God for preserving my life through another terrible & most awful battle. I have not time to give you particulars now. Suffice it to say I escaped without a scratch, but several of our officers have been wounded. Lt Rae had his leg broken, Capt Sheridan and his two Lts McMurtry and Griffin were all wounded. Capt Chickering is also wounded. Our Brigadier Gen Lytle was killed at the commencement of the battle. There seems to be a fatality in all the Brigade Commanders of this Division. The battle com. on Saturday the 19th in which our brigade was not engaged being held in reserve to guard a wagon train. Col Bradleys Brigade was in action however that day & they behaved nobly Col Bradley being severely wounded. Our position is the extreme right of the army. The engagement yesterday commenced in our front about noon the centre (Thomas corps) having been engaged for hours & the Heavens &

earth literally trembled with the cannonading & crash of infantry fire. At last they came at us. I was with my Co deployed as skirmishers & had the first chance at the Devils. They came up in mass & I held on with a good fire until they came within a few yards before I gave the command to retreat on the main body. It is a miracle almost that we were not all shot down in our tracks. The result of the matter was our Brigade was nearly broken up by a mistaken order in making a tactical evolution the Brigade "going in" nearly by the flank instead of the front. But I presume such things are all Greek to you. I believe I wrote you last from Look Out Mountain. Since then it was a continual effort to get down the Chickamauga valley (south east side of Look Out Mountain) in order to mass our troops on our own left, in front of Chattanooga. The "battle" yesterday was fought about 9 miles from Chattanooga. It will afford me material for the longest tale of battle to tell you that I have yet gathered up in my experience. Our army was badly cut up but I am proud of the pluck shown in the face of superior numbers. This army may be exterminated but it will fight to the last. There is a larger force here from Lee's army & it is but just to admire their bravery. It is worthy of a better cause. - - My men say I held them too long before retreating but they stood up to it nobly. The right of my Co rested in an open corn field. I was towards the left in the woods keeping back the fire of my men until they had a good chance to fire. Casting my eyes towards the right I saw the boys giving way. I ran back & ordered them to face about & advance. They did so as if on drill & went up a little in advance of the original line. The fact was they saw more than I did. The rebels were coming through the corn field & the result of my order was to bring us within a few yards of each other. I saw that if there was any virtue in legs now was the time. I told the boys to "go it" just as a whole regiment poured a volley into us tearing up the dirt, cutting off leaves & branches of bushes right where we stood. It was a race about neck & neck but we came out ahead. To tell you all the varying scenes of the day would be impossible. They are treasured up to be told you hereafter. I have only fifteen muskets out of 32 I took into action but I shall gather up

> most of them. I may attempt to describe the scenes hereafter. It was necessary for us to withdraw our lines nearer to Chattanooga & possibly we shall yet have a 3^{d} trial. If so may God protect us. It seems to me more & more & more that we are fighting the last battles of the Rebellion. Adieu I will write you again. May God bless us both. Love to all. Yours ever, John

In a later letter of October 1, 1863, John wrote:

> I know that our position was a remarkable one & no one at a distance without diagrams could well understand it. So far as myself was concerned I was left in my position to be sacrificed without an order from Col Chadbourne or notification of the movements of the regiment, & so I fought as it were on my "own hook," & extricated my command from the skirmish line on my own responsibility at the last moment of that battle. There are many things to say which I shall not commit to paper of my own share in it. I shall say no more than if I had it to do over again I would do the same. I am not ashamed of my record.

Immediately after the battle of Chickamauga, most of the Confederate generals urged Bragg to move forward against the Union forces before they could reorganize. Bragg said, "How can I? Here is two-fifths of my army left on the field. My artillery is without horses." Bragg was appalled by the losses his army had sustained: 21,000 casualties or 30% of his force to the Union's 16,000.[41] Many historians agree with Bragg's generals that prompt follow-up action by the Confederates might have finished off the Union Army.[42] This is comparable to the situation after Gettysburg, where many felt that Meade should have pursued Lee to destroy his army, but in both cases a pursuit might have backfired, turning victory into defeat. The casualties had been frightful on both sides, but worse on the Confederate side. Within 3 days, Bragg's Confederate army moved up to begin a siege of the Union forces in Chattanooga, cutting off all supplies for the Union Army.

By mid-October Bragg's siege of Chattanooga seemed to be succeeding as Union forces ran low on provisions and horses starved to death. But Secretary of War Stanton organized a remarkably rapid railroad reinforcement of Federal troops near Chattanooga. In mid-October Lincoln appointed General Ulysses S. Grant, who had triumphed at Vicksburg in July, as overall commander of a new Division of the Mississippi. Grant swiftly appointed General Thomas as commander of the Army of the Cumberland, replacing Rosecrans, and ordered Thomas to hold Chattanooga, prompting Thomas's famous telegraph message: "We will hold the town until we starve." Grant arrived at Chattanooga on October 23, and within a week his forces had succeeded in opening a supply line from the West to get essential supplies to the troops in Chattanooga; Union soldiers called it "the cracker line."[43]

On November 24, Union forces under Grant took Lookout Mountain from the Confederates and the next day won a spectacular and unexpected victory at Missionary Ridge, when Union forces, including the 88th Illinois, spontaneously, without orders, charged up the face of the heavily fortified bluff and routed the Confederate Army at the top of the Ridge, sending Bragg's army in retreat south into Georgia. Someone afterwards said to Grant that the Confederate position had been thought to be impregnable; Grant smiled and said, "Well, it was impregnable."[44] Chattanooga was now safe for the Union.

The 88th Illinois was one of the foremost regiments in the assault at Missionary Ridge, led by Col. Sherman, who had been absent because of illness during the battle of Chickamauga. But John was no longer with the Army of the Cumberland. On October 6 it was announced that he had been appointed by Governor Yates to be the colonel of a new regiment of colored soldiers to be raised in Illinois.[45] On November 1 he had been discharged as a captain in the 88th and assigned to volunteer recruiting service for the new troops; he had returned to Illinois to begin recruiting for the regiment he was to command, which would be named the 29th Infantry, United States Colored Troops. He had received the promotion he wanted. His leadership of the new colored regiment also demonstrated his personal commitment to the role of black men as soldiers of the Union Army.

NOTES

1. February 12, 1863.
2. Ibid.
3. March 18, 1863.
4. April 20, 1863.
5. February 1, 1863.
6. May 29, 1863.
7. June 27, 1863.
8. June 23, 1863.
9. April 20, 1863.
10. Tucker, *Chickamauga*, 32. Our abbreviated narrative of the Battle of Chickamauga relies mainly on this excellent one-volume history of the battle.
11. McPherson, *Battle Cry of Freedom*, 672.
12. Tucker, *Chickamauga*, 101.
13. Ibid., 29.
14. Ibid., 406.
15. Ibid., 104.
16. Ibid., 66.
17. Ibid., 69–70.
18. Ibid., 70.
19. Ibid., 71.
20. Ibid., 105.
21. Ibid.
22. Ibid.
23. Ibid., 118.
24. McPherson, *Battle Cry of Freedom*, 672.
25. Tucker, *Chickamauga*, 122.
26. Ibid., 123, 164.
27. Ibid., 196.
28. Ibid., 254.
29. Ibid., 314.
30. Ibid., 291.
31. Ibid., 291, 296.
32. Andreas, *History of Chicago*, vol. 2, 237.
33. Tucker, *Chickamauga*, 298.
34. Ibid., 304.

35. Ibid., 300, 309.
36. Ibid., 287.
37. Ibid., 332.
38. Ibid., 346.
39. Ibid., 359.
40. Ibid., 367.
41. McPherson, *Battle Cry of Freedom*, 674; Tucker, *Chickamauga*, 392.
42. Tucker, *Chickamauga*, 379.
43. McPherson, *Battle Cry of Freedom*, 676.
44. Ibid., 680.
45. *Chicago Tribune*, October 7, 1863.

CHAPTER 6

Late 1863 and Early 1864: Recruiting in Illinois

After the battle of Chickamauga, John was discouraged about his future in the army and was considering retirement from the regiment. There seemed to be no possibility of promotion within the 88th Illinois Regiment because of the political allegiance of the regimental leadership, and he thought that William's idea of his being commissioned as the commander of a new colored regiment was unlikely to materialize. In a letter to Belle of October 1, 1863, he wrote,

> I just let things take their course with a sort of blind indifference to my fate having given up anything like a hope for promotion or favors in this regiment.... I have thought seriously of tendering my resignation if I cannot get away otherwise.... I do not hope for anything from that proposed colored regiment, I do not believe it will be raised. I am afraid it was only raising false hopes when my brother wrote me about it. As to getting a command of that description here you might as well try to scoop out Rock River dry with a spoon unless you had the favor of certain army cliques.

Within five days of John's letter everything had changed. On October 7 the *Tribune* carried a "Special Dispatch" from Springfield to the *Chicago Tribune* dated October 6, listing several news items from the state capital, including the following:

> Gov. Yates has appointed John A. Bross of Chicago, Senior Captain of the 88th (Col. Sherman's regiment), Colonel of the colored regiment ordered to be raised in this State. Col. Bross has served with distinction, and was in the battles of Chickamauga, Stone River and Perryville, and other battles in which the gallant 88th has been engaged. All other recruiting for negro regiments in this State will now be stopped.

A *Tribune* article published the same day, October 7, reported:

> "The Illinois Colored Regiment"
> We have already referred to the plan on foot to organize and equip a colored regiment in this State, a movement for which orders have already been issued, and which, judging from the favor with which it is received among colored men, bids fair to reach a most satisfactory realization. By reference to our Springfield special dispatch it will be seen that Col. John A. Bross is to command this regiment, having been duly commissioned therefor by Gov. Yates. Col. Bross is thus transferred from the Senior Captaincy in the 88th Illinois, Col. Sherman's, with which he has participated with honor in the battles of Perryville, Stone River and Chickamauga. He is known personally to many of our city readers, and all who know him can attest the singleness of purpose with which he laid aside his profession of law at the call of his country. Believing in the war, in crushing the rebellion by hard knocks, in curing it by the eradication of its cause, Col. Bross will be heard from in his new position, which, if the present zeal manifested among the colored men is any sure token, will not be long removed from active service, for it is the desire and intention to have the regiment promptly in the field.

William had been at work, exerting his considerable political influence as a prominent Republican journalist with Governor Yates, urging him to raise a colored regiment in Illinois and to have John named as its colonel. In a letter of August 21, 1863, William had written the Governor: "A leading colored man has just left my office who says that a colored regiment can be raised in this state in six weeks at worst if it only has someone to head it. He further assured me that my brother John is, of all others, the man they want for Colonel. Now you can give them a chance."[1]

Like most people in the North, John started the war as a strong supporter of the Union but not an abolitionist. In the opinion of most Northerners, slavery was wrong and should not be extended but since it was recognized in the Constitution, it should be left alone in the states where it existed. Abolitionists were regarded by most people as dangerous extremists. In 1851, when a majority of the members of Third Presbyterian left the church in protest of the national church's perceived toleration of slavery, Belle's family remained with the church and John soon joined. However, like his brother and other Republican leaders including Lincoln, John began to change his thinking about slavery as the war went on with no end in sight—a war that almost everyone in the North had expected to be over within a few months, with the rebellion put down and the Union restored as it had been, including slavery as it then existed in the Southern states.

By July of 1862, as the war entered its second year, Union soldiers were becoming convinced that Southern property, including slaves, should be taken or destroyed if that was necessary to defeat the enemy, and Lincoln had begun to conclude that emancipation was a military necessity if the war was to be won. In July Lincoln said to a visitor, "This government cannot much longer play a game in which it stakes all, and its enemies stake nothing."[2] In the same month, he said to Secretary of State Seward and Secretary of the Navy Welles that emancipation was a "military necessity, absolutely essential to the preservation of the Union. We must free the slaves or be ourselves subdued."[3] On September 22, 1862, after the close victory at Antietam made it appear politically feasible to do so, Lincoln issued a preliminary Emancipation Proclamation and on January 1, 1863, although some had doubted that the administration would actually follow through, he signed the definitive Emancipation Proclamation. By that time, Lincoln's thinking had progressed so far that he was quoted as saying, "The character of the war will be changed.... The [old] South is to be destroyed and replaced by new propositions and ideas."[4]

The Emancipation Proclamation freed only the slaves in the states that had joined the Confederacy, not the slaves in the border states, but it changed the character of the conflict from a war about Southern independence to a war largely focused on abolishing slavery. Most people understood that the relatively small number of slaves not specifically covered by the Proclamation would also become free in one way or another.

A compelling political reason to make the abolition of slavery a stated purpose of the war was the impact Lincoln's administration knew it would have on the possibility of intervention by the European powers on the side of the Confederacy, which Confederate agents in England and France were working hard to achieve. In fact, Lincoln's decision to issue the Emancipation Proclamation was a turning point of the war: before it was published, England, France, and Russia were seriously considering an offer of mediation, which would have amounted to de facto recognition of the Confederacy and would probably have meant defeat for the Union. After the Emancipation Proclamation was published and the war became focused on slavery, it became politically difficult if not impossible for England to intervene, and France and Russia would not intervene without the support of England.

The preliminary Emancipation Proclamation made no mention of blacks as soldiers, but the final Proclamation, issued on January 1, 1863, stated that freed blacks "of suitable condition will be received into the armed services of the United States to garrison forts, positions, stations, and other places, and to man vessels of all sorts in such service." This seemed to imply limited rather than full military service, but black soldiers and sailors were soon being enlisted. Although the idea of black soldiers had initially been rejected by Lincoln's administration, by January 1863 Governor Andrew of Massachusetts had secured permission from the War Department to raise a black regiment. This was the 54th Massachusetts under Col. Robert Gould Shaw, which became the most famous black regiment of the war, fighting with conspicuous bravery at Fort Wagner at Charleston in July, 1863 and offering proof that African Americans made good soldiers who fought well. "[T]he organization of black regiments marked the transformation of a war to preserve the Union into a revolution to overthrow the old order. Lincoln's conversion from reluctance to enthusiasm about black soldiers signified the progress of this revolution."[5]

The *Memorial* describes the difficulty John experienced in changing his thinking about abolition:

> Looking alone to his earlier antecedents, Colonel Bross would not have been supposed likely to accept such a command. He was educated in the democratic faith, and held his political principles with the conscientious tenacity which characterized all his views. His mental tendencies were conservative; and he yielded but slowly to doctrines antagonistic to his long established convictions. He had been taught to regard everything which savored of what men were accustomed to call "abolitionism," with distrust; and it was only as the measures which contemplated a change in the status of the black population, underwent the deliberate scrutiny of his judgment, that he yielded to them. To become the commander of such a regiment, involved a change in his views and feelings, from those of his earlier years, than which nothing could more forcibly illustrate the *change* in the times. Yet for this service he was selected and detailed, and commenced recruiting in November, 1863. He established his head quarters at Quincy, in order to avail himself of the exodus of the black population passing from Missouri into Illinois, at that point.[6]

References to blacks in the military and the possibility of leading a black regiment, suggested by William, had begun to appear in John's letters during 1863. On May 29 he wrote Belle, "Well! What do you think of the policy of my applying for authority to raise a colored regiment? I could make an efficient one if anybody could." On June 20 he wrote, "As to the Black regiments, officers applying have to pass an examination and if approved govt. assigns a district for them to recruit in. I do not fear an examination so far as tactics in the infantry arm is concerned and I presume that is all that would be required." On June 23 he wrote, in answer to a letter from Belle, that he was pleased "to hear for the first time that Will was interesting himself for me about a colored regiment. I have not received his letter you speak of. . . . I shall be delighted if I can receive such a position and I will write him about it the first opportunity. But it is impossible to speculate about the future now." On July 5 John wrote to William, "My Dear Bro, Yours of 27th ult. reached me yesterday. I should be pleased to command a colored regiment if the opportunity offers. If I come safely out of this campaign I will write you more fully about it. In the mean time if you can make any arrangements for me, all right." And on July 12 he wrote Belle:

> I shall be ready at any time to come home upon an order of the Governor to raise that regiment. I have thought however that there would be such a rush for it that there would be no possible chance for me. All I have to say is that if I should have the chance I would make it a regt. that would be creditable to the State. I am a firm believer in the capabilities of the negro in the matter of soldiering. True it will require discipline but men of any color require it. My servant now will handle a musket better than some of the white men in the regt.

The letters suggest that John's interest in appointment to a colored regiment was also connected to his fervent wish to come home for a visit, since he had now been away for ten months with no leave. On July 6 he wrote, "I have written to Bro. Will in answer to his letter the 27th. If the campaign stops here I want to turn my attention to that matter and above all I want to see you. Language is not a vehicle to express my longing heart's desire to see my beloved and friends." And on August 1 he wrote from Alabama that he had heard that a board of examination for commissions in colored regiments might be set up and regiments raised in that department:

> If I passed a favorable examination I might get a chance to come home before entering on the business of recruiting. One thing I am convinced of is that a large mass of colored troops will be in the service before this year closes. And now dearest I hope this will reach you ere you leave N.Y. With a heart full of love.
>
> Yours ever,
> JAB

No opportunity arose for a visit home and by September 10, nine days before the battle of Chickamauga, John had been away from home for a full year.

References in John's letters during February and March 1863 indicate that at some point William met with Col. Sherman, commander of the 88th Illinois, that Sherman had suggested that John's performance was unsatisfactory, and that William had written a letter to John that implied some criticism of his performance, which offended John. On February 12 John wrote, "Sometime I will sketch the portrait of Col S. so that you and Br Will may see it in its true light—until then and perhaps always I may be misunderstood by Br Will who of all other men should know me." And on March 2 he wrote:

> The "Deacon" [William was often referred to in public as "the Deacon"] I am persuaded does not yet "know me." You know that to do good to my country I would willingly carry a musket & be commanded by anyone almost, but to be placed in this position is very trying indeed. Yet the Deacon can almost advise me to give up my manhood in order to use molasses & soap with the present Brigade Commander. It will be when my nature is changed very materially. The tone of his letter also gave me the legitimate right to infer that I should be careful to attend to military duties; giving an idea that I had been remiss in that! That was the unkindest remark of all the letter. I will leave that portion of my military life to the inspection of friend or enemy, yea all the world. Do not imbibe any feeling against William by reason of what I have written.... At bottom he is sincerely desirous of assisting me but he takes queer ways to accomplish it.

But he assures Belle that his reply to William "shall be respectful and without a speck of passion, couched in a tone of sorrow instead of anger.... I shall in the future as I have always in the past six months try to deserve success by my own efforts and if I do not succeed in getting a soldier's coveted distinction, promotion, the fault shall not be with me. I will follow your advice in that respect."

Over a year later, in a letter of July 3, 1864, two months after arriving in Virginia as commanding officer of the new black regiment, he would write, "I run over in my mind the past.... I am very thankful I am so much better situated away from the jurisdiction of a man who never appreciated me and was afraid of me as well." And on July 12, 1864:

> I felt that there would be casualties in the 88th & somehow was not disappointed at the news you send me of the death of Col Chandler. He was a brave officer, and after a year of service began to treat me as though he appreciated me.... This is not the place to speak of the merits of my comrade in arms. I would do him justice as I would mete out the same to Col Sherman. I cannot however in all my associations with my former brother officers forget the months of cool neglect and jealous fear with which some of them seemed to regard me. I have too much good sense to cherish up unpleasant feelings against a single one of them. It was but nature perhaps. My position here dearest only brings out in the strongest contrast some of the harder features of my captains life. Even the hard lot itself was not so hard to bear as false statements that went home, one of which Sherman put into Williams ear himself which caused him (Will) to write me so long a letter about my conduct, duties, etc. If I was ever provoked it was then. No one ever can appreciate my situation then. Too proud and independent to bow to the [illegible] set against me I could but show them all how little I cared for any of their sordid envy. Out of it all came good, for it stimulated me to be a good soldier if nothing else could. Here I have nothing of the sort to contend with, all the officers treat me with the greatest consideration and while I do not let down the least in my "military" I am much happier, much better situated in every respect, and to tell you the truth do not have to do half the hard work as formerly.

His thoughts ran on to the slain Col. Chandler, probably including some reflection about his own danger:

> Lt Chandler deserved the unqualified admiration of his friends for his cool determined bravery. He saved the rgt at Chickamauga. I admired

> his conduct when I joined it after I had been driven from the picket line of which I have said so much to you. If I could speak to the young men of Chicago over his dead body I would dwell upon his good deeds. It is no time to cherish unpleasant feelings when men of such coolness and daring as he possessed are stricken down in the midst of their usefulness.

Whatever had transpired between William and Col. Sherman, the incident shows that William was taking an active interest in his younger brother's military career. Probably, having decided that John was right about the political influences aligned against him in the 88th Illinois, William set about finding an alternative and began focusing his attention on the possibility of a command for John in the new colored regiment that was being proposed for Illinois. William's political influence was probably the main reason for John's selection as commander of the new regiment, but heartfelt praise of John's life and professional career by his fellow lawyers, and of his performance as a commander by his fellow officers and the men who served under him, many of which are published in the *Memorial*, are good evidence that he had amply demonstrated his fitness for the command and performed it well. Political influence was often exercised early in the war in the appointment of Union officers; in 1861 the herculean task of raising an army of several hundred thousand men virtually from scratch required attention to political influence because the efforts of local and state politicians and leaders of ethnic groups were essential in building the regiments. Some of the political generals turned out to be incompetent, but others performed well. By 1863, in the third year of the war, political support was no longer so necessary for building the army and performance in action, such as John's, was the principal criterion for promotion.[7]

On June 15, 1863, the *Tribune* had published an editorial calling on Secretary of War Stanton to authorize Illinois Governor Yates to raise a black regiment "that will stand as much hardship, and fight as desperately, and kill as many rebels in battle, as any equal number of men of purest Anglo-Saxon blood that have gone to the wars."[8] Joseph Medill sent the editorial to be shown to Stanton in Washington, and Stanton immediately signaled his approval. In late September Governor Yates was given final authorization "to raise a regiment of Infantry to be composed of colored men" in Illinois, on October 6 it was announced that John was to its commander, and on October 26 the Governor issued a General Order to begin the recruitment. The first enlistments were made on November 1 in Quincy, Illinois, for Company A, the first company to be organized. Companies B and C were to be recruited in Chicago and companies D, E, and F were to be recruited throughout the entire state.[9] Also on November 1, John was discharged as a Captain in the 88th Illinois Infantry and was assigned as "on volunteer recruiting service prior to muster" of the new troops, probably without pay.[10]

Although William had assured Governor Yates that a colored regiment could be recruited within six weeks, it took much longer than that to fill up the new regiment, which was initially named the "First Regiment Illinois Volunteers (Colored)."[11] The black population in Illinois was relatively small, only about one-half of one percent of the state's population, and this may have been because Illinois had "black code" laws that among other things made it illegal for any blacks, free or not, to reside in the state.[12] These laws, which were not finally abolished until 1865, were largely disregarded in the northern part of Illinois, but as late as 1863, six free blacks were convicted of living in the state and were sold to the highest bidder at a sheriff's auction since they couldn't pay the fine.[13] It was also true that about 700 black men eligible to join the military had gone to other states, especially Massachusetts, to enlist earlier in 1863. But as many as 22,000 slaves escaped from Missouri between 1860 and 1862, many of them coming into Illinois, so there were probably enough eligible black men in Illinois to raise a regiment of 900 or more.[14] Copperhead sentiment against black enlistments was high, especially in southern Illinois, which probably slowed recruiting, and news of Confederate death threats and actual massacres of black soldiers and their officers by Confederates cannot have helped.[15]

Another obstacle to the recruitment of black soldiers was the issue of discrimination in pay for black soldiers. When the War Department began enlisting blacks in early 1863, it offered to pay them the same amount as white soldiers, ranging from thirteen dollars per month for privates to twenty-one dollars for sergeants, plus rations and clothing. But in June 1863, the War Department announced that an opinion by the Department's Solicitor required pay for black soldiers to be governed by the Militia Act of 1862, which had envisioned the employment of blacks as laborers and specified pay of ten dollars per month, of which three was for clothing, regardless of rank.[16] This naturally led to outrage, on the part of both the black soldiers who had enlisted under the promise of equal pay and the abolitionists. Black soldiers took the only means of protest available to them as soldiers at war by refusing to accept the seven dollars per month offered them and serving without pay, which was a great hardship especially for their families, but there were also instances of insubordination and even mutiny, adversely affecting morale. Massachusetts Governor Andrew proposed to equalize the pay for black soldiers from state funds, but the soldiers refused to accept this because for them it was a matter of principle that they should not be treated as less valuable than white soldiers.[17] Republicans introduced a law for retroactive equalization of pay, but Democrats and conservative Republicans in Congress insisted on restricting retroactive pay only back to January 1, 1864, except for blacks who had been free before the war, so that many black soldiers could not collect their pay for service performed in 1863.[18] There can have been no reason for such discrimination in pay other than racial prejudice, but the Lincoln administration needed to proceed cautiously in the matter because of the considerable hostility in some political quarters to the idea of blacks serving in the military at all.

Two weeks after recruiting began, on November 12, the *Tribune* ran an editorial encouraging recruitment for the new black regiment: "We appeal to the colored men of Illinois to drive home and clinch the reputation of the slanders that have annulled their race and to prove in their own persons, as their brethren have elsewhere done, that beneath black skin rest the great qualifications now needed by the Republic to defend itself against the assaults of its foes."

A month later a dispatch from Springfield to the *Tribune* dated December 19, 1863, reported: "Capt. John A. Bross, of the 88th Illinois volunteers, has been relieved from recruiting service, by order of the War Department, and ordered to report to Governor Yates for the purpose of

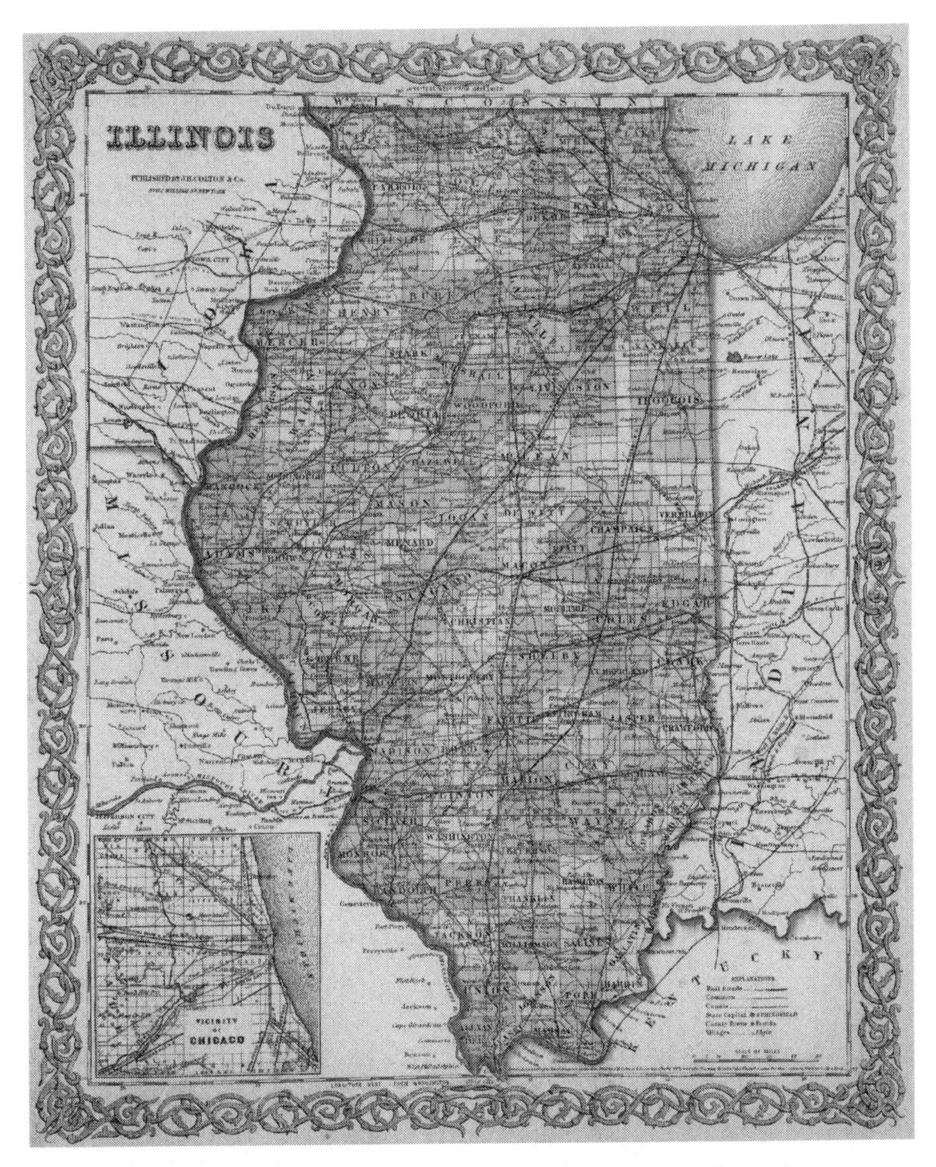

Map of Illinois, 1856, J. H. Colton (David Rumsey Map Collection).

organizing colored troops in the State. His headquarters will probably be established at Quincy." Evidently, John's mission was now organization of the new troops, although recruiting was by no means complete.

Because John stopped writing letters to Belle after he came home in October, we have no detailed account of his whereabouts until he again began writing letters when he left with his regiment for Virginia in April 1864. He was evidently in Chicago with his family at Christmas, since on December 28, 1863, the *Tribune* reported:

> The Negro Regiments – Lieutenants Hector H. Aiken and J.K. Conklin have opened a recruiting office at 203 South Clark Street, where they will receive recruits for the 1st regiment of colored Illinois volunteers. All those enlisted will receive $100 bounty, paid down in cash, and get clothing, &c.... and all enlisted here will rendezvous at Quincy, Illinois.... Colonel John A. Bross, of this regiment, will be at the recruiting office to day, between 10 A.M. and 4 P.M.

On the same day, a *Tribune* article explained that blacks enlisting from any county would reduce the quota of that county as well as any white recruit, and that transportation could be arranged for a recruit from any part of the state by telegraphing Colonel John A. Bross at Quincy. Soon after Christmas, therefore, John must have returned to Quincy to continue recruiting and organizing for the new regiment.

On January 10 the *Tribune* reprinted an article from the *Springfield Register*, which reported on the status of recruiting for the new regiment and also gave a vivid picture of the racist sentiments then prevalent in the area around Springfield. A friendly visit from John seems to have persuaded the *Register* to adopt an attitude favorable to the recruiting of black soldiers, evidently a change of heart for that newspaper. The Springfield article also reflects local distress about the social disruption caused by the influx of black refugees; in strikingly racist language it supports recruitment as a way of ridding the community of black newcomers, probably contrabands from Missouri, who were technically in contravention of the existing law against blacks residing in the state (although this law was apparently to be ignored for longtime black residents who were known and accepted in the community):

From the *Springfield Register*:

"The Colored Regiment"

Col. John A. Bross, of the "1st Illinois colored volunteers," called at our office yesterday, and gave us the first valuable intelligence we have had respecting the progress of the regiment recruiting under his command. There are about one hundred and seventy-five men in camp at Quincy, besides a number (125 men) enlisted at Chicago and some other portions of the state. Col. Bross has had much opposition to encounter, and but little assistance has been afforded him by the friends of the negro, par excellence, but he thinks that with a proper effort the regiment can be filled.

In Springfield, as well as in most other cities of this State, we have hundreds of negroes, amongst us contrary to law, and earning their living nobody can tell how. Col. Bross is here just after such darkeys; and as this war is a war for Sambo, Sambo ought to fight it. And if Sambo will not go except on compulsion let our city council investigate their cases and see how many of them are here in defiance of law, and if they won't go to the war, apply the penalty. "A bird that can sing and won't sing, must be made to sing;" and now that Uncle Sam has freed Sambo, let Sambo fight for Uncle Sam. The recent Congress will undoubtedly place them on the same footing with white soldiers, and they will have no excuse but their innate laziness or cowardice for refusing to enlist. We call upon Pompey, and Caesar, and Sambo to flock to Col. Bross' standard. A race that will not fight for their own freedom does not deserve to be free....

So far, notwithstanding our large colored population, Springfield has furnished not a single recruit for this regiment. We do not appeal to the old colored residents of the city, who own property here, and are engaged in legitimate business, but to the horde of late importations—great muscular stalwart fellows, who came from no one knows whither, who do not work for their living, and are liable to punishment for being here contrary to law.

The *Tribune* article, making clear that it does not share the racist views of the Springfield newspaper, comments: "We are glad to see the Copperhead

Register converted to the doctrine that negroes ought and must be employed in helping to put down the slave-mongers' rebellion" and suggests a "far better way" to induce local blacks to join Colonel Bross's regiment:

> When the Springfield Common Council gets together to "investigate," let the members follow the example of the Chicago Council and vote a bounty of $100 to each negro who will enlist into the Illinois colored regiment, and we assure our copperhead contemporary, that no other influence will be needed to cause those "great muscular stalwart fellows," to enlist by the scores. Black men like money just as much as white men. They equally dislike to work for nothing, and they are equally fond of wages. When Congress does pass the bill paying them the same bounty and wages accorded to white soldiers, there will be no room after that for complaining that colored men do not evince a willingness to enlist. Meanwhile let Sangamon county try the experiment that Cook county has found to work like a charm—offer each colored volunteer $100 in "greenbacks," and the offer will have lots of takers.

John was evidently going back and forth between Quincy and Chicago during this period and so would have been able to spend some time with Belle and Mason, although Belle had rented out their Chicago house and was living in Sterling with her parents. On January 21 a Special Dispatch to the *Chicago Tribune* from Quincy reported that "Col. John A. Bross of the Illinois colored regiment, left for Springfield to-day. His regiment is fast filling up, and from various parts of the State indications are that it will be filled up by the 1st of February without a doubt. By order of the War Department the regiment will be known and designated as the 29th Regiment U.S. Colored Troops." A special dispatch from Springfield dated the same day carries the announcement, "I shall be at the rendez-vous, Chicago, tomorrow, for transacting regimental business. John A. Bross."

The hopeful prediction that the regiment would be filled up by February 1 turned out to be optimistic. On January 27 the *Tribune* printed a rousing appeal for black recruits, blaming the slow enlistment on the delay in Illinois that had caused many Illinois blacks in previous months to enlist in other states and nimbly attempting to minimize the sensitive issue of lower pay for blacks, arguing that this discrimination would surely be rectified, but that blacks should in the meanwhile show their moral superiority and demonstrate their manhood by overlooking the surely temporary discrimination and seizing the first-ever opportunity to fight for their country:

> "The First Colored Regiment of Illinois"
>
> The 1st colored regiment of Illinois is now being recruited under Colonel John A. Bross, who has been commissioned for this purpose. Col. Bross was a lawyer of this city, a Christian gentleman, who went out as a Captain of the 88th Illinois, (2nd Board of Trade,) and has proved himself, as at Chickamauga and elsewhere, a brave commander, and an officer who takes good care of his men, and who will insist upon having qualified and sympathetic subordinate officers in the regiment. A good deal of progress has been made in the matter of enlistments. By delay in the movement in Illinois, some seven hundred colored recruits have already gone off to other States. But still there are enough left to fill up this first regiment, and more.
>
> Colored men of Illinois, Americans—falsely called Africans—while the physical bravery of your brothers in arms has become the admiration of the nation, now is the time to show your moral heroism. In this State your oath has not been allowed in court; your vote has been rejected at the ballot-box; your residence here is at the risk of a legally threatened penalty, with the alternative of being sold into bondage; you have been made the subject of a social proscription that has shut you out of all but menial occupations; you know that these laws and this diabolical prejudice yet remain in force. And then, when the Government has come to its senses, and calls on you for help, you find a discrimination made at which your better nature revolts—no bounty and only half pay—while you know that your men are as good soldiers as white ones; you know that any such distinction made against Germans, or Irishmen, or Yankees, would keep them out of the army. And yet there is a motive that should lift you above all this injustice and hatred. Now is the time to show your manhood. It has been the denial of this by the

> dominant race that has loaded you down with wrongs. Prove now that you are men, that you possess those noblest elements of humanity—exalted aspiration and the spirit of self-sacrifice in the attainment of liberty and the public weal. For this your anti-slavery friends have contended through years of obloquy. Your race now struggling up into its place among the nations, has thrust you forward to the Thermopylae of its advancement. Many generations of your sires, who have gone down under the burning stigma of chattels, now call upon you to redeem their memory from this horrid imposition. The first great occasion has come. It may soon pass. Nothing will so soon redeem your position among mankind as courage in the ordeal of war and in the exercise of those high moral qualities that shall enable you to rise above your wrongs and make you the world's heroes. At Yorktown on Thanksgiving Day, as I learn by a private letter, the colored chaplain of the 4th Virginia, who began his prayer "O God, we thank thee that the soil of Virginia is no longer too sacred for black men to unite and utter their praises to thee for freedom and victory on a national Thanksgiving day," said in his sermon, "some of you, I hear, are grumbling because you are not paid as much as White soldiers. Let the Government understand that we are not mercenary. Let us be grateful that we are allowed the great privilege of entering into the conflict at any price—that we are permitted to fight and die for the glorious cause of Freedom, Truth, and undivided Union." Meantime, if we are worthy of your aid, if we are worthy of the restoration of our Union, we shall hasten to remove the black laws from our statutes and to equalize the pay and bounty and protection of all soldiers under our flag. This is sure to come.

The encouraging words of the *Tribune* were only partially successful. A February 2 dispatch from Springfield reported that "Southern Illinois is likely to rival and eclipse northern counties in furnishing recruits for Col. Bross' Colored Regiment. The old 8th district has now two companies under way, and will fill them."

The *Memorial* explains that John went to Quincy to recruit because this was a place where black refugees, most of them runaway slaves still referred to as "contrabands," tended to cross over from Missouri into Illinois. It would have been possible to fill the regiment more quickly by accepting companies of contrabands from the government, but John wished to recruit as many "free blacks" as possible from Illinois or elsewhere in the North, believing them to be better educated and therefore "a more intelligent class of men," even though he could not be commissioned as a full colonel until the regiment was filled up.[19] Under army regulations, John could be appointed a lieutenant colonel when four companies of a minimum of seventy-five noncommissioned officers and men each were mustered in.[20]

In the end, as the *Memorial* reports, the regiment was summoned into action before it had been filled up. Troops were urgently needed by the newly appointed Union commanding general Ulysses S. Grant for the Virginia campaign against Lee's army, which he was planning for that summer. On March 22, 1864, the *Tribune* reported: "The Illinois colored regiment, Col. John A. Bross, now at Quincy, is ordered to report at Annapolis, Md. to be assigned to Gen. Burnside's 9th Army Corps." John was commissioned as lieutenant colonel of the regiment as of April 7; he was probably disappointed that his new regiment was incomplete. In fact, only five full companies and part of another had been raised when the regiment departed for Annapolis in late April. After arriving in Virginia, not wanting to spend more time of his own or of his officers in recruiting, John felt he had no choice but to accept four companies of contrabands, former slaves recruited mostly in Virginia and Maryland, but the order granting them did not come through until shortly after his death.[21]

The official mustering in of the new regiment is described in the excellent one-volume history of that regiment, *The Black Civil War Soldiers of Illinois: The Story of the Twenty-ninth U.S. Colored Infantry* by Edward A. Miller:

> On April 25, 1864 the unit, except for Company F, was formally "mustered into service of the United States by Charles C. Pomeroy, Capt USA," the Chicago-based recruiting officer, and the First Regiment Illinois Volunteers (Colored) officially became the Twenty-ninth United States Colored Infantry. On hand for the ceremony were about

> four hundred and fifty enlisted men—over two hundred of whom had been sworn in on the previous day—and a dozen officers, most of the latter still waiting for their commissions and so not mustered in. Companies A, B, C, D, and E had the minimum number of privates, sixty-four. Company F had but fourteen, too few for company muster. Each company had nearly all its authorized requirements of noncommissioned officers, musicians and wagoners, except F. As for officers, all companies were short two or even three; the regimental staff consisted of Lieutenant Colonel Bross, Major Brown, and perhaps a handful of enlisted men borrowed from the companies.[22]

On the afternoon of April 26, the regiment at Quincy boarded twelve coaches of the Chicago, Burlington and Quincy Railroad, heading for Chicago as the first stop on the way to Maryland.[23] A *Tribune* article on April 27 announced that:

> The 29th U.S. colored regiment, raised in this State, and under command of Col. John A. Bross, arrives in this city to-day from its camp of rendezvous at Quincy, en route for Annapolis. A number of Col. Bross' friends have united in the purchase of a horse and accoutrements to be presented to him to-day in front of the Soldiers' Rest. The animal was the property of a prominent Illinois cavalry officer, in the Virginia campaigns of the past two years. The presentation speech will be made by Col. F. A. Eastman. We are not able to announce the precise hour of the presentation, but we believe it is to take place at 11 a.m., should the arrival of the regiment render that hour practicable.

In Chicago, as in other large Northern cities, a "Soldiers Rest" building provided a place to stay for volunteer soldiers passing through the city. The Chicago soldiers rest was a building 250 by 50 feet, opened in January 1864 and run by a Board of Lady Managers whose "work was as arduous as it was onerous. Regiments were entertained at all hours of the day as they happened to arrive at the Rest."[24]

John's regiment arrived at 8 o'clock in the morning by train from

Quincy. After refreshments were served to the soldiers, the ceremony took place at 11:00 a.m. and by 1:00 p.m., the troops were again on their way east towards Pittsburgh. An April 28 *Tribune* article described the event:

"THE ILLINOIS COLORED REGIMENT"

"Its Arrival in Chicago—Reception—Its Departure to Join Burnside"

The Illinois colored regiment, 29th U. S. colored volunteers, Col. John A. Bross commanding, reached this city from its camp of rendezvous at Quincy, yesterday morning at 8 o'clock, en route to join Burnside's movement of the 9th corps from Annapolis, Maryland. The patriotic and generous ladies of the Soldiers' Rest had in readiness a bountiful repast to which the regiment did full justice. Their regiment is the first colored regiment organized in this State, and elicited high encomiums yesterday from all observers, by their soldierly appearance. Their regimental roster is as yet incomplete, and cannot be given in form. It would be doing injustice to excellent and devoted officers of strong Patriotism, to omit the names of Capts. Robert Porter, H. H. Aiken, W. E. Doggett, George R. Naylor, W. H. Flint, and Lieuts. J. N. Strickland, W. B. Gale, Fred Chapman, John Gosper, A. C. Knapp and W. H. Glint, as connected with its present rolls, and indefatigable workers for its proficiency and advancement.

The friends of Col. Bross in this city had prepared for him a pleasant and most appropriate proof of their good will in the shape of a horse and accoutrements of great value and beauty. The animal chosen was of the famous Kentucky breed, the "Gold Dust Morgan" which has already seen two campaigns of service in Virginia, bearing a gallant Illinois cavalry officer. The whole gift was procured at an outlay of $400, from some thirty or more donors. At 11 a. m. the beautiful and appropriate testimonial for an officer formed the centre of an admiring crowd of some hundreds drawn up before the Soldiers' Rest, where in behalf of the donors the deed of transfer was handsomely attended to by Col. F. A. Eastman, in the following address of presentation:

"Col. F. A. Eastman's Speech"

Col. John A. Bross: I had been in ignorance of a movement of your friends in Chicago, having in view the presentation to you of a horse and the requisite accoutrements, until last evening, when I was informed that the gift had already been purchased, and that it only awaited a few words from me, at this hour, to place it (at) your disposal. You have witnessed and felt the sublimities and dangers of battle. As Captain in the 88th—the 2nd Board of Trade—regiment of Illinois volunteers—God bless every surviving soldier of that noble band—you gave such evidence of martial skill and valor as secured to you the good opinion of your comrades and the commendation of your superiors in rank. The loyal citizens of Chicago have not been, and are not, slow to recognize merit or to evince admiration of bravery. This beautiful animal is yours, with the hearty friendship and bountiful good wishes of those who know you well. Permit me to remark, that your moral courage, as shown in your taking the Colonelcy of the 1st colored regiment of Illinois volunteers, is as creditable to you as honorable to our State. Regeneration is going on here; here, in Illinois, whose constitution and statutes are disgraced by the infamous 'black laws', light is breaking in. And the evidence of this is before us. A white man of good family, of culture, and of social position, does not hesitate to place himself at the head of a regiment of blacks, recruited in Illinois, to go forth to fight for the honor and freedom and unity of our country. Your peculiar position may involve you in peculiar perils. But I know—these numerous witnesses feel assured—that though perils and even tortures should come, in the name of humanity, you will not flinch.

Here, perhaps, I ought to conclude. But the memories of recent revolting cruelties, perpetrated by the rebels upon United States colored troops, impel me to proceed. History has many instances of one tribe of barbarians falling upon and indiscriminately butchering another tribe of barbarians. There are also instances of half civilized men visiting civilized communities, and in a moment of passion, mercilessly slaying their victims. These occurrences revolt, but they do not surprise us. Human nature is willing to supply provocations and palliations.

> But the slaughter, by the rebels in cold blood, of our colored soldiers! there is not, in all history, an example for it; not in the most depraved human nature can an apology be found for it. A run-away slave was the first man, when the outbreak of the colonies against England was imminent, to gather about him a company of patriots; he—the run-away slave Crispus Attucks—was the first to fire, and the first to fall dead in the opening fight of the Revolution.[25] Blacks were admitted into the Revolutionary army freely by Gen. Washington. Gen. Jackson employed them, and they defended for that old hero, and for the United States, New Orleans against the British. No troops did better fighting at Fort Wagner, Port Hudson, and Olustee, than the colored troops did.[26] Those terrible struggles awakened souls in black, as daring as were ever found in white bodies. Those men (alluding to the men of the 1st regiment of colored volunteers, and addressing himself to Col. Bross,) must be cared for and protected. They are ennobled by their aspirations to liberate their race from bondage—they are made like unto ourselves by the uniforms they wear. For every life surrendered by them to rebel cruelty, the life of a rebel shall be the forfeit. An act of torture for an act of torture—that should be the policy of our Government. But we must first get even with the brutal foe. These colored troops should take no prisoners until the massacre at Fort Pillow is avenged.
>
> At the conclusion of Col. Eastman's remarks, Col. Bross briefly and most feelingly responded, being received with hearty cheers. Shortly afterward the gallant regiment of "black and Blue boys" took up its march for the Fort Wayne depot, and at one p. m. they were off for the seat of war, followed by the good wishes of thousands.

The *Memorial* gives a little more information about John's response:

> His response being entirely extempore, was not preserved, but a sentence or two is remembered by those who heard it. "When I lead these men into battle, we shall remember Fort Pillow, and shall not ask for quarter. I leave a home and friends as dear as can be found on earth; but if it is the will of Providence that I do not return, I ask no nobler

> epitaph, than that I fell for my country, at the head of this black and blue regiment."[27]

Belle and little Mason were evidently present at the ceremony together with William, as a later *Tribune* article about John's death, probably written by William, refers to John's "little son of three summers, old enough to enjoy and clap his hands at the spectacle of the pageant of departure of his father's regiment."[28] So they were able to say goodbye to their husband and father, whom they would never see again.

Predictably, reaction in the South to the raising of colored troops was savagely hostile, since the idea of black troops fundamentally contradicted the idea of the racial inferiority of blacks, which was the foundation of slavery, and also touched the extremely sensitive Southern nerve of fear of a black insurrection. In May 1863, the Confederate government had threatened to re-enslave or execute captured black soldiers and their officers.[29] In July 1863, Lincoln had responded by ordering that "for every Union soldier killed in violation of the laws of war a rebel soldier shall be executed," but this policy was not carried out because the Lincoln administration did not think it was right to punish the innocent for the crimes of the guilty. Speaking to Frederick Douglass about retaliation, Lincoln said, "[I]f once begun, there was no telling where it would end."[30] The references to Fort Pillow in Col. Eastman's speech and in John's reply are to the notorious massacre of several dozen surrendered black troops and some white ones after Confederate General Bedford Forrest captured the Union garrison at Fort Pillow, Tennessee, on April 12, 1864, just two weeks before the stopover in Chicago of John's regiment and still vividly in Northern public awareness.[31]

Although the Confederates tended to keep few records about black prisoners because they did not acknowledge them as legitimate prisoners, it is known that hundreds of black soldiers were massacred at Fort Pillow, Poison Spring, the Crater, Plymouth, North Carolina, and other locations.[32] Not surprisingly, "Remember Fort Pillow" and "No Quarter" became battle slogans often called out by black troops going into battle, a reminder that they would receive no quarter and should give none, and there were several recorded instances where black soldiers killed white prisoners. "Most often, no action was taken against atrocities, and so the troops on both sides inferred that they had tacit approval for the use of the 'black flag.'"[33] Captain Charles Francis Adams wrote his father in reference to the fighting around Petersburg in June, 1864, "The cruelty of Fort Pillow is reacting on the rebels, for now they dread the darkies more than the white troops; for they know that if they will fight the rebels cannot expect quarter. Of course, our black troops are not subject to any of the rules of civilized warfare. If they murder prisoners, as I hear they did, it is to be lamented and stopped, but they can hardly be blamed."[34] It is noteworthy that Colonel Eastman in his speech at the soldiers rest in Chicago explicitly said that "the colored troops should take no prisoners until the massacre at Fort Pillow is avenged." But it was never official Federal policy that prisoners should be killed, and it appears that Union officers did their best to prevent it. It *was* official Confederate policy, supported energetically by Southern editorials, that black prisoners and their white officers should be put to death, but some black soldiers and their white officers were, in fact, taken prisoner.[35]

Even though black soldiers were taken alive and held as prisoners, racial prejudice also poisoned the process of prisoner exchange. A year previously, in May 1863, the Confederate government had refused to exchange black prisoners.[36] The Lincoln administration took the position that it would not exchange prisoners on any basis other than treating black and white soldiers alike; the exchange of prisoners then ceased and, as a result, many prisoners died in prison camps such as the notorious Andersonville near Atlanta.

When John's black regiment left Chicago, therefore, it was known that the officers of black regiments, all of whom were white, faced greater danger than other officers. The *Memorial* discusses this:[37]

> The perils of officers of his rank, in an active campaign, are always great; but in the service he had undertaken, they were felt to be largely increased. The cruel treatment of colored troops, and their officers, by the rebels, so far as their power went to reach them, was well known; and the massacre of Fort Pillow had recently occurred, to give intensity to the danger that adhered to this service. Of all this, no one was better

> aware than Colonel Bross himself. But his convictions of the rightfulness of arming the blacks, were clear; his faith in their efficiency, as soldiers, was entire; he had no doubt of his own duty, and he went forward to the sacrifice, without a murmur or regret.
>
> His pastor tells us, that in a conversation with him, as he was about to leave for Virginia, on reminding him that his connection with colored troops would expose him to peculiar dangers, a tear came into his eye, while he said, firmly: "If need be, I am willing to be offered."
>
> "There is nothing," as he was accustomed to say, "better expresses my idea of a soldier's duty, than Tennyson's description of the charge of the Light Brigade, especially the following stanza:
>
> 'Forward the Light Brigade!
> No man was there dismayed,
> Not though the soldiers knew
> Some one had blundered—
> Their's not to make reply;
> Their's not to reason why;
> Their's but to do and die;
> Into the valley of death
> Rode the six hundred.' "
>
> This he would repeat with such emphasis as often gave a pang to the hearts of loving friends, who remembered the dangers to which he would so soon be exposed, and now taken in connection with the manner in which he was sacrificed, seems almost prophetic. It clearly showed the direction of his thoughts, and what would be his course in similar circumstances.[38]

It has been noted that the additional danger for officers of black troops may have had a positive effect in that it served as a screen to weed out white men who didn't have a full commitment to service with black troops. One officer was quoted as saying, "The officers who accepted the command of colored troops were old soldiers in almost every instance. Death in their country's service was what they had been facing for years, and this threat of the rebel congress added no terrors sufficient to restrain them."[39] This was certainly true of John, who had served in combat with distinction for more than a year and had taken part in three major battles, facing death in his country's service.

NOTES

1. Dorothy L. Drinkard, *Illinois Freedom Fighters: A Civil War Saga of the 29th Infantry, United States Colored Troops* (Simon & Schuster Custom Publishing, 1998), 9.
2. McPherson, *Battle Cry of Freedom*, 503.
3. Ibid., 504, 558.
4. Ibid., 558.
5. Ibid., 565.
6. *Memorial*, 9.
7. James McPherson, *The War that Forged a Nation: Why the Civil War Still Matters* (New York: Oxford University Press, 2015), 129.
8. Edward A. Miller, *The Black Civil War Soldiers of Illinois; The Story of the Twenty-ninth U. S. Colored Infantry*. (Columbia: University of South Carolina Press, 1998), 5.
9. Ibid., 6, 21, 28.
10. Ibid., 13.
11. Ibid., 6.
12. Ibid., 12.
13. Ibid., 8.
14. Joseph T Glatthaar, *Forged in Battle: The Civil War Alliance of Black Soldiers and White Officers* (Baton Rouge: Louisiana State University Press, 1990), 12.
15. Miller, *The Black Civil War Soldiers*, 10.
16. Glatthaar, *Forged in Battle*, 169–170.
17. Ibid., 170.
18. McPherson, *Battle Cry*, 789.
19. *Memorial*, 10; Miller, *The Black Civil War Soldiers*, 34.
20. Miller, *The Black Civil War Soldiers*, 13.
21. Ibid., 34.
22. Ibid., 37.
23. Ibid., 38; Miller states that they boarded April 27 and arrived April 28, but the contemporary *Tribune* articles and the JAB letters indicate otherwise.

24. John Moses and Joseph Kirkland, *History of Chicago, Illinois*, Vol. 1 (Chicago: Munsell & Co., 1895), 197.
25. Crispus Attucks (1723–1770), an African American sailor, thought to be the first person killed in the Boston Massacre of March 5, 1770, is often referred to as the first American killed in the American Revolution.
26. Three battles in which black troops distinguished themselves: Fort Wagner, South Carolina, July 1863; Port Hudson, Louisiana, May–July 1863; Olustee Station, Florida, February 20, 1864.
27. *Memorial*, 11.
28. *Chicago Tribune*, August 4, 1864.
29. McPherson, *Battle Cry*, 792.
30. Ibid., 794.
31. Ibid., 748.
32. Ibid., 793.
33. John F. Schmutz, *The Battle of the Crater; A Complete History* (Jefferson, NC: McFarland & Company, Inc., 2009), 255.
34. Schmutz, *Battle of the Crater*, 254.
35. Richard Slotkin, *No Quarter; The Battle of the Crater, 1864* (New York: Random House, 2009).
36. McPherson, *Battle Cry*, 792.
37. *Memorial*, 11.
38. "Charge of the Light Brigade," first published in 1854, eight years before John went off to war.
39. Glatthaar, *Forged in Battle*, 202.

CHAPTER 7

1864: Virginia, Battle of the Crater

John's Twenty-ninth USCT regiment was assigned to the Fourth Division of the Ninth Corps, Army of the Potomac. Major General Ambrose Burnside, commanding general of the Ninth Corps, had organized his Corps into four divisions, three white ones and one black one. The Fourth Division, to which all the black troops were assigned, was commanded by Brigadier General Edward Ferrero and in early May had only five regiments of the planned nine, the others not yet complete or still on the way.[1] Ferrero organized the Fourth Division in two brigades, the first commanded by Col. Joshua Sigfried and the second, to which the 29th USCT was assigned, commanded by Col. Henry G. Thomas, a lawyer from Maine who was the first regular army officer to accept command of black troops.[2] In addition to the 29th USCT regiment, the Second Brigade included four other USCT regiments, the 19th, 23rd, 28th, and 31st.

The Ninth Corps had recently been transferred from Tennessee and had a reputation for indiscipline and disorganization.[3] It had at first reported directly to General Ulysses S. Grant, newly appointed as General in Chief of all Union forces, because General Burnside was senior to Major General George Meade, who was the commander of the Army of the Potomac, and Burnside had initially declined to report to Meade. Not until May 24, after

Burnside agreed to serve under Meade, did Grant place the Ninth Corps in Meade's Army of the Potomac. It was known that President Lincoln and some Congressional Republicans had been dissatisfied with the failure of Meade to pursue Lee's army after the Battle of Gettysburg and the presence of Grant, who outranked Meade, with the Army of the Potomac was seen by some as a reflection of that dissatisfaction; Meade was aware of this political threat to his reputation.

The 29th Regiment left Chicago at 1:00 p.m. on Wednesday, April 27 and after a journey of thirty hours, including some delay, arrived in Pittsburgh on Thursday, April 28 at 9 p.m. The *Tribune* reprinted an article of April 29 from the *Pittsburgh Gazette*:

> "Illinois Colored Troops"
>
> The 29th U.S. Colored regiment, of Illinois, arrived from Chicago last evening, and were hospitably entertained by the Subsistence Committee. The regiment numbers four hundred and seventy men, and is commanded by Col. John A. Bross of Chicago, a brother of one of the editors of the Chicago Tribune. Col. Bross was formerly Senior Captain of the 88th Illinois infantry. After the regiment had partaken of supper at the City Hall, Col. Bross returned thanks for the kindness extended towards them by the committee, and the members of the regiment sang a number of patriotic songs. The occasion was very interesting, and a large number of citizens were present. The regiment left in the eastern train this morning, for Annapolis, Maryland.

It would have been a "very interesting" occasion because a regiment of black men in blue Federal uniforms was a novel sight in the spring of 1864, as the inescapable implication of equal citizenship for blacks must have begun to sink in among the observers. And if the men of the regiment reflected the musical interest of its commander, it must have been a stirring concert, with the additional significance of black soldiers singing to a white audience patriotic songs about a republic of freedom and equality, which now for the first time might fully include them.

The regiment left the same evening at 11:30 p.m. for Baltimore, rather than Annapolis, arriving on Friday, April 29 at 9:00 p.m., where they took supper at the soldiers rest and were quartered in the Adams House, "a secesh concern the owners of which have been hunting their rights away down south," according to John's letter of May 1. Sergeant William McCoslin, one of the regiment's noncommissioned black officers, noticed that when they arrived in Baltimore "we marched up the identical street where the citizens mobbed the first white regiment. There was talk of mobbing the colored regiment." But "[w]e were treated with some respect by all the citizens."[4] John wrote that he spent part of Saturday trying to get orders about changing his destination and finally secured transportation to Washington.[5] The destination had to be changed because Major General Burnside's Ninth Army Corps, to which the 29th Regiment was assigned, had already marched from Annapolis to Manassas Junction in Virginia, south of the capital. The regiment was directed to proceed from Baltimore to Washington, D.C.; it arrived there at 8 p.m. on Saturday, April 30 and was quartered in the soldiers rest there.[6]

In his letter of Sunday, May 1, 1864, John gave Belle a description of his regiment parading down Pennsylvania Avenue that afternoon:

> We stayed there until after dinner today, when we marched down Pennsylvania Avenue in grand style and then to this point. I was pleased with the regt and the occasion. Little did I think three years ago when I sat on the steps of the Treasury building and looked down the Avenue to the Capitol and cried with indignation over the affairs of the country that I should at this day march a regiment of colored troops down that same avenue. The whole street was lined with an enormous crowd of whites & colored. I have the vanity to believe that your husband never appeared better or felt more keenly the promptings of a proud and joyous spirit. My charger performed his part of the play in gallant style. He is a noble animal. I shall always feel grateful to Mr. Smith for his efforts in procuring it for me.
>
> My regiment behaved well on the way—so much so as to provoke comparisons in their favor and to the detriment of white soldiers.

This morning I had religious services, a Scotchman of the Christian's Commission officiating. He is from Paisley and his name is Smith. I led the singing & it did me good to hear them sing. Tomorrow I make all arrangements for fitting out & next day I leave here for the Corps which is at present doing guard duty along the RR.

with the Regt and the occasion,
Little did I think three years ago
when I sat on the steps of the
Treasury building and looked down
the Avenue to the Capitol and cried
with indignation over the affairs of
the Country, that I should at this
day march a Regt of Colored troops
down that same avenue. The
whole street was lined with an
enormous crowd of whites & Colored.
I have the vanity to believe that
Your husband never appeared better
or felt, more keenly the promptings of a proud
and joyous spirit. My charger
performed his part of the play in
gallant style. He is a noble
animal — I shall always feel
grateful to Mr Smith for his efforts
in procuring it for me —

Portion of letter dated May 1, 1864.

John leads his 29th U.S. Colored Infantry Regiment down Pennsylvania Avenue. The reference to "three years ago" is the only known evidence that John and William attended Lincoln's first inauguration.

Two months after he arrived in Washington, John finally received a letter dated April 26, 1864, from John S. Loomis, Assistant Adjutant General of Illinois, which had been misdirected, informing John that he had left commissions for officers of the regiment at Willards Hotel in Washington. In the meanwhile, John had to undertake to replace the missing commissions. The letter, which is preserved along with John's letters, indicates that the commissions had been obtained after something of a bureaucratic struggle. Loomis writes:

> We have had a merry time with the War Dept. procuring these commissions. All West Point and other devotees of red tape have been dead against the issue without each officer being examined before General Casey's board after arrival of the regiment at Washington. This proposition of course the Governor objected to so strongly that Stanton finally gave in and made your officers an exception to the General Order. I presume all vacancies will be filled only by appointment of such officers as pass examination and I think it useless to try and get order to the contrary. I was fortified in my first application, made immediately after my arrival here, (after seeing you at Chicago) by the indorsement of Generals Grant & Burnside, but Halleck and the Adjutant Generals Bureau were strong against me and I think it will be easier and perhaps better to have all you propose, or wish to promote, examined.
>
> Hope you will receive commissions OK and that Brown will make you a good Major and the other officers merit the strong indorsement we have had to make to procure their commissions. Shall be glad to hear from, and at any time aid you, in accomplishment of your wishes.
>
> Wishing you a brilliant career with your gallant colored boys, I am
>
> Most truly yours
> John S. Loomis

As John's letter of May 1 indicated, the regiment proceeded to the soldiers rest at Alexandria on its way to Manassas. But John had not received an order sent by Major General Silas Casey directing him to report at Casey's headquarters near what is now the Fourteenth Street Bridge in Washington, and Casey complained to the War Department that John had ignored his orders.[7] The *Memorial* describes John's ensuing encounter with General Casey: "An order was thereupon sent to [John] direct, to report immediately at headquarters. He was received with much sternness by General Casey. 'Have you seen service before, sir.' 'I have, sir.' 'How came you to disobey that,' said General Casey, one of his staff at the same time presenting the order. 'Are you accustomed to obey orders?' Said Colonel Bross, with emphasis, 'General Casey, I obey orders with my life; your order never reached me.' The mistake was, of course, discovered and explanations were soon made. His air of resolute determination impressed the old general, and the colonel was thereupon placed in command of the colored brigade, then at Camp Casey, near Washington."[8]

The 29th Regiment had marched back from Alexandria to Camp Casey, one of the military bases established for the defense of Washington and a center for organization and training of recently arrived units, located not far from where the Pentagon now stands.[9] The understrength regiment stayed there for almost a month. John must indeed have impressed General Casey, as the morning after their arrival he was ordered to take command of the camp and of the colored brigade; John then appointed Captain Aiken, commander of Company B, as acting commanding officer of the regiment.[10] "Bross laid out the regiment's daily routine at Casey soon after arrival. Reveille was to be at 5 a.m., guard mount at 8, and company drill from 9 to 11 and, after lunch, from 2 to 4 p.m. At 5 a parade was scheduled; supper was at 6 and taps at 9." Instruction was mostly in close order drill and parade evolutions rather than combat training, with some basic instruction in the use of the .58 caliber Springfield Rifle Muskets, which were issued to the men a week after they arrived.[11]

In a letter from this period quoted in the *Memorial*, John indicates satisfaction with the progress of the training:

> My men are improving rapidly in all their duties. Captain Aiken is all I can desire in his conduct as commanding officer of the regiment. All the other officers seem to devote themselves to drill and discipline of their respective companies, while the men take pride in making all

> possible progress. It is with real pleasure I mount "Dick" for battalion drill. The evolutions are performed with animation, and without noise and swearing, which certainly renders it much more agreeable to me.[12]

In a letter of May 15 he writes:

> I have worked hard since I have been here but it has been with cheerful, pleasant anticipations of the future. I have felt a proud satisfaction of knowing that I am acting in a position that I could fill if I had the rank shining on my shoulder. I have as many men now under my command as Col Sherman. I fancy I am as strict as he is and yet a good deal more of a gentleman if I do say it myself. I would be glad to have any of my brother officers in that regiment see me on Battalion drill. Friday I made up a full regiment and spent the afternoon in Battalion evolutions. I was pleased with myself and the men. I would give a great deal if only I had my regt full. I am confident I could make a regiment equal to any in the service. The men improve rapidly in the use of the musket and in their general duties and should I stay here, I shall certainly have you here.

There were some issues of discipline. General Order No. 10, which he issued on May 21, stated, "The commanding officer has witnessed with pain and mortification the prevalence of gambling among a portion of the non commissioned officers & soldiers of this command and more particularly in the 29th regt U.S. Colored Troops."[13] And gambling was not the only challenge. In a letter of May 22 he writes:

> For your ear I am getting to be called "awful strict" which is pleasing to my military ear. I am proud of its effects upon my own regiment. It is the best by all odds in its discipline. ... I have issued some pretty stringent orders since I commenced operations about gambling & licentiousness. The other evening I had the guard house nearly full of soldiers for running into a contraband camp hard by. I also arrested one woman, kept her under guard all night & then with three others

> sent them over to "freedmans village" where they are living on bread and water. That evening there was a good deal of excitement among the men, and I took the precaution to have one of my own companies ready with loaded arms, at their quarters for emergencies. I was determined to stop this bad conduct of wenches at all hazards. I ordered all men to their barracks and enforced it at the point of the bayonet and every man who had slipped through the guards was arrested and clapped in the guard house without mercy. The camp wears a different aspect. I have some officers of other regiments engaged in the same nefarious business as the colored soldiers and as sure as they are caught wo[e] be to them.

On Monday, May 30, the regiment left Camp Casey for White House Landing, Grant's supply center on the Pamunkey River, east of Richmond.[14] The regiment marched to Alexandria, and there, late that afternoon, boarded a steamboat called the *George Weems*; it sailed through the night into Chesapeake Bay and reached Yorktown on the York River at sunset the next day. John reported in a letter of June 1 from the boat that "we have a cabin for the officers but I could not stay in it last night. I slept on the hurricane deck with the free air of Heaven circulating about my eyes and face.... We are just entering Chesapeake Bay and I may be sea sick.... I doubt if you can read this very well. It is caused by the jarring of the boat." The next day, which he reported as warm and sunny, the captain sent a party to find a pilot to take them up the York River and then the Pamunkey River, and they arrived later on June 2 at White House Landing.[15]

On May 11 at Camp Casey, John had reported with satisfaction that he had just had a visit from William and William's daughter Jessie, and he urgently expressed his desire for a visit from Belle: "I greatly wish I could see you and take not one but many, many kisses from you. I have had glimpses of you, not as in a glass darkly but as it were face to face. But that is nothing to the living breathing presence. You have my desires for you to come and see me."[16] On May 30 as he was about to board the transport for White House Landing, he wrote, "I cannot express to you how anxious I have been to see you but it is not to be." Then, writing on June 7 from White House

Landing, he has just learned that Belle had come to Washington to see him but had arrived just as, or just after, he was departing from Alexandria, and so had returned home without seeing him:

> My heart aches. Last night I received the first mail. I have no words to express my vexation at noticing the post mark & your superscription. Before I opened your letter I discovered all.... I could go to the front cheerfully feeling perfectly contented were I ignorant of the fact that you had come so far to see me & show your devotion. As it is I know I shall inwardly fret against the freaks of cruel fortune. Dearest, if I had only known I should have brought you here even if I had left an officer to escort you. You could have come this far without difficulty, and I could have returned you to Washington by any boat.... My beloved let us hope that we shall meet each other very soon. I would have given my commission to have met you. I cannot write you a long letter this morning as the mail is about to close. With a thousand embraces for my darling wife, I am always your loving husband John."

And on June 9:

> I do think it a great misfortune that I could not meet you at Washington. I shall not talk of my feelings towards you. Wait wait until I see you again. After this campaign is over if my life is spared we will be together for life. I do hope it will not be in the far future. I hope you will not be tired in reading my hasty notes from the battle field. Kisses for Mason & love for all. Yours Ever, John A. Bross

The 29th Regiment's arrival on June 2 at White House Landing took place a month after Grant had commenced, in early May, a seven-week campaign attempting to destroy Lee's army in Virginia and take Richmond. The campaign began on May 5 with the Battle of the Wilderness in northern Virginia, south of the Rapidan River, and ended on June 15 with the two armies facing each other over entrenchments south and east of the city of Petersburg, Virginia. During those seven weeks, Grant's army, superior in numbers,

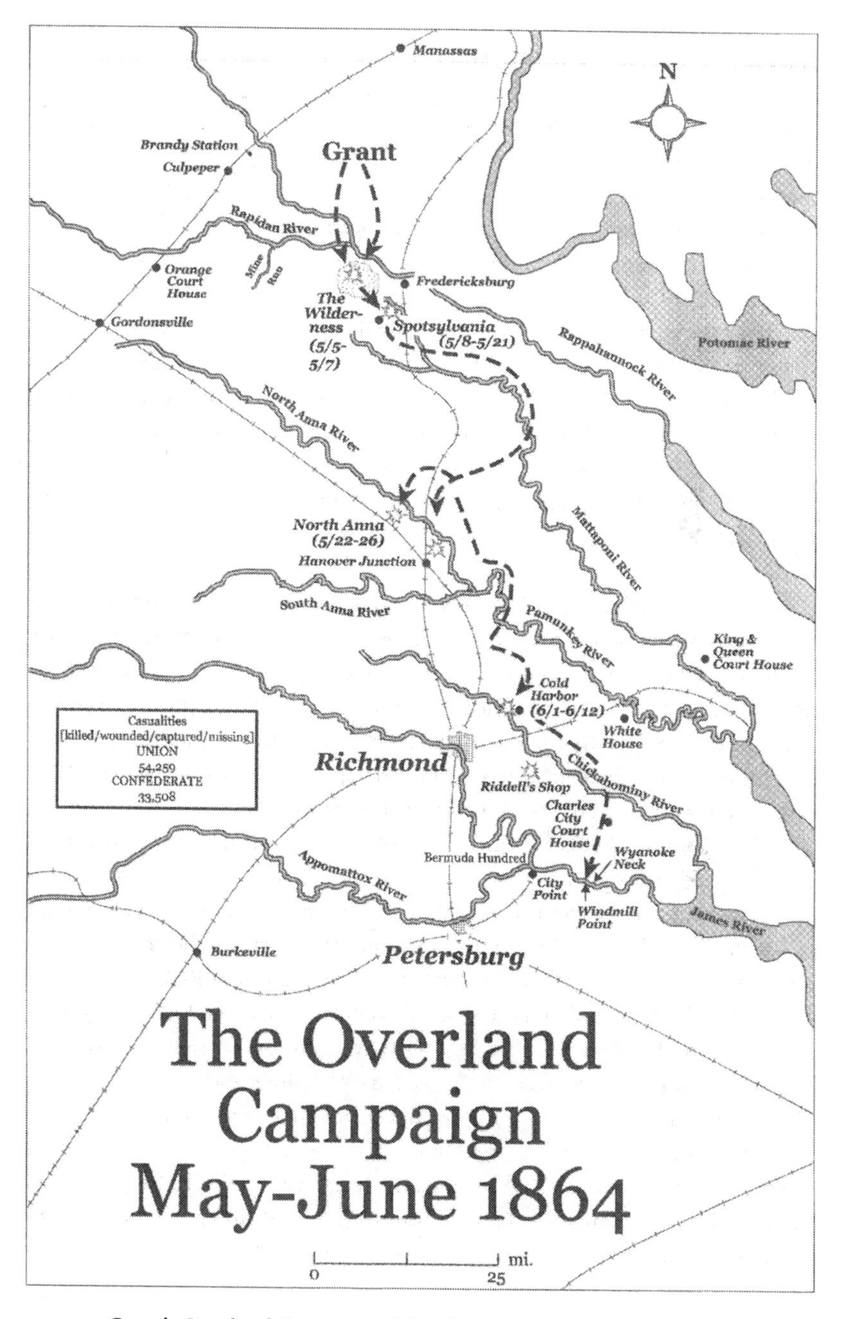

Grant's Overland Campaign, May–June 1864, from Noah Andre Trudeau's *The Last Citadel* (Courtesy of Savas Beattie LLC).

repeatedly attacked and was repulsed by Lee's Confederate defenders, and repeatedly moved south for a new attack. Along the way several major battles were fought: the Wilderness on May 5 and 6; Spotsylvania, from May 9–12; Cold Harbor on June 3; and the failed assault on Petersburg on June 15. The

General Ulysses S. Grant (Chicago History Museum).

casualties on both sides, but especially on the Union side, had been enormous. In one week, from May 5 to May 12, the Army of the Potomac lost 32,000 men, killed, wounded, or missing. At Cold Harbor on June 3, Grant ordered an assault on Confederate trenches, and the attack was repulsed with 7,000 casualties in one day. Before the battle, Union soldiers pinned notes on the backs of their jackets showing their names and addresses so that their bodies could be identified for the information of their families.[17]

Undeterred by the stunning losses at Cold Harbor, Grant devised a new plan to outflank Lee by moving his main army swiftly south from Cold Harbor, northeast of Richmond, to cross the James River and seize the city of Petersburg about twenty miles south of Richmond. Petersburg was of great strategic importance because it was a major railroad hub, linking Richmond, the Confederate capital, with the South. Once Petersburg was taken, Richmond was likely to fall within a few days, and that is what, in fact, happened at the end of the war in April 1865. This was apparently obvious to everyone. On June 19, after the 29th Regiment had arrived at Petersburg, John wrote, "Should we succeed in capturing this place it will make Richmond untenable." And on June 20: "I think if we capture this place it gives us Richmond."

Lee was at first unaware of Grant's movement south, which was brilliantly carried out, and although Petersburg was surrounded by formidable defenses, they were seriously undermanned and vulnerable to assault by the superior Federal forces, which arrived unexpectedly with remarkable speed. Confederate General Beauregard expected the city to fall within hours and lamented the approaching end of the Confederacy.[18] On June 15 the 18th Corps of the Army of the James, commanded by Major General William "Baldy" Smith, approached the defenses of Petersburg but paused, not realizing that they were manned by only a handful of men. The Union forces did attack near sundown and captured more than a mile of the enemy line but failed to push on because of false rumors that reinforcements had arrived from Lee. On the 16th and 17th, miscommunication and hesitation by superior Federal forces and a brilliant defense by Confederate General Beauregard, along a new line of defense, brought failure to uncoordinated Federal attacks.[19] By June 18 Lee had, in fact, arrived with most of his forces; a subsequent Union attack went badly and was called off. It became clear that the city could not be taken by assault, so Union troops settled down for a siege that would last for ten months. Extensive trenches were dug by both sides, and troops on both sides lived in the trenches under appalling conditions, always subject to deadly fire by sharpshooters. Europeans learned about trench warfare in the First World War, but it had happened 50 years before during the American Civil War at Petersburg.

During the seven-week Virginia campaign, the opposing armies, for the first time in the war, had been in constant contact with each other, rather than retiring after a major battle to rest and reorganize. Both armies were suffering from mental and physical exhaustion. Unlike previous Union commanders in Virginia, Grant never stopped applying pressure and never considered retreat. He had told Lincoln that "whatever happens, there will be no turning back" and during the battle of Spotsylvania, he sent a dispatch to Washington including the famous sentence: "I propose to fight it out on this line if it takes all summer."[20] But by June there was a "Cold Harbor syndrome" among the troops, a dread of attacking entrenchments and a sluggishness in the execution of orders; this attitude was probably a major factor in the failure of the Union Army to breach the relatively undefended fortifications of Petersburg and take the town on June 15.[21]

Because it was undermanned and untested, Ferrero's Fourth Division did not take part in the battles of the campaign but was assigned to covering the rear of the Army of the Potomac and guarding supplies.[22] For this purpose it was temporarily detached from Burnside's Ninth Corps during late May and early June and then returned to the Ninth Corps on June 19 on the front before Petersburg. During May the Fourth Division was stationed at Germanna Ford, the principal crossing of the Rapidan River, and thereafter in early June moved south with Grant's army. After arriving at White House Landing on June 2, John's 29th Regiment joined the Fourth Division, performing routine labor duties until June 7.[23] John was at the time commander of the Provisional Brigade; on June 7 he received an order to detach one regiment to guard a wagon train to the front and decided to select his own 29th Regiment, although that required him to give up command of the brigade.[24] Later he wrote:

> As commander of the Provisional Brigade all the orders for wagon escorts come through me. I was sure that we would all be moved from there & so I decided to go and let Col Russell come up when he wanted to. I did not like their conduct in wriggling to stay behind and I think they have got enough of it. I think you will now say I did right. True I would like to remain in the command of a Brigade but I was well aware that the one I commanded was only temporary.[25]

On the afternoon of June 7, therefore, the 29th Regiment left White House Landing as escort to a wagon train, arriving at Gen. Meade's quarters on June 8. The next day, they reached Old Church Tavern, a few miles above White House Landing on the Pamunkey River, at the headquarters of Brigadier General Ferrero, commander of the Fourth Division.[26] On June 12 the regiment began moving south towards the James River along with the Fourth Division, guarding the wagon train; by June 13 they were at New Kent Court House.[27] They then followed the wagons to Statesville and Coles Ferry, arriving at Charles City Court House on the north bank of the James River on June 16, where they were assigned to guard the 2,200-foot pontoon bridge, an engineering marvel that had been rapidly constructed on June 14 from Weyanoke Point on the north bank of the James River to Fort Powhatan on the south bank. The Army of Potomac's infantry was transported across the river on steamboats while its artillery and supply wagons on their way to Petersburg crossed the bridge in a fifty-mile line over the next three days; the bridge was dismantled on June 18. The Fourth Division crossed on June 17 and proceeded to Wilcox's House, still assigned to guarding supplies, and then to Petersburg, where it was returned to Burnside's Ninth Corps on June 19.[28]

The Ninth Corps was, at that time positioned to the southeast of Petersburg, initially on the left flank of the Union line, but the line was subsequently extended to the left by the deployment of other brigades.

John's letters provide a fairly detailed account of the regiment's movements and activity during this period, first at White House Landing, then as it moved south with the Fourth Division to Petersburg and then, for about a month after June 19, as it moved around Petersburg. The letters also offer personal observations on the state of the army, the progress of the campaign, his own growing proficiency in military matters, his continuing unshaken faith in the cause of the Union, and his undying devotion to Belle.

A letter of June 5, their eighth anniversary, reports that he is still at White House Landing:

> I know you remember this day. I know that eight years since I never thought of being here in the capacity of commanding officer of three Battalions of Colored troops. Yet it is real fact. How your dear self stands out before me as I write and how fixed in my memory is the day of our union. Time but shows me the value of your love and devotion, and the happy choice I was so fortunate as to make. I do not feel like referring to the events of the past eight years. While they are indelibly fixed in the store house of my memory, I yet from my peculiar position have my thoughts fixed on the present and future. ...
>
> Scattered all over the plain are the evidences of McClellan's army when they camped here two years since. I have been reading with great interest his report of that campaign and of course everything in the military view is deeply interesting to me. I devour everything that will give me information of the "situation." ...
>
> My heart has ached for the poor wounded soldiers. It is very different to be here and see the results of a hard fought battle. I have not felt the same in the enthusiastic tension of the mind on the field. Yet I also feel that in all history there is no such example as is now shown by our people in its lavish expenditure for the care of the wounded. I am glad that I have been here to witness it. I am also more than ever proud that I am one of the grand army of the union. Whatever be my fate I know I can give to my child this one thing, 'His father fought for the Union and the 'old flag.' " My beloved wife I pray Heaven to grant me life & health to see the end of this war, that again I may enjoy the sweet influences of your presence in peaceful times. ...
>
> Wishing that I could embrace & kiss you a thousand times to day and my dear boy. I am as eight years since your devoted husband
>
> John

On June 10, having moved near Old Church Tavern, John wrote that he was "not highly impressed with Army of the Potomac thus far," stating, "I see little ear marks of things that ought not to appear at all." Continuing the letter the next day he reported:

> Yesterday after dinner we had a genuine alarm caused by a dash of rebel cavalry upon our cavalry pickets in front.... The musketry firing was quite brisk for a time and we expected to have our cavalry fall back on us pell mell, but we did not get a chance to see a single "reb." My men behaved admirably, no desire to slink or shirk. They came into line promptly & on the "double quick." ... I will give my opinion of some of the officers hereafter. Don't consider me egotistical in what I have said before or will say hereafter. I feel my dearest a perfect consciousness of equality at least, with the best of them & if providence spares my life I shall hew my way among them all. I know you will encourage me in this.

A letter dated Sabbath June 19 announces, "We arrived in position in front of Petersburg this morning... near the rebels first line of defences.... From our position the spires of Petersburg are in full view."

During the month after its arrival at Petersburg on June 19, the Fourth Division was moved around Petersburg in support of different corps, guarding supply lines and building fortifications but also seeing action in the trenches. The Division arrived back again on July 22 at the same position from which it had started on June 19.[29]

If William's influence was helpful to John, Belle's father was evidently able to give some assistance to William, who was considering running for Lieutenant Governor of Illinois. John wrote: "Saw a Chicago journal yesterday with Williams name in it for Lt. Gov. I did not tell you I believe that Jessie wrote of Father Mason doing a great deal for his nomination."[30]

John was pleased to find that his regimental surgeon was from Scotland: "Enclosed I send you a photograph of Dr. Mackay my surgeon. He was surgeon of the 79th Highlanders which was mustered out of service this spring their term having expired. He is a full blooded Scotchman from Glasgow and is a very scientific man. I am fortunate in that appointment."[31]

The 29th Regiment seems to have been assigned mostly to digging trenches and building fortifications, but John's letters make it clear that for at least some of the time his troops were under fire.[32] On Sunday, July 3, John wrote a long letter from "Camp near Wells House, Norfolk RR 7 miles from Petersburg Va." in which he gave

> a short history of our operations since 19th. Monday night 20th we were ordered into the 2d Line of trenches. Our Division relieved the 6th Corps, which was transferred to the left. There was a good deal of picket firing during our movement but the men acted very well. At early daylight we were moved somewhat to the left, where we lay until night of 23d when we were moved still further to the left and rear. You should understand that this position we occupied was on the easterly side of Petersburg and nearly a mile inside the outer line of rebel fortifications. Our lines at this point & the rebels' are very close. We were in just as much danger from sharpshooters in the 2d as in the first line. All these nights there were attacks on our pickets and on Wednesday night especially the bullets went over my quarters and through the tree tops in a perfect hail storm. They were perfectly harmless however as they all went too high.

In a letter of June 29 from Prince George Court House John had already reported about these events: "We have been in the trenches in front of Petersburg for about a week where the bullets whizzed around our ears. One of my men was seriously wounded. It has been a good school to the men. In fact they became too careless of their persons."

Continuing the narrative in the July 3 letter, he states that on Monday, June 27th

> [a]t noon the Division marched for Prince Geo Court House, arrived there about 6 P.m. As Div Officer of the day I had to go the picket rounds which compelled me to ride a good many miles, taking me far into the night before I got through. Tuesday 27th [sic] my regt is one of the advance rgts of the line. I have a good place, near an ice house which I guard for officers use. … Thursday 30th called on Gen Sheridan

who was glad to see me, also his brother Capt Sheridan on his staff, also Major Forsyth 8th Ill Cavalry who was delighted to see me, Aiken, Gale & Chapman. He is a dashing soldier and enquired particularly for Jessie and seemed anxious to know whether she was really engaged to Charley Scannon son of Hon J.Y. I assured him she was not engaged to anyone. Jessie could do much worse in selecting others instead of him.... Yesterday July 2 we moved here which is about six or seven miles directly south east of Petersburg. We have been enjoying since yesterday, the shade of a grove of oaks & yellow pines trying to keep cool but it is awful hot nevertheless. We have found another ice house & while I am writing one of my Lts is making me a good lemonade. So you see we are not perfectly destitute. Yet our march yesterday was terribly severe upon some of the soldiers. In the afternoon a soldier of the first Brigade was found near my quarters in the woods dead. He had stood up to his duty, kept up with the rgt and died without anyone knowing it where he lay down to rest. It is one of the features of the service. It affects me more than the excitement & loss upon the battle field.... I think most of our operations now are in the nature of a siege. Our Division for the last two weeks has acted in the capacity of supports & to guard the rear. It looks as if that will be our duty. Yet in emergencies we may be put in the front. I don't think there is to be much more charging of breast works except upon some urgent necessity.

Earlier in the July 3 letter, John responded to Belle about a ceremony in Illinois she had described in her letter, probably in Sterling, where she had presided at the dedication and planting of an oak tree:

I was surprised and greatly delighted that you had acted as chairman and "poetess" of the occasion. I have always felt that under your self-possession and coolness, was a vein of the purest and richest poetical feeling, and I am proud to know that for once you have drawn upon it. Send me the verses in your next.... "Oakside" will be as deeply impressed on my memory as on yours. While you were dedicating & planting the

> oak I was "in the trenches" in front of Petersburgh. I hope that I shall be with you next year as you meet by the tree, & may we all be there.

At the close of the July 3 letter, John writes:

> You may think me forgetful of Mason, my heart is bound up in him. I am almost always fearful to read about him in your letters. I hope & pray he may be preserved. Yet I cannot become so much tied to him as to Cora. May God keep him & leave him with us. Kiss him dearly for me.

From a letter of "Monday pm July 5th[July 4th]":

> Yesterday was more like a northern Sabbath it was so quiet. The fact is that neither party I think dare make a direct assault on the others breast works. They are almost impregnable on both sides. We shall dig them out or Grant will play some game on them. As to our ultimate success I have no manner of doubt.

From a letter of Saturday, July 9:

> We are still located along the Norfolk RR where we camped one week ago today.... I am happy to inform you that I am making my way along in this Brigade. I am acquainted with all the "field officers" and I don't think I am too modest or carry too high a head. I only know I am not afraid to "pit myself" against any of them either in a knowledge of the military art or that other necessary quality of the officer & soldier "courage." This I could write to none other but yourself. I will make a further remark for your ear alone which I would not repeat. It seems to me that the colored troops has been made an asylum for some of the "poorest sticks" in the service.... I did have a profound admiration for the "regulars," but I must confess I have been sadly shocked in that respect for the past two months. I have sometimes felt in the last three years that the "Tribune" was too bitter in its attacks upon a certain class

> of regular army officers. Recently I have felt that their apparently caustic articles were drawn entirely too mild. Still what noble examples we have of a military education being the prelude to a splendid career as in the cases of Grant Rosecrans Sherman Sheridan and others.... I wish you could step into my "arbor" just now. I am located in the edge of a yellow pine and oak grove fronting on an oak field through which runs the Norfolk R.R. to the south east.... I don't wish you & Jessie to expend too much sympathy on us poor mortals in "these Hd Qrs" & thereabouts for the past week. After tonight you may let it flow again. Pardon dearest if I speak lightly but we have had so many good things that I wonder how I have been so fortunate. When I think of the privations I have undergone and those I may have yet to undergo I feel like being jubilant over the present. Sometimes I think a soldiers life has a tendency to make him adopt the Latin motto for his guide, "Dum vivimus, vivamus," and certainly "in campaign" so far as subsistence and sanitary supplies goes I generally act upon the principal use the best you have and enjoy it while you may whenever you can get them.

From a letter of Tuesday, July 12 at "Camp along Norfolk RR about 4 miles from Petersburg":

> I wrote you last Saturday. On that evening immediately after dark we had orders to be ready to march at a moment's notice. At twelve midnight our Division left its position and marched west & north westerly across and west of the Norfolk R.R. to the same position we occupied on the first of July when I wrote you near the house of a Mr. Williams just west of the Jerusalem Plank Road. We staid there Sunday & yesterday, our Brigade in the mean time being on fatigue duty building a huge fort towards the right of our then location about a couple of miles. Last night we were ordered to march at 3 A.m. this morning which was delayed until daylight, when we marched to this point being about 4 miles from town & two miles nearer Petersburg than we were located on Saturday last. The Brigade is now working on a new redoubt and I am located in a little copse of bushes resting & writing to you.

In a letter of Wednesday, July 13 he reports, "Our men are working like beavers on the fort I spoke of yesterday." Six days later, on Tuesday, July 19, he relates:

> Calling at Gen Fererro's Hd Qrs as etiquette requires he received me more cordially than usual. He soon mentioned that Gen White had called on him the day before and had spoken about me. Of course I did not ask what was said but presume it must have been favorable ... you see I am "getting on" in making acquaintance and showing that I deserve the good opinion of those who are in positions of influence. I am unable to fawn and blow my own penny whistle. Still I am pleased when my superiors take some interest in me. It is a greater satisfaction however to know and feel in my own heart that I am capable of occupying a higher position than at present. I am conscious of it, shall do what I can honorably to attain it, nothing more.

In the same letter he indicates that he has decided to turn to the government to fill up the regiment with contrabands:

> I shall apply to the Secy. of War to be filled up. I am done spending money for recruiting. Govt claims to appoint all the officers even if we spend our money in enlisting the men. I have no doubt if friends in Ill will help me I shall get the four companies. I have already written to Will to make application for me. I shall do it myself through the regular military channel. William can back it up especially if the state authorities and members of Congress will aid me. ... Gen Ferrero gave me yesterday three photographs which I shall dispose of to you Annie & Jessie. ... It is raining very hard today having the appearance of a settled storm & so I am keeping close in my "fly." You should see however how comfortably I can live under it. The rain is most grateful to the parched earth and it will be a grand thing in supplying the army with water. If it rains ten days I shall not regret it greatly.
>
> I shall take that trip with you someday down the St. Lawrence, possibly when I wear the "star." ... This army is better fed than I ever knew

the Army of the Cumberland to be. All kinds of vegetables are issued daily or at least some kinds daily.... I wrote you letters on the 3^{d}, 7th, & 9th, also the 12th. Some of them I am fearful may have been burned by the rebs as on that western mail [illegible] was burned. I hope however they will reach you.

From an undated letter, probably July 20, "in camp Norfolk RR":

Dearest

Yours containing the poetry reached me last night. I had been expecting it for several days and was sure I would get it last night. I was not disappointed. Of course I am proud of it. I have been reading it to Fred Chapman. I think you have exhausted the subject and shall not try to match you with any stanzas of my own.... You say well of Dr. Mackay. He has not been with the rgt much, he having been at the Division Hospital which is a couple of miles from us for nearly a month. He is considered the best operating surgeon in the Division. He is a "genuine Scot." By the by I wish you to get "Lucile" by Owen Meredith and read it. I was much interested in it having obtained it from Col Thomas comdg our Brigade. I would send you Gen Fererro's picture with this but he has gone to Washington for a few days & I wish to obtain his autograph.

On Saturday, July 23 "in camp near Petersburg Va":

My Beloved Wife

Your letter of 17th inst. came duly to hand last night enclosing five dollars which was very acceptable indeed. We left the Norfolk R.R. yesterday where we had been in camp on the extreme left and are now near Corps Head Qrs on the same ground occupied by us on 19th of June last when we first arrived in front of Petersburg. We have had a great deal said of our Division being about to make a "charge." Some of the Quid nuncs would have it that last night we were "going in" sure but I slept all night without being disturbed at all.... I am anxious as you are to fill up my regt. It does seem that the more a man works for the Govt

> & spends his means the less it cares for him.... Now a word of "home" matters. I am glad you give me details of Mason. I am rather amused as well as pleased that he has "temper." He would not be a Bross if he hadn't. I know that you will exhibit all the firmness necessary to direct that temper in the proper channel.... Tell him that papa will write him a letter some of these days, when he is not very busy.... I hope you will preserve all the notices of my regt. in the papers. I do not see them and they will be extremely interesting when I have an opportunity to read them. I am obliged for the stamps you sent me. Say to Annie that I am keeping a letter in my mind for her which will be drawn out some time. And now with much love to all my friends and with one more good bye I am ever your affectionate husband, John

These are the last words we have from him. No other letters are known to survive, although it seems likely that he would have written one or more letters between Saturday, July 23 and Saturday, July 30, the day of his death at the Battle of the Crater.

On that same day, July 23, the digging of the mineshaft and lateral powder galleries had been completed; by July 28 the blasting powder had been loaded into the galleries.

PLANNING FOR THE MINE AT THE CRATER

By the middle of July, the situation before Petersburg had become a stalemate.[33] Both armies had dug extensive trenches. Sharpshooters were an ever-present danger. The weather had become unusually and oppressively hot, often over 100 degrees, with men on both sides falling and sometimes dying of sunstroke. No rain fell for 47 days, and the dry earth became clouds of dust that settled over everything "shoe-top deep." There was a sickening and pervasive smell of sewage, garbage, and gunpowder.[34] Lee's Army of Northern Virginia had good morale, but all his regiments had been greatly reduced in numbers and the men were thin and overworked; no more recruits were available and there were desertions. Grant's Army of the Potomac had more recruits and greater numbers, but these were, in large number, conscripts and paid substitutes; after Cold Harbor, Meade said, the offensive spirit had been drained from the army.[35] Probably the only fresh and energized troops in the Union Army were the relatively new black regiments, including the eight regiments in the Fourth Division of Burnside's Ninth Corps. The political climate in the North was demoralized after a spring campaign that had cost over 70,000 casualties and still had not taken Richmond; Lincoln expected that he would lose the election in November to a new administration that would be committed to abandoning what seemed the endless butchery of a hopeless struggle and call for an armistice and negotiations leading to reunion. Lincoln's administration knew that once the fighting stopped, it could not be restarted; the Confederate states would never agree to reunion and would have effectively won their independence. A decisive victory would be a godsend to the Lincoln administration, while a decisive defeat would deepen the prospect of defeat in November.

What became known as the Battle of the Crater was an ingenious attempt for a decisive Union victory. It was a proposed operation to dig a tunnel and set a mine under a key fort of the Confederate line that was fairly close to the Union line; the explosion of the mine would allow Union troops to pour through the breach in the Confederate line and occupy Petersburg, which would probably compel the Rebels to abandon Richmond, their capital, and possibly bring the war to a victorious end. The operation should not have been too difficult if the mine was properly laid and exploded, which was accomplished in a remarkable feat of engineering.[36] Instead, it resulted in one of the greatest Union disasters of the war, failing totally and leaving the siege lines in exactly the same position as they had been before the assault, but costing 4000 northern casualties, including the life of John, and delivering a serious blow to Northern morale.

The failure was due to a combination of factors including poor judgment, incompetence, negligence, and even drunkenness at high levels, as well as a heroic defense by greatly outnumbered Confederate defenders, but the main causes of the debacle were the racist views and the professional jealousy of General Meade, the commanding general of the Army of the Potomac, and the incompetence of General Burnside. Burnside had confidence in the fighting ability of black soldiers but chose his black

Fourth Division to lead the assault because the troops were fresh and had high morale, not because they were black.[37] Meade assumed that Burnside's proposed operation was likely to fail because he doubted the fighting ability of black troops and also because he regarded Burnside and any plan of his with hostility and contempt; he therefore changed Burnside's plan only hours before the scheduled assault, ordering that the fresh black troops of the Fourth Division, who had been specially trained to lead the assault, should be replaced by tired and demoralized white troops of the First, Second, and Third divisions, who had no special training, with the Fourth Division following at the end. The line between believing something impossible and wishing it to fail can be hard to detect: assuming that the operation would probably fail if led by black troops, Meade went far to assure that it would fail by removing the specially trained black troops just hours before the attack. Perhaps he unconsciously wished it to fail, because of his reluctance to witness a victory led by blacks, because it had been planned by his despised rival, Burnside, and because failure would prove that he had been right to doubt the venture. The whole operation, including the digging of the tunnel and the assault, was regarded with doubt and contempt, rather than encouragement, by Meade and his regular Army of the Potomac staff. However, Burnside contributed to the disaster in several ways: by choosing the leading Division through drawing straws, the choice falling on a general whom Grant called the worst commander in the corps; by negligence in preparation for the assault; and by stubborn refusal to terminate the operation after the assault had clearly failed. Grant approved the removal of the black troops, probably because he was generally disposed to approve Meade's views in order to demonstrate support for the command structure of the Army of the Potomac.

Under such circumstances, it is not surprising that the operation did not succeed. Even a difficult operation could be successful, and many during the war were, when given single-minded support by the whole command, but when doubt and distrust and political infighting were present, even an undertaking with a high chance of success could be endangered. The Crater was a good example of a hopeful operation sabotaged by distrust, lack of cooperation, and, in the end, by racism.

The idea for the operation began in a Union regiment, the 48th Pennsylvania, many of whose men had been coal miners before the war. Some of them suggested to the regiment's commander, Lt. Col. Henry Pleasants, who had been a successful mining engineer in civilian life, that it might be possible to dig a tunnel under a fort in the Confederate line to plant gunpowder and to blow a hole in the line, making it possible to charge through and take the town. After discussing it with other engineers in the regiment, Pleasants decided that the plan was feasible and recommended it to Brigadier General Robert B. Potter, commander of the Second Division, in which the 48th Pennsylvania was located. Potter also thought it was possible and sent a report to Major General Burnside as commander of the Ninth Corps. At Burnside's invitation Potter came with Pleasants to discuss the plan with him on June 24. After listening carefully, Burnside liked the idea and told Pleasants to go ahead. The next day, June 25, Pleasants and his men began work on the tunnel while Burnside formally notified General Meade of the project.[38]

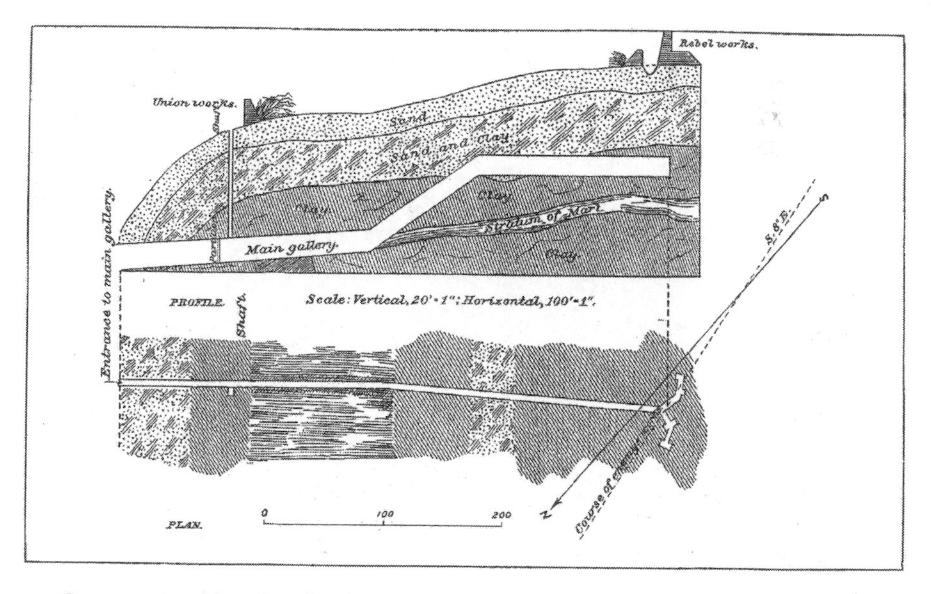

Cross section (above) and aerial view (below) of the mine, leading to the explosion gallery, outside Petersburg, Virginia, July 1864 (Library of Congress).

Meade initially liked the idea, since it offered the possibility of breaching the Confederate line without the butchery of another frontal assault, and sent sandbags to assist in the work. He also ordered his staff engineer, Major J. C. Duane, to take a look at the proposed project.[39] However, Meade soon became doubtful about the idea of the mine, although he had approved it, for two major reasons: his dislike and distrust of General Burnside and the opposition of his chief engineer, Major Duane.

General Ambrose E. Burnside (Chicago History Museum).

Meade's distrust of Burnside was based partly on Burnside's military record and partly on professional jealousy. Burnside had been Meade's superior at Fredericksburg and was still his senior in rank; he was careful to express his obedience and respect for Meade, but Meade was sensitive to any perceived slight.[40] Burnside was a genial and well-liked graduate of West Point, seven years younger than Meade; he had resigned from the army to engage in the manufacture of a good repeating rifle, the Burnside

General George G. Meade (Chicago History Museum).

Carbine, which he had designed in his spare time. In 1861 he had raised a regiment in Rhode Island and had soon been made a brigadier general. In 1862 he was put in charge of the Army of the Potomac, replacing his friend McClellan, in spite of his expressed reservations. In December 1862 he had led the Army of the Potomac to a ruinously bloody defeat at the Battle of Fredericksburg, where he had insisted on sending his troops on repeated futile assaults against the entrenched right wing of Lee's army, resulting in extremely high casualties at what the soldiers afterwards called Burnside's slaughter pen. He had performed better in the western theater, liberating Knoxville in eastern Tennessee in October 1863, but neither Grant nor Meade wished to put him in command of a major operation.[41]

Meade, on the other hand, who was, in any case, tightly wound and viewed as irascible by his staff, was under severe pressure from the hard fighting of the last few weeks. He was also under political pressure: he knew that Lincoln had been disappointed by his failure to pursue Lee's army after Gettysburg, and he felt that Grant's presence with the Army of the Potomac during the spring campaign implied official mistrust of his ability. He also knew that he was regarded with suspicion as a McClellan Democrat by radical Republicans in Congress who favored Burnside, known to be a Republican who was hostile to Copperheads and in favor of abolition.[42]

The other reason for Meade's distrust of the mining operation was the strongly expressed opinion of Chief Engineer Major Duane that a tunnel of the proposed length was "claptrap and nonsense," "all nonsense and an impossibility," because it had never been done before; even if the mine didn't collapse, he reported, the miners would suffocate for lack of oxygen.[43] As it happened, Duane had previously had a tangled relationship with Burnside, leading Burnside to the wrong ford over the creek at Antietam and managing to delay the pontoon bridges that Burnside was waiting for at Fredericksburg; perhaps defensiveness about these events led him to encourage Meade in disparagement of Burnside.[44] Pleasants had devised an ingenious plan for ventilation of the mine involving a vertical shaft with a fire under a grate that would force out the old air and suck in fresh air; Duane scoffed at the idea.[45] General de Trobriand, of the Second Corps, who had been born in France, wrote afterwards, "The chief engineers of the army and other authorities declared ex cathedra that the project was senseless and foolish; that a military mine as long as that had never been dug.... With specialists, the thing that has not been done cannot be done, and if you propose to them any innovation not found in their books, nine times out of ten they will tell you that it is impossible or absurd."[46]

Although Meade had promised to supply necessary tools and supplies for the mine, Pleasants's requests for even the most basic supplies, such as picks, shovels, and wheelbarrows, were ignored. Undaunted, Pleasants found or made his own supplies, including timbers to shore up the tunnel, and continued with the work. It was necessary to carry away the earth that was removed from the tunnel and hide it under freshly cut brush. When the fire was started at the ventilation shaft sunk about 100 feet beyond the entrance to the tunnel, but still behind the Union line, Pleasants had several fires built in the area so that smoke from the shaft wouldn't draw attention.[47]

On July 3, a week after Pleasants's men began digging, Grant asked Meade whether a successful assault could be made somewhere along the Rebel line because he wanted to increase pressure on Lee. Meade turned to Burnside, who replied that a surprise attack in his sector led by the black troops was possible but it would be best to wait until the mine could be exploded. He then offended Meade by suggesting that he, Burnside, be given authority over supporting corps in such an attack, and Meade interpreted this as something close to insubordination.[48] Meade sent Burnside's mine proposal to Grant without endorsing it; he had already become doubtful about the plan because of Major Duane's opinion. Grant, though, was interested and on July 6 had his own chief engineer, General J. G. Barnard, send Pleasants a list of technical questions about the project, which Pleasants promptly answered.[49] Major Duane had by then inspected the project and had officially reported to Meade his disapproval, even though Pleasants showed him that he had already completed 264 feet of the tunnel.[50] This did not surprise Pleasants since he knew that Duane had decided in advance that the proposal was impossible.

Nevertheless, Burnside was convinced that the mine was possible and would be necessary for a successful assault. While Pleasants pushed on with the tunnel, Burnside began to develop an operational plan in the days after July 4.[51] Considering the three white divisions in his Ninth Corps to be tired and demoralized, as well as understrength, and therefore unlikely to make an aggressive assault, he decided to select the colored regiments of his Fourth Division, whose commander was General Edward Ferrero. The black troops were fresh and enthusiastic; they were also inexperienced, but Burnside had confidence in their fighting ability if properly led. Burnside asked Ferrero if he thought his men were up to the task and when Ferrero said they were, asked him to prepare a tactical plan and begin training his men to carry it out.[52] Ferrero conferred with his two brigade commanders, Col. Henry G. Thomas (Second Brigade) and Col. Joshua Sigfried (First Brigade), and prepared a plan of attack that Burnside approved.[53] The plan was for two regiments of Sigfried's First Brigade to lead the attack through the breach in the Confederate line and then fan out to the right and left to sweep any defending troops out of the side trenches to avoid enfilading or flanking fire from any Confederate troops in the trenches. The remaining regiments were to charge ahead to the high ground of Cemetery Hill, from which Union forces could command the town of Petersburg and its bridges.

On July 9 two of Sigfried's regiments, the 30th and 43rd USCT, began intensive drilling to spearhead the assault.[54] Questions have been raised about whether there actually was special training for the black troops for the assault. Lieutenant Robert Beecham of the 23rd USCT stated in an article years later that the Fourth Division received no special training for the battle[55] and there are no references in John's letters to any special training. But the official report of the battle states that Fourth Division troops were drilled for the planned operation.[56] Beecham's 23rd Regiment, like the 29th, was part of Thomas's brigade, whereas it was the 30th and 43rd regiments of Sigfried's brigade that were selected for intensive drilling.[57] The plan for an assault after an exploded mine obviously depended on surprise, so there would have been pressure to maintain secrecy and keep discussion at a minimum. Capt. James Rickard of the 19th USCT (Thomas's brigade) stated, "[W]e had expected we were to lead the assault, and had been for several weeks drilling our men with this idea in view particular attention being paid to charging."[58] Even though John's letters do not specifically mention special training, Thomas's brigade was involved in the preparation, so there must have been special training for at least some of the Second Brigade regiments, including Rickard's 19th.

Col. Thomas wrote, years later:

> For some time previous to the explosion of the mine it was determined by General Burnside that the colored division should lead the assault. The general tactical plan had been given to the brigade commanders (Colonel Sigfried and myself), with a rough outline map of the ground, and directions to study the front for ourselves. But this latter was impracticable except in momentary glimpses. The enemy made a target of every head that appeared about the work, and their marksmanship was good. The manner of studying the ground was this: Putting my battered old hat on a ramrod and lifting it above the rampart just enough for them not to discover that no man was under it, I drew their fire; then stepping quickly a few paces on one side, I took a hasty observation.
>
> We were all pleased with the compliment of being chosen to lead in the assault. Both officers and men were eager to show the white troops what the colored division could do. We had acquired confidence in our men. They believed us infallible. We had drilled certain movements, to be executed in gaining and occupying the crest.[59]

On July 5 Grant's attention to the Petersburg front was distracted when a Confederate force under Jubal Early marched down the Shenandoah Valley, crossed the Potomac, and threatened Washington. There was panic in the capital, and Lincoln ordered Grant to transfer his Sixth Corps back to defend the capital. The defenses of Washington proved to be too strong for an assault, however, and Early retired his forces back to Virginia on July 13.

While this was going on, Sigfried's regiments continued to train and Pleasants's men continued to dig. After three weeks of backbreaking and dangerous work, without any assistance at all from Duane's engineers, the men of the 48th Pennsylvania on July 17 completed the main tunnel, exactly 510.8 feet long, twenty feet directly below the Confederate battery. Lateral galleries were dug at the end of the tunnel, one thirty-eight feet to the right and the other thirty-seven feet to the left, this work being completed by

Colonel Henry G. Thomas (Library of Congress).

July 23. The tunnel was now ready for loading with blasting powder, but no decision had yet been made by Grant on whether the mine was to be used at all.[60]

The Confederates had heard rumors that a Federal mine might be attempted and ordered countermines dug to discover it, but the countermines they dug were only ten feet deep, whereas Pleasants's tunnel was twenty feet deep, so it was not detected. After July 23 the Confederates felt reasonably safe in assuming that the rumor of a mine had been just that.[61]

On July 23 Grant decided that the mine should be loaded so that an explosion could be made either as a major assault or as a diversion from an advance he planned for July 26, moving Hancock's Second

Corps infantry and Sheridan's cavalry north against Richmond. On July 26 Meade informed Burnside of this and asked Burnside to submit his battle plan in writing.[62] The blasting powder was delivered to Pleasants on the morning of July 27, and he supervised the loading of the chambers that day.[63] Burnside had specified 12,000 pounds of powder, but Meade followed Duane's recommendation that 8,000 pounds would be enough.[64] Although Duane's engineers had refused any assistance for the project, they had so far not actively sabotaged it; now, when Pleasants was loading the powder, he discovered that Duane's department had sent him the wrong type of fuse. He had ordered thousand-foot lengths of moisture resistant safety fuse, but what was delivered was a load of ordinary blasting fuse in varying lengths, some as short as 10 feet, which would have to be spliced into one long fuse. Ordinary fuse was susceptible to damage by moisture in the tunnel, especially if it was not to be used for a day or two, and at every splice the spark might go out. To increase the chances of success, Pleasants ran three lines of spliced fuse with extra gunpowder at key points.[65] As it turned out, the lack of safety fuse resulted in delaying the attack by an hour and a half, since the splices did fail at one point and part of the fuse had to be replaced. Even Pleasants did not think that the wrong fuse was sent on purpose in order to sabotage the project, but the chief engineer's general attitude of distrust and contempt for the proposal must, at the least, have made it more likely that someone would make a negligent mistake about an important detail.[66]

Grant had been eager to make an attack on the Confederate lines but hadn't been sure where it could be made. Meade was unenthusiastic about an attack at Burnside's position opposite Eliot's salient because he thought there was a second fortified line at the crest of the hill, so that an attack would have to get through two lines. On July 25 he said an attack there would not "be hopeless," but that the chances of success weren't good enough to make it expedient to try it. Grant then said he didn't want to attempt anything so hazardous against the judgment of Meade and his engineer officers.[67] But the next day, July 26, Meade learned that there was no secondary line and gave Grant a favorable opinion of the proposed assault. Grant decided to go ahead with the mine and fixed the early morning of July 30 as the time for the assault.[68]

Grant also decided to go ahead with his plan to shift the Second Corps and two divisions of cavalry north towards Richmond, partly in the hope of a surprise capture of Richmond, but mostly in order to draw a significant number of Lee's troops away from Petersburg. This was the so-called Deep Bottom offensive, on July 26 and 27, which did not result in a significant victory before Richmond but did succeed in moving Confederate troops away from Petersburg; by the morning of the assault on July 30, only three divisions of Lee's army remained at Petersburg, facing three full Federal corps.[69] The Union Army had an overwhelming advantage in numbers for the planned attack.

Some twenty years after the battle, Col. Henry Thomas, commander of Ferrero's Second Brigade, contributed an article called "The Colored Troops at Petersburg" to *The Century Magazine*, the article afterwards being published in Volume IV of a work entitled *Battles and Leaders of the Civil War*, a significant collection of reminiscences of Union and Confederate officers published in 1883.[70] Thomas's article described the black troops' habit of greeting important news by jointly composing a song for a special command and, in particular, the battle song they made at the time when they were told that they were to lead this major assault, which would have been about July 9. The decision to employ the mine had not yet been made by Grant, and secrecy would have been highly important, so it seems likely that the troops were told that they were to lead an important charge, but not immediately given details about the mine:

> Any striking event or piece of news was usually eagerly discussed by the white troops, and in the ranks military critics were as plenty and perhaps more voluble than among the officers. Not so with the blacks; important news such as that before us, after the bare announcement, was usually followed by long silence. They sat about in groups, "studying," as they called it. They waited, like the Quakers, for the spirit to move; when the spirit moved, one of their singers would uplift a mighty voice, like a bard of old, in a wild sort of chant. If he did not strike a

sympathetic chord in his hearers, if they did not find in his utterance the exponent of their idea, he would sing it again and again, altering sometimes the words, more often the music. If his changes met general acceptance, one voice after another would chime in; a rough harmony of three parts would add itself; other groups would join his, and the song would become the song of the command.

The night we learned that we were to lead the charge the news filled them too full for ordinary utterance. The joyous negro guffaw always breaking out about the camp-fire ceased. They formed circles in their company streets and were sitting on the ground intently and solemnly "studying." At last a heavy voice began to sing,

"We-e looks li-ike me-en a-a-marchin' on,
We looks li-ike men-er-war."

Over and over again he sang it, making slight changes in the melody. The rest listened to him intently; no sign of approval or disapproval escaped their lips or appeared on their faces. All at once, when his refrain had struck the right response in their hearts, his group took it up, and shortly half a thousand voices were upraised extemporizing a half dissonant middle part and bass. It was a picturesque scene—these dark men, with their white eyes and teeth and full red lips, crouching over a smoldering camp-fire, in dusky shadow, with only the feeble rays of the lanterns of the first sergeants and the lights of candles dimly showing through the tents. The sound was as weird as the scene, when all the voices struck the low E (last note but one), held it, and then rose to A with a portamento as sonorous as it was clumsy. Until we fought the battle of the crater they sang this every night to the exclusion of all other songs. After that defeat they sang it no more.[71]

The following is the music of the battle song of the black soldiers of the Fourth Division before the battle of the Crater, perhaps written in Thomas's own hand.[72] John and the eight other regimental commanders of the two brigades would have heard it every night until July 30.

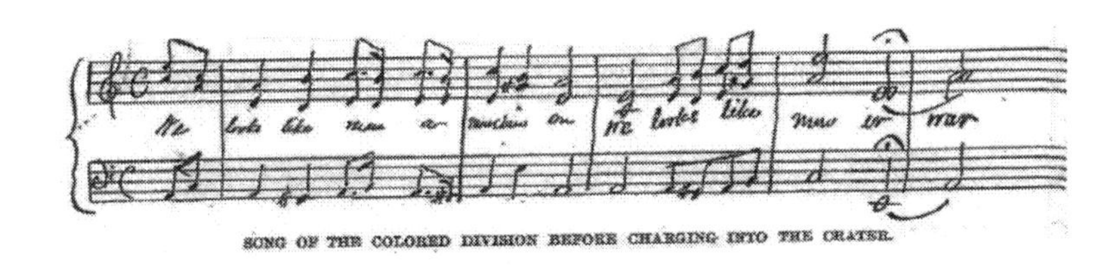

SONG OF THE COLORED DIVISION BEFORE CHARGING INTO THE CRATER.

The explosion of the mine and the assault had been set for 3:15 a.m. on Saturday, July 30. Burnside had sent his plan of attack to Meade on July 26, but Meade was occupied with the Deep Bottom campaign and was not available to review the plan until July 28, when Burnside rode over to meet him. Meade announced to Burnside that he would require several changes. The first was a change in tactics: the leading column should charge directly forward to Cemetery Hill, rather than fanning out to the left and right to clear the side trenches of enemy enfilading fire. Meade had reason to distrust complex maneuvers under combat conditions, but this would have been a prudent maneuver, and it was something the regiments of the Fourth Division had been specially trained to do.[73]

But Meade's major change to the plan was to say to Burnside that he could not "approve of your placing the negro troops in the advance, as proposed in your project." He said he "did not think that they should be called upon to do as important work as that which you propose to do, certainly not called upon to lead."[74]

This was a bombshell for Burnside, who had carefully considered the question of which troops were best for leading the assault and who had arranged for weeks of special training for those troops. He let the other changes go but argued vigorously for retaining the black troops as the leaders of the assault. He pointed out that the three white divisions, after months of decimation, trench warfare, disease, and exhaustion, were no longer reliable assault troops, and that the black troops, fresh and with high morale, were specially trained for the operation. Nevertheless, Meade insisted that Burnside should "assault with his best troops," clearly implying that, in his mind, exhausted and demoralized white troops were better than fresh, specially-trained black troops.[75]

Surely one reason for Meade's interference with Burnside's plan was his wish to assert his authority over a man whom he regarded as both a professional inferior and a political threat, an officer who had to be publicly kept in his subordinate place. But his main reason was probably racial prejudice. He was, in fact, a McClellan Democrat, and the political instinct of that group was generally opposed to abolition, certainly not in favor of the racial equality that could be implied by the existence of black soldiers. Meade was probably consciously or unconsciously reluctant to imagine a major victory headed by black troops. Like most generals in the Army of the Potomac, which had been formed by McClellan, he regarded black troops as mainly useful for labor in building fortifications or digging trenches, even after the bravery shown by black troops at Fort Wagner and other battles, and even though black regiments of the Army of the James's Eighteenth Corps had played a significant role in the initial siege of Petersburg.[76] Even Grant seems to have doubted the reliability of black troops, and in the Virginia campaign had used them mostly for guard and supply purposes, but he had acknowledged their ability in specific instances.[77]

Another possible reason for Meade's decision is given in John's letter of June 5. It has to do with Fort Pillow: "I mentioned the colored division of Burnside has not been in action also that Gen Meade is averse to putting them in because they will not take prisoners, fearing that the enemy will murder our white soldiers captured by them." If blacks remembered Fort Pillow and killed their prisoners, then Confederates might retaliate by killing white Union prisoners.

Burnside did not give up on his argument in favor of the black troops and Meade, to appear reasonable, promised to "report the matter to the lieutenant general [Grant], state to him my reasons, and those of General Burnside, and let him decide."[78] Burnside returned to his headquarters fairly confident that Grant would decide the matter in his favor since he knew that Grant supported the use of black troops in combat, and it was so clear that from a military point of view it would be better to stay with the plan as prepared. But when Meade met alone with Grant, he urged Grant to approve his removal of the black troops. He probably mentioned Burnside's thinking as to the demoralized condition of the white troops and his own doubts about the use of inexperienced troops, and he may or may not have mentioned the special training of the black troops, but his central point, as Grant later testified at the Congressional hearing, was a political one: "General Meade said that if we put the colored troops in front...and it should prove a failure, it would than be said, and very properly, that we were shoving those people ahead to get killed because we did not care anything about them. But that could not be said if we put white troops in front."[79] Grant and Meade both knew that that the use of black soldiers was a delicate political question; especially with a presidential election looming, what might be viewed as a careless slaughter of black troops could cause serious political damage to the administration.

It would seem that Grant should have wanted to confer with both generals on such a vital matter, and Burnside should probably have realized that he ought to be present at the meeting to present his case personally. Had Burnside been there, he might have pointed out to Grant that the assault could also prove to be a great success, and that even if it were a failure, its leadership could be seen as the honor that the troops considered it to be, and that, in any case, the most important political consideration was to ensure the military success of the operation. Grant said later that he thought his decision had been wrong but that he had gone along with Meade's political argument, which he, of course, did not have much time to think about. Grant was predisposed to support Meade's authority in order to counter any appearance that Meade's competence was in question. Whether Meade's decision to remove the trained black troops only hours before the assault was the rationalization of racial prejudice, whether he was really concerned militarily about the use of inexperienced troops, whether it was, at least partly, the result of personal and professional hostility to Burnside, or, in Grant's case, a purely political consideration, it ignored the obvious danger of changing a complex military plan at the last minute.

Burnside heard nothing more that day and by the next morning had begun to assume that this part of his original plan was still in effect. At 10:30 a.m. on July 29th, Burnside was conferring in his tent with two of his four divisional commanders, General Potter (2nd Division) and General Willcox (3rd Division), about plans for the assault. General Ledlie (1st Division) was not there and neither was General Ferrero, commander of the colored 4th Division, who was in Washington to straighten out the approval of his commission; General White was in temporary command of the 4th Division. Burnside was explaining to Potter and Wilcox that he had been "very much worried" that Meade would overrule his plan for the colored division but having heard nothing in 12 hours since Meade had conferred with Grant, "I took it for granted that he had decided to let it remain as it was." But just then Meade arrived and told Burnside, "I saw General Grant, and he agrees with me that it will not do to put the colored division in the lead."[80]

Burnside "felt, and I suppose I expressed, and showed, very great disappointment" and repeated his arguments against the use of the white troops, but Meade said that the decision could not be changed: "You must detail one of your white divisions to make the advance." To which Burnside replied, "Very well, general, I will carry out this plan to the best of my ability."[81]

Colonel Harris, Burnside's ordinance officer, wrote in his diary:

> Thus, at the eleventh hour.... The Negro division & its gallant commander, who believed they would be invincible & who had learned their duty by constant application to this single idea for the previous month, were informed "it wasn't best" and they must be replaced by white troops who had already their own instructions to do an entirely different thing.[82]

General Ledlie was summoned and the generals spent the next several hours trying to decide which of the three white divisions should be assigned to the lead, but each of the three generals was convinced that his division was not fit for the task. The genial Burnside, at least on short notice, did not have it in him to designate one of the three for the possibly fatal task. Unable to come to a decision, he decided to leave it to chance. He said, "It will be fair to cast lots." This was obviously not the proper way to make a military decision, but he tore three strips of paper, one shorter, and put them into his hat, "and so they did cast lots, and General Ledlie drew the advance."[83]

General Ledlie was afterwards described by Grant in his testimony as the worst commander in the corps. He was a civil engineer who owed his promotion to political influence and had recently applied to resign because he knew that he was not suited to military command. He was considered incompetent by his staff and was thought to have been drunk before every engagement; he had, while drunk, ordered a hopeless frontal assault against an entrenched position that resulted in many needless casualties.[84] But he seems to have been likeable and willing to protect his staff from danger, and they, in turn, protected his reputation so that Burnside may not have been fully aware of his incompetence.[85]

And so, battle-weary and dispirited white troops, untrained for this novel and challenging task and led by an entirely incompetent and distrusted commander, were at the last minute substituted for black troops who had been specially trained to lead the assault and were passionately looking forward to it. In his 1887 article, Col. Thomas wrote:

> It is an axiom in military art that there are times when the ardor, hopefulness, and enthusiasm of new troops, not yet rendered doubtful by reverses or chilled by defeat, more than compensate, in a dash, for training and experience. General Burnside, for this and other reasons, most strenuously urged his black division for the advance. Against his most urgent remonstrances he was overruled. About 11 P.M., July 29th, a few hours before the action, we were officially informed that the plan had been changed, and our division would not lead.
>
> We were then bivouacking on our arms in rear of our line, just behind the covered way leading to the mine. I returned to that bivouac dejected and with an instinct of disaster for the morrow. As I summoned and told my regimental commanders, their faces expressed the same feeling. [86]

This was when John would have first heard that the black regiments had been removed from the lead. Perhaps that explains the statement in the *Memorial* that "[o]ne who saw Colonel Bross, at eleven o'clock, found him walking back and forth before his tent, seeming somewhat anxious and agitated; but he at once controlled himself and joined cheerfully in conversation, talking over the coming struggle."[87] At 9 p.m. the regiments of the Fourth Division had marched from the rifle pits they were occupying to a bivouac on the open ground near the covered ways leading to the front Union lines, arriving in time for the meeting between Thomas and the regimental commanders. The line officers and the men were mostly asleep by the time the meeting was over and so were not informed of the change in plans until the Fourth Division was awakened at 3:00 a.m. on the morning of July 30th. When they heard about the change, Capt. Rickarts recalled, "We were terribly disappointed... officers and men."[88] On the other hand, Col. Weld, commander of the left wing of Ledlie's division, which had been substituted in the lead, wrote, "The officers and men were disappointed and discouraged at having to lead, as we had heard all along that the negroes were to do this, and we had no confidence in Ledlie."[89] So both the white troops and the black troops began the battle in a mood of disappointment and dejection, not a good state of morale before a battle attack.

For the battle John had put on the full dress uniform that had recently arrived with his baggage. This would make it easier for him to command from the front, as he would be immediately recognizable as an officer to be followed, although it also made him a target for enemy fire. At some point he had also trimmed his beard, shaving his chin in the style of Gen. Burnside's beard, probably as a gesture of support for the well-liked Burnside, who had assigned to the Fourth Division the honor of leading this crucial assault.

In a letter to Belle written a few weeks after the battle, Dr. Mackay, the 29th Regiment surgeon, recalled his last meeting with John on the evening of July 28:

> The last time we met was the night before they struck camp for the fight. He rode up to the hospital in company with Major Brown, to whom he introduced me. He looked and felt very happy. He was dressed, for the first time during the campaign, in his full uniform, his valise having just arrived from City Point. I chid him for having performed the anti-patriarchal operation of shaving, having donned the "Burnside cut"—shaving the chin, leaving side whiskers and mustache. I insisted on their staying to supper. It was a very hot afternoon, and I had some iced lemonade, with what we in army parlance called, "a brick in it." We sang some hymns and a few Scottish songs. I can yet hear his rich bass voice joining in the refrain of "My Nannie's awa." Those few happy moments were too soon spent.
>
> We supped—'t was the last I was to eat with my brave Colonel, and the last table he sat at for, in his tent, each one sat and ate and lay on

mother earth. He said to me, when about to start, "Now, Doctor, we have just got our valises up from City Point, and I expect a move soon. Will you have the goodness to take charge of them?" Of course I was happy to do so. He asked me to ride out to camp with him. I did so. 'T was a happy three miles' ride. The evening was beautiful and cool after the sultry day. We were very lively, and the horses seemed to partake of the spirit of the riders. I said: "Colonel, you'll have a fine staff when it's all full; you must have a pair of eagles at its head." He turned to me and smiling, said: "Doctor, I'm just going to have them too. Yes, Sir." He then congratulated himself upon having his clothes, as he "would not feel so bad on going to corps headquarters, as he did with that old blouse." He also remarked: "Doctor, I can see by the way things are going that you will soon be our brigade surgeon; and then" (laughing) "we'll have more transportation."

The regiment was camped in a pine forest. Captain Aiken and other officers were sitting around the Colonel's tent. [Here Mackay mentions that he asked Captain Aiken to let him have a certain young soldier for assistance in surgery, but the Captain refused.] The Colonel listened to all, but said nothing. He generally took things coolly. We changed the subject—talked of prospects. Colonel said that there would be an important move before long. It was now getting dark, and preparing to mount, my foot in the stirrup, the Colonel came to my side, and putting his hand on my shoulder, said: "Doctor, don't say anything more about that. I'll give you the boy in a day or two. I see how beneficial it will be to all of us." I thanked him, mounted, we shook hands. "I'll send the valises up in the morning, should we move." "All right, Colonel. Come and see us as often as you can at the hospital." "I will; but don't be a stranger, Doctor. Good night—good night." I yet see his tall, manly, broad-shouldered form turn from me in that darkening, dense, Virginian woods.

Ah! truly, what a loss is yours, when one who knew him so short a time learned so to appreciate.

His hospitality and uniform kindness, gentlemanly, straight-forward bearing, gained him the high esteem of all. But to me he was more than that. His admiration for everything Scottish, and his grasp of the very soul of Scottish poetry, making often the tear of enthusiasm dance in his eye, was something additional which makes me feel his loss so keenly. How he admired, and how thoroughly he lived out the following stanza of Burns:

"Preserve the dignity of man
 With soul erect,
And trust the universal plan
 Will all direct."

Often we wandered together in those woods, by turns arguing, philosophizing, or reading.... Let me tell you a conversation I remember, which struck me as almost prophetic. It took place in company with Adjutant Downing, for whom the Colonel had a very high estimation, and, I think, Captain Aiken, and myself. Our subject was "Death." The Colonel said: "One thing I wish, if it is my fate to fall before the enemy, I hope I may not have a long, lingering wound. If I'm to die a soldier's death, let me die on the field." Then, laughing, he repeated the last two lines of Campbell's "Lochiel."[90]

Truly do you say, how strictly did he perform his duty. With him, everything he did was a duty, and performed well and cheerfully. He has said to me: "How contemptible it is for us to distress ourselves about the littleness and frivolities of life—these things which generally distract the brains of humanity. Our great object should be duty energetically and cheerfully performed, unmindful of all consequences." "Yes," he said further, "it was an awful sacrifice for me, Doctor, to leave my wife and little one; but it was my duty, and that duty will be performed."

Intensity was one of his chief characteristics. He loved intensely that which was noble, pure and good; and he was what Carlyle would call a "superb hater" of everything low, vile or mean. Let the rising generation aim at the goal of my late noble Colonel, and farewell all doubt of human progress.[91]

THE BATTLE OF THE CRATER, SATURDAY, JULY 30, 1864

The fuse ends were 400 feet into the 510-foot tunnel; after 90 feet on the floor of the mine, the fuses ran into tubing that carried them through about

30 feet of sand bags that had been piled up to provide tamping so that the force of the explosion would not escape through the tunnel. Colonel Pleasants calculated that the triple line of fuse would take about 15 minutes to reach the powder chambers. At 3:15 a.m. Pleasants and two other officers lit the fuse and hurried back through the tunnel to the outside air and waited for the explosion, scheduled for 3:30 a.m. After 15 minutes, nothing had happened. Then another 15 minutes and still nothing. Probably the fuse had been broken at a splice, but possibly it was still sputtering towards the powder, so that anyone who went in to look might be buried in the explosion. At 4:15 a. m. two brave officers went into the tunnel to relight the fuse and found that the fuse had indeed broken at a splice about thirty feet in front of the tamping. They relit the fuse at 4:35 a.m. and ran back outside.[92]

At about 4:45 a.m. the ground under the 18th South Carolina Regiment gave a bump and then the earth cracked apart, letting loose a terrible uprush of earth and fire. A witness described it as "a great spout or fountain of red earth ... mingled with men and guns, timbers and planks, and every kind of debris, all ascending, spreading, whirling." It formed a mushroom cloud two hundred feet in height that peaked and collapsed downward in a deluge of earth, boulders, beams of wood, and human bodies. The enormous explosion formed a hole about 170 feet long, 60 feet wide, and 30 feet deep. More than an entire Confederate regiment was blown up or buried in the debris.[93] Fifty years later, during the First World War, the use of large explosives became common, but in the summer of 1864 nothing like it had ever been seen in the history of warfare.

The surprise was complete, but after that nothing else went right.

For one thing, communications were bad. It would have been sensible for Meade and Burnside to be together at the battle site for rapid consultation with each other and with Grant, but Burnside, at midnight before the attack, moved his headquarters to a bombproof shelter nearer the Union line while Meade moved to Burnside's former headquarters at 2:00 a.m. and set up a telegraphic connection to Burnside.[94] This was partly because Meade had insisted that he alone should have authority for command over the two corps supporting Burnside's, so he intended to get prompt and detailed telegraph messages from Burnside, and then telegraph orders to the supporting divisions. But it also fitted in with Meade's hierarchical and bureaucratic view of military command, typical of the Army of the Potomac, and it was probably also intended to reflect his superiority to Burnside in rank.

Burnside, for his part, failed to communicate effectively with Meade, fearing that he would be overruled and the attack called off. This resulted in orders from Meade based on a complete misunderstanding of the worsening situation, and even an angry spat between Meade and Burnside when Burnside understood the language of one of Meade's agitated messages to imply that he was not being truthful, all of this a waste of crucial time and highly detrimental to the success of the action.

Meade never came to confer with Burnside, but Grant did visit Burnside on the front line at 6:30 a.m. and advised that, in his opinion, the opportunity for surprise had been lost and the attack should be called off. But Burnside still hoped for success and cited Meade's orders to attack; Meade was not present and Grant did not want to circumvent the chain of command, so the attacks went on pursuant to senseless orders from Meade who was out of touch with the situation because of his absence from the scene and because Burnside didn't send him accurate information.

In addition, Burnside's orders were not effectively communicated. His written orders were often qualified by the phrase "if possible," which blurred their clarity, and he preferred to give his orders orally to his senior officers, which led to misunderstandings, especially in a complex plan that had been changed at the last minute.[95]

Perhaps the most important factor was another dimension of poor communication: the absence of any senior officers at the scene of battle. Burnside had not specifically directed his division commanders to be present at the action, probably assuming that they would be. In fact, Ledlie never was physically present with his troops, remaining in a bomb-proof shelter during the entire action. General Ferrero, commander of the Fourth Division, did go out to greet his advancing troops at the Union line, but he had only returned from Washington and been reinstated as divisional commander the evening before, and found himself in the middle of a complicated maneuver that was already underway, having barely been briefed on

Meade's change to the plan he had worked on. He seemed uncertain about the situation and spent most of his time during the battle in the bomb-proof, talking with Ledlie. The only divisional commander who actually went to look at the scene in the crater was General Turner, who was not even in Burnside's Ninth Corps but rather in the Tenth Corps, reporting to General Ord.[96]

Grant later testified that this was the major reason for the failure. When asked what he thought was the cause of the disaster, he said:

> I think the cause of the disaster was simply the leaving the passage of orders from one to another down to an inefficient man. I blame his seniors also for not seeing that he did his duty, all the way up to myself.... As I understand it, the troops marched right into the breach caused by the explosion without there being a single division commander there. They had no person to direct them to go further, although the division commanders were directed in the most positive terms to march to what is called Cemetery hill, which would have given us everything.[97]

One of Grant's objectives in testifying was to shield Meade from criticism, but it must have been obvious to everyone that Meade was ultimately responsible for the organization of the command structure during the battle.

Ledlie's behavior could be characterized as incompetence, but it was worse than that. Burnside had made it clear to Ledlie, both orally and in writing, that the task of the lead division was to charge straight to Cemetery Hill, behind the Confederate line, and establish a lodgment there. Ledlie gave totally different orders to his two brigade commanders, instructing them that their task was to secure the trenches around the crater and wait there, leaving it to the colored troops who followed them to go for the hill, so when the attack occurred, the commanders of the lead brigades were completely misinformed about their objective.[98] Ledlie was almost certainly drunk during the battle, as he had been during previous battles, and he replied to increasingly alarmed dispatches by mindlessly repeating orders to advance, orders that had no relationship to the actual situation. In his later testimony to the Joint Congressional Committee on the Conduct of the War, Grant said:

> I blame myself for one thing.... I was informed of this fact: that General Burnside, who was fully alive to the importance of this thing, trusted to the pulling of straws which division should lead. It happened to fall on what I thought was the worst commander in his corps. I knew that fact before the mine was exploded, but did nothing in regard to it. That is the only thing I blame myself for. I knew the man was the one that I considered the poorest division commander that General Burnside had—I mean General Ledlie.[99]

There was also the poor morale and general reluctance of most officers and men of the Army of the Potomac to make frontal assaults, after the blood-soaked spring campaign in Virginia had decimated most of the regular regiments. General Warren of the Fifth Corps, stationed to Burnside's left, could have relieved pressure on the assaulting troops by attacking the artillery stations south of the crater, which were raking the Union attackers; in fact he was at one point ordered by Meade to go in and take the two gun battery, but he delayed, insisting that there was a second line of defense, though there wasn't, and denying that rebel troops had been moved away from the line in front of him, though they had been.[100] He afterwards said that he had never believed in the idea of the mine and would not have authorized it.[101] In this, he seems to have reflected the general view of the senior staff of the Army of the Potomac: they distrusted the operation, expected it to fail, and therefore, if not explicitly wanting it to fail, were committed to its failure, of course with as small a number of casualties as possible.

Later, when the Federal attack had failed and Union troops were penned in the crater, the Fifth Corps could have made a diversionary attack on the left, and the Tenth Corps on the right, to support an orderly retreat from the crater back to the Union line, but Meade had ordered those troops to stand down and Burnside was specifically denied authority to command them, so the trapped troops received no assistance at all from the ample resources of the Federal Army. Meade did not know about the desperate condition of the men in the crater, in large part because Burnside had not told him.[102]

It is also true that Ledlie failed to provide ladders or sandbags for stairs for the troops to get out of the main Union trench, several feet above their head, so that at the beginning of the assault, they were unable to climb out until someone thought of sticking bayonets into the trench wall to form makeshift ladders; this cost time. And Burnside failed to carry out orders from Meade to clear the Federal abatis, defensive obstacles to an attack on the Federal trench, to chop down a grove of trees near the mine to clear the view for artillery, and to have engineers go in with the assault troops in order to dig in when they reached the top of the hill. Burnside ignored some of these orders because he thought removing the Federal abatis and chopping down the trees might alert the Rebels to the coming attack. The abatis did not turn out to cause much delay but leaving the grove of trees in place had serious repercussions in the battle because it prevented Union artillery from taking out a key Confederate artillery post, which was doing serious damage to the Union assault.[103]

Certainly an important factor in the Union defeat, in addition to the last minute removal of the black regiments from the leading position, was the failure to deal with the Confederate artillery. There were five artillery stations in a semicircle from south to north, all trained on the crater, on the territory between the crater and the hill and on the no man's land between the Union line and the crater. They began responding soon after the explosion and raked both no man's land and the territory beyond the crater with deadly shells and canister, causing the failure of several Union assaults. Nearly equal in importance was deadly rifle fire from Confederate infantry. The explosion of the mine had not done much damage to the Confederate trenches beyond 30 yards to the right and left, and the Confederate troops recovered fairly soon, so that the attacking Union troops had to face rifle fire in both directions from the major portion of the main trench and also from a honeycomb of Confederate trenches beyond the crater, unknown to the Union troops until they got there.[104] All of the Union advances that morning were stopped by a combination of artillery and rifle fire. Even a timely and well-led advance to the crest by the trained troops would seemingly have been subject to killing fire if the enemy artillery wasn't taken out and if supporting assaults weren't made to neutralize rifle fire from most of the Confederate trench line in that sector. However, in his testimony to the Committee on the Conduct of the War months later, Grant seemed to discount the importance of this factor. Asked whether it would have been necessary to take possession of the enemy's batteries and intrenchments on the right and left of the crater, he said, "Not at all. If they had marched through to the crest of that ridge, they would then have taken everything in rear. I do not think there would have been any opposition at all to our troops had that been done. I think we would have cut off entirely those of the enemy to our right, while those on the left would have tried to make their escape across the Appomattox."[105]

The Union and Confederate trench lines ran roughly north and south, so that the crater made by the explosion was roughly 100 yards west of the main Union line, on the other side of no man's land, which was increasingly raked with artillery and rifle fire as the troops clambered out of the trench and charged across it shortly after 5:00 a.m. Burnside's plan, as amended by Meade, was for Ledlie's division to charge across no man's land, pass through the breach, and then charge up to the top of Cemetery Hill some 300 yards to the northeast, securing a lodgment there with artillery to split the Confederate forces and dominate the town beyond.

What actually happened was that Ledlie's troops, after clambering out of the main trench, swept forward and then, instead of charging forward, followed his erroneous instructions and stopped to secure the position around the breach. The men went down into the crater, fascinated by the enormous cavity, becoming a "perfect mob" and losing all organization. Officers managed to extricate some of their troops and attack the trenches left and right but were stopped by deadly fire. Most of the troops were left in a disorganized mass at the bottom of the crater as enemy rifle fire was increasing and artillery shells began to drop on them. By 5:30 a.m. a messenger was sent to General Ledlie requesting reorganization or reinforcements, but Ledlie's only reply was to send an order to "move forward immediately."[106]

At 6:30 a.m. Burnside, prodded by a telegram from Meade, ordered his second and third divisions to "advance at once to the crest," not realizing

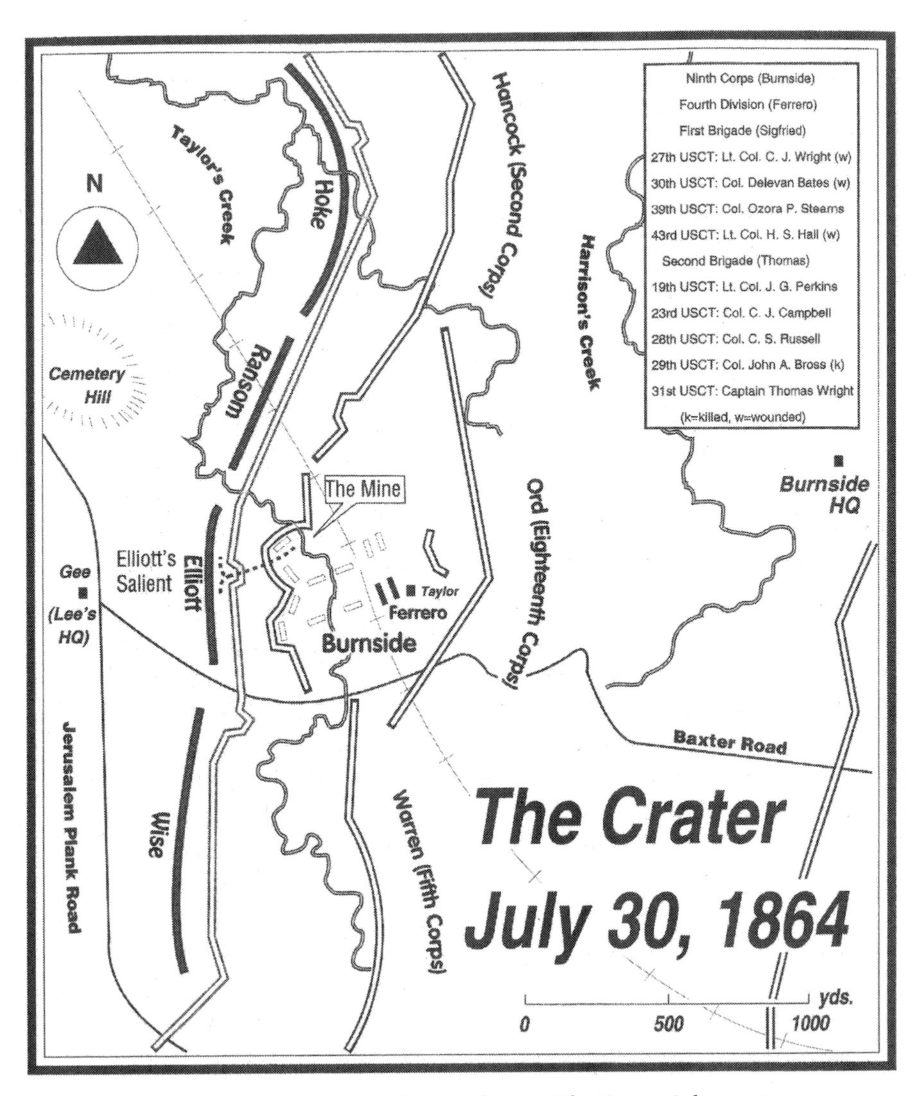

Diagram of Union and Confederate lines at The Crater, July 30, 1864, from *Like Men of War* (Courtesy of Noah Andre Trudeau).

that the troops crowded into the breach were entirely incapable of doing this. One brigade of the Second Division did succeed in pushing the Rebels back about one hundred yards from the breach, but artillery from the north stopped them, and the gridlock in the crater remained.

By 6:30 a.m. the colored troops had appeared at the beginning of the covered way leading towards the front line. Around 7:30 a.m. Colonel Charles Loring, a senior staff officer of Burnside's corps, visited with Burnside and reported that he had visited the breach and personally seen the gridlock at the crater and believed it would be dangerous to carry out an order to move more troops, the colored division, into the gridlock there.[107] But Burnside had just received a peremptory order from Meade ordering an attack and repeated his previous order, which Loring took to Ferrero, commander of the Fourth Division, who was sitting in the bomb-proof with Ledlie. Ferrero instructed Sigfried, leader of the First Brigade, to go through the crowd on the right side of the crater. Thomas's brigade was to follow him and support Sigfried on the left.[108]

By now the colored troops had been in the covered way for over an hour, watching an increasing stream of badly wounded men returning through the passageway, which Thomas thought was a serious strain on the morale of the troops. Shortly after 7:30 a.m., they were ordered forward; it was now almost three hours after the explosion, and the preceding white troops were gridlocked in and around the crater.

Sigfried's brigade was in the lead, four regiments beginning with the 43rd headed by Colonel Hall, followed by the 30th under Colonel Bates, then the 39th and the 27th. They had to make their way through a stream of wounded and demoralized soldiers going to the rear in the covered way then cross an open space, now under fire, to the main Union trench, where Ferrero cheered them on as they climbed down into it.

The men of the 43rd then fixed bayonets and clambered out of the Union trench, which was still short of ladders and sandbag steps. They charged across no man's land, following their colonel, through a cross fire of rifle and artillery. When they reached the crater and Hall saw the crowded men below him, he realized that his objective should be to widen the breach to the north of the crater. He led his men at the run along the base of the enemy parapet, some of them dropping under enemy fire. When his line reached the center of a salient, 200 yards north of the crater, he ordered the men to face left and charge the enemy parapet. Officers and men climbed over the parapet and overwhelmed the defenders.[109]

The black soldiers were full of fury and terror at their first battle and when they stormed the enemy trench, they began killing the surrendering Confederates until their officers, with difficulty, stopped them.[110] They had been urged on into the fight by their officers reminding them to shout the slogans "Fort Pillow" and "No Quarter" and, therefore, were probably assuming that they could expect no quarter and should give none. Lieutenant Steele stepped between his men and a group of prisoners being taken to the rear and physically pushed aside their muskets, saving the prisoners. Later he wrote that he understood their thinking: "There was a half determination on the part of a good many of the black soldiers to kill them as fast as they came to them. They were thinking of Fort Pillow and small blame to them."[111] But later in the day, when the tide turned, many, if not most, black prisoners would be ruthlessly killed by the Confederates.

Meanwhile, the 30th USCT regiment of Sigfried's brigade, commanded by Bates, had followed Hall's 43rd Regiment. Bates led his men to the left, roughly parallel to Hall's men, running along the main trench parapet, and again to the left, losing officers and men as he went, and then struck the rear of the salient that Hall's 43rd regiment was attacking from the front. The men of the 30th piled into the trench and took the position in fierce fighting, with cries of "no surrender to niggers" from the Rebels and shouts of "Fort Pillow" and "No Quarter" from the Union troops. The fighting was more violent than anything Bates had seen. He wrote afterwards, "It was the only battle I was ever in where it appeared to be just pure enjoyment to kill an opponent"; he blamed it on the hatred between black men and white Southerners.[112]

The position was successfully taken as the troops of the 43rd met those of the 30th, the result of a perfect pincers movement carried out by Hall and Bates in a flexible response to deadly and changing battle conditions, their troops prepared by the training they had originally been given.[113] The Union Army now controlled the front for about two hundred yards north of the crater, and Sigfried's brigade seemed poised for a further advance up the slope in front of them to the crest of Cemetery Hill.[114] The success of this first colored brigade, in spite of the disorganized preceding white troops blocking the way and of the ongoing deadly artillery and rifle fire, is evidence that the black troops were indeed reliable. Relatively inexperienced in battle but led by able and dedicated officers, they might well have succeeded in gaining the crest had they led the assault three hours earlier and been properly supported.

But as it was, the losses to the brigade had been severe; the lead three regiments had lost about half of their original numbers, either as casualties or from being mixed up with the bottlenecked troops, and the two best commanders, Bates and Hall, were both wounded and taken off the field by the end of that action. Their troops had become disorganized and remained under a steady withering fire from their right and their front.

Thomas's brigade had followed Sigfried after a delay of half an hour. The leading regiment was the 31st, led by Colonel Ross; followed by the 19th, led by Colonel Perkins; then the 23rd, led by Colonel Campbell; the incomplete 28th, led by Col. Russell; and bringing up the rear, the 29th, led by Colonel Bross "in his splendid full-dress uniform and Burnside whiskers."[115]

Colored Troops charging into battle at The Crater, drawing by Alfred R. Waud (Library of Congress). Figure at bottom left shows detail of boot.

As Thomas led his brigade at the run across no man's land to the berm of the crater, they were watched by Sergeant Harry Reese, the man who had crawled into the tunnel to relight the broken fuse, and who was now appalled by what he had seen of the incompetent assault. He wrote later, "If I had known what a blunder was going to be made in the assault.... I never would have gone into [the mine] to relight the fuse.... It made me still more furious to see a division of Colored soldiers rushed into the jaws of death with no prospect of success; but they went in cheering as though they didn't mind it, and a great many of them never came back."[116]

Thomas led his men up to the berm of the crater, and was taken aback by the crowded confusion he saw there when he looked down. He was able to keep most, but not all, of his men from going down into the crater and shifted their direction north, keeping the majority of them together. He led his men somewhat to the right, looking for Sigfried's troops, but found some rifle pits and took shelter in them to reorganize. But the rifle pits offered little shelter from the ongoing enemy fire, and he had lost contact with his regiments to the rear. The 31st and most of the 23rd were with him, but the 28th, 29th, 19th, and part of the 23rd had become separated in the confused mass of the white troops through which they had to pass and had gone to the left. Bross led the 29th, followed by the 28th, to shelter in front of a cavalier trench, a backup trench some 75 feet behind the first Confederate line with a high earth wall facing front; the two regiments lost men and officers to Rebel rifle fire as they ran. There was no room in front of the cavalier trench for the 19th, which remained further behind, trying to dig in for shelter near the north end of the crater.[117]

Thomas now felt that it was for him to carry the crest ahead. He did his best to organize the men of the 31st and 23rd who were with him and ordered a charge. But his troops were immediately hit with heavy rifle fire from the ravine ahead of him, as well as artillery shells and canister from the ridge beyond. All the senior officers of the 31st were killed and dozens of the men were hit. The attack stalled and the men took what cover they could find where they were. An effort to rally the troops for a second attempt was hit with devastating fire. An officer of the 19th to the rear of Thomas's position jumped up on the parapet and tried to lead the 19th forward in support but was immediately shot dead. Thomas ordered a retreat and the men ran back to cover in the nearest entrenchments.

Major Van Buren of Burnside's staff was still trying to organize a coordinated advance. He had conferred with Marshall on Thomas's left and Sigfried, to the far right, and then made his way to Thomas. Thomas agreed to make the assault but gave Van Buren a message for Burnside: "Unless a movement was made to the right, to stop the enfilading fire, not a man could live to reach the crest." Nevertheless, Thomas said he would attempt the assault in ten minutes, coordinating with Sigfried on the far right and the white troops who were between them. It was now close to 8:30 a.m.[118]

Thomas received no response to his request for support to the right, but he did receive an order from Ferrero that, like Burnside's earlier orders to the first three divisions, simply repeated an uninformed directive to "immediately proceed to take the crest in your front." So Thomas prepared to attack.[119]

There were to be four groups involved in a coordinated advance: on the left, the 28th and 29th USCT; then Thomas with the 31st and 23rd; next, to the right of Thomas, what was left of Griffin's Second Brigade of the Second Division; and finally, Sigfried's brigade on the far right. All of these units had become disorganized in getting through the crowded trenches near the crater, and all had suffered serious losses. The 29th, under Bross, was behind the parapet of the cavalier trench, with the trench on the opposite side of the parapet. To make a charge, they would have to climb up onto the parapet, jump over the trench, form up on the other side, and charge up the hill, all under heavy enemy fire. They would then be followed by the men of the 28th, who were sheltering in rifle pits slightly behind them. The 29th was about 50 yards further out than the 23rd, which would lead the advance under Thomas.[120]

The assault began. Thomas gave the order to charge, and the officers of the 23rd climbed out of the trenches and called on their men to follow. Fifty yards ahead and to the left, the officers and men of the 29th did the same. Both sections of the brigade were immediately hit by heavy fire. As Bross's men of the 29th mounted the parapet, a shot splintered the flagstaff of the colors and hit the man carrying it. Another man lifted the colors and was shot through the neck. A captain picked up the broken staff and climbed onto the parapet and was shot through the ankle. The men hesitated.[121]

Then, as described in Richard Slotkin's book, *No Quarter*,

> Colonel Bross, conspicuous in his full-dress uniform complete with yellow sash, grabbed the colors and hopped up onto the parapet of the cavalier. "The man who saves these colors shall be promoted," he cried. The regiment rose to his call. He turned and jumped over the ditch on the far side, and as he did, a bullet thumped hard into his body. "Oh Lord!" he cried, and as the troops rushed past him, he called out, "Forward, my brave boys." The flag was taken from his hand by the seventh man to carry it that day. Neither flag nor bearer returned. Of 400 men who had followed Bross into the battle, only 128 came back.[122]

Slotkin records that on the Confederate side, General Mahone and Colonel Rogers of the 6th Virginia "saw a Union colonel—almost certainly Bross—standing on a parapet encouraging his men. They saw him 'seize his colors and spring over the protecting ditch, and by every gesticulation showed the way to the front—and perhaps to victory.' "[123] John F. Schmutz writes in *The Battle of the Crater* that as Mahone's officers conferred,

> "a magnificent looking Federal officer [later identified as Lieutenant Colonel Bross] stepped out from the occupied works, and grabbing a flag, called upon his men to form a line preparatory to a charge, which order appeared to be very indifferently obeyed." Here and there a man would jump out from the works, but the great mass of the men in the trenches failed to respond. The colonel was using all means to induce the regiment to charge from the broken line he held on the heights in his front. It was hard to encourage the black soldiers out of the sheltered trenches, which presented a double line of ditches at least four feet deep and just as wide, capped by heavy, thick sandbags. However, this colonel was so energetic that Mahone worried that he might get them to charge, as he seized the colors and sprang over the protecting ditch "and by every gesticulation showed the way to the front—and perhaps to victory."[124]

It is difficult for the historian to construct a coherent narrative about a battle involving the complex maneuvers and uncertain motives of thousands of officers and soldiers, and it is also difficult to be accurate about a single battle event, such as the death of John, since there are often conflicting recollections by several witnesses. In the *Memorial*, there are four accounts of John's death. The testimony of Captain McCormick is given that "Colonel Bross had advanced to the parapet, and planted his colors upon it. But seeing how matters stood, gave the order to retreat, and just then he was struck by a minie bullet, in the left side of the head, and fell dead, uttering, as one says, in falling, the words, 'O, Lord.' "[125] The *Memorial* then reports

> a touching account of the manner in which the Colonel became possessed of the colors, given in the simple language of one of the Sergeants. "... [The flag] was then taken by Colonel Bross, who planted it upon the parapet of the works, the furthest point reached by our troops. The Colonel then drew his sword, took his hat in his hand, and cried, '*Rally, my brave boys, rally!*' The men pressed up to him, but he quickly fell."[126]

A letter from the brother of Lieutenant Ridenour, too disabled to write himself, is quoted, stating that "My brother was wounded in five places, and as he lay on the field the Colonel fell quite near him. He was shot in the left side of the head, and died instantly without a groan."[127]

Finally, the *Memorial* gives portions of a letter to Belle from Lieutenant Chapman, including the following:

> My last interview with the Colonel was while we were halted in the covered way. Captain Aiken and Lieutenant Gale were also there. Few words were exchanged, our thoughts, as usual at such times, straying homewards. We little knew then that by incapacity and wanton neglect, thousands of lives were to be sacrificed. Again we were moving forward. The outer line of works was passed, and we were hastening up the hill to the fort. Here, friend and foe, living and dying, were heaped together, causing us to halt in the midst of a destructive fire of both musketry and artillery. I well remember how he looked, standing in the midst, his

> countenance lighted up with steadfast hope and an almost superhuman courage, he cried out, "Forward, 29th," and we moved on over the mass. The men were falling thick and fast, and soon my turn came. Lying on the field, I felt the auspicious moment had passed. His form was ever a prominent mark. Turning to Captain Brockway, he said, "bring forward the colors." Then seizing them in his own hand he cried, "Follow me, my men." But it was in vain; the enemy were concentrated. It was madness for us to charge where three Divisions had already failed. As we were ordered back, the Colonel was seen endeavoring to rescue the colors. Standing upon the parapet he said, "The man who saves those colors shall be promoted." The fatal ball came, and he fell, but the legacy of his bright example and the memory of his noble deeds remain. The intense sorrow and grief of that night I will not attempt to portray.[128]

These accounts of John's death vary as to where he was hit, what, if anything, he said, and whether he was in an advance or a retreat when he fell. They are mostly in agreement that he had the regimental colors in his hand and was standing on the parapet when he fell. The "colors" were the two flags carried by every infantry regiment of the Union Army in the Civil War: one was the national flag, the stars and stripes, with the regimental number and name embroidered in silver on the central stripe; the other was the regimental flag with the seal of the United States on a dark blue background and the regimental name on a scroll under the eagle. These regimental flags stood for the honor and courage of the regiment; it was a disgrace to the regiment if they were captured and a notable victory to capture the colors of an enemy regiment. Each flag was carried by an unarmed corporal, called a color sergeant, and the color sergeants were surrounded by 6 to 8 corporals, called the color guard. It was a great honor to be named one of the color guard, but it could be a dangerous assignment since enemy fire was often concentrated on the regimental colors. The colors may have been especially important for this regiment's black soldiers, whose uniforms offered the promise of a new level of citizenship and equality.

It is not certain which of the two flags John was holding when he was shot down, probably the stars and stripes, but it is clear that he was courageously taking personal leadership of his troops in a situation of extreme difficulty and danger, holding high a flag that symbolized its honor.[129] Having learned a few hours earlier that the battle plan had been abruptly changed, and apparently sharing Thomas's doubts of its success, he may well have been recalling the lines from Tennyson that he had often quoted:

> Was there a man dismayed?
> Not though the soldier knew
> Someone had blundered.
> Theirs not to make reply,
> Theirs not to reason why,
> Theirs but to do and die.

It must have been clear to John as the attack began, before he died, that someone had blundered.

The 28th followed the 29th into the advance and other units, including Sigfried's troops on the right, also started forward, but these units were too separated for a coherent charge and too decimated for effective strength. Within three minutes, a double line of 800 Confederate infantry under General Mahone suddenly rose out of the ravine some two hundred yards away, moving downhill at the double quick with bayonets fixed, giving the chilling falsetto howl known as the rebel yell.[130] General Mahone and the rest of the Confederate high command, including General Lee, had responded rapidly and efficiently after the explosion. Mahone had shifted two brigades north unseen into the ravine and began his charge in order to break up the Union advance. In fact, John's demonstrative leadership action may have precipitated the Confederate assault: Schmutz reports that Mahone was waiting for a Georgia brigade to join the assault, but "Wiesiger simultaneously observed Bross' actions and told Girardey that the charge really needed to commence at once, without waiting for the Georgia Brigade, and indicated that 'if we do not move forward promptly all would be lost.'" Mahone thereupon gave the order to charge.[131] But Mahone's men, against orders, had begun firing, and it was probably one of these shots that brought John down; if so, he did not live to see the attack of the Confederate line.

In short order, the troops of the Union line broke before the downhill

Confederate charge and began running in disorder to the rear, some to the crater, some to trenches near and north of the crater, and some all the way back to the Union line. “The black soldiers, particularly Thomas’ men in the front lines, were hit very hard, and the majority of their officers fell in the first few minutes, thereby leaving the inexperienced blacks without leaders: thus many quickly gave way to the rear.”[132]

The Union troops, both black and white, who fled were not cowards. After four hours of heavy fighting and courageous advance in stifling hot weather, in confused circumstances and under punishing fire, having lost many of their men and most of their officers, the units no longer were able to stand against a downhill charge by fresh and well-organized troops. But the Union troops who retreated to the area of the crater found defensive positions and repulsed an assault by Mahone’s troops in heavy fighting. It was now about 10:00 a.m.

At 9:30 a.m. Meade talked with Grant and concluded that the attack had failed. He wired an order to Burnside suggesting that he withdraw, with subsequent wires making the order mandatory but permitting him to postpone the withdrawal until nightfall to make it safer for the troops to withdraw. Burnside still thought the operation could succeed. As a student at West Point, he had gone into debt losing money at cards because his instinct was always to double down, never to fold his cards, and this was his reaction now.[133] He rode to Meade’s headquarters and angrily demanded that the order be changed. But Meade’s opinion that the crest could not be taken was backed up by General Ord of the Tenth Corps, who had been stationed to Burnside’s right, and by General Grant, both of whom were present, so Meade made his order to withdraw peremptory. Meade offered no help in arranging the withdrawal, perhaps because Burnside did not tell him how desperate the situation was becoming, and perhaps Burnside himself did not know, or refused to know, since he assumed that his troops in and around the crater could hold out until nightfall and then retreat under cover of darkness. The withdrawal order had also gone to the Fifth Corps under Warren, to Burnside’s left, and to the Tenth Corps under General Ord, to Burnside’s right, on both of which he had counted for possible support during the attack, so they were no longer available for help with a withdrawal. By 10:30 a.m. Meade and Grant had returned to their own headquarters and Burnside was left in charge and alone. As Slotkin points out, it was strange for Meade to assume that Burnside could handle everything by himself when he had made it so abundantly clear that he had little confidence in Burnside's ability.[134]

Burnside sent along the order to withdraw and directed his division commanders to have the officers on the line work out a plan for withdrawal. But these officers were largely cut off from contact with headquarters by heavy fire over no man's land and so had no idea whether or when the support they were hoping for would be forthcoming or how to coordinate with it.

In the crater an active defense was still in progress. Colonel Thomas had joined a Pennsylvania regiment at the angle of a picket line 100 yards north of the crater and they were holding out there but were isolated and running low on ammunition. In the northern half of the crater, an officer tried to get men up to the firing line along the berm, but the only soldiers who would go up were twenty five or so black soldiers, of whom a Lieutenant later wrote, "[T]hat from noon until the capture of the Crater two hours later, the firing was kept up almost wholly by the colored troops."[135]

The situation grew steadily worse. Ammunition was running low. Confederate artillery began again, canister and shells being fired directly into the open north end of the crater. "Soldiers screamed as body parts that were torn from their comrades became projectiles, or a man might be 'dashed in the face with a hot steaming mass of something horrible that covered his eyes and filled his mouth ... a mass of brains, skull, hair and blood' from a comrade decapitated by flying metal."[136] Then mortar shells began to drop in among the crowded men, doing still more damage. Men were also incapacitated or killed by the terrible heat as the sun bore down directly into the crowded crater. Even worse than the heat was the dreadful thirst, for most of the men had gone into battle with just one canteen of water and that was now gone. Wounded men begged for a little water. A few soldiers, including some of the blacks, volunteered to bring back water from the Union line and actually did so, but most were killed or wounded crossing no man's land. General Bartlett and the men still believed that some action would be taken by the Federal reserves to rescue them.

But no such action was taken:

> Conditions in the crater were intolerable. At 1:00 p.m. the intense heat and glare of the sun poured straight down into the pit. Dead and wounded men were strewn all over the bottom and up the sides of the crater.... The clay floor of the crater was baked hard by the sun and it held the blood in pools that dried slowly. Parts of dismembered bodies were scattered everywhere, abuzz with flies, and the stagnant ovenlike air was thick with a horrible stench from bodies and parts of bodies that had been rotting in the heat for eight hours, and from human shit—it was impossible to make or use latrines or sinks, and diarrhea was chronic in both armies.[137]

The 97th Pennsylvania and Colonel Thomas and his black troops abandoned their isolated position north of the crater, successfully dashing back to the Union line. As the Confederate troops prepared for a final assault against the crater, Generals Hartranft and Griffin, now commanding in the crater and having received no answer to their request for supporting attacks, ordered an immediate retreat for those willing to risk the run across no man's land while a rear guard stayed behind to hold off the assault.[138] Confederate infantry stormed the northern and southern ends of the crater and Union troops soon surrendered in both places amidst the confusion of the assault, shortly after 2:00 p.m.[139]

The final battle and surrender at the crater were made more complicated and much more deadly by the racial factor of black troops. The assumption on both sides was that no quarter could be expected or would be given; Northern officers had encouraged their black infantry to remember Fort Pillow and many of the Southern troops were enraged at their first sight of black troops and by having heard that the black troops had shown no quarter to them that morning. In addition, many white Union soldiers feared that they would be killed by Confederates if they were captured together with the blacks, and there were ugly scenes of white Union soldiers actually killing their fellow black Union soldiers. A Union captain later testified "that White Federal soldiers 'bayoneted blacks who fell back into the crater. This was in order to preserve the whites from Confederate vengeance. Men boasted in my presence that blacks had been thus disposed of, particularly when the Confederates came up.'" Slotkin points out that the underlying cause of these particularly disgraceful killings was not fear but the racial prejudice of the Northern white troops.[140]

When the Confederate troops entered the crater, they immediately began to bayonet wounded blacks. Confederate "Colonel John Haskell observed, 'Our men, who were always made wild by having negroes sent against them ... were utterly frenzied with rage. Nothing in the war could have exceeded the horrors that followed. No quarter was given and for what seemed a long time, fearful butchery was carried on.' Though he did no killing, Haskell's coat became so sodden with blood that he threw it away in disgust."[141] Many of the blacks fought back, refusing to surrender; one Confederate private said of them, "They fought like bulldogs, and died like soldiers."[142] But when Confederate and Union officers alike assured them that they would be treated like POWs, the blacks eventually put down their guns. It might have become another Fort Pillow, but finally the killing was stopped and many black soldiers were sent to the rear as prisoners.

But the killings of blacks did not end there. As the disarmed black prisoners were marched back to Petersburg, many were randomly killed by Confederate soldiers who met them on the way. One Confederate officer later said that he thought that fewer than half the black prisoners made it alive to the rear, that they were lying dead all along the route.[143] Such unjustified killing of unarmed prisoners, clearly an atrocity, would of course not have happened except for the racial factor.

The battle was over, a major defeat for the Union. "In addition to the loss of life, the moral effect was intensely calamitous. It spread a gloom over all the land. It was widely felt, as a result, that we were making no progress in the war, and were likely to make none."[144] "For Lincoln, it was one of the worst moments in a bad summer. The Crater fiasco tainted Grant's reputation and caused people to doubt the will and ability of the soldiers themselves."[145] The Ninth Corps had lost some 3,800 killed, wounded, or missing.[146] In a telegram of August 1, Grant wrote Meade:

> Have you any estimate of our losses in the miserable failure of Saturday? I think there will have to be an investigation of the matter. So fair an opportunity will probably never occur again for carrying fortifications; preparations were good, orders ample, and everything, so far as I could see subsequent to the explosion of the mine, shows that without loss the crest beyond the mine could have been carried; this would have given us Petersburg with all its artillery, and a large part of the garrison beyond doubt.[147]

In a message two days later to Chief of Staff General Halleck, Grant wrote, "It was the saddest affair I have witnessed in the war. Such opportunity for carrying fortifications I have never seen and do not expect again to have."[148] The siege lines remained as they had been before the battle. And the war would go on for another eight months.

Although he had not planned it, John's life had become inextricably involved with the important strand of American history that involved racial relations, the glaring conflict between the universally accepted American ideal of all men being created equal and the fact of black slavery, which so plainly showed that men of different races were *not* considered equal. As an officer in a black regiment, he became directly engaged in the important step Lincoln had taken to bring black Americans to full citizenship by making them soldiers of the United States Army. John's life was ended at the first and only major battle of the war in which race played a decisive role, a battle that stood at a key point of influence on the future course of racial relations in America. The assault at the crater might have been a glorious victory for the Union that ended the war, led by the very black men whose oppression had caused the war; this could have dramatically changed public opinion about citizenship and equal rights for black people, whose soldiers and officers would have been seen as heroes of a decisive battle. Instead, there was a disastrous defeat associated with black troops, caused by racist assumptions as well as incompetence and professional jealousy, which not only tainted with racism the events that immediately followed but also had the effect of prolonging and hardening racist attitudes in much of the public mind. The road that led from the fiasco at the crater pointed toward the abandonment of support for reconstruction, with its goal of racial equality, and the consequent establishment of the era of Jim Crow and lynching in the American South for the next hundred years.

The *Memorial* observes, "If a soldier falls in a successful battle, his name is imperishably linked with whatever of lustre it sheds about it. History, poetry, and oratory dwell upon it. But to fall in a failure, is to go down in comparative darkness, and history refuses to linger upon the theme." This was evidently true of the battle at the Crater. "This was a battle Northern historians and writers preferred to minimize or forget, not simply because it was a defeat but because it so forcibly displayed the intransigence and complexity of the race question that puzzled or ultimately repelled them."[149] The "comparative darkness" could be as true for a cause as for an individual. The North won the war and assured the abolition of slavery as well as the integrity of the Union, but the relative oblivion to which the defeat at the Crater was assigned seemed also to include progress towards racial equality. John's heroism and his manifest Christian commitment to racial justice were largely forgotten. They are easier to remember more than a century later after the cause of racial justice in American society was revived in the 1960s by Martin Luther King and the Civil Rights Movement.

One of the events in which racial prejudice made itself felt immediately after the battle was the care for the wounded lying between the lines before the establishment of a truce on August 1, which incredibly had been postponed for a day due to Burnside's attempt to avoid the appearance of defeat. General Warren observed with outrage that water and assistance were being given to white wounded men but not to black ones.[150] Another was the treatment of the prisoners in Petersburg, where General Hill, Lee's senior corps commander, organized a parade of the black and white prisoners, including the one-legged General Bartlett, through the streets of Petersburg in order to humiliate them. Such treatment was unheard of, entirely inconsistent with accepted rules for the treatment of prisoners of war, and was clearly caused by racism. "Like a circus parade they were marched down and around all the streets of the town for two hours or more, 'taunted by the women, stoned by the boys, and cursed by the men.' The merging of officers and men, Whites and Blacks, was (from the Southern point of view) the essence of the humiliation: 'See the white and nigger equality soldiers!' "[151] This was the dark opposite of Jefferson's and Lincoln's ideal of equality: blacks and whites in equality together were viewed as a hateful perversion of decency.

The battle's long-term effect on racial relations was also corrosive. A military court of inquiry was arranged a week after the battle, really for the purpose of exonerating Meade, the judging officers having been appointed by Meade. The court's findings unsurprisingly laid most of the blame on Burnside, though not by name, and Burnside went on a leave from which he never returned. The performance of the black troops was not mentioned in the findings of the court, but in the Ninth Corps and in the army as a whole, blame for the fiasco was generally put on the black soldiers for the route that had followed Mahone's charge and for disrupting the defense of the crater by piling on top of the white soldiers there:

> This belief was especially favored by the officers of the routed regiments, and by their brigade and division commanders, whose actions would be scrutinized by the court of inquiry. Their testimony turned the court of inquiry into an investigation of the strengths and weaknesses of black soldiers, as well as a tribunal on the performance of general officers. It became customary in descriptions of the battle to describe the timing of events in relation to "the stampede of the darkies." In contrast General Hartranft, who came out of the battle with some credit, described the black soldiers as having been no more or less disordered by conditions around the crater than any troops would have been.[152]

Slotkin points out that the colored brigades were, in fact, able to bring more men through the disorganization at the crater than any of the preceding white brigades, even though the crowding was worse when they got there, that Sigfried's brigade made the most successful assault of the day, and that Thomas's brigade also got through the jam in the crater and made one assault, and then was ready to attempt another after the first one was broken up. Of 504 men in the Ninth Corps listed as killed in action, 209, or 41%, were from the Fourth Division, which was engaged for the shortest period. The units of the Fourth Division were "green" and yet many of them did rally after Mahone's attack, even without their officers. Colonel Thomas reported that after Mahone's charge, "One little band, after my second charge was repulsed, defended the intrenchments we had won from the enemy, exhibiting fighting qualities that I never saw surpassed in the war. This handful stood there without the slightest organization of company or regiment, each man for himself, until the enemy's banners waved in their faces. Then they made a dash for our own lines, and that at my order."[153] He added, "The 4th Division were good soldiers, and they performed as well as or better than any of the other divisions on the field."[154]

But the narrative accepted by most of the public was that the defeat was chiefly caused by the failure of the black troops and that this was a result of their racial inferiority to whites. This was the story in much of the national press in accounts of the battle of the Crater, both immediately after the battle and in subsequent years. Four days after the battle, the *New York Herald*, a conservative Democratic paper, stated that blame for the defeat must rest with "the President and his whole cabinet, with its nigger-worshipping policy.... Niggers are not fit for soldiers. They can dig, and drive mules; they cannot fight, and will not fight." Even the Republican *New York Times* also put much of the blame for the defeat on the Black troops.[155] A *Tribune* article of August 3, however, stood up for the black troops:

> Let those who would decry the valor of the colored troops because they did not carry the crest of the hill at Petersburg last Saturday, remember Fredericksburg and Vicksburg on the one hand, and Malvern Hill and Gettysburg on the other. Where has better blood been spilled than by our white soldiers in charging up steep hills surmounted by earthworks and cannon, vomiting grape and canister into their ranks by the ton?

And a *Tribune* letter dated August 9th from Petersburg and published August 17, probably written by William, stated, "As to the negro troops, they followed their officers into the very jaws of death, and not until their leaders were nearly all shot down, did they flinch from the contest. Any other statement is purely a malignant lie, come from whatever source it may."

In the two decades after the Civil War, the initial work of Reconstruction in establishing civil rights and property rights for black citizens was overthrown by violence. Regimes dedicated to white supremacy were established in most of the Southern states. Initial federal support for the rights of Southern blacks waned as the Southern "Lost Cause" myth of the Civil War grew popular: it was better for everyone that the South had lost since the fires of war forged a united nation that became a world power, and generally better for everyone that slavery had been abolished, but the valor of Confederate officers and soldiers and the enduring social values of the Southern way of life should be cherished, including the social value of white supremacy. President Wilson was fond of the movie *Birth of a Nation*, which glorified the rise of the Ku Klux Klan, and everyone was fond of the novel *Gone with the Wind*, which presented a romantic view of plantation life, its black slaves well cared for and happy with their lot. There was general acceptance of the idea of "the white man's burden." Northern and Southern veterans met on battlefields of the war to fraternize and reminisce, but not about the black slavery that had caused the war, and black veterans were usually not included.

In the North the lingering implication of the blood-soaked failure at the Crater was the association in the public mind between black troops and failure. In the South the Union defeat at the Crater played into the universally accepted theory of white supremacy: the barbaric attacks of "crazed" negroes, shouting "no quarter" and killing their prisoners, were easily overwhelmed by heroic white Southern soldiers who were justified in killing black prisoners of war even well after the battle had ended. The only mention of black troops at the crater in later Southern accounts was to stigmatize them as uncontrolled and vicious, offering proof that blacks ought to be suppressed by exclusionary laws and the threat of lynching. Slotkin points out that "[i]n effect, justification of the massacre at the Crater symbolically justified the use of lynching to terrorize Blacks and keep them in submission in the contemporary South."[156] But the officers who had fought with the black troops in the battle, including Colonel Thomas, always and officially affirmed the courage and dedication of the black troops on the battlefield.[157]

Burnside's Republican friends in Congress insisted upon a congressional inquiry. It was assigned to the Committee on the Conduct of the

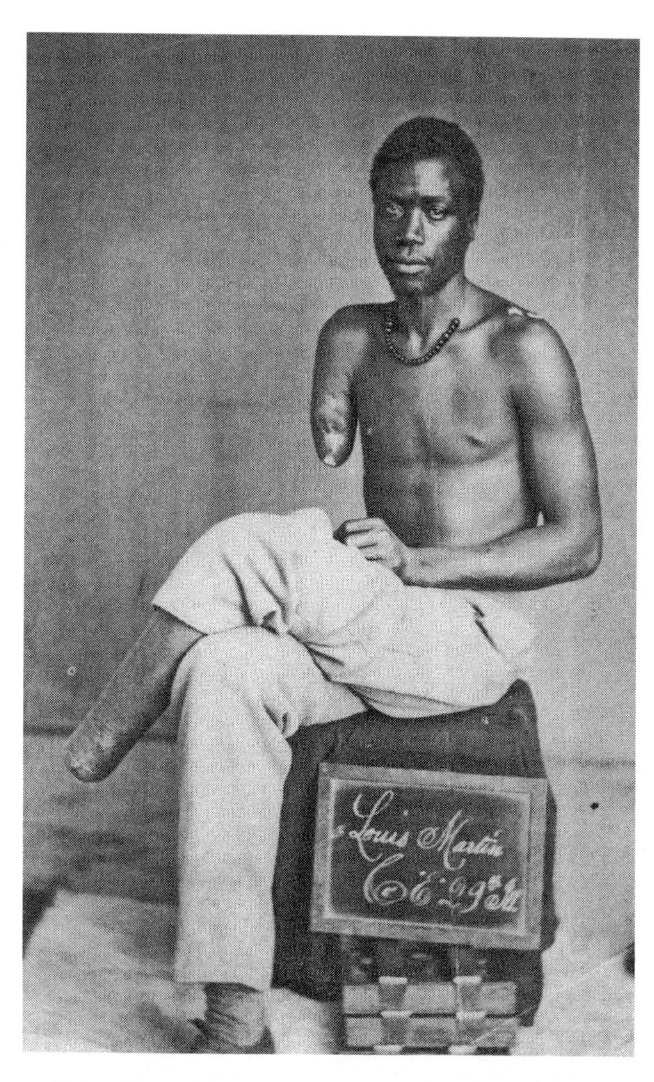

Private Lewis Martin, Company E, 29th Infantry, United States Colored Troops (National Archives).

War, which held hearings beginning in December in Washington and in Petersburg. The main finding of that investigation was that the "first and great cause of disaster" was General Meade's last-minute order forcing Burnside to remove his specially trained Fourth Division from the advance. This was consistent with Grant's testimony to the Committee, but what Grant actually said illustrates the complicated political calculations about race in planning for the assault:

> General Burnside wanted to put his colored division in front, and I believe if he had done so it would have been a success. Still I agreed with General Meade as to his objection to that plan. General Meade said that if we put the colored troops in front (we had only that one division) and it should prove a failure, it would then be said, and very properly, that we were shoving those people ahead to get killed because we did not care anything about them. But that could not be said if we put white troops in front.

The last question put to General Grant at the Committee hearing was: "Question. He [Burnside] desired to use his colored troops for the advance? Answer. Yes, sir; and that part was changed, I thought then very properly, and I think so yet; for we had but one division of colored troops in the whole army about Petersburg at that time, and I do not think it would have been proper to put them in front, for nothing but success would have justified it." [158] In other words, had black troops been used for the advance, the attack would probably have succeeded, but a failure by black troops would not have been acceptable, whereas a failure by white troops was acceptable, so it was proper to remove the black troops from the advance. Grant was, of course, committed to supporting Meade.

The Committee's report put most of the blame on the removal of the black troops from the advance. Grant put most of the blame on faulty leadership. Of course, these views were not inconsistent: use of the trained black troops for the advance might still have failed if the leadership were flawed, and the white troops might have succeeded had they been properly led. Whether white troops or black troops were in the advance, they would have been hampered by the lack of support in neutralizing Confederate artillery, and this was another leadership issue, at the level of General Meade and, really, General Grant: it is understandable that Grant felt obligated to respect the authority of Meade, but Grant knew how important the outcome of this battle might be, and he could presumably have taken more direct charge of the assault. Slotkin observes, "The Battle of the Crater could have been won, and putting the 4th Division in the lead would have made it more likely—but far from certain, given the weakness of Meade's battle plan and Burnside's limited skills as a corps commander and tactician."[159]

The findings of the Joint Congressional Committee, issued in late January 1865, did much to exonerate Burnside's reputation. They also could have, perhaps should have, changed the public mind about the performance of the black troops, but this did not really happen because the findings came months later, when public opinion had already been formed and when the Committee's proceedings were being overshadowed by dramatic ongoing events in the final months of the war.

Definitive news of John's death reached Chicago on August 2. William went to Petersburg to visit the battlefield, probably to decide for himself what had happened, and to search for his brother's body. On August 13 the *Tribune* reported a letter from William informing them that he had little hopes of obtaining the body, as it was buried inside of the Rebel lines. A published letter of August 9, probably by William, stated:

> So far as we could learn, Col. Bross, his Adjutant, a brave young officer from Poughkeepsie, N.Y., and a small portion of his command, reached a point further inside of the enemy's lines, towards Cemetery Hill, than any who had preceded him. Here the Colonel and his Adjutant fell, and as all were driven back by the deadly shower of rebel grape and canister, his body could not be reached and brought in. In the afternoon the rebels established their pickets beyond where he lay, and they therefore buried him and his Adjutant side by side, a colored sergeant of the regiment taken prisoner, assisting in the service. This sergeant was met by some of our officers on Monday, under the flag of truce, said he knew precisely where Col. Bross was buried, and a rebel Major

> with whom Gen. Julius White became acquainted that day, promised that the spot should be carefully marked, so that at some future day the remains might be recovered.

It is possible that John's body was buried together with his adjutant on Saturday afternoon, after the battle, or on Sunday, July 31, when there was an informal truce to allow water and whisky to be distributed to the wounded. Most of the Union dead were buried either in a trench on Saturday night, after the battle, or on Monday, August 1, when a truce for that purpose finally went into effect.[160] Since John had been conspicuous by his uniform and his gallantry, it is possible that he was given special attention for burial on the field. But his grave was never found, so he may have been buried in a mass grave trench with the many other Union dead lying behind the Confederate line. The Confederates did not usually return the bodies of officers of black troops and, in this case, might not have been able to do so.

It appears that William fired a final defiant salute to the memory of his younger brother whose life he had done so much to guide. His letter report dated August 9 contains the following:

> "An Incident"
>
> Last evening, after tea, a party of reconnaissance to the front, consisting of General Julius White of our city, and the writer, was formed and marched in good order, though frequently a Minnie ball would whiz overhead, a shell would go screeching by and explode in our rear, and the tall pines torn off, or speckled with bullets, told but too plainly that there were rebels about, to the fort in front of the one blown up by our troops on Saturday, the 30th. There, with glasses, we made a most particular examination of the ground where so many brave men fell on that fatal day. The rebels have repaired it, and now hold it with a strong force. Our reconnaissance completed, we took the covered way to the fort occupied by Capt. Reaumer's battery. We found the gallant soldier and his comrades at supper. He received us most cordially, and after his repast was over, Gen. White asked the captain "if he could not wake up that fellow" (a fort about a mile a little to the left.) The guns were manned,

and some half a dozen shells were sent, with no very definite results. The last one was carefully aimed, and the writer requested permission to pull the "lanyard." The Captain gave the words, "left face! ready! fire!" the proper muscle was expended, and away sped "the compliments of the Chicago Tribune" to the rebel den, Gen. White and Capt. Reaumer watching it carefully with their glasses. They reported that the death-dealing "compliment" went directly through the embrasure, where it exploded, and a moment after there was a loud second explosion of a rebel caisson or something equivalent. A loud cheer from our picket lines and a cloud of dust in the rebel fort told plainly enough that something, if not somebody, was hit.

Bidding a cordial good-bye to Capt. Reaumer, our party retired in perfect order, not in the least demoralized by the incidents of our expedition to the front.

John's body, therefore, was buried with his fallen men somewhere on the battlefield within the Confederate lines. The same thing had happened to the body of Colonel Robert Shaw, of the 54th Massachusetts Colored Division, after his death at Fort Wagner in July 1863. Colonel Shaw's father had said, "We hold that a soldier's most appropriate burial-place is on the field where he has fallen."[161] The *Memorial*, written probably by Belle in early 1865, says of John: "The ground at this time is still within enemy lines; and whether his body will be recovered by his friends, is uncertain. But his is a

Whatever be my fate I know I can give
to my child, this one thing, "His father
fought for the Union and the 'old flag'."
My beloved wife I pray Heaven to grant me life
& health to see the End of this war, that again I
may Enjoy the sweet influences of your presence
in peaceful times.—

Portion of letter dated June 5, 1864.

His reference to "the old flag" reflects the significance of the American flag as a symbol of the Union and what it stood for.

soldier's grave; and no fitter spot could be selected than that where he fell, in the service of his country, and in obedience to his God."[162]

NOTES

1. Miller, *The Black Civil War Soldiers*, 42.
2. Ibid., 51.
3. Ibid.
4. Drinkard, *Illinois Freedom Fighters*, 19.
5. May 1, 1864.
6. Miller, *The Black Civil War Soldiers*, 42.
7. Ibid., 43.
8. *Memorial*, 12.
9. Miller, *The Black Civil War Soldiers*, 43.
10. Ibid.; *Memorial*, 12.
11. Miller, *The Black Civil War Soldiers*, 43.
12. *Memorial*, 13; May 27, 1864.
13. Miller, *The Black Civil War Soldiers*, 44.
14. Ibid., 46.
15. June 3, 1864.
16. May 18, 1864.
17. McPherson, *Battle Cry*, 735.
18. Ibid., 741; Schmutz, *Battle of the Crater*, 29.
19. Schmutz, *Battle of the Crater*, 21–31.
20. McPherson, *Battle Cry*, 726, 731.
21. Ibid., 741.
22. Miller, *The Black Civil War Soldiers*, 49.
23. June 5, 1864.
24. June 7, 1864.
25. July 3, 1864.
26. June 7–9, 1864.
27. June 15, 1864; Miller, *The Black Civil War Soldiers*, 48.
28. June 19, 1864.
29. July 23, 1864; Miller, *The Black Civil War Soldiers*, 52.
30. June 20, 1864.
31. June 29, 1864.
32. Miller, *The Black Civil War Soldiers*, 55.

33. Our short narrative relies mainly on two excellent detailed studies of this battle, both published in 2009: *The Battle of the Crater* by John F. Schmutz; and *No Quarter, the Battle of the Crater, 1864* by Richard Slotkin.
34. Slotkin, *No Quarter*, 38.
35. Schmutz, *Battle of the Crater*, 49.
36. Miller, *The Black Civil War Soldiers*, 54.
37. Ibid., 53.
38. Schmutz, *Battle of the Crater*, 53.
39. Slotkin, *No Quarter*, 25.
40. Schmutz, *Battle of the Crater*, 59.
41. Slotkin, *No Quarter*, 28.
42. Ibid., 24.
43. Schmutz, *Battle of the Crater*, 53.
44. Ibid., 59.
45. Ibid., 61.
46. Ibid., 59.
47. Ibid., 61.
48. Ibid., 63.
49. Ibid., 63.
50. Slotkin, *No Quarter*, 45.
51. Ibid., 68.
52. Ibid., 73.
53. Ibid., 74.
54. Ibid., 74, 96; Schmutz, *Battle of the Crater*, 97.
55. Drinkard, *Illinois Freedom Fighters*, 37; Noah Andre Trudeau, *Like Men of War: Black Troops in the Civil War*, Boston, London: Little, Brown and Company, 1998.
56. Drinkard, *Illinois Freedom Fighters*, 33.
57. Slotkin, *No Quarter*, 96.
58. Schmutz, *Battle of the Crater*, 114.
59. *Battles and Leaders of the Civil War*, Edited by Robert Underwood Johnson and Clarence Clough Buel, Vol. 4, New York: The Century Company, 1884, 563.
60. Schmutz, *Battle of the Crater*, 65; Slotkin, *No Quarter*, 127.
61. Schmutz, *Battle of the Crater*, 71–72; Slotkin, *No Quarter*, 127.
62. Slotkin, *No Quarter*, 131.
63. Schmutz, *Battle of the Crater*, 66.
64. Slotkin, *No Quarter*, 138.
65. Ibid., 139.

66. Ibid.
67. Schmutz, *Battle of the Crater*, 89.
68. Ibid., 90.
69. Ibid.
70. *Battles and Leaders of the Civil War*, Edited by Robert Underwood Johnson and Clarence Clough Buel, Vol. 4, New York: The Century Company, 1884.
71. *Battles and Leaders*, 563.
72. *Battles and Leaders*, 564.
73. Slotkin, *No Quarter*, 140.
74. Schmutz, *Battle of the Crater*, 97; Slotkin, *No Quarter*, 141.
75. Slotkin, *No Quarter*, 141.
76. Schmutz, *Battle of the Crater*, 94.
77. Slotkin, *No Quarter*, 141.
78. Ibid.,
79. Trudeau, *Like Men of War*, 251.
80. Slotkin, *No Quarter*, 145.
81. Ibid., 146.
82. Ibid.
83. Schmutz, *Battle of the Crater*, 100; Slotkin, *No Quarter*, 147.
84. Slotkin, *No Quarter*, 69.
85. Ibid.
86. *Battles and Leaders*, 563.
87. *Memorial*, 16.
88. Schmutz, *Battle of the Crater*, 114; Slotkin, *No Quarter*, 176.
89. Slotkin, *No Quarter*, 169.
90. The last two lines of Thomas Campbell's "Lochiel's Warning" are: "And leaving in battle no blot on his name,/ Look proudly to Heaven from the death-bed of fame"
91. *Memorial*, 80.
92. Schmutz, *Battle of the Crater*, 128; Slotkin, *No Quarter*, 172–173, 175.
93. Slotkin, *No Quarter*, 182.
94. Schmutz, *Battle of the Crater*, 116; Slotkin, *No Quarter*, 149, 171.
95. Schmutz, *Battle of the Crater*, 105; Slotkin, *No Quarter*, 151.
96. Schmutz, *Battle of the Crater*, 197; Slotkin, *No Quarter*, 232.
97. U. S. Congress, Joint Committee on the Conduct of the War, *Report of the Joint Committee on the Conduct of the War on the Attack on Petersburg, on the 30th Day of July, 1864*, Washington: Government Print Office, 1865, 125.
98. Slotkin, *No Quarter*, 165.

99. U. S. Congress, *Committee on the Conduct of the War*, 124.
100. Ibid., 323.
101. Ibid., 221.
102. Slotkin, *No Quarter*, 298.
103. Ibid., 193.
104. Ibid., 192.
105. U. S. Congress, *Committee on the Conduct of the War*, 125.
106. Slotkin, *No Quarter*, 197.
107. Schmutz, *Battle of the Crater*, 192; Slotkin, *No Quarter*, 229.
108. Schmutz, *Battle of the Crater*, 213; Slotkin, *No Quarter*, 230.
109. Slotkin, *No Quarter*, 232–233.
110. Ibid., 234.
111. Ibid.
112. Slotkin, *No Quarter*, 237.
113. Ibid.
114. Ibid., 237–239.
115. Ibid., 240.
116. Ibid.
117. Ibid., 241.
118. Ibid., 243.
119. Ibid., 249.
120. Ibid., 249–250.
121. Ibid., 252.
122. Ibid., 253.
123. Ibid.
124. Schmutz, *Battle of the Crater*, 234.
125. *Memorial*, 17.
126. Ibid., 18.
127. Ibid., 31.
128. Ibid., 33. Frederick A. Chapman, born in 1843 in New York or Massachusetts, went to work at age 13 as an errand boy at the office of William's *Democratic Press* to support his widowed mother. He moved to Lake Forest, Illinois, in 1858 to attend Lake Forest Academy, graduating in the first graduating class in 1861 and then attending its college class until 1862, when school was terminated because of the war. He joined a Chicago Board of Trade battery and later became a lieutenant in John's 29th USCT Regiment. After the war Chapman worked at the Board of Trade in Chicago. In 1874 Chapman and his wife, Ellen,

had a son whom they named Jesse Bross Chapman, who died at the age of 2. Chapman died in 1880, aged 37, nearly the same age as John (38) at the time of his death.

129. At the Proceedings of the Chicago Bar in John's memory three weeks after his death, George Herbert said that "on the parapet of the enemy, planting the flag of the country—the flag he so much loved—he fell, covered with the folds of that flag and with glory." At the same event, Major Stevenson said, "He fell as heroes fall, with the old flag, so dear to him, in his hand, nearest the enemy."
130. Slotkin, *No Quarter*, 254.
131. Schmutz, *Battle of the Crater*, 235.
132. Ibid., 240.
133. Slotkin, *No Quarter*, 273.
134. Ibid., 274.
135. Ibid., 277.
136. Ibid., 280.
137. Ibid., 285.
138. Ibid., 288.
139. Schmutz, *Battle of the Crater*, 292.
140. Slotkin, *No Quarter*, 290.
141. Ibid., 291.
142. Ibid., 290.
143. Ibid., 294.
144. *Memorial*, 15.
145. Slotkin, *No Quarter*, 335.
146. Miller, *Black Civil War Soldiers*, 83.
147. U. S. Congress, *Committee on the Conduct of the War*, 52.
148. McPherson, *Battle Cry*, 760.
149. Slotkin, *No Quarter*, 351.
150. Ibid., 305.
151. Ibid., 309.
152. Ibid., 330.
153. Thomas, *Abraham Lincoln; A Biography*, 567.
154. Slotkin, *No Quarter*, 333.
155. Ibid., 334.
156. Ibid., 352.
157. Ibid., 350.

158. U. S. Congress, *Committee on the Conduct of the War*, 125.
159. Slotkin, *No Quarter*, 325.
160. Ibid., 303, 312.
161. McPherson, *Battle Cry of Freedom*, 687.
162. *Memorial*, 19.

CHAPTER 8

Memorials

On August 3, 1864, four days after the battle, the *Chicago Tribune* printed on the front page a detailed account of the battle and its results, and also the following article about John, probably written by William:

> "Lt.-Col. John A. Bross"
>
> The dispatches received yesterday, both in private and news telegrams, make certain and prophetic the boding chill with which the friends of Lieut. Col. John A. Bross in this city, read the earliest advice that his command, the Twenty-ninth Colored Volunteers, was among the seven devoted colored regiments thrown into the "imminent deadly breach" in the operations before Petersburg on Sunday last. The briefly outlined picture of the extremity of that peril, the general statement of the appalling struggle, and the cloud of gloom that at the end rested on the ill-starred portion of that day's undertakings, were all melancholy suggestions of fears as to the fate of this gallant officer. Concerning him it was known that he would do his whole duty, even in that hour when the path of duty was the road to death. He has fallen. The accursed rebellion has claimed another victim from among our sons and brothers.
>
> John A. Bross, the fifth son of Dea. Moses Bross, now of Morris, in

this State, was born at Milford, Pike county. Penn., February 21st, 1826. He received a thorough academic education at the Chester Academy in Orange county, New York. He entered as a student the law office of Messrs. Booth & Jansen in Goshen, New York, and completed his studies with Hon. Grant Goodrich in Chicago, coming hither in December, 1848. He at once entered on the practice of his profession in this city, winning and holding an honored position among his brethren at the bar. In June 1856, he was united in marriage to Miss Belle Mason, eldest daughter of Hon. Nelson Mason, of Sterling, Ill. The fruit of their union is a little son of three summers, old enough to enjoy and clap his hands at the spectacle of the pageant of departure of his father's regiment, not old enough to realize the blow that has made him fatherless.

The breaking out of the war for the Union very early called the attention of the subject of this sketch from private pursuits, in which he was winning honor and success, and from a home whose happiness was unmarred. Actuated by patriotism, not ambition, by a desire to serve his country in her peril, he recruited a company for the 88th Illinois regiment, Col. Frank Sherman commanding, and as its Captain led it in the battles of Perryville, Stone River, and Chickamauga, participating in the thickest of these battles, and winning high encomiums from his brother officers and renewed confidence from his men, by his heroism and self-devotion.

His views and insight into the nature of this struggle, his hatred of the cause of the rebellion, his sympathy with the oppressed race for whose oppression he saw our nation visited with direful penalty, had, at the outset, prepared him for the stage in the war, reached by others through a conquest of bitter prejudice. He believed in the manhood of the colored race, and recognized in them a powerful agency, under Providence, for turning against themselves the devices of their oppressors and our enemies. Thus in favor of the arming of the blacks in the cause of the Union, he interested himself with a zeal in the formation of the colored regiments accepted from this State. The regiment rendezvoused at Quincy, and under his command was mustered as the 29th U.S. Colored Infantry. While he wrought with zeal to further recruiting in this State, his influence and attention to his recruits in camp rapidly advanced them in soldierly acquirements. When the regiment was ordered forward, its numbers yet unfilled, it won high praise for its perfection in drill, and reflected high credit on our State and city, as accorded by all who saw it en route to the front, in the Virginia theater of war.

It was with a perfect realization and most complete acceptance of the enhanced perils of his position that Lt. Col. Bross thus went forward a second time in the service of his country. In his farewells to his friends, in his partings with relatives, he took no pains to conceal his convictions that the path that lay before him was one along which his returning footsteps might not pass. Fort Pillow still shone freshly red in the annals of rebel ferocity; but the malignant brutalisms they held in store for all colored troops and their officers he looked calmly upon, and went forward. Then followed a brief and unimportant connection with the campaign against Richmond, chiefly in guard duty, the regiment, meanwhile, receiving further accession to its numbers, until it would shortly have been full.

Suddenly from out of the comparative lull of the arms, comes the springing of the mine in the enemy's center, and our devoted columns are thrown forward in an assault, the details of which will thrill coming ages and be read in the history of earth's battles, long after more peaceful pages in our national history shall have been turned. In this assault, which became a carnage, among the slaughtered victims of his own regiment and the hero-dead of the Ninth corps, fell John A. Bross. It is a melancholy but genuine relief that he died as a soldier would wish to die—on the field—and escaped that other fate we know he had dreaded yet more—the tortures and butchery that our enemies hold in store, as yet unrebuked by this Government, for our officers and men of our colored regiments.

Thus has ended another young and promising manhood passed from among us into the history of this peril and salvation of our republic. None have met the death of the soldier more heroically or calmly. He recognized the nature of this struggle and the priceless sacrifices it would cost, and did not shrink to contemplate the possible record of his own among them. Nor was he ever disturbed or swayed by the timid question of doubtful patriotism, "*Is it worth all this?*" A Christian, recognizing a Providence in all the concerns of nations as of men, we believe it of him that had the question been asked in his moment of extremest pain and peril, when death raged about him, when shot and shell plowed furrows through the ranks of living men at his side, when his own life was ebbing, and the thought of loved ones came nearer to his mind—"*Is it worth all this?*"—he would have looked beyond the present peril and anguish of the hour, to the happier state of a nation rescued through such sacrifices, and answered, "Yes—worth this and a thousand fold more to purchase Peace under Liberty, and the perpetuity of our institutions for the millions who are to come after us."

From such sacrifices that are falling thick and fast among our homes, by the purchase of these lives laid down that a nation may live, will come the reward of all this suffering—a rescued country, its foundations cemented anew in the blood of its patriot sons. Of these Chicago has a share, the present desolations of which rest heavily upon many hearts and homes.

The next day, August 4, the *Tribune* printed another article about John:

"Col. John A. Bross"

This lamented hero who fell in the assault on the rebel works at Petersburg at the head of the 29th regiment U. S. Colored volunteers, was a pure, brave, earnest patriot. He accepted his command, not from motives of personal ambition, but from a religious sense of his duty to his fellow men, and from that sentiment of true chivalry which inspires the Christian martyr to give his life for the oppressed and to brave prejudice in behalf of the lowly. Our country has lost no truer, nobler son. He went forth knowing his fate. No earthly reward—no common patriotism would have induced him to make the certain sacrifice, for such he regarded it—such it has proven. He fought not only for the integrity of our Government—a motive at best of enlarged and enlightened

> selfishness—but for the freedom of the slave, a motive Christ-like, unselfish, and which less noble minds cannot even appreciate. He has gone to the reward which his deep convictions of truth and duty ever presented to his mind and heart as the highest to which mortal could aspire, for had not Christ taught "Inasmuch as ye have done it unto the least of these ye have done it unto me."

Also on August 4, the *Tribune* carried a dispatch from Springfield dated August 3 containing several items, including the following:

> "The news of the death of Col. John A. Bross before Petersburg, which was brought to this city by Col. Mann, of the 39th, this morning, created a very painful sensation here. Governor Yates was much affected at the tidings, and had the National flag at the Executive Mansion raised to half-mast, as a mark of respect to the deceased."

On August 6, the *Tribune* reported a meeting of the Chicago Bar:[1] "The Late Lieut. Col. Bross. Meeting of the Chicago Bar. A meeting of the Chicago Bar was held on Thursday last in the Tremont House, for the purpose of taking action with regard to the death of the late Lieutenant Colonel John A. Bross, 29th U. S. Colored volunteers. There was a full attendance." A committee of seven was appointed by the Chair to draft "resolutions expressive of the sentiments of the Bar in relation to the deceased," and a committee of three was appointed "to confer with the friends of the deceased on the subject of making arrangements for the funeral, and to report their action to an adjourned meeting of the bar."

The meeting of the Chicago Bar in John's memory was held on August 18. The proceedings of that meeting, including speeches, were printed in the *Tribune,* but the *Memorial* includes a fuller account, some twenty printed pages of resolutions and sixteen speeches offered at that meeting and in two later court appearances about John's life, character, and selfless patriotism. The *Memorial* has recently been reprinted, so the full text of the speeches is available there.[2] The following few quotations give a sense of the respect in the Chicago community for John as a lawyer and citizen of Chicago and for the cause to which he gave his life. John was neither a high elected official nor the head of his professional organization, nor a man of great wealth, but so many and such heartfelt tributes indicate that he was a prominent and beloved figure in the community and that his loss was sincerely mourned.

From the "Resolutions":

> Whereas, Our friend and brother, Lieutenant Colonel John A. Bross, 29th regiment U.S. Colored Troops, has fallen upon the field of battle—another victim upon the altar of our country,
>
> Resolved, That by his glorious death this Bar has lost one of its most cherished members, his regiment an able and fearless commander, the country a brave soldier, and humanity an earnest advocate and uncompromising friend....
>
> Resolved, That though we shall miss Colonel Bross in the halls of Justice and in other walks of our common profession, we shall not cease to remember the urbanity of his deportment, the geniality of his companionship, the integrity of his purposes, and the honesty of his heart.[3]

From Remarks of George Herbert, Esq.:

> You all know his industry, his urbanity, his genial spirit, his integrity, his sense of professional honor, and the truthfulness of his unostentatious life.... His conviction of the great fact that "God had made of one blood all the nations to dwell upon all the face of the earth," had early been with him a settled principle of faith; and when the Government decided to call forth that great element of power representing four millions of our population and give them their position as men in this conflict, no one was surprised that Captain Bross applied for power to enlist a regiment in Illinois.... With him the great brotherhood of man had its foundation in a common Creator, a common ancestry, and a common destiny, and anything that practically denied that, was to him infidelity.[4]

From Remarks of Hon. Grant Goodrich:

> His virtues were well known to all who were honored by his friendship.... In his private life he was a slave to no vice, and was almost a perfect model of manhood. All who knew him well, speak of him with feelings of respect and affection. While they, his professional brethren, mourn his death, there is mingled with their sorrow, a feeling of pride that another member of their profession has distinguished himself as a soldier patriot.[5]

From Remarks of Major Stevenson:

> I must say here, not because he is dead and I would speak in eulogy of him, but because truth compels me, that he was one of the best, most temperate and efficient officers in the division.... In the rain and tempest, and under the scorching rays of a Southern sun, he lived with his men, doing his duty as a soldier and a patriot.... In battle there was none braver than he. At Stone River and Chickamauga, battles historic for the bravery of our troops against heavy numerical superiority of the enemy, he displayed that coolness and determination which fitted him so much for a higher command....
>
> But it seems to me Colonel Bross had still greater moral courage than we gave him credit for. He has shown it in taking command of colored troops. To take this step required a man of nerve and fortitude, for he knew that to the officers of colored troops there was no imprisonment like unto others, but certain death awaited them should the chances of war cast them into the hands of the enemy. But with full knowledge of all this, he went bravely into the contest, because he believed it to be his duty to his country and his God.[6]

From Remarks of L.B. Taft:

> He always had a kind word for every one, true as steel to all his friends, and whenever he met those whom affliction or adversity had visited, he consoled them with words of sympathy and kindness.[7]

From Remarks of Hon. I. N. Arnold, Member of Congress:

> I remember very vividly my last interview with him. It was the Saturday before he marched from his camp, near Alexandria, to join the forces of Grant, confronting Lee. I drove over with my family from Washington to his quarters. It was a most beautiful sunny afternoon, and I saw him with great pride review his regiment on dress parade. He had received his marching orders, and was full of enthusiasm and very proud of his regiment. He assured me that in capacity for service, endurance, courage, and all the qualities of a soldier, his regiment of negroes would not be outdone by any regiment, white or black, in the service. He took a seat in my carriage and rode with me a short distance towards Washington. I parted with him as the sun sunk behind the blue hills of Virginia, and as we shook hands in farewell, I never was more impressed by any man He was sun-burnt and manly—his large, fine, manly form full of health and vigor, filled with the martial ardor of the soldier and the hero. He struck his tents that night—led his gallant regiment to Petersburgh, and found there the death of a hero and a martyr. I can truly say that in all the rich sacrifices of this war there has fallen not one more manly, brave and true: none more patriotic and disinterested: no more worthy Christian soldier than John A. Bross.[8]

The *Memorial* includes extracts from several letters that Belle received from fellow officers and soldiers of John's regiment. The following few quotations are typical:

> The Colonel was endeared to us all. His virtues, his noble, open and frank heart, attracted all, and compelled admiration.... He was not only brave on the field, but possessed that moral courage which sustained him in the camp. Throughout the whole Division he was known and loved, and the universal expression is, "had he only lived." ...[9]

> We know your loss is great; but we too miss him, and you hardly know

> how sadly. I had learned to love him as brother, and in memory of him, tears will come. All who knew him, were forced to respect his superior character. ... [10]

> Our Colonel was a man universally beloved by officers and men. His life among us was so fee from any fault, so consistent as a Christian, that it challenged and won our entire confidence and love. In the management of his men, he was firm, yet kind, and though, as becomes an officer, a rigid disciplinarian, he happily had the judgment to blend kindness with discipline, and justice with moderation. His associations with his officers were of so generous a nature, that they seemed more of a friend than commander. ... His name is often heard among the men, who think, and truly, that they will never again be led by a man in whom they can have such perfect confidence as they had in Colonel Bross.[11]

Finally, the *Memorial* includes a memorial sermon preached at Third Presbyterian Church, Chicago, on December 11, 1864, by Arthur Swazey, the pastor of the church since 1860, succeeding Ashael Brooks, who had married John and Belle in 1856.

The sermon, which fills fourteen printed pages, reflects on the abolition of slavery as an example of the nature of truth, which is "always antagonistical, more or less, to the prevailing order of things," always likely to cause strife. Characteristically for the times, the pastor distinguishes between abolition and equality: "Whether the negro be equal or not to another man, (which need not be asserted nor denied,) suppose him to be born free, having the natural right to liberty and the pursuit of happiness." That first step of freedom, which was not the same thing as equality, was bound to produce conflict. "Truth gets her charter from God, but, sorrowful to say, her seal is blood. This he [John] knew full well." John is remembered as "a good husband, a tender father, a kind and generous neighbor. ... He was a faithful and much-loved member of this Church." The pastor ends with a prayer for "victory to our arms," for a speedy end to days of national trial and domestic anguish, and for repentance: "May we all learn that life is not in length of days, but in deeds; that an early grave found in the service of our country and of God, is better than a long life of self-indulgence; that he who dies with uplifted arm against iniquity, dies not, but becomes immortal!"[12]

A stone obelisk memorial to John was placed in Rose Hill Cemetery in the same family lot which holds the remains of Cora. The inscription on the front of the monument reads:

to the memory of
JOHN A. BROSS
Col. 29. U.S. Colored Troops
Killed at the assault
on Petersburg Va and buried
on the battlefield July 30, 1864
---------- o ---------
virtute vixit - memoria vivet
gloria vivet
---------- o ---------

Perryville	Oct. 8, 1862
Murfreesboro	Dec. 31, 1862
Chickamauga	Sept. 19, 1863
Petersburg	July 30, 1864

On the south side of the obelisk there is another inscription:

CORA,
only daughter of
John A. & Isabelle
BROSS
died July 6, 1861
aged 2 ½ years

After the war, in 1886, Union veterans in Springfeld, Illinois, who had been in the U.S. Colored Troops, formed a post of the Grand Army of the

William Freeman, Recruit, Company A, 29th Infantry, United States Colored Troops (Courtesy of Kathleen Heyworth).

Republic. Most had been members of the 29th USCT and when they applied for a charter, they named it the John Bross Post in honor of their fallen colonel. The John Bross Post 578 existed until 1913.[13]

On April 14, 2003, a memorial plaque for John was dedicated at Lake Forest College, Lake Forest, Illinois, of which William Bross was a founder and for many years a trustee. Prior to the dedication, Dorothy Drinkard-Hawkshawe, Professor of History and Director of the African and African American Studies Program at East Tennessee State University and author of *Illinois Freedom Fighters: a Civil War Saga of the 29th Infantry, United States Colored Troops* (1998), gave a lecture at the college's Lily Reid Holt Memorial Chapel; the lecture was entitled "Illinois Freedom Fighters: A Dedication to the Soldiers and Officers of the 29th Infantry, USCT." She began the lecture in a communal African way, with a libation invoking the ancestors who fought in the 29th USCT Regiment, the gathered community saying Amen. At the dedication of the plaque in the courtyard of Deerpath Hall, there was a presentation and retirement of the colors by military personnel from Naval Station Great Lakes in Waukegan, Illinois. The presence of a U.S. military color guard at this memorial to a fallen soldier, some 140 years after his death, expresses the official ongoing memory of the U.S. federal government for those who fought and died for the flag of the United States and the freedom and equality it stood for.

The text of the memorial plaque is as follows:

In Memory Of
LT. COLONEL JOHN A. BROSS
February 21, 1826 – July 30, 1864
Regimental Commander of the
TWENTY-NINTH INFANTRY, U.S.C.T.

An Illinois Regiment of African American troops

who was killed in action while planting the American flag on the enemy's
parapet at the Battle of the Crater, near Petersburg, Virginia

"Whatever be my fate, I know I can give to my child this one thing,
'His father fought for the Union and the old flag.' "
(from a letter of June 5, 1864 to his wife.)

NOTES

1. This was prior to the formation of the Chicago Bar Association.
2. The *Memorial* has recently been republished three times, online by Big Byte Books and in paperback by Sabin Americana and by Kessinger Legacy Reprints. An online description of the book by Big Byte Books (2016) noted: "John A. Bross is forgotten today, while Robert Gould Shaw, the commander portrayed by Matthew Broderick in the film *Glory* gained fame immediately upon his death that has endured. Both events are remarkably similar—two young Union colonels who led African American troops and who died very nearly one year apart"(February 2016).
3. *Memorial*, 58.
4. Ibid., 59.
5. Ibid., 61.
6. Ibid., 63.
7. Ibid., 65.
8. Ibid., 67
9. Ibid., 33.
10. Ibid., 34.
11. Ibid., 35.
12. Ibid., 54.
13. Kathleen Heyworth, *Private Lewis Martin and African-American Civil War Soldiers in Springfield, Illinois* (Springfield, IL: Bluelily Press, 2015), 46.

CHAPTER 9

What It Meant, What It Means

The story of John's life and death is representative of many Americans who moved west during the 19th century and of many men who volunteered to serve as officers in the Union Army during the Civil War. However, his decision to take command of an African-American regiment places him in a smaller category of Union officers who personally embraced the acceptance of blacks as U.S. soldiers and, by implication, as citizens. Not all officers of black troops agreed that blacks should have the right to vote, and there is no positive statement in John's letters or in the *Memorial* that John was in favor of suffrage for blacks.[1] But the general tenor of the letters and resolutions about John, and the statements in the *Tribune*'s front-page memorial article, probably written by William, about John's "sympathy with the oppressed race" and that he "believed in the manhood of the colored race" suggest that he would have approved the passage, five years later, of the fifteenth amendment to the Constitution, which specifically affirmed the right of all citizens to vote regardless of their race, color, or previous condition of servitude.

What was the real cause of the Civil War? How could one find some meaning in the unexpected and dreadful conflict? And what should be done as the war came to an end? President Lincoln's Second Inaugural Address gives perhaps the best and wisest answers to these questions and they all involve racial slavery and the racial prejudice on which it was based.

As to the cause of the war, Lincoln said: "One-eighth of the whole population were colored slaves, not distributed generally over the Union, but localized in the southern part of it. These slaves constituted a peculiar and powerful interest. All knew that this interest was somehow the cause of the war." There has been lengthy discussion of whether the war was about states' rights or really about economic rivalries such as Southern cotton versus Northern wheat. Lincoln's view seems better. The states' right for which the Confederate States were prepared to dissolve the Union was the right to hold human beings of African descent as slaves.[2] As to underlying economic causes, it seems disrespectful to the men and women of that or indeed of any time to ignore their stated reasons for risking their lives and property in a war and to claim instead that they were "really" fighting for some other unspoken cause unknown to them. Southern leaders stated very clearly that they intended to dissolve the Union in order to protect their peculiar institution of slavery. Leading voices among Northern political leaders and in the Northern press stated equally clearly at the start of the war that their purpose was to save the Union and two years later that their stated purpose had been expanded to include the abolition of slavery, partly because that was right but mostly because it was necessary in order to save the Union.

As to the fundamental meaning of the war, how it might be generally understood, Lincoln offered a mystical view from Old Testament sources that were known and accepted by virtually every American, both North and South, at the time:

> The Almighty has his own purposes. "Woe unto the world because of offenses; for it must needs be that offenses come; but woe to that man by whom the offense cometh." If we shall suppose that American slavery is one of those offenses which, in the providence of God, must needs come, but which, having continued through his appointed time, he now wills to remove, and that he gives to both North and South this terrible war, as the woe due to those by whom the offense came, shall we discern therein any departure from those divine attributes

> which the believers in a living God always ascribe to him? Fondly do we hope—fervently do we pray—that this mighty scourge of war may speedily pass away. Yet, if God wills that it continue until all the wealth piled by the bondman's two hundred and fifty years of unrequited toil shall be sunk, and until every drop of blood drawn with the lash shall be paid by another drawn with the sword, as was said three thousand years ago, so still it must be said, "The judgments of the Lord are true and righteous altogether."[3]

As to what should now be done, Lincoln ended his brief speech with words that have become part of the American heritage: "With malice toward none; with charity for all; with firmness in the right, as God gives us to see the right, let us strive on to finish the work we are in; to bind up the nation's wounds; to care for him who shall have borne the battle, and for his widow, and his orphan—to do all which may achieve and cherish a just and lasting peace among ourselves, and with all nations."

Racial slavery appears clearly in the first two of these observations. Lincoln points to it as "somehow" the real cause of the war and offers, as a way to comprehend the terrible trial, the view that it was God's punishment imposed on the whole nation, both North and South, for the offense of racial slavery.

The racial element is also present, by implication, in the third point. Lincoln's vision of what the American Republic stood for was famously and briefly summarized in the Gettysburg Address, but there has been much discussion over the years about the meaning of the phrases he used in that short speech. Does "conceived in liberty" refer to individual rights, such as the right to own guns, or does it refer to the right of the nation as a whole to be free and independent? The "proposition that all men are created equal" enshrines Jefferson's phrase from the Declaration of Independence, which Lincoln clearly considered central to the new American form of government and a beacon of hope to the world. How does the "new birth of freedom" relate to those two concepts? Did "freedom" at the end of the speech mean something different from "liberty" at the beginning? If slavery based on race was, in his view, the real cause of the war and the essence of the way to understand it, then his vision for the road ahead must have rejected both slavery and the racism that underlay it. He had already concluded that slavery had to be abolished to save the Union, and he clearly implied several times that his decision to enlist black soldiers meant that those soldiers, having fought for the Union, must be permitted to become full citizens of the republic they had fought to save. The "new birth of freedom," then, would refer not only to the idea of liberty enlarged to include the abolition of slavery but also to a society with a new understanding of equality in which men of all races would enjoy legal equality and probably eventually social equality. This would be fully consistent with the obvious meaning of Jefferson's phrase, although Jefferson himself shrank from acknowledging it. And this is probably what Lincoln had in mind when he spoke, in the Second Inaugural Address, of doing "all which may achieve and cherish a just and lasting peace among ourselves and with all nations." It would imply a sweeping change in Southern society but also a major change in Northern society, where racial prejudice, if not slavery, was almost as firmly entrenched as in the South, if not more so.

Lincoln probably understood better than anyone else the background and politics as well as the military situation of the war. It is one of the tragedies of American history that he was murdered shortly after the military victory since he was the only person who had the political authority, and the political wisdom and skill, to guide the nation towards a creative new beginning. George Washington led the nation to victory in the War of Independence, but he also acted as its leader for the first two presidential terms that were crucial to its formation. Had Washington been killed soon after Yorktown by an embittered loyalist, the American colonies might have remained a collection of separate political entities tenuously connected by the weak confederation that existed at the end of the war; there might have been no effective national union. Had Lincoln not been killed by a vengeful racist shortly after Appomattox, had he survived to complete his second term, the sour legacy of a failed Reconstruction and lingering economic depression in the South, bound together with the officially supported racism of white supremacy, Jim Crow, and the Ku Klux Klan, might have been at least to some extent avoided.

But racism was hard to kill and was itself a deadly killer. It caused the murder of Lincoln, and it arguably caused the disaster at the Crater. It has been recognized that Grant, when he became President, had two major challenges: reconciliation and emancipation; that he successfully dealt with the first but that the challenge of true emancipation, which would have included equal citizenship for all races, was not met.[4] In effect, the price for successful reconciliation in late nineteenth century America was acceptance of white supremacy and Jim Crow. The new birth of freedom did not begin to arrive fully until the civil rights movement of the 1960s led by Martin Luther King. And racism is undeniably still a powerful force in American society as this is written in 2017.[5] President Obama said in his farewell address in Chicago in December 2016, "After my election, there was talk of a post-racial America. Such a vision, no matter how well-intended, was never realistic. Race remains a potent and often divisive force in our society." He also said, "For every two steps forward, it often feels we take one step back. But the long sweep of America has been defined by forward motion, a constant widening of our founding creeds to embrace all and not just some."

The white officers of the Union Army, including John, who served with black troops, were the ones most closely connected with the underlying racial character of the conflict, most directly committed to the establishment of a new birth of freedom in accordance with Lincoln's vision, even if many of those officers were not at the time in favor of giving blacks the right to vote.[6] The disaster at the Crater may have contributed to the white supremacy opinions that did become prevalent and officially supported in the late nineteenth century and the first half of the twentieth century, but John, as a committed commander of free black soldiers, was prominent among those who laid the foundation for an American society in which all men (and women) would be viewed as fully equal, even though significant progress on this was to be postponed for at least another century.

One of the black privates in the 29th Regiment wrote his own letter to Belle, stating his view that John was a "friend to everyone"—meaning a friend to the black soldiers—who "tried to deliver his people out of Egypt."[7] Presumably such a leader would have favored the free and equal society that Lincoln had in mind.

Camp near Petersburgh

Mrs. Colonel Bross:

Respected Madam: You will please excuse this letter, that I pen to you, but as I am one of the soldiers brought up under his discipline, I deem it my duty to address you. Allow me to say, that although a colored man, a private in the 29th, I found in Colonel Bross a friend, one in whom every member of the regiment placed the utmost confidence, for, and with whom, each one would help defend the country to the end. Yes, I can say with truth, they would willingly die by his side. I was with him from the time the regiment left Quincy, until he reached the land of liberty or death. He loved his country, and fought for it, and may the Almighty never suffer his name to be blotted out of history. The 29th, with its leader gone, feels there is no such commander under the sun, to lead it forward and cheer it up. He was loved by everyone, because he was a friend to every one. God has received him unto himself, and may he give peace to the hearts of us who loved him. Weep not for him who was one of God's chosen ones, who tried to deliver his people out of Egypt. But his appointed time had come to be changed, and God works all things for the best. Fearing I might tire your patience with my poor letter, I will close.

Respectfully,
Willis A. Bogart

NOTES

1. Joseph T. Glatthaar, *Forged in Battle: The Civil War Alliance of Black Soldiers and White Officers* (Baton Rouge: Louisiana State University Press, 1990), 228–9.
2. James M. McPherson, *This Mighty Scourge: Perspectives on the Civil War* (New York: Oxford University Press, 2007), 94.
3. This was not a new thought for Lincoln. In a speech at Columbus, Ohio, in September, 1859, he said, "In contemplation of this thing, we all know he [Thomas Jefferson] was led to exclaim, 'I tremble for my country when I remember that God is just!' We know how he looked upon it when he thus expressed himself. There was danger to the country—danger of the avenging justice of God in that little unimportant popular sovereignty question of Judge Douglas. He supposed there was

a question of God's eternal justice wrapped up in the enslaving of any race of men, or any man, and that those who did so braved the arm of Jehovah—that when a nation thus dared the Almighty every friend of that nation had cause to dread His wrath." Abraham Lincoln, *Speeches and Writings 1859–1865* (New York: The Library of America 1980), 41.

4. Joan Waugh, *U. S. Grant; American Hero, American Myth* (Chapel Hill: University of North Carolina Press, 2009), 1–8; 303–8.
5. A December 24, 2016, *New York Times* article quoted Carl Paladino, "one-time Republican candidate for governor of New York and political ally of President-elect Donald J. Trump" answering "in response to an open-ended feature in which local figures were asked about their hopes for 2017. 'Obama catches mad cow disease after being caught having relations with a Herford', said Mr. Paladino, who ran unsuccessfully for governor in 2010, making an apparent reference to the Hereford cattle breed. He said he hoped the disease killed the President. Asked what he most wanted to see 'go away' in the new year, Mr. Paladino ... answered, 'Michelle Obama.' 'I'd like her to return to being a male and let loose in the outback of Zimbabwe where she lives comfortably in a cave with Maxie, the gorilla,' he said." It appears that the racist campaign of Republican presidential candidate Trump in 2016 created an atmosphere that encouraged the open expression of such "politically incorrect" views, previously kept under cover. It is ironic that the party of Lincoln came to use racism as a tool for building and protecting a white oligarchy.
6. There were approximately 180,000 black troops, with 7,000 white officers, out of a total of approximately 2,200,000 Union troops with an estimated total of approximately 86,000 officers. Glatthaar, *Forged in Battle*, x; 250
7. *Memorial*, 32.

PART TWO

The Civil War Letters of Colonel John A. Bross

CHAPTER 1

Letters from September 29 to December 31, 1862: Kentucky and Tennessee, Battle of Perryville

Camp near Louisville Ky
Sept 29th 1862

My Darling Wife!

Yours of the 22^{d} reached me yesterday on my return from "picket duty" with the regiment. How glad I was to hear from home you can scarcely appreciate. We went out on Saturday in a hard rain staid all night and the only effect it had on me was to make me as hungry as a bear. My Company was one of three in the extreme advance in the post of danger. 1st Lieutenant Abe Longworth of the 36th step son of Aunt Julia[1] at Morris was also with us. I have been so busy in camp I have had no time to do anything in the way of writing home or to any one else. Last Friday was the first day I was out of camp, in town to see about the soldiers' bounty. I saw Buells army come in & it was a sight worth seeing—while one of the regiments was marching past all begrimed with dust & dirt, James Curtiss Jr recognized me and was extremely glad to see me. It was the 15th regulars. We have moved our camp several times & are now located on the east side of the city near the river being the extreme left instead of the right as last week. To day there was a very sad occurrence resulting in the death of Gen Nelson. Almost every body says served him right. I am very well indeed. I do not know what will come of it when we go on a long march, but I think we shall be all right. I will always tell you whenever I am indisposed. I am careful of my diet & I am getting enured to it. My heart was somewhat stirred at hearing & reading Mason's letter. One of the first men I met at Louisville on Friday last was Col Wilson & son. He told me of seeing you & Mason & all the folks. We are getting ready to march and are expecting orders to move every hour. Our destination is unknown to us, but it is supposed to be Lexington. I am very glad the pictures are good. I should like one myself but I suppose they are all spoken for. You may stop the Evangelist and Herald & tell them I shall pay the balance due them as soon as I can. I would like father to see about recutting that 40 acres in DeKalb Co. What to do with my dress coat I do not know! All the officers trunks are ordered out of the regiment, and I have no fitting valise to take my things. I have about decided to store them in Louisville & yet I don't wish to. I received a package of papers from father & one from you this morning. I read the resolutions of the inevitable Cobbey and Shaeffer with various & sundry comments. Chickens will roost at home in time. The ladies of the regiment never got over the river but one & she as a hospital nurse. To day I am "officer of the day" & have comparatively easy times. Herbert Blake called to see me to day. He is looking very well. I hope you will find something to occupy and amuse you. It is a pleasant thought to know that your loving heart is going out towards me while I am in camp or on the march far away from you. I forgot to mention above that I saw the 34th that Friday. Lt Col Bristol of Morrison & Robinson of Sterling & all of Co A. I did not know them all. I wish Sterling could see them just as they were.

Tuesday Eve Sept 30. I will now try and complete this letter. Have been making ready for the march with "light baggage" which means no tents & no baggage of any account. I will send my trunk home by express and key in this letter. We must "rough it" and have the open sky for our tents. We have already had a taste of it, and I think we can stand it. We must move quickly and with little impediments if we expect to meet and overtake the enemy and I am in favor of coming right down to sudden and quick marches and hit the hardest blows whenever we can. I want to be a good soldier and I am glad to see you approve my desire. Yours of the 24th reached me last night after I had written the 1st sheet. I threw down my eating utensils for the purpose of perusing it and I was truly rejoiced to receive a letter again so soon. To day we have had more changes in our brigade and division & corps. Our brigade is now the 37th Brigade 11th Division composed of the 36th & 88th Ills, 21st Michigan and 24th Wis Col Greusel comdg. Our Division is commanded by Gen E. Dumont an Indianian. We are in the 3d army corps. I understand that rations were issued in Louisville to day for 225,000 men. I would like to have two woolen shirts such as you bought me but at least six inches longer. I do not know however when I shall get them. I shall write again the first time a mail is sent back from the advance. Will Dinsmoor[2] is well. Bressler is sick in hospital not dangerous however. Give my best love to father & mother, Mason a thousand kisses. Annie I should love to see you & Em. I am hoping to be home at the interesting time when I will wear my "store clothes." May God bless you all is my earnest prayer.

Ever Yours
John A. Bross

1 Julia Winfield, the youngest sister of John's mother, Jane Winfield Bross, was married to Thomas Alford and was living in Morris, Illinois. In 1863, all but one of their children having gone west, Moses and Jane Bross also moved to Morris from Milford, Pennsylvania; they spent the rest of their lives in Morris.

2 John W. Dinsmoor, evidently a younger friend of the Masons from Sterling, was born c. 1842 in Lowell, Massachusetts, and entered military service on August 12, 1862, in Chicago.

Bivouac about 12 miles south of
Louisville. Oct 2d daylight.

Dearest.

We have been in "line of battle" ready to receive a visit from any band of secesh since 4 o'clock A.m. The regiment is now getting breakfast and I am writing you a line on a knapsack. We are on the road to Newburgh but we do not yet know whether we go to Bardstown or Lexington. Yesterday we took up the line of march from camp about 11 A.m. I rolled up my shawl, rubber blanket, a common soldiers over coat, strapped them on my back & with my haversack filled with crackers, a piece of chicken, two lemons, a towel, a little soap, a toothbrush, a pair of stockings, a little tea sugar, a small bottle of that Bourbon that Bro Will gave me, a pen & some ink, my sword & belt, you may imagine my appearance. Our march lay through a beautiful country & some fine old Kentucky homes made me feel like owning some of them. I trudged along at the head of my company & the scene together with thoughts of home and friends the talk of Orderly Rae & Capt Chickering[1] about the Chicago girls, the gay laugh of some, the swearing of others, the "falling out" of those who were unable to proceed further all kept my attention. Beside my other burdens I carried Rae's knapsack & gun for some distance. I feel sorry for the boy & Dinsmoor yet they are "gay" & merry although Rae complains hugely about his living. We arrived here about sundown, & as soon as I could I went off about ¼ of a mile & washed myself. It was very refreshing, after which you might see me seated beside my camp fire with a piece of fat bacon on a stick broiling over the fire. Directly the Col comes along and laughs heartily and approvingly at my situation. Some of the line officers cannot yet come down to a soldiers life. I assure you that the bacon, hard cracker and a cup of tea made in a tin cup was eaten with a relish unknown to dyspeptics. Directly after this comes up one of my boys who is a perfect mischief. I asked him if he got along well on the march. He hesitatingly said yes & reached over to my ear & said he had 4 of the <u>dangdest</u> nicest pullets & a nigger that ever he <u>seed</u>. I am just now stopped to eat the pullets (not the nigger) together with sweet potatoes, good soup &c. This is a specimen of camp life. I slept on the ground with nothing but the stars above me. It was a glorious nap. I will finish this further on the march good by... Forenoon—after breakfast we fell in and left at ¼ to 7 & are now a mile or so in advance resting by the side of the road waiting for some other division to move. It is a very pleasant morning but it will be hot. My boys are in good spirits. I do not forget the scene two years ago this day in Chicago.[2] Little did I then think at that immense gathering of wide awakes of the change so soon to come over our beloved land & that I should be fighting for the preservation of our government, that I should leave the sweetest wife and dearest friends & bear trials hardships & exposure that our son may enjoy the same privileges under a beneficent, God given Republic. I sometimes have an anxiety that you may think because I sought a position in the army, my love for you was not of that all absorbing engrossing nature which we expect from each other. And yet I am sure you appreciate my motives. Nothing could take me from you but my country. While writing here two men of the Sterling Co Capt McMoore of the 75th passed with their canteens to get water. They knew me & spoke to me. The Regt is about a half mile from us. The call attention is made & I must be off—I halt. 11 A.m. We are now about 16 miles from Louisville the whole brigade have stacked arms and are resting by the side of the road. Perhaps you do not yet understand our marching with "light baggage." I have no clothes with me except my blouse pants shirt boots & stockings & my pack. Two ambulances to a regt, 5 officers tents for 30 line officers & only one team for a whole regt to carry the valises of the officers, tents, &c. If the team does not get up with the regt we sleep in the open air as we did last night. It is hot today and I have just learned that we have passed the point where the rebel scouts were last night. I have also learned that we are to return to town. It may be all right but this kind of marching back after making a forward movement I do not like. I would like to see secesh and give him a slight evidence of my regard. So perhaps I shall mail this in Louisville myself. - - Saturday morning Oct 4th. On the march. I have had no opportunity to close this letter. After writing the above I learned that the road we were then on had been blocked up by the rebels and the whole Division had to countermarch a mile or so from our stopping place & then take a by road in order to get on another. We started about 4 ½ P.m. it having rained considerably while laying by the road and it was about 9 o'clock before we reached camp, wet hungry & jaded & nothing much of anything in the mens haversacks to eat. I had a good cup of tea & hard cracker & lay down in the corner of a rail fence with some cornstalks on the top which was but little protection however from the rain. My rubber blanket however was just the thing to keep one dry. Was called precisely at 4, to form line of battle which was soon done & then, breakfast. There was some geese chickens & another nigger stolen the owner of which tried to get but the boys would not allow him to go back.[3] We were early on the move yesterday & passed through "Mount Washington" and camped last night in the valley of the east branch of salt river, a beautiful location. I had not been in camp 30 minutes before two of my boys brought in a full dressed sheep, an old bake kettle & salt to cook it. You may think my morals are getting rather loose in the way of gathering things for the palate. I tell you I have but little respect for Kentucky unionism. One man in Louisville told me, who is in the P.O. department that Lincoln's proclamation was worse than 30,000 rebels to Ky. & that as soon as we were through with the rebels he wanted a crack at the abolitionists. I was thoroughly disgusted & as for the unionism of this state I do not believe there is enough of real patriotism in its people of themselves to keep it in the Union. It is more the fear of the north than any thing else that keeps them in the Union. So I at least am ready to look after something to eat & not wait always the red tape of Uncle Sam or his QM wagons. We have been waiting on the bank of the stream for some regts ahead of us, forward is called & I am again off. We stop again & I write again. I ate two suppers last night, fried mutton & soup, tea &c. again just before going to bed took more soup as a lunch. It was delicious. It reminded me of the man whose face was made to shine with grease & gladness. This morning I luxuriated but cannot particularize. I do not forget Mason & yourself today, it being his birthday. How I would like to embrace you both & tell you again & again how much I love you. There is an immense force moving southward but I presume you know much more of the main movements than we do. I mention again we are in the 37th Brigade, 11th Division, 3d Army Corps Major Genl Gilbert comdg. I am in first rate health could not be better & one of my old whiskerando's this morning "reckoned I was tough as steel." Yesterdays march was very hot & poor Rae was nearly used up. I carried his gun a long way for him. These things do not injure me among the men. Dinsmoor is in good health. Willie Bross[4] is also very well. We are on the road to Bardstown. Will write more if I can get time & paper.

2d sheet

Sunday Oct 5th Noon. Bardstown Ky. When I stopped writing yesterday I did not quite expect to be here not knowing in which direction we should move. We had quite a long march and after striking the Louisville & Bardstown pike we had a fine chance for marching. We were kept on by roads hitherto & on our first gaining the road we passed the head quarters of Gen Buell. We camped last night seven miles north of this on ground occupied in the morning by the enemy. In the afternoon our advance Division (Woods) had a skirmish with Texan rangers. 5 companies of the 1st Ohio Cavalry were tempted beyond artillery & infantry support and were cut off by a large force of cavalry hidden from sight. As it was our cavalry did nobly in cutting through, about 40 of our men were taken prisoners the balance all safe. The major was wounded. I saw our men this morning already paroled—we took 13 prisoners. Genls Bragg, Hardee, Duncan & other rebs left yesterday. Our advance entered town from the north as the rebs left on the south. I have never realized until this morning that we were on the road to catch the enemy. It has seemed like parade more than anything else. I have seen a great many troops but this morning, the arrival of Divisions from various roads fills the mind with the power & resources of the Govt. I slept well last night & we were quite early on the march. I am also officer of the day & so do not have to be with my Co all day. It is something like Sunday being on the march & nothing to do but visit along the line. We are now waiting in the centre of the town for the passage of another Division & hence I write. We passed over the scene of yesterday's skirmish & the first sign of battle was a dead horse in the road & that was all, as only one man was killed & five or six of the rebs wounded who were carried off. As we were passing the scene of the skirmish the 4th U.S. regular cavalry were ordered to the front and as they filed by us I began to feel that we were on the track of the rascals. I felt pleased and am now ready to "pitch in." To day is the Sabbath but the steady tramp of infantry & the passing of artillery at a gallop is indicative of anything else but "peace on earth." The last regiment of the brigade we had to wait for is filing by us & I shall have to stop in order to "fall in."

Oct 9th Dearest since the above we have overhauled the enemy and I have been in a "fight." I shall not claim anything more than that I did my duty. Dinsmoor, Willie Bross & myself are safe. You will see a letter of mine in the Tribune. The courier is about to leave & I must close. Will try & bring up as I have time the occurrences from Sunday. I am well & hearty. Yourself & Mason was in my mind more than once yesterday. I thank God for his care of me. Will Dinsmoor & orderly Rae are heroes. Good bye. Love to all. Kisses for Mason

John

1 Orderlies were soldiers selected for intelligence and ability to attend on generals or officers. John W. Chickering was the captain of Company F in the 88th regiment.

2 A massive meeting of Chicago Wide Awakes, of which John served as Chief Marshal, was held in Chicago on October 2, 1860, a month before the presidential election.

3 Lincoln's preliminary Emancipation Proclamation was issued on September 22, 1862, but neither this nor the final Emancipation Proclamation, which took effect on January 1, 1863, applied to Kentucky because it was not one of the states in rebellion. Prior to January 1, 1863, Union forces generally took the position that escaped slaves from behind Confederate lines were "contraband," or enemy property, seized according to the rules of warfare, but Kentucky was not behind enemy lines. Kentucky did not abolish slavery during the Civil War, as did Maryland and Missouri, but about 75% of the slaves in Kentucky were freed or escaped to Union lines. Slavery legally ended in the United States on December 18, 1865, when the Thirteenth Amendment became part of the U.S. Constitution, but the Thirteenth Amendment was not ratified by Kentucky until 1976.

4 "Willie Bross" was John's nephew, the 13-year-old son of John's brother Josiah, who had enlisted as a musician in Company D. He deserted shortly after the Battle of Perryville in October 1862. There were no musicians in John's Company A.

Camp near Lancaster Ky
Oct 15th 1862

My Dear Sweet Wife!

I have a little time this morning to send you a line. I recd yours of Oct 2d at the secesh hospital camp near Perryville, & of the 7th this morning. You cannot appreciate the pleasure I received from them. Never have you appeared to my minds eye in so favorable light & father & mother & all of you, and my dear boy. I hope he will never forget his papa. You are never forgotten on the march or at night. I write while the roar of cannon is heard in our front and we may be ordered up at any moment. Still I will devote every moment to you. I cannot relate all the incidents that occurred on our march from Bardstown to the Battlefield. Sabbath eve we camped a few miles south east, next day we had a long and wearisome march as rear guard of the Division train of wagons, an endless string passing through Springfield & beyond about six miles eastward toward Perryville, reaching camp about midnight. I was tired & very hungry, but all of us as soon as we stacked arms, lay down in our tracks & slept, entirely oblivious of all around. I awoke in the morning as bright as a new dollar, made me a cup of coffee, soaked some hard cracker & with a little sugar made what I thought a capital breakfast. It only whetted my appetite. I borrowed some bacon, broiled it over the fire with a stick & took course No 2. After that, with expectations of being ordered off I run the risk of cooking some rice, which I succeeded in doing admirably making course No 3. With that I was satisfied. We lay there until afternoon when we took up the line of march & reached camp in the evening, where we remained until next day, Wednesday, the day of the battle until about 11 A.m. My cooking then was eminently successful. The last thing I did when the regiment was moving out of Camp was to almost drink a splendid dish of beef soup enabling me to go into battle on a full stomach. Do not think that I am entirely given to eating. Yet it is one of the points in a soldiers life. I often wish that you & mother & the girls could see us cooking. I have made a reputation among the boys in this respect. We marched from camp about two miles eastward on the Perryville road where it passes over a rise of ground between two hills. These hills to right & left of us were held by two batteries of artillery & we were their support. We were resting where we could see the battle raging on the left, (our position was the centre) & it was grand beyond description. On the left the 75th was placed & you have heard ere this of their calamity, the direct fruits of incompetent field officers. They went into action a mob & were cut to pieces like a flock of sheep. Their first fire I was told by one of their corporals was upon our own men. I have not seen the regt at all having met one of the corporals on the road.[1] While laying in the road our batteries kept up a continuous fire, between two & three P.m. we were ordered to form line of battle & advance over the hill on the right to repel a charge of a rebel brigade which was advancing to capture our battery. It was the key post of the centre. The enemy comd by Hardee were ordered to take it at all hazards. We marched over the hill & as quick as we appeared we were met by a shower of balls from the rebels hid in a cornfield in front of us & behind a rail fence. The hill between us fell away in a graceful slope about 50 rods with a few large oak trees growing on it. Down the hill we went about halfway when we halted and poured in our fire the men laying down on the ground. We had not advanced a rod from the brow of the hill before one of my best dutchmen was shot down close by me in the eye the ball lodging in the brain. I thought he was dead but strange to say he revived a little after the battle & lived three days. I wish I could describe the sound of the balls as they passed by me. I was so anxious for my men & to keep them in line that I had no time to stop & think of the dangers of the situation. The regt held its position bravely, loading and firing at will until the enemy took to their heels & then such a shout you never heard. The regt was ordered up the hill, reformed & marched down to the rail fence where we lay on our arms all night. The first thing when we reached there was three cheers & a tiger[2] for Capt Bross from my men. It was praise which came to the heart. I had done my whole duty as far as I could & I lay down thankful to God for preserving me to you and friends. I ate a hearty supper & slept as if I never had been away from your sight. The boys however could not sleep until all the incidents of the battle had been told over. One instance of coolness of one of my corporals is related by Mr Rae. The corporal fired 4 times & now said he I will stop & take a drink, which he did with all the coolness of camp life. I have many things to say about my first experience in battle if I live to get home but cannot now. I had seven wounded out of 52 men in action.

Crab Orchard 12 miles south of Lancaster, Ky. 16. We had a fine march yesterday of 14 miles. We stay here one day. The enemy are on a galloping retreat & we shall not catch them I fear. They are bound for Cumberland Gap. The 9th and 10 we camped near by the secesh Hospital and such a shocking sight I never saw or wish to again. With Longworth I visited the secesh line of battle the 3d day after the battle in a drenching rain. I cannot describe it. I was only affected to most indignant feelings as I saw piles of dead rebels. How vast the responsibility of the wicked leaders of this rebellion & I wished for the power of omnipotence to crush the satanic crew at a single blow. Never did I feel more like devoting our son body & soul to a life time of labor against this cursed pack of scoundrels who have spilled so much of brothers' blood. The heaps of dead showed the accuracy of our fire. In passing through the hospital I caught the eye of a wounded man who anxiously beckoned me to him. I stepped into the shed in which he lay. He asked me in a whisper to raise him up, he was shot through the lungs. He asked for a cup of water which I procured for him. He looked his thanks. I saw he was dying. I commended him to his maker told him to make his peace with God. I laid him gently down & in a moment he was in eternity. I cannot tell my feelings as we lay on that camp ground. I did not feel those solemn thoughts that would naturally arise. Rather was it a stern joy that we were victorious and that there lay all around us the evidence of justice asserting itself right through the heart & brain of rebeldom. I must now close this letter. I now wish a few articles, 2 pair of woolen undershirts of good length, 2 pair of drawers, a big woolen night cap to cover my head in sleeping out doors in winter, 2 pair of woolen socks, & that big pair of boots. I want them made very wide & 10 ½. Si will know what will suit me. Do them up in the smallest size package you can & direct to our Col Sherman 88th Ill vol. 37th Brigade 11th Division Louisville to follow the army, "Clothing" on outside. I know not when you can get any money from me as long as the campaign lasts we shall be on the march & no one will draw anything. Buells army was not paid for six months. I send this letter back by favor of Col Greusel. Love to all dear friends. Father mother sister Annie, Em &c. & Kisses for Mason.

Ever your affectionate husband
John A Bross

1 This reference is mystifying since most accounts of the battle indicate that the 75th Illinois, raised in Sterling, Illinois, many of whose men were known to the Masons, performed bravely under fire.

2 This was a contemporary cheer, apparently three hurrahs followed by a rising growl.

Camp near Crab Orchard
17th Oct.

Dearest!

I write a note this morning to tell you how to direct my package when you send it. Have it directed to care of N.S. Boutosi Brigade Quarter Master 37th Brigade 11th Division Louisville Ky, and it will then be forwarded on any of the teams in our train that go back to Louisville for supplies. We are bound I think for Cumberland Gap yet there is no certainty that we shall go directly there. I shall need the things by the time they reach me especially the boots. I am very well indeed. Have no time to write more. Love to all.

Ever your husband
John A. Bross

In camp Bowling Green Ky
Monday Nov 3d 1862

My Dear Sweet Wife!

Yours & fathers letters of Oct 17 came to hand to day and I was filled with joyful excitement as I hastily perused their contents & again and once again did I scan the pleasant words and familiar handwriting of those I love. We have now been more than a month on the march & I know from experience what a soldiers life is. We are here in camp to rest and re-clothe ourselves after chasing Bragg out of the state. I wrote you from Crab Orchard a long letter, which I hope you have received ere this, although Jack Morgan with his cavalry made a raid on Bardstown about that time & stole a large mail. At Crab Orchard we stopped the pursuit of Bragg, staid a couple of days then returned to Lancaster, thence to Danville, thence to New Market Ky. There we staid a couple of days and a storm of snow unprecedented for the time in this state occurred. It made us all shiver but nevertheless I got along nicely, in the big hospital tent. New Market is north of a high range of hills which we crossed on our march reaching Green river, the Little Barren, & camping on the 30 & 31, within 8 miles of the Monmouth cave but I did not get time to go and see it. We reached here the 1st last and we are recruiting our strength fast. I have stood it first rate except that I was a little sick at New Market because I ate too much & was bordering on the jaundice. Dr Coatsworth & asts have been very particular to help me out of this and I am again all right. My appetite is huge & I fear if I should come home all of a sudden, Mothers delicious table fare would be swept away in a twinkling & before she could recover her astonishment. Just imagine me sitting by the side of the road all covered with dust eating Government Shingle and bacon. The picture is not very attractive but you can "see it." Once in a while we "press" a good dinner on the march & then if ever, we should remember the injunction "put a knife to your throat" but we forget sometimes.

We are all heartily rejoiced to have a change in the command of our army. Rosecrans is satisfactory to us all. We are expecting to be on the march to Nashville in a few days. I will try & drop you another note ere we go. I am happy to know that you have seen & talked with Washburne.[1] It may have a favorable effect upon my prospects hereafter. I should like to get a good staff position although I like my present one very well. I am becoming familiar with its duties & getting the co affairs in good condition. There is an immense amount of labor to be done, but it is stirring, active life and it agrees with me. If I could get detailed on Rosecrans staff I should be pleased. I see Ducot is one of his aids, my friends at home may do me a great deal of good in this project if I enter into it. Post Quarter Master at some procurement point would be worth something in a pecuniary point of view in which I might call for the services of father.

Now as to Uncle Carlile the matter I thought was thoroughly understood as I spoke to him several times about it. My note is to be applied on Jansen & Bross' co account,[2] which I understand Uncle Carlile has to pay. I have nothing in the world to do with N. Macons individual a/c & do not wish my a/c to be mixed up with his. All that is necessary to be done is to let the note offset so much of Jansen & Bross' bill, over half of which is mine and more than balances the note and interest if I remember rightly. I hope this is plain enough. I never dreamed of making an arrangement by which my indebtedness should settle another mans claim against the person I owe. It takes three—all the parties interested to make such a settlement & Uncle Carlile will never claim that I ever did make such a request. I always spoke of J & B's bill. I hope this is plain enough. You do not mention Annie and Emma. How I would like to see you all and my boy Mason. May God bless you all. My heart yearns for you all and I hope to see you soon if I can get a furlough. It is not easy for that though in these campaigning times. Love to you all. Let me hear from [you] soon. Direct as before.

Yours ever
John A. Bross.

[In the margin] Will Dinsmoor is well & sends regards.

1 Elihu B. Washburne was an influential Republican congressman (Member of Congress) from Galena, Illinois. A political ally of Lincoln, he advocated for the promotion of Grant in the Union Army.

2 In 1848 William Bross started a bookselling firm in Chicago called Jansen & Bross; Jansen was probably a brother of William's wife, Jane Jansen Bross.

In Camp Nashville Tenn
Nov 8th 1862

My Dear Wife!

We arrived here yesterday in the afternoon and pitched our camp about a mile from town. We left Bowling Green Tuesday the 4th. I mailed you a letter there which I hope you recd. I am very well indeed & am "officer of the day" hence cannot go to town. There is an immense force concentrating here and I understand our destination is Chattanooga. I am very willing to go there but I hope the paymaster will come first. To day Maj Raymond of the 51st, Capt Haydon 19th & other officers visited our camp. I omitted to return thanks to father for his kind offer to send me some money. I need some but I hope to get some soon. We must forage on the enemy if we can do no better. I am going to try to get a furlough to come home Thanksgiving & Dec 1st but am not very hopeful as our campaigning for the fall months is just about to begin in reality unless something occurs, and if there is to be any "big thing" to happen I want to be where it is. I hope you have found a tenant for the house, also that Uncle Carlile will settle up that matter without any more words about it. I see by a stray Tribune that young John Phillips has a decree in his favor. I think I gave him a receipt in full of all demands but I made an agreement with Windett to deduct ¼ & if he succeeded I was to have the full amount. The deduction was about $45, if I mistake not, & he ought to pay it. I did not think of this, of his succeeding, when I gave Si a small order on John making it a receipt in full. That of course may be explained. I know not when we shall be paid off if we do not get it here, & in that event I shall be compelled to get Br Will to get my note at Scammons renewed. I will devote every cent I can towards that object. One great anxiety I have is that you may be shortened for means & father also on my account. I know Br Will will favor me in this respect. If I do not get the furlough to come home I wish you to assure Sister Em & my new (to be) brother of my earnest wishes & prayers for their happiness in their new relation. Nothing could give me greater satisfaction & pleasure than to come home to see you & Mason, father mother & Annie & witness Em's nuptials.[1] May she be blessed in her choice.

Our march from Bowling Green to this point was a pretty hard one. Thursday we marched 23 miles, but I did not feel so fatigued as on some other days when we marched a shorter distance. Somehow we all felt glad when we got out of Kentucky. Dinsmoor is very well & is "growing" on his marches, being a little more fleshy. So also Rae. They both send regards. I sent from Crab Orchard for some clothing. If you have not sent them do not send an overcoat as I expect to get one from the Q.M. that will serve every purpose & cost but little. In fact while campaigning I do not wish to spoil good clothes. Good socks are very desirable. I run out entirely & Abe Longworth gave me a pair. He is a capital fellow but oh how he does swear. It makes my hair stand on end almost as I hear such profanity from almost all. Yet there are a few that hold fast to their convictions and I love to see their consistency and once in a while it does me good to be with such & to unite our voices in praise to God for his goodness. When we shall move from here is unknown to me. If we could stay a couple of months, I should certainly have you here on a visit. I would be pleased to see father down this way if he could have time money & a permit to enter the lines. If I cannot get home this winter, I am going to send up a requisition to mother for a little butter & other "fixings" to delectotate my appetite with. How does Mr Dinsmoor get along? I was pleased to see by a Tribune one of my boys got Mr D's name attached to the address of the Rep State Com. By the by I get no papers from Chicago. I will be obliged if you will cut out of the Tribune any thing of importance, put it in an envelope & send it. Papers do not come regularly at all. Letters do however, or comparatively so. You might send me nearly a whole paper that way, cutting out the advertisements, although when we do get a paper I read it clear through. It is expensive I know to envelope letters but I must have some news once in a while. The RR north or rather south from Louisville is open to a little place just this side the Tennessee line where there is a tunnel blown up by the secesh. All our supplies will for the present have to be brought in team wagons until the RR is repaired. The distance is about 35 miles from here. We may be put on short rations for a few days but I hope not. I am ready for another march, although we have already marched 300 miles. It looks short by rail but let any one try it on foot & he will see the country & no mistake. When I get back I will be in trim for a series of "views afoot" either in Illinois or Europe. I will write again soon. Am hoping to hear from you soon. Kiss my dear boy a thousand times for me. How I should like to step in very suddenly upon you all. Love to all the dear ones.

Yours Ever
John

1 Nelson and Desire Mason had three daughters, Belle, born in 1837, Emily, born in 1840, and Ann, born in 1842. The Masons had moved back to Sterling in 1855, shortly before Belle's marriage to John. Emily married Zadok (Zed) Galt of Sterling on December 19, 1862. Belle and Mason moved back to live with her parents in 1863 for the duration of the war.

Nashville Tennessee
Nov 12, 1862. Evening

My Dear Wife!

I have just learned that the Sergt Major of our regiment goes to Louisville tomorrow and I take the opportunity to send you a note. I wrote you several days since but do not know whether it will ever reach you so I write very soon again. We have a beautiful camp here a short distance north of the Cumberland, in a large grove of trees belonging to secesh and we are using them for firewood &c. Our regiment is quite thinned out by sickness & exposure on the march. We arrived here on the 8th and do not know how long we shall stay. Hope it will be until we can get our pay from Government. I have recd nothing from you since your letter of 17th ult. and it being nearly a month you may judge that I am somewhat anxious to hear from you. I hope you and Mason and all friends are well and enjoying yourselves. It must be quite cold with you. The day we reached here was raw & a little snow fell but not enough to whiten the ground. Since then the weather has been delightful. To day our Division was reviewed by Gen Rosecrans. We stood on the ground about three hours and when he did come we were all pleased with his appearance and good nature. I do not know that I can write you any thing in the way of news from this quarter. We are all lying still waiting for our line of communication to be opened to the Kentucky line, that is the RR from here to Louisville. Since I wrote you the boys of the 19th & 34th have been visiting us freely among others Charley Wheeler. He is orderly of Co A. & at one time was in command of the company. They have been cooped up here nearly two months without communication with the north & scarcely any supplies, no coffee, tea nor sugar & other necessaries. We gave Charley a pretty good dinner and he was pretty thoroughly pleased. Charley Davis, Henry Howland & others have been over to see us. Nashville is fortified in such a manner that it would be impossible for any amount of secesh to take it. We have just got some news from the election in Ill. In truth I have not been much disappointed with the result in the state. We get no papers from Chicago and have no other newspapers except some very small affairs here. In reference to coming home I have no faith in it, and you need not count on my returning in time to witness the nuptials of Em & Zad. How greatly delighted I would be if I could do so and mingle my wishes with yours for their happiness & prosperity. I wish I could see you all on Thanksgiving and eat a dinner in a home once more. I expect to go out on picket tomorrow and as it is getting late I must close this hasty scrawl. My best love to you all. Kiss my boy. May he be spared to grow up to a useful & honorable life.

Yours Ever
John A. Bross

[Addendum at top of letter]

Nov 13. 6 A.m. I have only time to say that I have just rec[d] your letter from Chicago also one from Will & father. How delighted I am to hear from you & that you are well. We are going out on picket & I shall take time if possible to write of things of which I have not heretofore written. Your love and devotion to me is more gratifying than tongue can tell. Unless I could get detailed for some duty to go to Louisville there will be no use of Zad & Em attempting to come to see me. I am very well and you must not be anxious for me. I shall always let you know if I am sick. Thanks to dear mother for her words of cheer. Again love to all. The things will be acceptable. The overcoat I want saved as I have got a cheap one.

In camp near Nashville Tenn
Nov 14th /62

My Dear Father![1]

Your letter of 1st inst. reached me near midnight yesterday, together with one from Belle & Bro Will and you may well imagine with what eagerness I devoured the contents, so grateful and pleasant to my heart. I have some moments of leisure and will write you a line. I sent a note to Belle yesterday morning by a messenger who went to Louisville on business of the regiment. I hope she will get it although it was all written before I rec[d] your letters. To day is a lovely, balmy day and I wish it may be the same with you although it must be colder. We have frost here & cold nights but the days when the weather is clear are charmingly delicious. I believe I would give up Lake Michigan for the Cumberland River if this people were my people, & I was about to say their God my God. Yet one God rules over all; the rebels as well as Loyal. The face of the country is very attractive, and in spring time must be beautiful in the extreme. I wish Belle Zad & Em might visit me here if we should remain here so long but I do not anticipate any such pleasure. If Rosecrans is the man we take him to be this army will be thrown against the rebels just so soon as our line of communication North to Louisville is completely opened. He reviewed our Division the other day and his manner exhibited a great deal of familiarity with the soldiers and bon homme generally. As to the generals we have been under little need be said. I have not spoken of them from the fact that in writing I have had so little time when I have sent you hasty letters. Our Division when we left Louisville was part of Gen. Gilberts army corps, a special pet of Buell. Gilbert made himself thoroughly hated by officers & men. His regulations with regard to the movements of trains, baggage, supplies, officers baggage &c were extremely hard on us all, while he had 21 wagons for his own personal convenience & his escort of cavalry must sleep on the ground. He was nowhere at Perryville as also Buell. The latter was miles in the rear & late in the afternoon wanted to know what those guns were firing for in the front. I saw his army come into Louisville & slept with a member of his signal corps. He told me how bitterly the officers & soldiers denounced him for his conduct. It was the same with us after the Battle of Perryville. We lay three days after the battle near the scene of action chafing like a spirited horse that wishes to dart off upon a gallop after the enemy. Our blood was all up, and our prestige gained in the recent battle would have impelled us like a whirlwind upon Bragg's retreating forces. But no, we must absolutely do nothing & not even crawl after the enemy. Curses loud & deep were muttered all through the army. It was a magnificent sight the morning after the battle as our Division formed in line & marched forward a short distance in the order of battle. A few guns about 7 A.m. to our right wrought up expectations to the highest pitch and the ball we thought was again open. We lay on our arms all day except towards night when we marched through cornfields, threw down stone fences &c & camped near the secesh hospital of which I have spoken in a former letter to Belle. Here we lay two days & then started again after Bragg who had in the meantime got well off towards Crab Orchard with all his plunder. We followed him to that point, where the good roads stop & there we stopped & let him go. We retraced our steps to Lancaster thence to Danville, thence towards Lebanon—within about six miles of that town the whole Division turned off into a by road to the left of that town where we got lost & Major Gen Gilbert besides. That day we marched twenty miles and when we found out our ludicrous march we were too indignant to contain ourselves. We had got around on another road and was going back nearly in the direction we came from. Such was Gen Gilbert who could issue a brutal order to prick up with the bayonet every soldier sick or shirker who should fall out of the ranks and get behind. It was at that camp on Rolling Fork of Salt Creek that we got word of Gilberts being superceded by McCook who now commands our Corps and that Rosecrans would probably be Buells successor. This was great news for us. We marched to New Market & thence across high hills to Green River. We crossed that stream about 16 miles above Munfordville. I wrote Belle a letter from Bowling Green showing our arrival up to that point. I gave it to a citizen there as we left town who promised to mail it. We left Bowling Green on the 4th inst. & reached here the eve of 7th one days march being 23 miles. I was glad when we passed the State Line & we were out of Ky; Union so called, but whose Union inhabitants I have but little respect for. I felt as I entered Tennessee we were getting towards Dixie, although she has a glorious Governor. -- I believe this will give you an idea of our marching in Ky. You will see by the map that we have been pretty well "around" in that state, having marched over three hundred miles to get to this point.

I am doubly grateful to you for the interest manifested in my welfare. I am heartily glad that "Mason" is so well. It would give me inexpressible pleasure to witness the development of his mind and body. I have received no papers from Chicago except a couple from Si. By the by, Willie was not under my care but was detailed as a regimental drummer along with all the other co musicians, & were all in a squad under the charge of the Drum Major. I looked after him however as much as I could. He was in the habit of doing what he pleased & going where he would. The morning of the battle he strayed behind and away from our camp which was about two miles from the battlefield, & have not seen him since. He deserted along with another boy and walked to Louisville where he got across the river somehow. The truth is there was no way of keeping him to his work. He would or he would not and the drum major did not try to control him. When I was near he would do his duty properly when I was out of the way no one was more saucy or could swear harder oaths. I am fearful he is a "gone case." I am pleased that you have seen Messrs. Gurley & Washburn & that he was pleased with

Belle. I knew he would be and it is a matter of pride that so distinguished an M.C. should appreciate her. The postage stamps were very acceptable. In addressing letters do not send them to care of Q.M. they will come directly by simply putting my name & no. of Regt. I rec[d] your package of papers & was thankful for religious as well as secular news. It was a sort of "comfort" I cannot describe to get a report of this kind. I do not see why William does not send me some Tribunes but I suppose he is so full of other things that he cannot think of it. We have just heard of McClellans removal. We are all satisfied with Burnside. We hope something will now be done on the Potomac. I wish I could be with you thanksgiving to eat mothers turkey and more than all enjoy the pleasure of friendly, filial intercourse. I have filled my sheet and as I expect to write to Belle I will speak to her of other topics. Love to all.

Ever your affectionate son
John A Bross

1 This letter was to Belle's father, not his own. In usage of the time, it was common to refer to a spouse's parents as "Father" and "Mother."

Nashville Tenn
Nov 17, 1862

My Dear Wife!

I write you of one or two things which may surprise you a little but of which you may not be ashamed. I am under "arrest" which simply means that I am at my quarters & not in command of my Co. Now for the facts. The other morning I spoke of going on "picket" the Regiment went. My Co. & Co. "H" Capt Chickering were placed as reserve. I was on duty with my co in P.m. until 6 o'clock. Chick then went on duty until 12, relieving me & my Co. I let the Co lay down to rest as is usual supposing that Chickering would do his duty. He & his whole command went to sleep also. The consequence was that the Guard Officer of the day who happened to be Col Sherman caught our two companies in that predicament. We were placed under arrest, I was off duty but was like the unfortunate dog. Very well, I have tendered my resignation & if it is accepted I may see you soon. There are some reasons why I greatly wish to get away from this regt & go into another. For my desire to serve my country is still as strong as ever. I do not feel that I have committed or omitted any act that will disgrace you or my sword. I am in a cheerful mood, am well and if I can get to see you soon I will have long stories to tell you. The mail is just ready to leave and I cannot wait longer. I will write you again to day or tomorrow if I can get the opportunity. Please to have no unpleasant thoughts about this matter. It is providential for something or other. Love to all.

Yours Ever
John A. Bross

In Camp near Nashville Tenn
Nov 18th 1862

My Dear Wife!

Yesterday I sent you a line stating the fact of my arrest and the how of it, also that I had tendered my resignation. There has been no result as yet & I cannot tell how long it will be before I shall know how it is disposed of. I am doubtful of its acceptance and will wait until its final disposition before I go into particulars. In the meantime I hope your mind will rest at ease as I shall say nothing more of it until I may enter fully into details. Until then I dismiss the subject. Yesterday a Mr. Wicks a messenger of the B. qt. called and left me a note from Jno Hitch Br of "Tim." He is at Hd Qrs. of Gen Rosecrans on secret service of the Govt. I expect him over here to day to dine on "Shingle." I believe I wrote you at Bowling Green that we had recd our tents. From that point we had them along with us all the time, also my mess chest. Here we have been living a good deal better than on the march. To give you an idea how that is done I will first state the modus operandi. About every day there is a foraging party organized from the 4 regts of the Brigade who take their guns to escort as many teams as is required to get hay oats etc. Now the rule is that all forage is to be taken for the U.S. but the rule is more "honored in the breach than in the observance" for we officers generally send a man who will bring us under the hay a leg of veal, mutton or chickens, potatoes or any other substantial, all this the Lieutenant in Command never sees although his eyes are wide open. Secesh are thus gulled but no union men. We would not hurt a hair of the Union men's heads, but those who do not have protection papers have but little sympathy. In this way in camp we rub along quite respectably. I have got my tent in half decent shape. To day I made some stools out of ash blocks for us to sit on around our mess chest, and we took solid comfort in using them. I have also a good writing desk in the shape of the inside box of my mess chest set on stakes and it is very handy in that position. Our camp is in a beautiful grove of ash, poplar gum, hackleberry & other woods. We have cleared out the underbrush and you would be pleased to see us. - - Well, since writing the above, I have heard from Col Sherman who paid me a visit to my tent returned my resignation and restored me to duty. The whole thing has its ludicrous aspect although a recent order of Rosecrans about guard duty & some other things is very severe upon the shoulder straps. I have no time in this letter as I supposed I should to enlarge upon it. The Regt is ordered off on a three days excursion somewhere, I believe to Mitchellsville, which is north to the State Line to guard a provision train. I may send you a line from there.

I am deeply grateful for your love which shows itself in works. The package will be very acceptable. I am glad you are so hopeful of our meeting again. Let us trust in Heaven that we may hereafter enjoy many years of happy domestic life in each others society and with our dear boy, and our dear parents, and all our dear friends. I am glad you have rented the house to a good tenant. It quiets my mind a good deal and I can rest comparatively easy. I wrote Br. Will about my note. I do not know that I shall get any money by Dec 1, & I have written him to have it renewed if necessary. I shall devote all I can to dispose of that, at the earliest moment. I have as much as $300, coming from Govt, if I could only get it. I have however something to pay the Quarter Master, if we get paid before Dec 1. I will remit to father if not in time, or to Will if there is time to take up the note—I am pleased that you have disposed of the furniture in such nice shape to Uncle P. & stowed the balance in the house. I gathered from your letter that Chicago has charms yet for you and that you are in the "right place." I do not wonder and how gladly will I in the future make a home & house which you will be pleased with & in which we will "enjoy a green old age." But perhaps the idea of old will grate harshly on your ears. It will be better to enjoy it while we're young & in middle life. - - I hope you can get that present for Em. That was rather characteristic of Jeanne Wicker. I am surprised at Mrs O. I hope you will keep my military coat & pants all right. I believe I got some [illegible] against one side of the coat which will need a little cleaning, but your quick eye will discover all that. I am glad you have had so pleasant visit at Uncle Carliles. I know you will enjoy it at Br Wills. Please remember that I will carry out your suggestions about position &c, &c. And so you saw Mr Washburn! What else could I think, knowing of your correspondence with Gov Yates[1] that you wished to make a friend of W. for my sake! You are quite a politician already. I was particularly pleased to know that you had met him & "produced an impression." Arnold goes back. I did not think his majority would be so much. About my overcoat I do not want it unless I stay here sometime, but will write you if I do. - - Father Mason can collect that bill of Tafts client. His agent is in the rooms on LaSalle street where the British Consul formerly had his office. I hope he will do it. All that is necessary is to show his power of atty. Has anything been done with the 40 acre tract of Judge Marvin in DeKalb Co? It was to be rented from Oct 1. I am not anxious about praising Col. S. & will never do it unless he deserves it. I am obliged to you and father for your stamps. Of course I will send them back home again outside of letters. I should like a little money now but I do not wish you to be strapping yourself & father too. The words of mother were like drops of honey to the taste. I should just like to hug her as a dear good mother. Hope she will not be surprised at my strong language. And little "wide awake" Mason I do not cease to think of him. I suppose I shall be very much surprised at his advancement in knowledge and physical development, I am glad to know that his teeth are all right & that he is so healthy. Papa hears drums enough in all conscience, he sleeps, eats, drills, & rests at the tap of the drum. I am getting so accustomed to it that if I should get away from it I would be lost almost. I have not yet seen Nashville although from an eminence near our camp we can see the Capitol. I had hoped to go over tomorrow but this P.m. comes our order to go on this expedition. We are to go without our tents, leaving everything here in charge of a guard, and we shall be back again in three or four days. I hope to have a chance to write again along the road. We do not anticipate any trouble along the way although the guerrillas may attempt a dash on us. Lt Longworth is well. He took tea or rather coffee with us. If you could only send me a pound of good tea I should like it first rate, I am sick of coffee. Dinsmoor is well. I have him for my clerk & will promote him when I can. He goes out foraging for us. Yesterday he cramped a bushel & more of sweet potatoes which we have enjoyed greatly. He is out again today & has not yet returned. I leave him in my tent in my absence. I hope to hear from you again soon. Love to mother & father, Em & Annie, & Regards to Bro Zad. Hope he will prove all right now. I hope this will find you dearest in good health and spirits. Indications are that we shall have an active campaign. John Fitch called today, & I had a pleasant chat with him. Good bye,

Ever Yours
John

1 Richard Yates (b. 1815) served as Governor of Illinois during the Civil War, beginning in 1860.

In Camp 7 miles south of Nashville
Dec 4th 62

My dear Sweet wife,

Yesterday I sent you a letter & in the P.m. recd your letter & the package of papers by Mr Stevens. I was vexed at some of the news and sorry to know that business matters have so troubled you. I would fly to you if I could to quiet your uneasiness. I am afraid my visit home will be after this winter. I was anxious all day for you but your letter & Bro Wills of 29th ult. made me feel better. I wrote you from the camp near Nashville which I hope you got soon after you wrote your last. I have no particular news to write except there was some breeze stirred up at the news. I am glad to have Gov Hoffmans[1] letter here although I have kept perfectly quiet and shall. We have not yet got any commissions & I do not yet know where they are. It places me in a delicate situation & I have to be very careful what I say or do. I cannot decline the position & yet for one man I am sorry & that is Capt Smith of the present Co A. He is a gentleman. I suppose I have the opposition of the Major & Lt Col who by their influence in the present arrangement jumped their Lts when I was Capt over my head. For them I am glad that I may have the opportunity of walking above them. I will write you whenever anything is developed about it. I am very thankful for your care of my interests. I have a good pair of gloves that were too large for Rae. The stockings, & milk were very acceptable. Now that you are at home I would like a tin can of butter if I could get it safe through and a package of ginger snaps and some dried beef. If I had some of mothers pickled pork I would consider it one of the greatest of luxuries. I often picture to myself our last winters life and my mouth waters almost when I think of those delicious buckwheat cakes which I cannot now get.

Yesterday the 36th was paid off & they feel very rich I assure you. The sutler gets a great deal of the money however. Abe Longworth was over to see me this eve & we had a good time. I would like to have you drop in & see me now in my tent. It is quite neat I assure you. Then I have a contraband for a "servant" whose lips are as thick as Masons arm. By the by your report of Mason is very agreeable. I can only see him as I left him & I often wonder if I should know him were I to drop in somewhere where I could not know it was him. - - I wrote Will this eve about our not getting paid until January. I am glad you have made so long a stay in C. Wish you could have made a longer visit. I wish you & Sister Mary could visit me about Christmas also Em & Zad. Mrs Lt Cushing, & Lt Col Chadbourn's wife are in camp & have been for nearly a week. They are quite interesting but in features do not at all compare with my bonnie wife. I should love to have you here & in my letter to Will suggested that he bring you. I have not yet been in Nashville except to march through it. I want to visit Rosecrans' Hd Qrs. & will act upon your suggestion. I wrote father two weeks since. I hope has recd it. I am always glad to hear from them. Give my warmest love to them all and believe me ever

Your devoted husband
John A. Bross

1 Francis Hoffmann served as Lieutenant Governor of Illinois from 1861 to 1865, when William Bross became Lieutenant Governor.

In Camp Mill Creek
Dec 8th 1862.

My Dear Wife!

I send you a line this P.m. not knowing how soon we may be ordered away. We have been in Camp here now about two weeks and all indications of the Camp are significant of an advance. To day I have been hugely disappointed in one thing. I made application to be detailed to Illinois to get deserters & bounty for my co. Cols Sherman & Greusel approved but Genl Sheridan disapproved & that ends the matter as it lies in his breast. Well I had hopes of coming to see Em married but this knocks it all endwise. I had hoped to see my dear wife & child & all my friends but I now give it up and shall go forward committing you to the care of Him who rules all things for good. Of course I know not how far we shall go but I anticipate seeing Murfreesboro before we make much of a stop. I received fathers letter two days ago. We all know his familiar hand. It does me good to hear from him. The commissions have not yet come. They were sent by Capt Miller of Miller's battery, who has not forwarded them. I have had a private confab with the Adjutant who is a friend of mine & he says all the field officers are angry about my being Captain of Co A, & they will resist it to the last. This is as I expected as Co B, & C, are the Cos raised by Lt Col Chadbourn & Major Chandler. Chandler is a Long John[1] toady & has no love for our name. I have not tried to make friends with either of them nor shall I. When the Coms come I shall demand my place, & if I do not succeed I will resign. I will not serve under such men any longer than I can help. I have not written to Josiah yet about Willie for the simple reason that I have been pressed greatly for time. I shall tell him however the whole facts very soon. Suffice it to say that I never gave him permission to leave. I had no power if I wanted to.

I wish you to extend to Em & Zad my warmest wishes for their prosperity and happiness. I shall be thinking of you all about Christmas wherever I am. Dinsmoor & Rae are well. They are both busy this P.m. making preparations to leave. It is astonishing how things accumulate in a short time & as we are expecting to move "light" again we are at a loss almost to decide how & what to take. We expect to leave our mess chest & tents all behind and sleep again in the open air for sometime to come. At least that is what is given out though no orders have as yet come to that effect. Be assured I shall do my duty. I hope you & Will rec[d] letters from me in relation to that note. I will say again that I do not know when we shall be paid. I will send you all the money I can just as soon as I can get it. Please to remember & be as easy as you can about me. Trust Heaven that in due time I will see you again. Mms. Bouton, Sherman, Cushing & Chadbourn are here. They will have to leave though pretty suddenly. Love to all friends & kisses for Mason. May Heaven bless you all. I will try & keep you advised on the march if we go as to our whereabouts.

Yours Ever,
John A Bross

1 This is evidently a reference to "Long John" Wentworth, who had recently served as Mayor of Chicago and who, as a Republican and strong opponent of slavery, should have been in political alignment with William Bross and the *Tribune*.

On picket 8 miles south of Nashville
on Nolensville pike. Dec 10, 1862

My Dear Sweet Wife!

Since I last wrote you we have broke up camp where we have been for the last two weeks. It was done this morning. All our tents & baggage have gone to the rear & we are again on the extreme outpost in the advance without tents & the Canopy of Heaven over us for our roofing. The 36th & 88th are guarding the road today. Yesterday the long roll beat just as we had finished our last mouthful of dinner. Our two regts were into line in five minutes. We marched out of camp along the road some distance & deployed to the right & left of the road & lay on our arms all the P.m. when no secesh appearing we returned to camp. As I dismissed the Co Charley Wheeler & a Mr Fletcher of the 19th called at my tent. I was glad to see them. I gave them a soldiers supper which they seemed to enjoy not withstanding they live in town & we are in the country. Our supper was made up of pancakes, sweet potatoes, tea, crackers, cheese, beefsteak & other "fixins." Charley is a fine, manly looking fellow and every inch a soldier. We had a pleasant social chat over matters & things in the north, of friends &c in which Charley said he would like mighty well for us to meet at my house, or Charley's to a good supper at home. Dearest: we know how to appreciate you the further we travel from home & the longer we remain away. This morning we struck tents at 4 ½ o'clock while we were getting breakfast and the tents were the first thing off the ground. I had a good breakfast nevertheless. We saw every thing leave & then we came up here to watch the road. For days we have been getting rumors of an attack upon us & we have been on the alert all the time. We went into line yesterday in gay style. I cannot account for it but there is something exciting in the chance of having a dash at the rebels & most everyone is ready to jump at the chance of giving them a round or so. I cannot yet tell the movement that is going on, but I hope we shall be permitted to go forward towards Murfreesboro, where the rebels are said to have been massing their forces for some weeks back. It is said that Rosecrans is actively engaged in making preparations to drive them out of that. I hope we shall. - - I suppose you have a little colder weather than we have here. Today is most beautiful and delicious. The air comes up from the south in zephyr-like breath, & literally fulfills the line of the poet "December as pleasant as May." I have become enamored of this climate. The last time we were on picket we came out in a snow storm which lasted until noon. It was about two inches deep - - since then the weather has been very pleasant indeed. My company is one of the advance today, & deployed to the right of the road facing south. I am in a nice grove on the edge of a stubble field "sitting on a rail" & writing to you on my memorandum book which serves for a writing desk resting on my knee. I have no overcoat or shawl around me so you can judge how nice the weather must be. My boys are frisking about who are not on duty—capering like young colts. You may consider this rather monotonous life. It is in some respects & yet there is variety about it sufficient to spice our daily routine. Open air life is beneficial to my health provided I do not expose myself unnecessarily. I often think how I can stand it to go back to sleep in tight rooms. This morning I had just "turned over" on my side & was enjoying a sort of indescribable comfort in the rest of a new position when the stirring reveille came. I disliked to move but there is no chance to shirk. Officers & men must get up & be about their business. It is altogether better though we feel at times we should like to lay snugly by in our couches. - - I know you would like this country except perhaps the want of water to give variety to the landscape. The tallest corn I ever saw is to be found here & the largest sweet potatoes. The latter we like to get whenever we can. I will tell you an incident which you must not mention to Mr Dinsmoor. One night about two weeks since, Willie D. went on an excursion to replenish our stock of potatoes. He & three of my men & 14 of Co B. had just nicely loaded themselves with as much as they could carry when they were pounced upon by a co sent out on purpose and arrested. Back they came to camp. Sherman gave them a "particular cussing" & sent them over to Col Greusel. He sent them back to quarters immediately, & all the punishment they got was to do a little policing of camp. Moral—I got the potatoes. I should tell you that Willie messes with me. I suppose our dear mother may think this rather impinging on the moral law—I should myself if it were foraging on a true Unionist. But I am somewhat of the opinion of Old Brownlow—Secessionists have but two rights—to be hanged & be d—d.[1] I wrote a long letter to Josiah a few days ago detailing the facts about Willie. My Co business is in such a state now that I will not have so much to do here after when we get in camp & I hope to devote more time to correspondence & even write a letter or so occasionally for the Tribune. - - Dec 12. I stopped writing the above in order to attend to my co duty. That night was light moonlight & frosty. One of the companies of the 15th Missouri could see the rebel pickets about 800 yards off so you see we are close by the outposts of the enemy. We were returned from our picket yesterday morning & marched back to our new camp which is only about a mile nearer Nashville. How long we shall remain here is unknown to us but from appearances it will be very brief. Yesterday shelter tents were brought into the regiments. Ours have not yet been distributed. They are nothing in the world but square bits of cotton cloth & I do not see what good they will do. Each two men is to carry a tent. We expect to have the present ones all taken from us. As I said before this indicates an active winter campaign. I must again mention the climate. Today seems to be the sunniest of all the year. Yesterday I recd a letter from Will. Father Mason had taken tea with him.

I hope you are not exercised about my not doing my duty as I might infer from an expression in Wills letter. I hardly think he thought so although his letter or a sentence of it rather, is liable to that construction. When you hear of another battle in which this regiment is engaged you shall hear of my doing my duty. I will promise no more. I wish you will not omit to write me again soon. I do not expect much however until after the wedding when you will please give me all particulars. Once more I send my greetings to Em & Zad. I should like to give them some brotherly advice but I cannot get time. How is it none of your letters contain any allusion to Sister Annie. What is she doing? Mother I hope has good health. Will speaks of my "boy." I shall be intensely gratified when the time comes for me to see him and your own dear self. With a heart full of love for you all I am as ever yours

John

1 William Gannaway Brownlow (1805–1877) was a Methodist minister, a newspaper editor, and a politician in Tennessee; he was a fiery and bitter opponent of secession.

In Camp on Nolensville Pike
Dec 13, 1862.

My Dear Wife & Father Mason!

Your letters of Dec 7th & 8th reached me this evening with letters of Farnum & Mann & Nolker, both of which I have just answered. I was delighted to hear from you and that your face Belle had become better. It is interesting to Willie & myself to know that the wedding is on Thursday eve next. We shall be with you in spirit that evening wherever we are and if this should happen to reach you on that day you will remember my oft repeated wish that you give them the hearty good wishes and blessings of a brother. May happiness ever be their lot. I wish you to give me full particulars of the affair immediately afterwards, and what they are going to do & where they will reside. I hope you have received my letters by this time informing you of the receipt of those articles—they were all right except the boots which were entirely too small. Lt Gibson takes them & pays the price when I can know what it is. I am glad to hear a good report of Charley. I will write him when I can get an opportunity. I should like to hear my chatter box of a boy. Sometime I shall I trust and dear Mama & all. Kiss him for me. I will bring him a drum perhaps when I come—or a small cannon or other implement of war. Now a matter of interest to us all. To day the commissions came & were distributed. The changes were as follows. A to B, B to C, C to D, D to A. The question instantly arose as to rank. Col Sherman took the ground that the companies were mustered for pay on the 31st of October Smiths as Co A mine as Co D & that settled the rank. I informed him that I cared but little where my Co was placed in line of battle but that I should claim my rank to command whenever field officers were not present. I so informed Capt Smith & he got mad & his Lieutenants—also Col Sherman stormed like a mad man because I spoke to Smith about it. I knew a breeze would be raised as I told you. Col Sherman refuses to allow me to have my place on the right of the regiment—so far as fighting is concerned I don't care where I am placed but my rank from the Gov. I will never abandon. I have advised with Col Greusel & other officers of the 36th. I also went to Genl Sheridans Quarters to advise with him but he was absent and not expected to return for some hours. I propose to have no difficulty, but shall write to Gov Yates through William. I shall never give up if all the field & line officers are against me in this matter. I can write no more as we ordered off on a foraging excursion tomorrow. 4 regiments & artillery. Love to all and my whole heart for yourself

Ever Yours
John

"On Picket" Dec 19th 1862.

My Ever Dear Wife!

We are located where we were when I wrote you last, that is our camp is in the same place & we are out today on picket duty at the same place where we have guarded the roads for a couple of weeks past. The weather has been unpleasant for a few days but today is one of "pleasantness" if not peace. I take this occasion to report our doings last night. Your letter which I answered gave us the day of Ems wedding & as I wrote you I determined to get up a little celebration on my own account. Yesterday was spent in Battalion drill in the morning and Brigade drill in P.m. It was one of the sunniest days of all the year though a little muddy under foot because of frost the evening previous. This was pretty well dried up about sundown. I was thinking of you all the whole day and imagining the little labors you were all performing in order that the affair might go off in good style. Mason chattering around, perhaps getting into places where he was not wanted. Then the dressing hour, then the hour of assembling, then the parlor filled with friends & then the ceremony. But I will not imagine any further but tell you what I did. In the afternoon I had some nice biscuit made or rather just before tea; these with butter beef steaks, crackers, cheese, tea & sugar constituted our tea to which we sat down at 6 o'clock P.m. I had only one guest which was Lt Longworth. The company consisted of Longworth, Bross, Cole, Rae & Dinsmoor, my 1st Lt being absent on detached service. We sat at table nearly an hour mingling war matters with Zad & Em wives children friends, &c. At 7 I had to attend recitations at the Col's tent. The "tactical school" of the line officers being held every evening. At 9 P.m. we sat down to an "oyster supper." This was the feature of the evening. To say that we enjoyed the oysters would but ill convey the sensations of pleasure which were derived from the bivalves. The supper was graced with two kinds of splendid cake a present from Miss Nellie Davis, Dr. Davis' daughter of Chicago, to Orderly Rae. He has been sick in Hospital for several days and of course could not eat his cake until he recovered which happened yesterday just in time you see. The cake was fruit & jelly and plenty of it. In imitation of all chroniclers I will say that "after the cloth was removed the intellectual feast began." Capt Bross as host & Chairman of the meeting rapped to order with his knuckles upon the mess chest and proposed as a toast "Our wives and children," when "Abe" broke in (in parenthetic style) "you're just right!" It was drunk in silence as became the dignity and true hearted devotion, esteem, & regard which Longworth & myself bear to the dear ones at home and the virtue and worth comprehended in the name of wife & mother. The young men honored you with the most evident respect and without a movement or intonation to mar "expressive silence." The next was "sweethearts" drunk with all the honors. The next toast was given after I had stated that this occasion was in honor of the nuptials of my sister & I gave "Zad & Em: Long may they live to enjoy the sweets of wedded life and never regret the step which they this evening make and publish to all the world." This was received with demonstrations "long & loud" of mirth & jollity, so much so that we had a gentle reminder from the Col that what was passing in my tent could be heard outside. We came down of course to gentler language or rather our voices were pitched to a lower key & the hilarity of the occasion continued. The next was Miss Nellie Davis who contributed so unexpectedly to provide our table with the "luxuries of life." We gave her a bumper and wound up with another toast to "Em." After a very pleasant evening spent in this manner, Lieut Longworth separated from us at 10 ½ P.m. just about the time you were eating your supper I presume, and we retired to our sleeping apartment which was simply to move our mess chest to one corner of the tent & lie down in our blankets. I rested sweetly doubtless enjoying my slumbers long before any of you thought of retiring. But we rise earlier than you and we can sleep earlier I presume when not on "picket." Thus ended "my celebration" of an important family event. I used all the influence I could command to get leave of absence in order to be with you but I could not accomplish it. I wished you could have "looked in" upon us, it would have been a pleasure indescribable to me. I have given you an outline of what the (now) "elder son" did upon Em's taking her husband & I expect in a few days to have particulars of the event from yourself or Sister Annie. I presume you are engaged in that today if you are not too fatigued with the work of yesterday. You have never told me where Z. & E. go upon their wedding tour, nor where they are going to reside. I presume however it will be sometime before they will go to keeping house. I believe I told you in a former letter that I have written to Josiah about Willie. I am sorry to make him feel bad but I must tell the truth. I am certainly glad to be relieved of any responsibility with regard to him.

Sunday evening Dec 21. After writing the above I had to go on duty and had no good opportunity to finish. We did not get back to camp yesterday until about noon. The P.m. was spent in washing & cleaning up generally. We have just read the news of Burnsides defeat.[1] It throws a chill of disappointment over us all and a great many are ready to censure every Commander on the Potomac. It was heroic bravery though to rush on those fortifications. - - I received three letters today from William in one of which he speaks of his present to Em. Yesterday I rec[d] a very good letter from Jessie. She is very flattering to me. Will speaks very highly of you & says that in the event of my falling in battle he will take care of you & Mason. I have received my commission but Col Sherman sees fit to side with his "lettering" & ignores my claims. He will yet be taught to do the right thing. After my standing by him as I have this is a poor return for my efforts in his behalf. We go out on a forage excursion tomorrow morning at 4 ½ o'clock. I heard a capital sermon this P.m. over in the 36th by their chaplain. It did me good—our own chaplain I like less & less, in fact he has no sense or discretion. I hope to hear from you soon. "After Christmas" you will hear from me again till which time I bid you adieu. I send lots of love to mother & Annie, father & "Mason" & always I am yours

John A Bross

1 The Battle of Fredericksburg (December 11–15, 1862) was a disastrous defeat for the Army of the Potomac under General Ambrose Burnside, who ordered repeated frontal assaults uphill against strong Confederate fortifications. Union soldiers spoke of "Burnside's slaughter pen."

CHAPTER 2

Letters from January 5 to October 8, 1863: Tennessee and Georgia, Battles of Stones River and Chickamauga

Jany 5, 1863—near Murfreesboro

My Dear Wife

I have only time to say that myself & Dinsmoor are safe, having been in battle on the 31st ult & 1st instant. It was terrible yet God has saved us through all the storm. Can say no more. Love to all

John A Bross

In Camp three miles south
of Murfreesboro Jany 7th 1863

My Dear Sweet Wife!

I seize a moment of time to give you an outline of recent events. I sent a single line several days ago saying I was safe. I am still well & safe through the good Providence of God. We left our camp on the Nolensville Pike Dec 26 & drove the enemy beyond Nolensville that day. Next morning we advanced about 3 or 4 miles in line of battle in a drenching storm driving the enemy before us & taking a few prisoners. We camped that night near the Pike & next day being Sunday we rested. Monday morning we left the pike eastward over a dirt road to the Murfreesboro pike & as we debouched into that road it was a magnificent sight. The whole of the right wing "McCooks Corps" in which is our Division had concentrated there. That night our Brigade was thrown forward a mile or so & deployed as picket in a muddy cornfield. Rain all night but the presence of the enemy kept us on the alert. We were about 4 miles from Murfreesboro and we could distinctly hear all night the arrival of rebel teams & great lights along the southeastern horizon. Early in the morning our Division advanced on the pike about a mile or so & deployed to the right of the road the 36th & 88th in front. Skirmishing & cannonading continued all day without much effect on either side except that we drove in their pickets upon their line. We lay in line at night in a cotton field gently sloping down to a meadow across which in a thick cedar forest the rebels lay. Early on the morning of the 31st, the enemy came out of the woods & advanced upon us. We peppered them nicely & they fell back in disorder at the same time the 36th became engaged & they also drove back the enemy. But the two Divisions on our right were entirely surprised & routed. This exposed our own right flank & so we had to retreat. The whole right wing fell back upon the left our line being in the shape of a horse shoe. They having heard what was going on were ready & as we fell in their rear they became engaged. It was well for us that we got there as we did as the enemies' right & left were just closing in upon us. This was the most sublime sight I ever witnessed, & oh how my blood boiled to feel that wicked carelessness on the part of one of our Divisions had nearly lost us the whole army. The left & centre stood firm under the example of Rosecrans & their Generals but it was a desperate game. I have trembled since to see how nearly we were lost. But "Rosy" saved the day. We held the enemy at bay & at last repulsed him handsomely although our loss was great in men & artillery. I felt like shooting the stragglers some of whom never stopped until they saw Nashville 27 miles off. Rosecrans said that the check given the enemy by the 36th & 88th saved the day as it gave the left & centre time to get ready for the fight. Next day, Jany 1, was an anxious time for us. We traced a new line of battle & lay there expecting an attack but none came. We threw up barricades of stones & logs & were just mad enough to fight like tigers. Jany 2d all was quiet in the forenoon, but it only was the prelude to a terrible storm. They now attacked our left. But "Rosy" knew their intent & had prepared for it by massing a great force at that very point. My Co was on provost guard duty that P.m. & I had a fair chance to witness a battle & not be in it. I cannot describe my feelings but will try at some other time. The enemy were literally butchered, mowed down in heaps & it at once changed the rebs movements as on Saturday last they left Murfreesboro with great haste. Yesterday we moved up here & to day we again have our tents. Such in brief is what we have been about. I have known & felt what soldiers life is. I have done my duty & have not a single thing to regret in my conduct. Yet the scene is one that I never care to see again. Not that I would refrain from fighting just as quick but it is horrible after all to see this bloody work. If I ever see you I will have long tales to tell you. I am very well, ready to fight at any moment & wish to "go ahead." Kiss darling "Mason" a thousand times & love to all, all my dear friends & yourself. I forgot to say that I received your letters with the receipt for things. I hope to get it soon. Dinsmoor is well. He always has everything that I have & is more favored than others.

Yours Ever
John

[Written in top margin] Excuse this dirty paper. I will try & get letters when I get settled. Have lost my shawl & blanket in the battle. The officers baggage was taken by the rebs. Our Co papers & tents were in the rear & not touched.

On Brigade picket, Shelbyville pike
5 miles south of Murfreesboro Sabbath
January 11th 1862 [1863]

My Dear Father!

We are on Brigade picket to day that is all the regiments of our Brigade are out on the picket lines in front of our camp. I avail myself of the occasion to answer your letter sent with Belle's dated Christmas day. First I know you will rejoice with all our friends that in the late terrible battle God preserved my life. The raging Storm of human Strife was succeeded by days of rain in which our duty and watchfulness was never intermitted in the least until the glad tidings came that the rebs had got up and run. I have given already to Belle an outline of events in that week of toil and privation, one which to appreciate the like must be endured in order to know what a thing of horrors a Great Battle is. You will ere this have read all sorts of letters about the battle & know perhaps from them the general features of the field. I will only attempt to give some details which may interest you all. I send a little diagram which may aid you in imaging our position. The figures 36 & 88 represent our regiments laying down in a cotton field in front of a meadow across which in the edge of the cedar forest the rebels lay. We had the enemy beaten back near their left centre & if we had had proper support we should have broken their line in two parts. Mind you this was by the bravery of the 36 & 88, but just at that moment the two Divisions on our right had been driven back. Johnston's by his traitorous carelessness & Davis because he was outflanked & then ours had to give way in order to save themselves from being taken prisoners. It was too bad thus to have victory snatched from our grasp and so many of our two regiments killed & wounded. Our right wing being compelled to fall back swung round & over onto the left. Here as the broken right wing fell in behind the left the battle again became obstinate & bloody. It was a large open corn field & cotton field in which our regiments were massed one behind the other & all laying down on their faces. To their rear on a slight elevation by the Rail Road our Batteries were placed in long lines which did terrible execution. I shall never forget my enthusiasm or the sublime scene as we retreated through a cedar forest came out into the open field in front of our left, with the enemies left just behind us and their right wing coming forward over a large open field in splendid array advancing to the charge. Their two wings might be compared to a huge vise that was about to close up & crush our army and the Union at one turn of the rebel screw. The scene is engraven on the tablets of my memory & will ever be as vivid as the noon day sun. We had just time to get out of the way of our own guns when the heavens were rent by the artillery of both sides & such horrid din never before met my ears. This was more on account of my being a witness than an actor perhaps. But the feeling uppermost in my mind was that of exultation as I saw such a mass of our own men ready to receive the advancing wave of rebeldom. Consider that our right was retreating, I was literally mad with indignation at the result thus far. 3 great Divisions giving way by reason of carelessness on the part of a Kentucky General & I felt just like invoking on the head of the criminal all the curses that had ever been uttered from Cain to Calhoun & if he had come within reach of our muskets that day he would have been shot like a dog. At that point "Old Rosey" exposed himself with perfect carelessness to the enemy's shots. His Chief of Staff was instantly killed by a cannon ball. The Gen. conversed with the common soldiers telling them what to do to give them a good volley, then the bayonet & they would never stand. His example was inspiriting & he saved the day but the struggle was awfully severe. Back & forth across that field went our forces at times driving the enemy clear into the cedar forest then they would rally & drive us again back towards the rail road, and so the fortunes of either side swung from side to side like a pendulum until night drew its veil over both armies and we slept exhausted. Meantime that afternoon the broken & failed remnant of our Brigade under Col Greusel were sent to the rear to guard our train of wagons which were at one time of day actually captured by the enemy's cavalry who had turned our right. A timely charge of the 4th Regular Cavalry however sent the Texas rangers kiting and we did nothing but listen & watch the scene on our left. You may get a good idea of the extent of our line of battle by thinking of the distance from Sterling to Como. I have not said much of our mornings work. I shall look back to it with stern pleasure on many accounts. I know I did my duty & think I have shown one or two things of which you may not be ashamed. Enclosed I send you a secesh infantry button I cut from a dead rebel after the battle who lay directly in front of where my Co lay in line of battle. To do the rascals justice they came across that meadow with great bravery but they met men as brave who gave them more than they could stand against. You should have heard the exulting cheers of our men as they turned & sought their cover. But it was momentary as in less than five minutes we had to get up & leave. I wish you could have seen the activity of my mind in this battle; its grasping every little passing circumstance & taking note of every thing that occurred. The little rabbit that darted across the field, the birds that flew from tree to tree, the porkers that grunted around as if nothing could disturb them, nay every thing in animate nature within the scope of my vision I noticed. I have been amused frequently since then in recalling that electric state of my mind in contrast with "abstractions" out of which Belle has rallied me at times. It may be the shock of arms is the best and only thing that can bring all the dormant, latent, powers of my mind into play. I speak of these things for the family, it would have the appearance of egotism for strangers perhaps to see it. Even Bro Zad might misconstrue it. I can say also that with all this I never had better command of my company & myself, never cooler in the true sense of the term, & never in a better state of mind for the judgment to have its full sway. "Things present" were not the only things present to me; you, Belle, "Mason" all seemed nearer in my heart than ever before. My hands had not been washed for two or three days, very slovenly mother would say, & so I thought how ridiculous it would look, & what Belle would think if I should be wounded and taken prisoner or if my corpse should be taken up with an awful pair of dirty hands. Then again, as shells, cannon balls & bullets of all kinds whistled & hurtled by in very dangerous proximity, was it not peculiarly pleasant to think of a little angelic form whose mortal remains are sleeping on the shores of Lake Michigan, hovering around and warding off the death dealing instruments of the enemy? And so the early morn passed. It is rather ludicrous to have you Belle speak of my using caution on the Battle field. Where one can avail himself of the nature of the ground you may lie down but to attempt to get rid of bullets on such occasions savors of cowardice rather than control. It never helps one in the least. I give an instance: one of my men on the afternoon of the 30th got scared at some of the enemies pickets firing on us & he skedaddled to a barn just in our rear where he stayed all night. The battle commenced early in the morning & when we retreated he was shot dead at that barn. He might have been with me had he stayed with his company. One of the most disgusting features of the battle was the cowards who ran away. I also had a fine opportunity on Friday afternoon Jany 2 when the battle raged on the left to witness the effect of fright upon humanity. My Co was detailed as provost guards to watch & guard the Murfreesboro pike. One soldier came running past to the rear without gun cartridge box blanket or anything in the way of accouterments. He stopped very suddenly at my command to halt which was given in the sharpest kind of style. Whats the matter said I, "Oh my back" is shot through with a shell. I grabbed hold of him threw up the cape of his over coat & there was no rent or hole in any of his clothes, but his features exhibited the very extacy of fear. I set him down by the side of the road in short order & so with many others who thought our army was cut to pieces. I can not understand how men can be guilty of such poltroonery. Thousands of Johnstons Division in the first days battle went helter skelter through woods and fields & never stopped running until they reached Nashville & there secesh ladies unsexed themselves by gloating over the scene. It was a burning disgrace & I hope to never see such conduct again. Rather would I have seen the whole of them die in their tracks. It would have been to them an honorable end of their career. The scene made me feel like shooting the whole brood. But thank God we stopped the flow of that mass of human sheep & beat back the enemy also and that is glory enough. We are ready for the march again & I expect we shall move forward soon. I want to see Alabama & Georgia & that soon.

I thank you for that printed letter of Cobbey. His regiment is located a short distance from us yet I never call there. I shall treat him as a stranger if he crosses my path. Providence doubtless has some good end in view in causing him to be my tormenter last summer. I hope He will send me no more Methodist preachers if I undergo any more trials such as I had then. I wonder Worthington printed his silly stuff. I thank you heartily for that box of butter &c. It has not yet reached us from Nashville. The postage stamps are very acceptable.

The Tribune reporter Mr Curry came into camp to day bringing a letter from Wm. He is to be with the "Right wing." You will hear from him soon. The Fox River valley will be in mourning for their friends of the 36th. I saw 42 of their dead buried in one grave. Oh how sad it is & yet I could not shed a single tear for these brave hearts who have gone down to an early tomb. Honor to their memory & curses for the traitors who caused their untimely end. Near by a much longer pit contains the dead of the 30th Mississippi.

I am pleased to hear that "Mason" was made so happy on Christmas. Some time when you get an ambotype of him I wish you would send me one. My dear mother I presume you have many anxious thoughts for me and I am grateful for all your motherly kindness. I trust that when this horrible war shall cease I shall be so happy as to meet you again with all our friends. Annie I hope you have received my letter & that you are writing me an answer. Say to Em that I should like to drop in upon her at the Wallace House & receive some cake at her hands out of that Cake Basket. My Dear wife I will write you soon. Meantime remember that this letter is all in the family. Dinsmoor is well except some cold that he got during the fight. My love to all. Ever your affectionate son

John A. Bross

[In margin at top] I send two cotton balls taken from the battle field. It looked very nice when I got it but it has got some specks of dust in it by being in my pocket.

In Camp on Stone River
Three miles south of
"Murfreesboro" Tenn.
January 22d 1863.

Dearest.

Yours of the 1st came to hand three days ago and the first opportunity I have I seize to write to my own cherished love. I have been on "picket" & engaged on other duty, so much so that I have been too fatigued at night to write with any kind of interest to myself or you either. I have been at one thing that makes my tent comfortable. Dinsmoor & myself have built a brick chimney to our tent and fire place included which works to a charm. We can sleep dry and warm, and what is more it is real, old fashioned down right cheerfulness. True, we may leave it any day but we will enjoy it while here, and invite friends to call with some show of hospitality. It is decidedly agreeable. So while we are here in damp or cool weather imagine us sitting by our (soldier's) fireside as happy as we can be "under the circumstances," but ever and anon "at home" in spirit with those we love so well. We have a very pretty camp. Yesterday the things from Chicago arrived & I was very glad indeed to get the hat & cap. It was all the better as I expected they would be "gobbled up." By the by we have never received that box & I am afraid we never shall. Dinsmoor has been extremely anxious about it for the butter he has been very desirous to taste.

Friday Eve Jany 23d

To day the regiment went beyond the picket lines on a foraging excursion. We marched about 12 miles. It was a pleasant jaunt although I am a little tired. I wish you could enjoy our pleasant weather. It would make you love the climate. - - Last Sabbath was a very pleasant one for me. Capt Longworth & myself got leave of absence & securing horses we rode over to the "left wing" Crittenden's corps. We called on Lt Knox who is on the staff of Crittenden & had a most pleasant chat with him. He looks much like his sister. I was not aware that he was there. Capt Longworth became intimately acquainted with him while the 13th & 36th were at Rolla Mo. My object in going over to the left wing that day was to call on my friend Parsons of whom you have heard me speak. He has a battery of his own now and it did most splendid execution on that terrible day of Wednesday the 31st. I passed him that day & did not know it was my friend. I did not see him as he had just left for N.Y. to see his young wife and bear in person his own blushing honors. How sorry I was that I could not see him. We next called on Henry Howland Q.M. of Palmer's Division same Corps. We took dinner with him & such a dinner! It was worthwhile to visit him if for no other purpose than to enjoy the creature comforts of this life. But the pleasure of talking with an old friend was the best treat of all. He showed me pictures of his wife & children. Enclosed I send you lines written by a secesh lady widow of Ex Gov A.V. Brown,[1] Polk's P.M. General, with whom Howland boarded sometime while in Nashville. Pretty ain't they! But it makes me have some queer thoughts to think of such ones fattening on the public & then be such traitors. Mr H. sends all sorts of regards to you. I have also a message from him to Em which I shall send in a letter to her in answer to her letter of 1st inst. which I received yesterday.

Well my little sweet wife you will not ask me to write any more of the fight will you? I entered into that sufficiently in detail in my letter to father which I intended for you all. The more I think of it the more I thank God for giving me strength of mind & body to go through it as I did. Sometimes I think I was too careless & yet it was all for the best perhaps. When we had to retreat I never felt so vexed in all my life. But let it pass I will not continue the subject. We whipped them at last & that was sufficient.

This morning just before we started out on our forage excursion I was weighed for the first time since I joined the army, & I was much surprised that I have gained in flesh in the 4 ½ months since I left you exactly 20 lbs. I now weigh 161 lbs a greater weight than I ever attained before. I shall be a "weighty character" at the end of a year if I go on increasing at that rate, and a pretty good mark for secesh to shoot at. I hope with my increased physical proportions I shall be able to wear a broader smile on my countenance than usual, & I know I shall whenever I meet my dear friends at home.

I was sorry to hear of Mason being sick with a cold. Hope your next will report him well. I should like to see him in a little Scotch dress. I feel very strongly already about his education & future prospects, but it is useless to set our hearts on anything of that nature. All I can do is to pray that God will protect him & you and guide you both. Do not dearest be exercised about what I wrote to Will. I was fearful he would mention it & yet I know you have judgment beyond that of many women. I want you at least to bear witness in after years should the Supreme being take me away from Earth on the field of battle that I died a "brave man." Of all things I detest a coward, and it is my pride above all things to have you love me for any good qualities I may possess. I promise you I will not be rash, but I will be found wherever my duty calls, whatever be the consequences.

I should like if I could get it here a sole leather valise about 22 inches long with steel springs. It costs a good deal I presume but they are the only ones that will stand banging about. You may send it if you can whenever any one comes as messenger to the regiment. Have my name painted on it. Put in it a little broom brush, & a small oval hand mirror, & I wish you could just come with it yourself. With much love to all I am as ever your affectionate husband

John A Bross.

Note: The following page, evidently the final page of a letter to Josiah Bross, was probably written on January 22nd or 23rd, at the same time as the above letter to Belle. She may have kept it with the other letters because, on the reverse of this page, John has sketched the positions and movements of Union troops during the Battle of Stones River.

A word on other matters. I was weighed a few days ago & I come up to 161 lbs avoirdupois a greater weight than I ever attained before. So you see the army agrees with me physically having gained exactly 20 lbs in 4 ½ months. I wrote to Belle to send me a valise. I think my dress coat might be sent in it as I am fearful that if I go on increasing at this rate I will never be able to wear it out. My vest I have already split open about four inches on the back & it is tight now. Perhaps if she could get a good chance to sell it she had best do that as it will not be quite large enough for me unless I pinch myself considerably. I have never worn it but twice on dress parade & one afternoon in Louisville. The hat & cap are just right. Capt Longworth of the 36th is a right jolly good fellow, & we train together a great deal. We are unable to tell when we shall move from here but we are not expecting to march immediately. We are hoping something from Burnside.

Since writing the above, my 2d Lt. L. B. Cole has been detailed to go to Louisville to bring up the convalescents & I wish you would see to getting me a sole leather valise about 22 inches long with steel springs. Print my name on it. Send to Belle by telegraph if necessary for the coat & pants. This is the only opportunity I will have perhaps to get them for a long time. Send by express to Louisville care of 2[d] Lt. L. B. Cole, 88th Ill Vol immediately. He will be at Louisville only a few days & you will need to use dispatch. I send this by him & he will mail it. I have only time to say that I will see you repaid as soon as I can get my pay. I write you instead of Belle as she is too far out of the way to reach in time.

Ever your brother,
John A. Bross

1 Aaron V. Brown served as Governor of Tennessee from 1845 to 1857 and as Postmaster General in President James Buchanan's cabinet from 1857 to 1859.

In Camp Stone River Tennessee
Jany 26, 1863.

My Dear Wife!

Since I wrote my last letter two Lieutenants of which 2[d] Lt Lewis B. Cole of my Co have been detached to go to Louisville & intermediate places to bring forward the convalescents, & I seize the opportunity to send you a line. Firstly. I have written to Josiah to purchase a valise sole leather about 22 inches long & steel springs & to telegraph if necessary to you to send my coat & pants to him. I might as well wear out the coat, as I am afraid it is too small for me now. You will need to use despatch as Mr Cole will be in Louisville only a very few days & the valise will be sent to his care by express, at least I wrote him to do it for me & send letter with Cole to Louisville. I would like it if you could also send an oyster can full of mothers butter or some approaching to it if she is not making any, just to enjoy it once but don't delay sending the other things on my account. This is the 4th letter I have written you since the battle. I hope you have received the others. I also wrote in my last letter for a little broom brush & a small oval hand mirror—but you need not delay for them. I am sorry I could not slip home to see you just for an hour as you say but I have about made up my mind to be content with my lot & wait events. Col Sherman complimented me on my conduct on the field & has seemed very polite ever since. I only meet him officially & bide my time.

Yesterday Capt Blake 89. Ill. called to see me. Also Lt Blakeslee 74th who took dinner with me. Capt Longworth was also over & we went to church together that is to hear the 36th chaplain. He is a magnificent man, while our chaplain is a mere stick, a perfect useless piece of furniture. He is a Methodist.

I wish you would do one thing for me. Aunt Julia & Mattie Longworth sent me in a box to Capt Longworth two cans of preserved peaches a can of preserved currents, apples, butter and some head cheese. All these things were very thankfully received & I wrote a note of thanks addressed to both. I think it would please them very much if you would also send them a note thanking them for it. I got the things on Christmas afternoon. Had a huge supper with Capt Longworth & next morning we broke up our camp & started for this place. I ate that butter along the route & enjoyed it hugely. The last morsel I ate on Saturday P.m. after the battle ... Our box has not yet come although I have sent to Nashville for it time & again. I am afraid it is lost. I get no papers from Chicago. Great many wonder at it, while others frequently get them. Cole leaves in the morning & I must close. Love to all.

Yours Ever
John Bross

Camp Butler Stone River Tenn
Feby 1, 1863.

My Sweet Wife!

Your letter of 19th ult. & fathers of the 20th reached me on Friday last. I was extremely gratified & delighted to hear from you as I had not heard from you since your letter of Jany 1. a month since. I presume father has recd my letter to him written nearly three weeks since. The mails have not been regular since the battle until within a few days and we hope we shall now get our letters direct. It is difficult for you to appreciate the earnest longing we have suffered as day by day passed and no word from those we love. Officers & men watch the mail with intense eagerness, and when the well known hand of father appeared on a letter to me I was more than gratified. - - Col Sherman has gone to Springfield & Chicago to procure recruits. Several of the Lieutenants have sent in their resignations for various causes, & one got mustered out in disgrace for giving as a reason his opposition to the Presidents proclamation. You speak of the diminution in our regiment. It is rather sad to see what havoc has been made in it since we left Louisville. We can now scarcely muster 200 for Battalion drill, & yet we are much more efficient than you would suppose. The weak & worthless have gone into hospital or skedaddled and most of what we have left are good men & can stand a great deal of exposure. I went into battle with 36 men & lost ten, but have now 32 again for duty. Look at the figures: 19 in hospital, 15 deserted, 2 died of disease, 19 lost in battle in killed & wounded, & 32 for duty. My Co is an example for the others. The item of deserters includes about ten who were utterly unable to keep up on the march and fell out. Not having heard from them I put them down as deserters in order to get them off the muster roll. 1st Lt Gibson is on detached service in the pioneer corps, & 2d Lt Cole is on special duty for twenty days to bring up the convalescents & so I am alone for twenty days. All there is of it, it keeps me close at home. The hardest work we have at present is picket duty & forage duty. It is the rainy season and mud is the rule. However we are pretty well cared for as we have drawn rubber blankets from both the U.S. & Board of Trade. We are as comfortable now in our tent as you would desire. We can also live quite cheaply & easily getting rations from the commissary at Govt price without cost of transportation. Whenever we can get flour we live first rate that is, if we are smart enough to get soda & cream tarter from the Sutler. I could furnish you griddle cakes or biscuit which I imagine you would relish with mothers butter. My men have become thoroughly accustomed to look out for themselves in this particular. They are sharp in helping themselves to all the necessaries of life whenever an opportunity offers. Do not imagine that such life with me is at all in comparison with that I have left. I would fly to you instantly if it were so that I could with honor to myself and my convictions of duty. Still is it not a great deal better while I am in the army to try & be contented with my lot & to make the best of circumstances. A cheerful mind goes a great way in reconciling me to absence from you and I look forward with the utmost faith that I shall be with you and enjoy again those domestic joys that cluster so thickly in my memories.

Privations & hardships do not express all of camp life. No one but the actual endurer of them all can really appreciate how hard it is. It is enough to draw tears from a heart of adamant at times to witness sufferings of the poor soldiers on the march or in camp, or in a living grave of a hospital. "I would rather be shot than go in a hospital" is a frequent expression. It has more terrors than all the horrible butchery of the Battle field. I know you do not consider me insensible to these things when I talk of being cheerful amid all these scenes. I keenly feel it all & yet while I am a soldier in the service of my country I must be a man. It is but an evidence of your devoted love as I read of your longing for my society. It does not discourage me. On the contrary, I know you have strength of character to bear our separation for a season, and that devotion of yourself to me challenges my most profound regard. Six years of domestic life & happiness I ascribe to you and with all my patriotic feelings I do not hesitate to tell you how much I would be glad to resume it again. I feel all over the same as when I went into the army that I could serve my country as a soldier. I feel so still. When the time arrives I shall most gladly lay aside the sword for that dear sweet smile of yours which is all powerful with me.

I wrote you in my last letter of the reception of the hat & cap. They are very nice. I also wrote in a hurry about a valise. I suppose there will be opportunities to send them if you cannot get them to Lt Cole in time. - - To day has been literally a day of rest for our Regiment. It rained hard last night & this morning & we have had nothing to do but sit by our "own fireside." Rather ludicrous ain't it to talk of such a thing here. By the by Col Greusel called at my tent yesterday. He asked who made my fire place! I told him & he complimented me highly. How I wish you could drop in & see me if it were but for a day. I did not lose my "haversack" on the battle field. On the contrary in the morning of the 31st, between day dawn, & the secesh making their attack upon us which was perhaps ten or fifteen minutes, I was busily engaged in cutting off the remaining pieces of meat from a leg of mutton which had been given out to the company the night before & filling my haversack with it. This stood me in good stead that night. This was while the regiment was lying down in line of battle. I was determined to have a good meal at some time & I did when night closed o'er the scene. I dont know that I told you how I lost my blanket & shawl. On the Sunday previous to the battle Col

Greusel offered to have them carried in his wagon which generous offer I accepted. On the day of the battle, it was captured & recaptured but a lot of the things had been stolen out of it among which mine was not to be found. I hope you did not think that I retreated from the field leaving those behind. I carried off the field one of my private's blankets which he had forgotten to pick up. That said haversack is very convenient. It carries my "night cap" when on picket or the march, a little tea, coffee, sugar, meat & crackers, & a tin cup, knife, fork & spoon. - - You say well that we must admire Rosecrans. Never can I forget that sublime sight of the artillery massed on a gentle elevation between the pike & Rail road & in that mass of artillery young Parsons' battery was placed. I felt in my bones as our right wing came out of the cedar woods in to the open field in front of the long line of bristling cannon that we had a commanding general however much I felt indignant at one of our Division generals. I felt that that point was the key & there old "hold fast" was bound to stay. That artillery & the stubborn bravery of the infantry massed with it saved the day. Rosecrans has a strong hold on this army & I admire his generalship but there is one thing that makes me fear sometimes when I think of what might happen should he eclipse every other general in military reputation. He is a Catholic of the Jesuit order & "Father Tracy" his confessor is one of the most bigoted as I understand of the same order. Suppose he should dazzle the country by his military genius so as to become a successful candidate for the presidency & be elected, I should have great misgivings on account of his religion. Not on account of himself perhaps, but of those who would be apt to control his councils. And does not the spirit of faction at home indicate that we may drift into military despotism. I frankly avow that I prefer a strong government to anarchy & if we must lose our present Union & Government I prefer a head & an arm that can control. Already we have heard it in the army that if necessary hundreds would gladly march home & clean out a la Cromwell the miserable secessionists of our northern legislatures, and it would be done too if the men were only "let loose."

And now a word as to the end of the war. Of course no one but Providence knows that, but it does seem to me that if we could have our regiments filled up with new recruits we could crush out the rebels in less than six months with ordinary leadership. The army as a mass want to go home. They are in a measure sick of the war because it is lengthened out. The old regiments thought they would be at home long ere this and officers are continually dropping out for one cause or another. Many I doubt not came into it thoughtlessly & enthusiastically little dreaming of what the actualities of war really are and hardships have cooled off whatever of enthusiasm they ever had. Then again some things in the management of the war has had great effect on others, and political favoritism and corruption in high places is enough to fill the mind with anxious forebodings. If Senator Wilsons bill shall become a law to consolidate regiments many officers will thereby have a chance to retire honorably, & in that event if there was a chance to do better in a new regiment I should gladly get out of this one. Capt Longworth & I have discussed the project of trying to get permission to raise a Cavalry regiment. There will be more needed of that arm of the service. At least we think there ought to be a great deal more here in the west. Especially if we succeed in breaking up their armies there will be need of cavalry to chase down the guerrillas. - - I suppose you will be glad if we have a consolidation which will leave me out. I shall not be sorry to get out of this with Col S. at the head. - - I am sorry to hear of father being unwell it makes me feel very anxious whenever I hear of his indisposition. It is rather ludicrous to hear of Sister Em shaking with the ague. You know I cannot appreciate that disease. - - I hope Annie will not wait to write me because others tell the news. I hope she will have a good visit in Chicago. By the by would it not do you good to visit Chicago again? I am sure it would be agreeable to you & would tend to satisfy my mind. Not that you are unpleasantly located at home, but because a change will do you good. I know you will be welcome at Br Will's and a months stay in Chicago will be short. - - You speak of Bressler? He was in the battle of the 31st & escaped without injury. He is the worst man in the Co & cordially hated by all the privates. At Bowling Green on Nov 2d I ordered the Co to go to the river to wash their clothes. He refused unless he could have a kettle for himself. I told him to go with the rest, at the same time taking hold of his arm. He immediately flew into a passion & said "don't you strike me sir!" There was a scuffle immediately in which he struck at me three or four times. I had him arrested instantly & taken to head quarters where he was tied up. At Mill Creek this side of Nashville he was tried for "disobedience of orders" & for "striking his superior officer" the extreme penalty of which for the latter offence is death. His case has not yet transpired but it was intimated to me by one of the members of the court that he was convicted. What his sentence will be I know not. I do not expect him to be punished much & do not wish it, but he will learn one lesson before he gets out of the army & that is to obey orders or he will get his head broke. He has a poor reputation among the boys for fighting on the day of the great battle. - - And now a word about Dinsmoor. You have spoken in one of your former letters about his promotion. I would gladly do it if I thought he would sustain himself but he is so utterly heedless & careless that he almost forgets at times whether he has a head on his shoulders or not. He is generous to a fault. He would give away the last stitch of clothing he had to accommodate anybody & is always apologizing for the short comings of this or that delinquent, two or three times he has lost the greater part of his clothing. In battle he is as brave as any, but he does not seem to have the slightest idea of good business habits. I write this for yourself & to let you know why I have not promoted him. I must have officers on whom I can rely. I have made some mistakes in that line & I shall make no more if I can help it. Dinsmoor is better cared for than any other private, so much so that the men have grumbled of course at what they knew nothing about. I relieve him from guard duty. He messes with me in my tent, sleeps with Rae in my tent & there is nothing that I have but he has his share. He has a general oversight over the cooking. This may appear menial but it is no more than I do myself. Whenever there is a chance to get him in the QM. or commissary department I shall gladly do it. Now if father has anything to advise about him I wish he would. I feel anxious for Dinsmoor & will do anything I can for his advancement. My "nigger" wanted me to tell you what a good soldier he would have made in the last battle if he had had a gun. He formerly was a servant of the wife of Gen. Rousseau. I shall never forget his almost super human leap to the rear on the night of the 30th, when the reb pickets came across the field & suddenly fired upon our pickets. - - The postage stamps from father came duly to hand. Billy Kilgour I hope will recover from his wound. I wish him no harm but he is no friend of mine. The 75th is right by us, yet they are strangers to me. Their treason to me as well as that of some of the civilians at home I shall never forget & I was about to say I shall never forgive. I avoid thinking of it as much as I can for it is abominable to see how essentially devilish were all their acts in regard to me. But what have they gained by it? Their Regt is a mob & nothing more. I have nothing but scorn & contempt for the whole crew. It (the Regt) will never be any thing & never can while such officers as they have control it. I have sympathy but for one man & that is squire Besse over the loss of his son. Let father present to him my regards and sorrow for his loss. As for Cobbie all his meddling, busy body, snake in the grass conduct has come to no good end & all his views are come to naught. His patriotism is bounded by the extent to which his promotion goes & no further. If he ever attempts to speak to me I shall insult him regardless of consequences. This may appear vindictive in your's & mothers eyes but if ever there was a case out of the ordinary line of treachery & meanness this case of Cobbie is one. It seems to me that I am specially delegated to chastise him at some day. But I will dismiss him lest I say too much about him ... I saw the marriage of Miss Nichols & Ed Frey in a paper—but was surprised to learn of the union of Vernon & Miss Graves. Who next I thought in our church? - - I always read with avidity anything from mother. It makes no difference how it is written! I am glad you gave "Tim" a Roland for an Oliver. - - Capt Whiting goes home on leave of absence for fifteen days, cause his new wife is in "an interesting situation." He says he will take this! Capt Chickering is under arrest upon grave charges & both of his Lieutenants have resigned. Give my best love to all & kisses for the dear boy, & as ever I am your ever affectionate husband

John A Bross

Head-Quarters Fourteenth Army Corps,
Department of the Cumberland
Office Chief of Police

Nashville Feb 4th 1863

Dearest!

You will be a little surprised to find me writing from this place. The regiment is here as escort & guard for our Division train of wagons. I am writing from the office of John Fitch, who is "Provost Judge." He is very well. I am enjoying a little rest in his office after the fatigues of yesterday. It has been awful cold for this climate. I have brought my letter to this place & will mail it here. Capt Whiting has already gone home. He left camp before I knew it. I expect to return with the regiment tomorrow. It seems pleasant to meet an old friend and to sit down in a comfortable office again. It is the first time since I left Louisville. This is a hard looking town except a few localities. Nothing scarcely but soldiers & niggers; here & there you will see a citizen. All the way from the front to this place shows signs of desolation & war. I hope the North will never experience its effects as Tennessee does wherever the army goes. I have many things to look after & I must be short. Again love to all. Just hug Mason for me.

Ever your affectionate husband
John

On "Brigade Picket" Salem Pike
5 miles west of Murfreesboro, Thursday
February 12th 1863

My Beloved Wife!

Yesterday afternoon my heart leaped with joy when I received your epistle of Feby 3d & fathers also of the 4th by mail! I had not heard from you for some time & I devoured your letters with greediness. I presume you have received my letter mailed at Nashville on the 4th, by this time. I expect the things with Mr Cole whose time of absence is not yet expired. I am much obliged for the valise. It will be of great benefit to me. After I mailed your last letter at N. I sallied out on business and as Dinsmoor says had a square meal with a friend. At dark I returned to the Regt which was camped in the "floral hall" of the state fair grounds outside of the city. I was so fortunate as to find at the express office that box of butter. Young Scudder Q.M. Sergeant & myself had bought some bread, sausages & head cheese & we had a grand supper of our own manufacture buttered with fathers & Mr D's present. While you & friends were enjoying yourselves at

Uncle P's I was luxuriating on buttered toast etc etc. We did not have much moonlight that night for it snowed like the mischief, but we slept in our blankets as unconscious of all our surroundings as if we had no sensation at all. But believe me dear you all were in my thoughts that evening. While nothing is necessary to the vivid mental impression which will embody you all in actual presence almost, yet there is something in the tangible evidence of the love and remembrance of friends. I buttered & toasted & toasted & buttered in true epicurean style oblivious of almost anything else, thanking my stars the while for such friends. I did think that I would never mention "appetite" or the "good things of this life" again in my letters, but your oysters set my "mouth watering" & Uncle P's good cheer by way of contrast made me think that your husband had something good all the way from Sterling at the same time you were partaking of the generous viands. Next day Feby 5th we started for the front a two days march. It was drizzly & sloppy & through it & over a horrible road we marched 15 miles, half way & reached our bivouac at Lavergne about 4 P.m. I expected to sleep on the wet ground but luckily we had a brick dwelling house to stay in. The town had recently been burned by the East Tennessee Union Cavalry leaving but two or three houses standing. I had a room by myself & a fire already in it having been occupied by a court martial in session for the Brigade stationed there. Lucky for me as it was the first house I have slept in since I left you. However I have no bed of down but the soft floor was good enough for me. At 4 A.m. next morning I was up bright and cheery as the lark & among other things toasted a spare rib ("cramped" by my boys from a living animile the night before) on the clean side of a shovel before a rousing cedar fire. You must know that salt & pepper is a part of the "stores" in my haversack. With this I basted the "ration" and young "Scud" pronounced it some of the most delicate eating of his experience albeit he is very particular in his appetite. You see I am at it again. Well I will not quote scripture about it. We started just at the peep of day and as the bright moon was descending the western slope of the sky. It had frozen up hard & with the bracing atmosphere we went forward at a pace that surprised ourselves. The sun rose "in unclouded majesty" & at nine A.m. we reached the vicinity of the battle ground. How changed the scene!

All was desolation & as silent as the grave. Scattered all over are the graves of the dead while the carcases of the horses yet lie in every direction & cannon balls can be picked up almost every where. We were a long while in crossing Stone River to Murfreesboro but we arrived in camp south of M. at about 3 P.m. We were glad to get back and rest. Who should call on me on returning but my friend Capt Longworth with his resignation accepted. He is now on his way home. He said that I must have you go down to Morris & have a long visit with him & Aunt Julia. It would do you good I know & I hope if you can feel like going to do so. I feel under the greatest obligations to Capt L. He has been a true friend from the start & it would please all our relatives there to see you. Next morning Feb 7th we were ordered out here for three days on Brigade picket. This pike is one of the approaches to Murfreesboro from the west. The object of our being here is to protect the rear of Davis' Division who has been out on an expedition to the westward for the past ten days. Instead of staying three days we are here yet & am not certain when we shall go back to camp. Our stay here although without camp equipage has been delightful. Yesterday I was Brigade officer of the day & so "rode a horse." The duties are to look after the whole camp, & more particularly the whole picket lines around our Brigade. You should understand that we are considered in the enemies country away from our regular lines, and as it is only one Brigade we have to be on the alert. Our lines are about 3 miles in extent & so I had a grand ride going round 4 times in twenty four hours, twice in the day time & twice at night in order to see that all is right. I know you would be glad if I could ride one all the time & so would I. Perhaps the time will yet come. - - Our Lt Col Chadbourne is in com of the Brigade, Col Greusel having resigned. Col Sherman will take command when he returns. I have thus given you a little history of occurrences since I last wrote. Feby 13th. Yesterday Col Sherman returned & this morning came out here & took command bringing your letter of 5th & one also from Bro William. I am much gratified at your evidences of devotion in writing so often. Last eve there was an officers meeting of the 4 Regiments at Brigade Head Quarters to express their sentiments upon the resignation of Col Greusel. Unexpectedly I was appointed Chairman of the com on resolutions, with a Lt Col & acting major as my associates. No resolutions had been prepared & the other members of the com threw it all on me. It placed me in a quandary for the time being. A feeling came over me that I should not do the Col or myself justice. I threw off an effusion however in the shape of a preamble & resolutions which pleased the committee not a word being changed. They also met the unanimous approbation of all the officers. A copy signed by the officers is to be presented to Col G. today & also copies sent to the papers at Chicago, Milwaukee, Detroit & Aurora for publication. If you get a copy in the papers send me one for preservation. The administration have done wrong I think in overlooking his services & he resigns I think because of it & ill health! Say to father I am pleased with his disposition of the DeKalb property. I see by Bro Wills letter that Father & Mother Bross are to live at Morris. I have already written you about Bressler. Set your mind at rest about my losing my commission. Mrs Bressier may sing a very different tune ere long. It is all balderdash about Bressler's vaporing. He does his duty now very well. I only require him to do his duty & that he has got to do, you may rest assured of that. Not a man in the Co likes him. - - I have never called on Gen Kirk & I do not propose to do so. His conduct at S. last year was unfavorable to me all the time & I do not propose to flatter his vanity at all. I care not how much of a hold he has upon the people of Sterling. I shall not forget his conduct towards me, or that of any other of the sycophantic traitors that are continually "blowing his horn." Mother I am afraid will think me vindictive. I trust not! You will never find me detracting in the least from the well earned laurels of a brother officer or soldier were he my bitterest enemy & it is equally as impossible for me to forget injuries that are literally burned into my soul. Do not suppose I brood over these things of last year. On the contrary I am a firm believer in the rulings of Providence & I know that it is all for the best. I do not regret my present place believing that I am here to fulfill some design of the Supreme being. I try to make the most of my position & contentment & cheerfulness is the very best of medicines! - - And so my little "chatterbox" wants to "lite to papa"! I saw at Nashville two or three little toddlers neatly dressed and their cheerful sunny countenances made my heart leap with yearning desires to embrace my own dear boy. How any human being can dislike children is a mystery. - - Saturday morning Feb 14, 5 ½ A.m. In camp. Yesterday afternoon, we were relieved on Salem pike by Col Bradley's Brigade & we returned to camp. At 7 this morning we go out to our old picket ground on the Shelbyville pike. I thought I would finish this letter. Last night I was again gratified by a letter from Sister Annie. Two in one day was too much almost for me to expect. I know she must enjoy herself in Chicago & I hope you will make arrangements to go there soon & also to Morris. Did father get the letter with the balls of cotton. You or he does not speak of receiving it. In your last you also speak of a pair of boots. When & how were they sent? I will write to father soon! I expect Mr Cole to return next week & then I shall be pretty well fitted out! William it seems had quite a "blow out" with Col Sherman the result of which was they "kissed & made friends." Another result was a long letter to me susceptable of two constructions, of which I shall of course look to the better one. You also speak of looking after the good graces of the Col! I shall do what I can consistent with my sense of right to be agreeable as I always have done; but beyond that do not ask me to go. If I am but a Captain the whole of my period of service I shall not be a sycophant, lick the hand that smites me and "crook the pregnant hinges of the knee that thrift may follow fawning." I know you would not have me do that! Sometime I will sketch the portrait of Col S. so that you & Br Will may see it in its true light until then & perhaps always I may be misunderstood by Br Will, who of all other men should know me. - - My best love to our dear parents. Kiss papa's darling boy & with love to Em & Zad.

I am always your devoted husband
John A Bross

In Camp on Stone River
Saturday Feby 21st 1863

My beloved Wife!

Yesterday we went out on our usual picket duty and was relieved about 9 A.m. to day. I came back to camp feeling that I should hear from you to *day* & sure enough your letter of Monday last came with todays mail. I have thought several times whether you remember that *this* is my birth day. I take it for granted you will. I was happy to hear from you & extremely gratified to know that father is now recovering from his attack of sickness. You will say I would have been likely to be alarmed if I had not known that the crisis of the disease was passed. I am *so* glad to know that he is not dangerously ill. Now at the outset as to coming home I am almost sure it is impossible to attain the object yet to accomplish it I will do almost anything to see my beloved ones at home. We expect to be paid next week & if we get more than two months pay I shall be able to pay that note of Scammons beside leaving something for you & settling with the Q.M. besides. How *dearly* I would love to bring my money in person *you* can well appreciate. I will take the first opportunity to see Sherman. It is not *all* who ask for leave of absence that can get it. Favoritism is in the army as elsewhere, and you may gather from my letters that I am not in the habit of bending to the footstool of power because men *have* the power. Still, I would do almost anything as I said before to make a short run home. I will make the effort & let you know the result. This morning was very beautiful—it is raining this afternoon very hard accompanied with thunder. It is in strong contrast with the remembrance of former birthdays. By the by have you read the proposed plans of Eli Thayer for colonizing Florida? It has attracted my attention from its novelty, or rather an old thing in reality applied to the resuscitation of a slave state, & because my friend Judge Morris resides there. I believe I will write him & get his opinion as to its practicability. How would you like to live in a sunny clime amid bananas, guava, oranges & tropical flowers & fruits? I am inclined to think that your gentle nature would be charmed with it, provided we had a peaceful home & a competence. I throw this out merely as a suggestion. Of course it is useless to make plans when I have 2 ½ years yet to serve in the army & we know not yet what is to come out of the present and the near future.

As to business matters I am sorely anxious at times about them and especially for your sake. But you see how difficult it is for commanders of companies to get away. Capt Whiting got home by private representations with regard to the condition of his wife. The ostensible reason was *business*, but the personal representations outside of the written reason, were the real reasons that procured him the leave of absence. There is a disposition among Division & Corps Commanders to keep the Captains with their Companies. One Lieutenant in command of a Co in the 36th for nearly a year past & never since he enlisted away from the Co was refused leave of absence for 20 days while Capt Longworth's resignation was accepted. This is the way it works. Now if I cannot come home, why can not Bro Will & you come & see me? I can get you through I presume as far as Nashville without difficulty where I can get a pass to see you for a day or so. I want especially to see you & Will for business reasons & to pay you all the money I can spare. Suppose it does cost a little money for you to visit Nashville? I think it would be well spent. Will ought to see Nashville, look around, become acquainted with Gov Johnson and Rosecrans all of which might in the end help your husband. I would like to see the baby—my darling Mason, but I would much rather you would not be encumbered with him if you should come. I shall certainly propose to William to run down if I cannot get leave of absence. I must see Will to set his face right about my situation in the regiment.

Sabbath Feb. 22d

To day has been interesting to us! A general order from Rosecrans was read on "dress parade" about the day which was truly eloquent & patriotic. There has also been a grand salute from batteries in every division of the army. It was magnificent indeed. By another order an election in each co was had for five privates in each co who have distinguished themselves for soldierly conduct bravery &c to be placed upon a "Roll of Honor," three of whom from each co are to be detailed to form a co & with the same no. from the three other regiments of the Brigade to form a "light Battalion" to be models & the elite of the army. They are to be mounted & carry revolving rifles. It created of course great interest. Dinsmoor was one of the no. on the Roll. I of course very quietly had his interests in my keeping. He is very desirous of getting into the "light Brigade." As they will ride & have some advantages which infantry will not have. He is worthy of the Honor conferred although he was extremely fearful that he would fail because some have grumbled because he was with me & so relieved from the common duties of a soldier. No one was braver or did every duty required at Stone River than Dinsmoor. If he goes it will be a post of danger but he is not the man to flinch in such a position. Some one will be hurt when that light Brigade makes a charge, for it will be composed of men who cannot show the white feather. Rosecrans has touched the right cord in this movement & I confess I wish I had a command in it. I would take pride in doing what I could to make it as famous as the English "light Brigade," celebrated in the poem of Tennyson.

Wednesday 25th February

I have had no time to finish this letter since Sabbath. Monday our Brigade changed camp from the east to the west side of the river. We are in a much better location on the immediate bank and we have been all the time getting things in shape. Yesterday we went on a long march for forage. It was a beautiful day. Enclosed I send you a couple of the first flowers of the season I picked up on my way. They will all be faded when you get them, but I know you will accept them in the spirit that prompts my sending them. How beautiful they looked on their stems & cheerful, amid the desolation that war brings in its train. We returned at night having marched nearly 20 miles & procured a hundred wagonloads of corn & other produce. To day we have been making preparations to get paid for the 1st two months service. We are the last Regiment in the Brigade & it may be next week before we get it. We are also promised two more months pay in a few days. This is good news to us. I wish we could get it up to March 1st, which is another muster day. - - We have had a specimen freak of the mail bags, yesterday & to day. Last evening on my return I found yours & mothers letters of January 13th. To day I received one of Bro Wills of Jany 16, one from Guilford of Jany 29. Willie also recd one from Carrie of Jany 19th. I had supposed there was such a letter somewhere but your not having mentioned it in subsequent ones I thought I might have been mistaken. But along it comes at last, fresh as when first written, & full of a mothers love, and my wifes devoted, affectionate nature. I am inclined to think I prize them more than if I received them directly.

Thursday morning

It is raining hard and Stone River is booming high. How I wish I could be with you this morning. I am just as contented here as any of them & do not allow myself to become disheartened at my long prospective absence from you. Yet I long to be with you all again—to thank my mother for her goodness father for his whole hearted kindness and you all for the interest continually manifested in my welfare. So far as health is concerned I think you may all rest easy. There is no one in the regiment, perhaps, capable of greater endurance than myself. If I ever get through this war I do not wish to be confined in an office. I must have out door exercise. I do not like the thought of giving up my regular business, yet I never can be content to rust out in sedentary life. But there is ample time for deciding on the future. I will write you as soon as I get my pay in hand & forward it by express. I cannot tell yet how much you will receive but every cent I can spare you shall have to liquidate claims. I shall have enough to clear all up I hope with six months pay, except Uncle Pennington. The little Daguerreotype of yourself I so much prized I have lost in consequence of the old valise I have used having a hole in it. I would not have parted with it for anything. We expect to go on picket tomorrow. I will write again soon. Love to all and a thousand kisses for Mason.

Yours Ever
John A. Bross

In Camp on Stone River Tenn Monday
March 2^d^ 1863

Dearest!

To day is one of the brightest and fairest & sunniest I have ever enjoyed. I write you the labor being that of love. The brigade is out on drill. I am president of a Brigade Court martial and consequently am relieved from other duty. We have adjourned for the day, and you may well imagine that you are in my thoughts. Saturday your letter of 26th Jany & fathers of same date came to hand in answer to mine of 11th Jany. Yesterday, yours & fathers of 22[d] and 23[d] Feby came to hand making my heart light & cheery because of hearing so directly from home. The former as well as other letters have been laying all the while in Nashville I presume as I understand they have only three clerks there to transact the business for this whole army. It is a nuisance that should be abated at once. I thought I had acknowledged the reception of the pair of boots. They are capital and with them I can go on any march. - - And so Aunt Ann would have me resign! I fully appreciate the kindness intended and her desire to keep me safe from harm knowing that it arises from that feeling but for that cause I can have no face to leave this position. I counted the cost at the beginning. I know well its dangers and the possible sacrifice. Yet I am one of those who thoroughly believe that blood must be shed in order to bring this controversy to a close. Let me commend to your notice to Mother & especially to Aunt Ann an article in the March No. of the Atlantic Monthly a copy of which I was favored with yesterday addressed to the women of the North. If all would be as sacrificing as yourself we should hear no more of the contemptible conduct of base men behind us. I am heart sick sometimes to witness the indifference & detestable meanness of men & women in the North. Your sex have not exhibited that devotion & abnegation of self which characterize the southern ladies. Don't think I confound such as you & mother with those who would basely give up all that we hold dear in order that cotton lords & their female friends should domineer & crack the whip over our fair land. No. I well know how much you are willing to do & to suffer for my sake & the cause in which I am engaged. - - As to the misunderstanding with Col Sherman, yourself & William I know you could not ask me to play the coward. As to the letter of Br Will I shall pay him my respects in a reply that he will remember. Be assured it shall be respectful & without a speck of passion, couched in a tone of sorrow instead of anger. I shall not very soon seek anything from the Tribune. You are well aware that it has always been an injury to me instead of an advantage. I shall in the future as I have always in the past six months try to deserve success by my own efforts & if I do not succeed in getting a soldiers coveted distinction—promotion—the fault shall not be with me. I will follow your advice in that respect. As to your enquiry, it is not always true that a captain is acting major when the Col becomes

Brigade Commander. 2 field officers is considered sufficient. Yet the fact is if such thing becomes necessary, Col Sherman always puts his own appointees in Command. There is the rub. With my desire to create no fuss here in the front & in the presence of the enemy it yet wounds my feelings to an extent that you may appreciate but scarcely anyone else. The "Deacon"[1] I am persuaded does not yet "know me." You know that to do good to my country I would willingly carry a musket & be commanded by anyone almost, but to be placed in this position is very trying indeed. Yet the Deacon can almost advise me to give up my manhood in order to use molasses & soap with the present Brigade Commander. It will be when my nature is changed very materially. The tone of his letter also gave me the legitimate right to infer that I should be careful to attend to military duties; giving an idea that I had been remiss in that! That was the unkindest remark of all the letter. I will leave that portion of my military life to the inspection of friend or enemy, yea all the world. Do not imbibe any feeling against William by reason of what I have written. He is a [illegible][2] in some things & always will be. At bottom he is sincerely desirous of assisting me but he takes queer ways to accomplish it. - - As to getting an appointment to carry dispatches it is out of the question! If I had a staff appointment it would be practicable perhaps. Now in all I have written do not be yourself distressed. I tell you all my feelings as near as I can commit them to paper but above & beyond all I follow the great requirement of a soldier—obey, & do your duty. It is but for three years. I know it seems an age to you but with my active life time passes rapidly. I cannot realize at all that I have been six months in the army. But I am tired of this theme. - - Yesterday I procured a horse & rode over to Murfreesboro to see about my valise. It had not come. I stopped & called on Col Mihalotzy of the 24th Ill. The Brigade to which he is attached is composed of the 1st & 21st Wisconsin, 24th Ill & 79th Pennsylvania, commanded by Col Hambricht. The Brigade is commanded by Col Starkweather of the 1st Wis. They had a Brigade inspection & at its conclusion a magnificent stand of colors & guidons were presented by a com of Lancaster Co men to the 79th. The Brigade was drawn up in hollow square within which were the field & staff officers & Gen Negley & staff & 3 batteries of artillery. The 79th was raised in Lancaster city except one co. Its Col is a very fine looking man pretty much after the style of Gen Bullock whom he resembles very much from the eyes down to the chin. While the Brigade was being inspected I was introduced to the three gentlemen from Lancaster who brought the colors. They seemed much pleased when I told them I was a Pennsylvanian. They felt at home at once. They are well acquainted with Smith Patterson, the Hendersons the Wallaces, Galts &c. We had a pleasant confab and I was pleased that I happened there to witness the presentation. Lewis Halliday a very large man read the address of presentation & Col Starkweather replied for Col Hambricht. Gen Negley also made a neat little address. On being introduced to him "Ah!" (said he), "I saw you in the cedars!" Yes, you did! General! And the pressure of hands told more than words could, how his language meant the battlefield. - - Andrew B. Meixell & Walter G. Evans were the other members of the com. One of them has a sister, a Mrs Sheets living in Freeport. I was going to enquire of some of the officers of the 79th if they had any relations in Whiteside Co. but on 2d thought I thought it useless to enquire as these were soldiers before me, while (begging Zad's pardon) up your way they are men of peace; & so there is not much relationship. I must have the humor of it anyway.

I am very glad to hear that father has recovered sufficiently to get out again. He must be very careful of his health. It is one of the most depressing thoughts to know that he or any of you are unwell. - - Capt Longworth resigned because his wife has been long desiring him so to do, she having three children & because Lt Col Jenks came on to take command. There is a long tale to tell of Jenks' appointment as Lt Col of that Regiment. He has now resigned and some are very sorry that Longworth did at this time as he might have been made major. I do not wish to commence soliciting Gov Yates in my behalf. He knows the situation of affairs & if he does not see fit to right it I shall not try and I hope you will not either! I have never run after the "powers that be" and I shall not. - - Now as to a furlough. I wrote in my last that I would try. There has been no opportunity yet to see Col. S. Yesterday a friend of mine in the 36th saw Goddard Rosecrans' Chief of Staff & he said no officer could get a furlough unless he had a certificate from the doctor that he was "about to die"—this is a strong expression of course but it shows how difficult the undertaking is. - - It was rather singular that

Annie called on Mrs Sheridan. She is entirely too good I have heard it said for her husband, who happens to rank your husband (according to S) & I know I would not have anything to do with him in Chicago & no lady would. - - McClurg is one of the best captains in the regiment. Chickering has been under arrest ever since we left Mill Creek in December but is now in command of his co again. His two Lieutenants have resigned and gone home. At the Battle of Stone river he "Skedaddled" & put out for Nashville along with the miserable rout of cowards. He was not in command of his co. His father was here a few days ago & the charges I presume were withdrawn. - - All the articles in the box came safely to hand. We have been enjoying that butter & tea. Do not be anxious about living. As long as there is anything in the Commissary Department, or produce in the county, we will live I hope. - - I would give almost anything to see you but for a day. I could make you understand more of my position in one hours talk than in writing a quire full of paper. - - I have a long letter to write to Annie when I know of her getting a stopping place. I am glad she is enjoying herself, I hope she will not be in haste to get married. I want an unmarried sister yet awhile. But that is selfish perhaps. - - To show you how uncertain is a soldiers life we all expected this morning to remain in our beautiful camp having just got nicely settled, & this afternoon comes an order for "five days rations," & to be ready to march at a "moments notice." This does not look like a furlough! We have a rumor that we march at six A.m. tomorrow and in that case you may not hear from me for a week or two. I did not get my valise yesterday—I hope it will be forwarded soon. - - Tuesday morning, 3 March. Last eve the order to "advance" was indefinitely postponed but we are to keep five days rations on hand nevertheless. I think a movement will be made soon. We have been here two months and if the weather remains fair we shall go ahead. There is a desire either to remain here or make a movement into Georgia or Alabama. We do not like to go a short distance and then stop by the way. - - A word more about my "difficulty." I do not wish you to gather from what I have written that I am preventing by my own feelings & conduct any advantage or prospective promotion or otherwise. I am not blinded in any manner. I do all I can to make myself agreeable to all about me & to treat my superiors with proper respect but beyond that

I shall never go. Now I hope this will make it plain enough so that you at least may rest easy about my conduct. - - I shall send this letter by Surgeon Pierce the successor of Coatsworth as far as Louisville hoping thereby you will get it direct. He is a fine scholar and a perfect gentleman & was lately assistant surgeon of the 36th. Coatsworth was a fine surgeon & from Bowling Green about Nov 3^{d} when he had a great drink up to the time of his death he was a perfect example of propriety. He was considered the best surgeon in this "wing." - - Bressler's sentence has at last been made public. He was convicted & sentenced to 14 days hard labor. So much for my losing my commission. - - I was disposed to feel indignant when I read your statement about old Linder making a speech for the Copperheads but on second thoughts what is he? nothing but a tool. I would rather put a bayonet to the breasts of the scamps who urge him on. The army has a "broad grin" upon it in consequence of the passage of the Conscript bill. The whole brood of cowards & traitors at home may rest assured that the army would enforce it with a will if the civil authorities are unequal to the task. We want our thinned ranks filled up. I believe in my very soul if the women of the North would drive their able bodied friends into the army we should crush out rebellion in three months. The draft properly executed will act like a charm. The south has scraped together their last man and we have ample resources yet to rely on. I am in favor of an armed emigration if nothing else will do. Let Northern mind & muscle "root out" what is left of the Oligarchy & then we shall certainly have a homogenous people. - - We expected to be paid yesterday but the paymaster is sick in Murfreesboro. Hope to get it tomorrow—when I will express some money home. - - Mason! my darling boy! do you remember Papa? Papa is way off—very far away! but he hears the birds sing every day, & the flowers are beginning to peep out & to look sunny as your own little face when mamma has a present for you. The band of music is now playing the "Ingleside"[3] for guard mounting & it almost makes papa a "baby" like yourself. Ask Grand Pa what "Ingleside" means & "guard mounting" also. Tell Grand Pa and Grand Ma & mamma that Papa loves them all very much & you too & that I want your picture and mamma's too.

Good Bye
John

1 John's brother William, active in the Second Presbyterian Church, was often referred to in public as "Deacon Bross."

2 Several words here have been erased.

3 This is, perhaps, a band tune named for the town of Ingleside, Illinois.

Bivouac near Franklin
Tenn. March 9th 1863

Dearest,

We are just about to go forward again on the march and as there is communication from here I send you a line. We left our camp on Stone River on the morning of March 4th the day appointed for our Regiment to be paid but we were not. We have been on the march westward by easy marches but it is a hard muddy road. We were in sound of the cannon the other day; the fight resulted in the loss of a Brigade. It makes us all fighting mad at some of our own officers. We do not know our destination as yet but probably you will hear of our being in a brush before this reaches you. I am very well and hope you are all the same. It is impossible now to give you any idea when we shall be paid. I am sorry on yours & Will's account but you know that "orders" are inexorable. It has been very unpleasant rainy weather since we left. This morning however it is delightfully pleasant. - - I left Dinsmoor back at Camp expecting only to be out on a 4 days scout, all the tents & camp equipage having been left standing. I must leave all to your imagination as to our destination, but do be cheerful & not too anxious for my welfare. Let us trust in Providence that he will preserve me safe through all the events I shall have to be a participator in. You may direct your letters as heretofore to Murfreesboro, Tenn. We are expecting to go back to camp but if not our correspondence will be sent us from that point. I hope I shall hear from you soon, but it may be ten days yet before I get back to camp. Rae is well also Barber. He is a capital soldier, being 2d Sergt he is acting orderly whenever Rae is not on duty. It is time to close this letter & with the greatest love to all & kisses for "Mason." I am ever & always your devoted husband

John A Bross

In Camp on Stone River
Tenn. March 16, 1863

Dearest!

I simply write you a short note now to tell you of two things. 1st our Division arrived back to camp safely last Saturday evening. The particulars of our "tramp" I may detail hereafter. I am very well. Found the valise had arrived, & I enjoyed the luxury of reading three letters from you at once. The next thing is I have got my pay to Dec 31 & I expect to send to Bro Will by the allotment comr of Ill by way of Louisville & the express from that point. $400 to Bro Will to liquidate that note, the balance he can pay to you. I am so full of business just now that it is scarcely possible for me to snatch a moment to devote to you. I found a large mass of official correspondence & with the endless daily routine, & looking after the interests of my men in sending their money home I am literally tied hand & foot as it were. I have made it a point to do my duty first. We were paid yesterday. I send Bro Will all I can & hope next payment to send you a like amount. The mode of getting the money to Will is as follows: I pay my money to the comr. He pays it to the paymaster at Murfreesboro. The paymaster there draws on the paymaster at Louisville. He makes up a package of like funds & amount & deposits it in the express office at Louisville directed to Will. This avoids any danger of loss or capture between Murfreesboro & Louisville. I shall take the first opportunity to write my sweet wife a long letter. You may imagine how my heart bounded with joy at reading your sweet letters. Love to friends & kisses for Mason.

Yours ever
John A Bross

P.S. I found on my return Uncle Penningtons Aunt Annes[1] & Florence's letters. I shall be most happy to answer them when I have leisure.

JAB

1 Anne Barnett Pennington was the sister of Belle's mother, Desire Mason.

In Camp on Stone River
Tenn. March 16, 1863

My Dear Bro!

I write you a short note to say that we were paid yesterday, up to Dec 31, 62. I intend to send through the allotment com[r] for Ill by way of Louisville & the express co $400.00 to your address with which I wish you to take up that note of Scammon. If there is a balance left after paying that & reserving the price of the Tribune you can pay it over to Belle. This is all I can send you reserving only about $20.00 for myself after settling up my commissary bills. The mode of sending the money is this. I pay the money to the allotment com[r]. He pays it over to the paymaster at Murfreesboro. He draws on the paymaster at Louisville who puts up in a package a like amt of funds & deposits it in the express office at Louisville addressed to you. This is to avoid risk bet. Murfreesboro & Louisville. I send you this note in order to let you know it is coming. I have no time to write you anything else save that I saw Cury on the march to Franklin & Spring Hill & Columbia. We returned here Saturday night. I have a large mass of business to straighten up which has been accumulating since March 4th when we left here on our expedition, which I am determined to get off of my hands first. At the proper time I intend to notice your letter sent me by the hands of Col Sherman. Don't think that because I do not answer your letters that I am forgetful. It is not always I can do so. I rec[d] a very good letter to day from father Bross. Give my love to sister Mary & as soon as I can snatch a moment of time you shall hear again from your affectionate Bro

John A Bross

In Camp Stone River
Tenn March 18th 1863

Dearest!

Two days ago I wrote you that I intended to send to William $400 by the allotment com[r] for Illinois. Yesterday the money was sent. It was a pleasant thought that it will make us both feel better as it arrives at its destination &

wipes out indebtedness. The whole amount of my pay to Dec 31 was $550. I have paid all my commissary bills to date, sutlers bills, and some borrowed money to pay for "mess chest" & other little expenses, leaving me square with the Government & every body here except my "clothing account" which is not settled by any one in less than six months or the end of the year. I shall be able to get along with what I have left until next pay day I think. If I don't do not trouble yourself about it as I can always command all I want from friends here who are desirous to lend in order that their money may be safe. In looking over the six & a half months I have been in the service I may I think congratulate myself on having contracted no debts of any account & my record is clear so far as that goes. If I could only dispose of the old matters at home my heart would be light indeed. Yet let us trust that time will bring it all around right. So much for business.

As to coming home it is impossible now. Lt Gibson is permanently detached to the pioneer corps & since McClurg has been sick, Lt Cole has been detailed to command his company thus leaving me entirely alone with the company. For that reason alone I could not get away. The reason for Cole being detailed was that Mc has no Lieutenants left, one having resigned & Lt Bool being on Shermans staff. McClurg goes home this morning on leave of absence for twenty days on a/c of disability. A thought of bitterness or of sarcastic feeling will come over me sometimes when I see others having the great privilege of visiting their friends while I must stay with my company. Well! be it so. I thank God for health & strength to be a soldier, and a disposition to be contented with my position. It requires some patience however.

I hope you have rec[d] two letters from me one sent part of the way by Dr Pierce & the other written near Franklin, Tenn while on the expedition. I should like to describe that march. If there is any enjoyment in "soldiering" I had it, although the way was long & fatiguing to a great many. I lived better than at any period since being in the service, having the best kind of "ham" pressed along the way, together with eggs, chickens, mutton, fresh pork, beef, &c & even potatoes. Ah! if the secesh in the north could but feel what war is at their own doors they would hurry up troops to end it here in doubly quick time. Our last days march was about 25 miles, and many gave out by the way. You might have seen me trudging along with my own "traps,"[1] &

a musket of some one of the tired boys. I had a feeling of pride in my muscle & endurance & it is with feelings of thankfulness that I can say so. As to that my reputation is the first among my brother officers.

I thank you heartily for the valise & contents. I appeared in my dress clothes on Sunday last & I had many congratulations on my complete metamorphose— and many compliments on your husbands fine appearance. The coat cannot be buttoned around the waist by two or three inches & the pants are also tight in that locality. Still I shall wear them as I am not compelled to button the coat only at the top. We have had quite a little feast over that good butter & Maggies cake & sugar. The cake was remarkably good after so long a time.

2^d Sheet
Wednesday Evening

Since writing the first sheet this morning we have changed our camp. We have been located on the south side of one of the forks of Stone River. To day the "right wing" moved from the south to the west of & nearer town. We have been at work all day & have got things to rights. It is a very pleasant evening the day has been hot especially in the forenoon. The peach blossoms are out & the foliage begins to come out & the grass looks so pleasant & the birds sing so gaily that I do wish you could enjoy it with me. It all reminds me of home, of Mason & you & Sister Annie & all. Yet how gladly would I leave them to see you.

I am glad you have written to Mrs Longworth & I hope you will accept their invitation at an early date. Captain L. can tell you many things that I may omit in my letters. We contracted a very close intimacy & he deserves our confidence. I received the Gazette to day sent by father at the same time with your last letter. The Tri weekly Tribune comes quite regularly now. I shall write to "Tim" soon. And so Mason writes to "John" & asks him to come home! Did I not write to him the very day he asked papa to come home? Yes, & I was thinking of him & mamma all that day & the next while on a long march. Sometime I shall see my darling boy. And then that great stick of nice candy for papa! It was sweeter to papa's taste than all the honey he has eaten here or at home. - - I should like to see Judge Arrington's speech if you have it send it to me. I have the printed resolutions I wrote about Col Greusel—there are some errors of printing. You speak of Leavitt. I heard through Willie that he will be dismissed the service also some other officer in the 34th. There is injustice in the way some officers slink away from their duties, draw pay from Government as long as possible & then get out of the service while those who do the work of a campaign must remain at their posts.

Sister Annie must be having a very pleasant visit to stay so long a time. I shall write to her soon; also to Florence. - - That can of butter I have been tasting with great gusto you may be sure. I am afraid you will think me a real epicure but I can't help it. We do enjoy such things from home—because we know it is good. Allow me to thank you for the tone of your letters & to hear from others what a patriot you are. It just nerves me up to my duty to know of what a gentle delicate creature like yourself is capable of doing.

I received a very warm hearted letter from Cap Longworth the evening before I left on the expedition. He was one of the most popular Captains in his regiment—always full of good nature the only drawback is his profanity--of course you would never hear it on visiting him. - - The Board of Trade have been quite liberal with the regiment. A few days since a large quantity of articles came for the regiment among other things dried apples. - - I am hopeful that fathers health will be good again. I was not aware before that Zad contemplates opening a dry goods store. I hope he will be successful. I see Colby is again in the Gazette. I thank him for the statistics of the company. While our Division was passing through the little town of Eagleville last week on our way home, we passed Davis, who was out there to support us. While waiting for some of the regiments of our Brigade to cross a slough young Woodburn came up to me while I was reading a paper by the road side. We had passed close to the 75th & I did not know it. The young man seemed very much pleased to see me. - - I send to Mason a specimen of the postage currency being a part of my first pay. Of course you have plenty of it there but I think you will appreciate it as coming from me. Willie also sends him some. The clipped corners is his. With much love to all I am ever yours

John A Bross

1 "Traps" is a nineteenth century word for personal belongings.

"Brigade Picket" Salem Pike
March 28th (Saturday) 1863

My Beloved Wife!

Your letter of 20th instant reached me this afternoon & glad was I indeed to receive it albeit I was somewhat disappointed at first thought that you had not received a short note stating my arrival back to camp from the Franklin Expedition & of our being paid. I hope you have received it ere this. I have been expecting to hear from you for several days & so have delayed somewhat to write you. There has [been] nothing of special note in the way of news or movements on our post since we came back to camp, except that we have again changed our camp nearer to Murfreesboro. In fact the whole army that has been advanced for several miles on the different pikes ever since we occupied Murfreesboro has been drawn in to the suburbs, so that it is all compact. Immense fortifications have been in progress of erection for months all around the town. Rosecrans is determined to hold this point at all hazards. Piles on piles of supplies & subsistence stores are daily increasing here & stand within the intrenchments. If the rebels presume to attack us here an event which we would all rejoice to see come to pass—they would be annihilated. Last Monday our Division had a "Grand Review" Rosecrans being present accompanied by a magnificent Staff. It was one of the most splendid military spectacles I ever beheld. The Genl was highly pleased. Our division has a first rate reputation and it will give us a position in the front when we move. In fact there are very few in it but what would prefer to be there than to remain behind to garrison a town or among the reserves. I hope you will not "dread" too much another encounter in which I shall be engaged. Let us trust that Providence has a long life in store for me after this rebellion has come to an end. Yet if otherwise I hope I am ready to lay down my life for the good of my country.

On the 17th of March in accordance with my intention expressed to you & Bro Will I forwarded to him through the Ill allotment comr & the Express the sum of $400.00 to take up that note of Scammon—to pay for the Tribune & the balance to pay over to you. I hope it will reach you in good time & I know it will relieve us both of one cause of anxiety at least. It may also be of some moment for you to know that I have paid up all my commissary bills & am square with the world excepting my clothing account which is settled once in six months! I don't know whether I told you how much I rec^{d} but I will state it here. I received $550.30 to Dec 31. Out of this I paid $35 for little expenses of recruiting at Chicago which I knew nothing about. It came pretty hard to pay them but I did so in order to close them out. I am glad I can assure you of my being so square with the world here. Then I think you will say also that I have done pretty well in laying by nearly $100.00 per month of my salary & paying for commissary bills 2 ½ months after the date to which I was paid. I had about $15 left which I can rub along with I hope until I am paid again. I should say also that I paid Willie $15 for attending to matters about my tent. By the by I have made him 1st corporal jumping him over several others. On the 21st Rae was promoted to Sergt Major. Barber I made "orderly" in his place. This gave me a good chance to promote Dinsmoor. I may have an opportunity soon to make him a sergt. He is with me now on Picket, the first regular duty of the kind he has done. I think his friends may be satisfied that I have taken pretty good care of him. - - While on the expedition to Franklin I was placed in command of the "right wing" on picket duty one night. Capt Sheridan refused to obey my orders & for which I reported him I do not know why I was placed in this position but so it was. He went home two days ago having obtained a leave of absence on the strength of a dispatch that his child was dying & his wife was very sick. It is a little singular that so many can get furloughs & I cannot.

Sunday 28th[1]

I wrote the first sheet last night while the officers were "making merry" & cracking all sorts of jokes in our "Sibley tent" which is brought out for our use. We are here for five days. Yesterday the Reb Cavalry came up very close to reconnoiter & it would have pleased you to see how quick we all jumped into our places thinking that we might have a chance for a slight brush, but they made off very suddenly. And now a word about coming home. I have tried all I could & I do not see any chance for me at present. Perhaps it is better for me to wait awhile yet. Soon after we returned from Franklin I called on Col Sherman & asked him about going home, told him the reasons for going etc. He said he would recommend my application with pleasure but he was almost certain it would not be granted—that this army is waiting movements at Vicksburg & we may move any day—that the next two months will be active spring campaigning & after that the army will do but little during the hot summer months when there would doubtless be a chance. So much that. Now as to my position here. At present I am the ranking officer any way or soon will be. Major Chandler is selected to command the Light Battalion from this Brigade. Capt Whiting Co "B" by some special favoritism is made the honorable one from this regiment so they will be out of the way which will leave the way open for an "acting major." When Sheridan returns the selection I presume will be between him & myself. Now ought I to try & get home in view of all these things? Be assured I would fly to you in a moment if I could but if all things seem to hedge me up in my regiment for the present I think I had better quietly submit to my fate especially if by remaining I may have the chance of being an acting field officer. Then again by waiting two months I may almost be sure of a short furlough! I would gladly see you here but I see that you cannot arrange to have William come with you as in a letter to me he says he is going east to be gone to the 20th of next month. - - I am making up a list of "little notions" which I may send for by my next letter. I mailed a letter very hurriedly to Annie the other day with some flowers & cedar twigs from the battle field. I had no time to arrange them in proper style. - - I can well imagine that "Mason" needs your care and attention. I do most strongly hope that the time will not be long until I can see you both. I have written to Uncle P. Aunt A. & Florence. Please add to my long letter the personal assurance of yourself how greatly I appreciate Aunt Anns letter. I know it must be painful for her to make any effort at labor of any kind. I wish I could say to her all I wish in reference to her great affliction. I believe if she could only have a peaceful & undisturbed home in the south that it would have a most beneficial effect upon her health. I have written letters recently to "Tim"—O'Hara—& Capt Longworth & Sister Maggie in answer to one she sent me in the valise. We had a merry time over her cake & sugar along with some lemons & other things Rae got. Now dearest write me what you would like to do about coming down to see me. I must see you at some date. Ever your own

John

1 This sheet is most likely misdated; should probably read "Sunday 29th."

Camp Schaeffer. Tenn.
April 1 1863

Dearest!

To say that I was delighted in coming in from "Picket" yesterday & finding yours & fathers letters with the "ambotypes" of yourself & "Mason" would but illy express my feelings & emotions. You will not misunderstand me when I tell you that it was many minutes before I thought of reading your letters. There was your own clearly defined countenance, lit up with that genial, never-to-be-forgotten smile—the light of a loving devoted wife. And the rogue of a boy! Though the eyes are not distinctly defined and his little mouth almost wide open yet I recognize it as his picture, and the contour is like yours which makes it not the less interesting. I had "curiosity" enough to scan everything—the dresses, ribbon, &c & while I loved the persons I could but have the old admiration for the taste, amounting almost to intuition displayed by my gentle wife. However defective it may be as a picture I yet prize it very very highly and am greatly obliged for it. Do not forget to send me a good one of your own, two or three copies of a photograph if you can. And by the by I should greatly like a reg small Album containing yours Em & Zad's, Annie, Father & Mother DV, Florence, & Aunt Ann, together with Williams, Mary Janes, Si's, Maggies &c. It would put you all to too much expense on my account I presume, but it would be deeply interesting nevertheless!

April 3d—I have been unable to finish this letter until now. That note of Bishop that Will speaks of was given to Thompson & Bishop on settlement of that Seely matter for their costs or rather fees. It was no more than right that the defts should pay it, as I would ask it under the same circumstances. My recollection is that I told you of all the facts relating to this settlement. I do not propose that you shall pay the note now unless you think best. I feel that father is better entitled to it all than any body else. Still you can do with the money what you see fit; only I insist that you shall keep a portion for any emergency that may arise in my absence. We expect to be paid for two more months soon & after settling my clothing account I will send you all I can. Do not think that I shall shirt myself.[1] I really do not need a great deal of money & in fact if any accident should happen to me especially upon the battle field I would rather have but little on my person. So you are in every point of view the best one to have the cash. If I need anything here I have as much credit as any one can wish & I can always get money of friends to supply all little wants.

I received a most beautiful letter from Mr Swazey[2] yesterday, one that did my heart good. He paid your husband a compliment which was as gratifying as heart could wish. He says he shall keep my letter to him among his papers for his "children's children." I learned from him that Sister Maggie has been much prostrated with the typhoid fever. - - Wednesday Evening. Capt Spaulding & myself attended a meeting of all the Evangelical Chaplains in our Department at a church in Murfreesboro. It was the first time I had entered a church since I left Chicago. The house was full of men & one solitary woman. The speaking was very good. Col Moody of the 74th Ohio who is a minister made a very fine speech. My thoughts wandered frequently to the church prayer meeting where we so often gathered with our friends. - - I wish I could have had you with me the other day in a visit to the battle field. It seemed as if I saw you in every peach & rose bud & blossom that smiled upon the scene. You will see in Harpers Weekly a representation of McCooks Head Quarters. It is somewhat like the house but is very poor otherwise. It is a beautiful situation but war has made desolation all about it. I have a long letter to write you if I can ever get at it. So you must be content with a sheet full this time. I shall write father a note in a day or so. I hope that Aunt Ann has received my letter by this time. Tell Mason that papa did laugh at his little face and that he will keep his picture until he will sit still & get a better one. With love always I am ever yours

John

1 This is a little pun!

2 The Rev. Arthur Swazey was the pastor of the Third Presbyterian Church in Chicago, of which John and Belle were members.

"On Picket" Stone River
Tenn. "Sunday" April 5th

Dearest!

Yours of March 28th reached me yesterday. I read it with great interest, & then read portions of it to Willie & Barber. To day our Regiment is out along Stone River on a 24 hours picket. The day is most beautiful & pleasant. I have two companies (Chickerings & mine) & have the command of one "Station" the balance of the regiment being off towards the left under command of Col Chadbourne & Major Chandler. I have thus a sort of independent command although small. While speaking of this, let me give you an idea of how we "picket." The "Station" is the point to or upon which all the sentinels from that command retreat in case of their being compelled to fall back by a superior force of the enemy—it is generally located behind a clump of trees or a small elevation so as to hide the few small fires which are allowed by night and to mask our position and numbers by day. In front of the station from 150 to 250 yards are from one to three "outposts" according to the force at the station and the extent of ground to be picketed. There are generally a sergeant and six men, three of whom are deployed in front of the outpost from 100 to 150 yards according to the nature of the ground forming the "chain of sentinels." The sentinels remain on duty two hours when they are relieved by the three men at the outpost who stand two hours, the first sentinels remaining at the outpost. The Sergeant and six men having been at the outpost and picket line for four hours are relieved by the same number from the station, that is, a relief for the outpost is sent out from the Station every four hours. I send you a small diagram which may assist you in getting an idea of how a regiment does picket duty. My station is deployed to day according to the diagram. It should also be stated that no fires or lights of any kind are allowed at the out posts & chain of sentinels. You can easily see that we are spread out somewhat in the shape of the folds of a fan or the spokes of a wheel & if sentinels—men on out post—& those at the station are on the alert & do their duty in case of attack, there can be no surprise of the army. In case of serious attack it is the duty of the men at the out post to move up & take position in the intervals between the chain of sentinels thus forming a double picket line while the reserve at the station either remains in position or advances towards the sentinels if necessary in order to be within easy supporting distance. Having written you so frequently on picket, I thought I would explain it for once. There are generally commissioned officers enough who take turns of duty during the night.

I said that the day was beautiful. All nature seems to rejoice and bask in the beams of a southern sun. I cannot my beloved wife look at the violets that are joyously showing their pleasant faces along Stone River without thinking of you & your fondness for flowers, and pleasure runs through my veins because nature & you are in my thoughts. And mother too will excuse this letter written on the Sabbath because I have thoughts of you & no testament to read. But she will say I should have had one! True but I cannot always think to put it in my haversack. Well I have the tract Journal for April with a long communication in it from "Mr Savage" one of the "Reverends" whom she has recently entertained. In it was a little item that was a strong commentary on a portion of your letter. It was what the little boy said about his father, & because of the conduct of his father thought that "God couldn't see in the back shed." Appropos of that paragraph in your letter I am pleased that you have spoken of my contracting habits here that might not appear well at home. Perhaps there may be something in expressions in my former letters that suggested your speaking to me about it. I hope you will never fail to be my little monitress. I shall endeavor to follow your advice. I entered the army with some idea of its vices determining at the same time to avoid them. I think I may say for myself that I have tried to so conduct myself as to meet the approbation of the purest being I have ever known on Earth. [Note: The following parenthetical text was evidently added by Belle in pencil over an erased sentence of John's original penciled text.] (I was never afraid with his refined mind, that he would change or become what I would not have him. He mistook my meaning. Belle) It is the silken & golden cords that keep me from any harm. As to loose habits of expression in conversation & writing I shall try & be more particular on your account as well as my own. Often have I criticized sharply & very severely at times the language of Willie & Rae & of course the critic should not lay himself open to their criticism—and for that reason I have endeavored to set them a good example as well as others. I like very much the idea of being well prepared for anything if I am spared to go back to civil life & will endeavor to devote all the time and opportunity in the direction you wish. As a means for this I ought to have a pocket dictionary & some work on English composition, which I will send for with a list of small articles I am making out for you or Si to purchase.

I was amused & gratified with your desire that I should live in a style corresponding to my dignity & position. I shall endeavor to do that, but I do not wish to run up great bills at the sutlers. Only think of paying $9.50 for a barrel of potatoes in Nashville. Why I could spend more than my salary at the sutlers & not half try. We purchase meat, coffee tea flour hard bread & all that government furnishes to soldiers at the same price for which Government gets it—the officers paying nothing for cost of transportation. Thus sugar is 13 ½ cts, flour 3cts per lb. Everything we get at the sutlers we pay an enormous price for. Butter 6/per lb, eggs 5 cts each & to day being "Easter" I go without even an egg in consequence. I have a good recollection however of the splendid secesh ham & fresh eggs that I enjoyed on the Franklin Expedition and that is some compensation; for I paid nothing for them. That reminds me that I have an idea that I can teach you how to broil ham when I come home. Don't you think me assuming a little? Well I became an adept in that when on that scout & I am perhaps a little vain of my accomplishments in that line. Perhaps you may smile at my frequent allusions to the art of cooking but you know I have a numerous family to take care of & I have labored to show them that I am capable of discharging my duty in every respect.

I smiled at your remark in reference to Major Henry. He arrived in our Division yesterday and is to pay off our Brigade to the first of March. I am happy to inform you that I shall be able to send you some more money soon. I am perfectly willing to economise for the express purpose of "owing no man anything" & for that I cheerfully labor, albeit it is hard earned money. It helps me to appreciate its value, and moreover I want to be just as well as generous.

It seems ridiculous to raise home guard regiments to "protect the state from invasion" & to do guard duty! & then to appoint such men! Well, I would like the position of Col but I tell you frankly I should feel out of my place to be stationed with a regiment in Illinois for three years while my comrades were undergoing the realities of war. It is too much like playing at war in your snug parlors at home—Carpet Knights—who show themselves off in glittering uniforms to the gaping crowd. I do not wonder that such men bring disgrace upon the profession of arms. No! if I had the command of a regiment I should feel like welding it by discipline into a huge hammer & then hurl it upon the enemy. It is enough to make one indignant to think of the hundreds like Capt Longworth who are so abundantly capable and deserving of a command left in the shade, while men bankrupt in character & purse, the meanest rascals & sycophants of the country are foisted by politicians into positions which they are perfectly incapable of filling. B.G. Wheeler to raise a regiment for Illinois & Henry to pay out the government money! Begging Cowles' pardon I venture the remark that the inside of a certain establishment at Joliet[1] is a better & more fitting place for Mr W. than the interior of a Colonel's dress coat, while I have no doubt certain R.R. men would gladly give Henry a "free ticket" to the same place. But I must not speak too freely of my "associates in the Cause"! Pshaw!—Oh! this political demon that controls the army should be exorcised at once, and merit, bravery, and competency exhibited in the service the only road to preferment in the military profession. I shall never cease to admire the conduct of Napoleon in this respect. It is the curse of our government that it is otherwise. These regiments to be raised in Illinois may be needed to enforce the conscription & yet I am thoroughly of the opinion that a regiment of old troops if there is no more than 200 of them left would be worth more for that purpose than a full regiment of raw troops of more than a 1000 men. The reason is that we have seen the worth of discipline & we are all, privates & officers in favor of punishing deserters & making a conscription that will utterly & forever crush out rebels & copperheads if need be at one and the same time.

It is now nearly sundown & I will allude to the manner of spending our afternoon. At Noon, Lieutenant Boal Inspector on Sherman's staff rode up with flushed face saying that the enemy were advancing in great force & that we should keep a sharp look out. You should have seen the effect on the men. All were aglow with a smile of incredulity & yet mixed with pleasure at the thought of having a brush. I told the Inspector that we were all ready. At the same time all was quiet yet energetic action in the camps as I have since learned. The whole army turned out under arms on their own parade grounds in less than ten minutes. Rosey is not the man to be caught napping, and we all like him for that trait. Well we waited & waited as you do for a train behind time, but we got no sight of the rebels. We went on with writing & reading in the shade of our "shelter tent" as usual, while the birds sang merrily in the big oaks over our heads & all seemed as peaceful, bright & sunny as if man never took the life of his fellow, & yet we were here for that very purpose, ready like the lightning's flash to spring to our arms & deal death into the ranks of our Country's foe. While so waiting our chaplain came up. I laid aside writing & reading, gathered up my little Command on reserve at the station & the chaplain talked to them in an earnest manner for about twenty minutes while I stood listening with one ear to the address & the other for the report of the enemy's cannon. It was quite an interesting little incident. When he concluded it was time to send out a relief, which being attended to I gave up any idea that we should receive any visit from the enemy to day. About 5 P.m. Col S. rode up with all his retinue, the Command "fell in" & I received him with all the "Honors." He talked a few minutes, rode off, & so has passed the afternoon. How different from your own quiet Sabbath & yet I know our hearts have been with each other in spirit. It has been with you all, & though I rejoice that I can write in cheerful mode—a buoyant spirit—& feel that vigorous manly strength is given to my physical frame, yet, oh! yet at this very moment, how I long for an interview with those I so dearly love.

I learned from Mr Swazey's letter that Maggie had been sick, also a great many particulars about the church & congregation. I hope Aunt Ann will be benefited by a tour to the East. If she could go to Havana for a season it would be good for her health if she could stand a sea voyage. - - I do not wish you to regret sending that ambotype. I was very glad to get it. Send me another of you both when you can. - - My pay will amount to about $250, of which I hope to send home about $200, but cannot yet tell exactly. I wish you to be sure & keep enough to pay any expenses you may incur & also to pay me a visit if I can not get a furlough. I will follow your directions about remembering my position. I have to see that 34 men look well & I want to set them a good example. By the by Mrs Pierce is here quite gay and dashing & I learn she has complimented the good looks & appearance of your husband. I have been introduced to her yet never have called upon her. She has a riding habit & creates quite a sensation. You may remember she is the wife of our present surgeon. She has been twice captured while on her way to visit her husband.

In Camp Monday 6th.

I hope you will not be frightened at the length of this letter. I left off writing at sundown yesterday and will finish to day. Dr Dunham of Chicago has been here since Saturday & left for home to day. I believe I told you that Rae was promoted to Sergt Major! Lieutenant Meacham of Co I died last week and Rae has been recommended for the place. I presume he will get it without any doubt & it is a deserved promotion. This leaves no one in the way of Barber for the 2d Lieutenantcy in my Co in case I am promoted at any time hereafter or the 2d Lieutenantcy becomes vacant. Barber makes a first rate "orderly." Dinsmoor prefers being a private in the Light Battalion than to be a corporal in the Co & he will most probably be in it. - - Today we have word of a large force concentrating in our front a reinforcement to Bragg. Well, we just want them to come and try us. There will be such work as was never known before in the history of this war. I do not attach much importance to the rumor however. You need not have any anxiety about it. Recd a letter to day from Hawley about the deed to that church property known as the Williams Street Mission School. The deed is to the Trustees of the 3d Pres Church. You can send it to him if he writes for it. Sister Annie must have enjoyed herself hugely in Chicago this winter. I am extremely glad that father is better. Mother need not have any delicacy about writing if you do write frequently. Mason! Papa looks at your little picture every day! I want another & so you must sit still to get a good one when you go with mamma. Go up & kiss mamma & Grandma for papa. - - Hoping to hear from you soon I am always & truly yours

John

1 The Illinois State Penitentiary was located in Joliet, Illinois.

Monday Eve, April 20, 1863.

My Beloved Wife!

I sit down to write an answer to yours of 10th inst. but I hardly know where to begin. First of all I thank you for the 2d picture of Mason. It is a vast improvement on the first. It produced most varied emotions. It seemed as if I could discover in him strong resemblances to Cora although perhaps if I were with him as you are all the time I would not notice it. Your picture in the group with Zed is one of the best I have seen except the favorite one I lost. I discovered in the first one you sent me what mother mentioned that you look much better than usual. That set of furs made me shrug my shoulders with an ugh! "how cold it is up North" & yet I do think nothing ever became you more than my "present." Mothers letter was just like her. I shall reply to it soon. - - You have seen by the papers the death of Adjt Ballard. It is a great loss to this Brigade. None named him but to praise. I have called on Miss Stebbins & the particulars are chronicled in a letter to Em. I send with this, letters to Em & Zed because I have no postage stamps, if you will please run your eye over the one to Zed & approve its tone & spirit you may hand it to him otherwise burn it. We have a new sensation in camp tonight. Brig Genl Lytle of Ohio formerly in command of the 10th Ohio & who made a reputation at Carnifex ferry Western Virginia has been assigned to the command of our Brigade & takes command in the morning. Col Sherman returned to the regiment to night. We have had very pleasant relations with Col Chadbourne. He has done every thing he could to make it pleasant with the line officers. I hope Col Shermans return will not re inaugurate the scenes of former days. - - On the 17th Willie was detailed as clerk for Capt Whiting who has been appointed "assistant Commissary of Musters" at Sheridans Head Quarters. This is a permanent detail & but little if anything to do. The business of Whiting is to muster out an officer & muster him in again when promoted to a higher position. It is a Staff appointment detaching Capt Whiting. Willie is very much pleased. I have given him some of the best advice I could & he is now in a position of no great danger except possibly through an unoccupied mind. It relieves my mind of one anxiety. It is all with him now if he gets advancement in that department & he feels it himself. He has been looking forward to some such appointment for some time. Capt Whiting seems to be pleased with him.

I received my two months pay on the 12th to March 1, & on the 13th sent you $200.00 in the same manner I sent the $400 to Bro Will. By the way I do not remember that I told you I was satisfied with Will's sending you that note. I would just as quick he or father would have all you do not wish to use. In ten days we will be mustered again for pay but I do not expect to get any more very soon. Paymasters are generally from three to six months behind hand. It seems very queer however that I have been eight months in the service. If I see Gov Yates I will talk to him. I have a letter from Will however in which he says he has the personal assurance of the Gov that it is fixed & no one can cheat me out of promotion the first opportunity. - - And now my dear I begin to think we are going to have a forward movement soon. John Fitch says that we shall most likely cooperate with Burnside who is about to make his way into Eastern Tenn. I want to be ready to go ahead and to bring up all my correspondence to date & to keep my business in such shape that I can march at any moment. So while we may not move at all yet do not be surprised if there is a movement at any time. I have written thus far feeling a little "sleepy" and will finish this in the morning. Tuesday 21. How beautiful all nature is this morning. Poets have sung of the attractions of the advancing sunlight as it throws its glad beams over hill & dale while they themselves are spending their time in bed. Nothing can be more grateful to the eye than the sight of day dawn and the cheerful flood of light that comes from the open gates of the East. I rejoice that "Reveille" comes at day light. Yesterday on Picket I awoke just as the first faint streaks of the coming dawn were visible, at the same instant I heard two musket shots in quick succession next on the left of my station. Throwing aside my blankets I sprang from my "Shelter tent" (we always sleep on Picket with our side arms on & in full dress ready at a moments warning) to meet the enemy if necessary. All was quiet after however, but I went out to the out posts first to see that all was right there, & then to the chain of sentinels. I soon forgot all about secesh in watching the approach of the glorious old orb and wondering if my beloved wife & babe were enjoying a fairy, refreshing sleep, while husband & father was a small part of the periphery of the power of "Uncle Sam," watching on its utmost verge to defend the household of loved ones far away, and the inestimable birthright, the gift of our fathers, our free institutions. I trod the soil of Tennessee with the proud consciousness that this is my country, this my native land, that my love of country was not hemmed in by any narrow contracted views of imaginary straight lines, state boundaries, no "pent up Utica" but that I could exult in the glorious thought, the "whole boundless continent is ours," and for that I am willing to deprive myself for a season of that best of all, dearest of all spots on earth, the sacred little domestic circle. - - I showed the "group" this morning to a young Lieutenant. "Pshaw!" said he! "Why don't such a man have "shoulder straps" on?" That is the feeling here of young men, & I hope Z will not feel bad if I do "poke a stick" at him sometimes. I shall now write to father about that little matter of business. I will also write to day to Josiah to see about it. We are expecting several more ladies in camp soon. I should not be surprised if they had to go back as quick as they came. With many kisses for Mason & a husbands love for yourself I am yours always.

John

P.S. I shall have to make a small draw on you for some "postage stamps" as I am out, & we can get none in Camp or in Murfreesboro. Of course you will furnish father the funds to arrange that matter with "Kussell brothers." I succeeded in getting a postage stamp for Em's letter & so mailed it here.

On Picket Stone River Tenn.
Monday morning May 4, 63

Dearest!

Yours of 24th ult. reached me four days since but I have been closely engaged until yesterday which I kept as a day of rest except to call with some friends upon that Mr Miller who used to reside nearly opposite Aunt Jane's on Ann Street. He is sutler of the 42[d] in Col Bradleys Brigade & Saturday he insisted that I should come & see him. I am sitting directly on the south bank of Stone river under the shade of a magnificent elm in command of four companies & writing to you on a "drum head." The day is beautiful & sunny & plenty of music over our heads. My "station" is just to the right of the "Shelbyville" pike & bridge across Stone river. We guard the pike a post of danger, one that requires vigilance, and your husband is equal to the task. - - Last Thursday being the 30th was our regular muster day for pay. It brings with it a great deal of labor in making out muster rolls & pay rolls which are forwarded to Washington, & the paymasters. When we shall get the money on the rolls is a question none of us can answer. We do not expect it at least for two months to come. - - I was glad to receive notice of your receiving my last package. You said you "stole out" to write me but did not describe the company present if there were any. I wish I could send a couple of hundred of what is due me to you right away. It is rather amusing that I have heard through you & some others that father is busily engaged in building a ware house & yet you do not say whether he is to have a store in it or what it is to be used for, & where located. I suppose you have received my last letter ere this & one to father & one each to Em & Zad. - - Last week all the Sibley tents of the men were turned over & our camp is now entirely made up of little "Shelter tents." Each line officer commanding a co returns his wall tent & has also a shelter tent for the march. The "shelters" are portable a half one being carried by each man & so "baggage" will not be very large. We are all ready for anything, but our movements I presume depend upon others now about to be made east & west of us. I am very nicely situated in my tent & would be glad to introduce you to it but as I wrote to Annie I was hugely disappointed in asking for a pass for you. You ask in a former letter if the ladies here sleep in tents? Certainly they do, & you would wonder at their convenience also if you should "inspect" one. Let me describe one for you. Dr. Pierce has a wall tent for his parlor & reception room. Joining to it on the rear is a wedge tent with a large "fly" over it: this is the sleeping apartment. In front of the wall tent is another large "fly" serving as an awning to keep the sun off & here or in the parlor

Mrs Pierce receives co. She is one of the "gay & festive" ladies perfectly at home anywhere not at all equal in good looks to you or sisters yet she is well thought of. Mrs Whiting has short hair, she was the wife of E. W. Tracy a lawyer in Chicago. I have not called on her. She does not look so well as any of the four ladies. Mrs Sherman is the most womanly as she is the best looking of all of them. It is becoming unpleasant for me to think of their being here "cutting about" & I am deprived of the privilege of seeing you, so I avoid calling on them although of course I see them all the time. No one knows the bitter feelings that will burn as if set on fire from the lower regions at times within my breast as I think of my sacrifices for the good of my country, how all my heart thinks for its success & yet I must be placed in a position that would try the patience of a Job! I sometimes think it is a part of the penalty that all must pay & yet as the soldiers say "I don't see it" at all times "in that light." I have thoroughly given up any idea of promotion for the present. I shall never ask the "deacon" or the "Tribune" for any assistance in anything I shall ask for hereafter. If I remain as I am for three years I will try to content myself. If any good luck happens to me it will be by my own exertions and no thanks to them. Let us change the subject. Yesterday I received my first letter from Ira[1] in answer to one I sent him a short time since. I must copy you an extract from his letter reading which set me in a perfect roar of laughter. It was good for the brain. "P.S. I forgot to mention that Katy Wallace was down here last winter & spent two or three days at the house where I board. She was on her way to Monmouth. We had a merry time while she was here. I never was so astonished at anyone in all my life. You remember how still & quiet she was at your home in Chicago. Here she was a perfect chatterbox and I'll be hanged if I could put in a word edgewise. A cousin was with her Miss Mary Wallace. We had a regular romp while they were here. Kate sings first rate, dances well & in fact is not the same Kate that I saw in Chicago and my opinion of her has undergone a change. I like her first rate but I don't think she is long for this world." There! Isn't that rich? Now if Kate will put off her exit out of this world for Ira's benefit I may be invited home to a wedding some of these days. Of course you will be a little careful to whom you show the above morceau! - - Yesterday P.m. Fred Chapman & Charley Garnsey of the

Board of Trade Battery called to see me & staid some time. I was glad to see them. They are very healthy. They are about going into Negleys Division. I wrote Annie a "notice" of my calling on Capt. Howland. He is one of the gayest men in the army and the best ladies' man, I take it. He seemed to be particularly anxious that you & Em send your "cartes" to him. Not being so well acquainted with Annie he did not dare to ask so particularly for hers. I must say I was particularly pleased with my visit to him. George Knox also made enquiries for you all. I learned from him that Capt Parsons has recently been ordered to West Point as one of the instructors of artillery. - - I wrote the foregoing in the forenoon since which I have had a visit from Gen Lytle & Staff. I have also been out on the out posts & picket line. From the out post on the pike I saw our post bag coming & so I returned & met your letter of 29th. Oh! how glad was I to get it "on Picket." It does make my heart so light to hear from you & home. I was rejoiced to know that my letters were appreciated & that Zed was pleased with his. The only motive I had in sending the postage currency was a thought that crossed my mind that perhaps you did not get that kind of currency very easily, & I thought gold was out of the question.

I shall not hesitate to ask my dear wife for any little favors of that kind and "currency" I'm fearful will not be in every letter. I was much amused at your sage advice about "comparisons & compliments." Pardon me when I tell you that I cannot take it. I felt just like calling you my "darling little simpleton!" What, have me dam up my hearts best affections? Your own little magic self opened up the flood gates of my heart and no straight laced prudential motives shall ever prevent me from speaking & writing just as my hearts impulses flow. No dearest. I only wish I had a new vocabulary to express the love devotion regard esteem and all the most gushing feelings of my heart for my wife my mother & my sisters. Think you father Bross will except to my devotion to you all? Not he! I never will be cramped in my love & admiration for you all. It may appear ridiculous to an outsider but I care not for it. In fact I am proud to tell it to all the world. So don't please don't ever again ask me to measure my words upon a theme upon which I love to dwell. As to father's sending for my letters I do not think he can ask for them. While I do not care for myself yet there is no reason why he should see them any more than a stranger. As to your going to Chicago I hope you will certainly go there in June to be at the convention. Go & enjoy yourself & if by a smile you can help on the notional work do so. Also do go & see father & mother Bross. I have tried to give you an insight into their peculiarities. Be as "free & easy" with them as you can & I know you will be fathers pet. I am afraid Aunt Jennie will be as crabbed as any old maid can be but do not mind her, & I think father is very liberal to give you each a lot. I sat & looked a long while over Masons letter, & will not describe my thoughts over it. - - Tuesday evening. We were relieved from picket this morning. I could not complete this out there by reason of attending to duty. I hope you will be at ease about me, that is as much as you can. I speak of unnecessary anxieties. We are acting as if we were to stay here all summer & yet we are ready to leave at a moments notice. Tomorrow our Brigade goes out several miles on the Salem Pike to remain five days. I may not have so much opportunity to write you until I return. Tell Mason Papa will send him a letter some day. I wish I could have him with me sometimes. I have been trying to make up a little list of things I want but have not got at it yet. Will soon send for them however. I am happy to know you answer my letters so promptly. You ask about Mrs Pierce staying all the time in her tent. All the ladies make their home in camp. There is no house close by. With love to all I am ever your affectionate husband

John A. Bross

1 "Ira" refers to John's ten-year-younger brother, Ira Bross, who was living in Illinois.

In camp Sabbath May 17, 1863

My Dear Wife,

Since I wrote you last I have rec^d^ yours of the 5th & 9th inst. for which I am very much obliged. I have been very well indeed. Nothing of importance has occurred in army matters save that baggage of men & officers are being cut down to the lowest standard. The dress & overcoats of the men have been sent to Nashville for storage & when we move it will be light enough in all conscience. However there is no necessity of having anything extra. If we do move I do not want any anxiety about baggage. We are waiting events & do not be surprised at either an advance or a long stay here. Either is among the possibilities. But wo[e] to any rebel force that attempts to force our lines in front of Murfreesboro. We should just literally butcher them. We never can be whipped in this position.

Your last letter I received on picket Friday. We were at the same place when I wrote my last letter, but I had no time to write. The day before a Brigade had been sent out to support the picket line as we expected an attack and I was more than usually careful & vigilant of the Shelbyville Pike. Nothing occurred however to disturb our wonted quiet & my command came off yesterday in fine condition. In the afternoon I stepped over to the 36th which is a few yards from the right of our regiment to see Capt Austin who is now the Captain of what was Captain Longworths Co. After some time Capt Cass came into the tent & told me he had a map of "Stone River." I went down in a few minutes & judge of my surprise when I learned that he had a brother just come to see him & that he preached at Como. Of course I was immediately introduced to him & told him of your mentioning him in your letter. Mr Savage sent him down here to look after the wants of this army. I had quite a pleasant conversation with him last night & this morning. I shall certainly have him go & see you when he returns & "report" me among my dear friends at home. Capt Cass is young & has only recently been promoted to the captaincy.

I am anxious about the Small Pox in Sterling. I hope that none of you will be attacked with it. Do not fail to keep me advised about it.

I had a few days before your letter came received an intimation from Si that the Curtiss suit was decided in our favor, & had got a copy of Windetts self laudation in the Tribune by express. It was characteristic of the little bag of vanity.

As to that Kussell matter there is certainly a receipt from them of one hundred & two 50/100 dollars if I mistake not. I know I paid them a $100 in gold for which I had some premium. I know I had the receipt just before

I left. It may as well lay some time until I come home as it is no lien against real estate. They must be rascals if they think they are going to cheat me out of the amount of that receipt.

I hope you will not fail to go to Chicago this month & stay a good long while. Perhaps you may get a chance to come & see me. It requires a pass from Rosecrans in order to "come into our lines." This you must have in order to get here. I do not know what the fare is but I presume I can find out. I wish you could come with father.

Capt Stevenson's brother & his bride are here now, on a visit to him. I saw them on horseback this morning but have not called on them. Did not know they were here until yesterday. I received a letter from John Butler yesterday. I hope you will make yourself at home among the "old folks" when you go to Morris & do not be shy of Capt Longworth. The "ladies" in our regiment are still here. They may "get off" very suddenly some of these days. Willie comes over quite frequently & I will certainly not forget him. You should understand that he is liable to be sent back to the Company at any time but if he does his duty well he can serve his whole time in some such position.

I am waiting somewhat to know whether we shall move or not before sending for some articles. When I send I will have you forward the collars. If we go forward I may not see a package sent me for weeks possibly months. I heartily respond to Sister Em's dream in one respect, that I may come home sometime to lay some deserved honors at all your feet, that all of us may at least have the proud consciousness that brother son & husband has done his duty to his country faithfully & deserved honor even if he don't get it. Tell Masie that Papa will kiss him day & night when he comes home, that Papa thinks of him every day & Mamma & Grand Ma & Grand Pa & all his dear friends.

Mr Cass told me he thought Kilgour would soon be back to the regiment. I wonder that Cobbey has sense enough to stay in doors. Let me know when you go into Chicago. I hope you will see that our cemetery lot is properly taken care of & that you lay above our little Cora one bouquet in behalf of her father. Ever yours

John A Bross

Camp Schaeffer May 29, 1863

My Dear Wife

Your letter with that of Glenns inquiry about some old notes was rec[d] a few days ago. I was happy to receive it albeit I think that you mistook the tone of my letter somewhat about my own position here. Of course it is almost impossible to pass over all the past. Yet I am following out your suggestions and the dictates of my own judgment in looking to the sunny side of affairs. As to "promotion" in this regiment there is absolutely no chance unless all the field officers die or resign, events not likely to happen very soon. I use philosophy and determine to let the "world wag as it will" according to Charleys old song—and try to be "gay & happy." If sometimes I let some expression slip that betrays a lower stratum of discontent, please remember that it is only in your ear that I pour my thoughts. It is hard sometimes to bear it all alone. Yet I do enjoy myself here as much as most anyone I think. However with my somewhat suffering disposition I look forward to a time in my history when justice & judgment shall be meted out with no unstinted hand. You may set that down as burnt into my very soul. Do not think because I allude to these things that I allow my mind to brood over these things so as to make myself unhappy or that I treasure up a spirit of revenge. Far from it. I cannot go out in the woods & fields without admiring all around me and the natural action of the mind is to have you there as well as other friends. I have sufficient resources of animal spirits and control of my mental faculties not to become misanthropic. I look upon such a state of mind as you allude to as a weakening that men should avoid. But I shall not proceed further on this point hoping that this will reach you in Chicago where I trust you will not fail to enjoy yourself to the fullest extent.

Those old notes are among my papers in Chicago or else returned to Halloway & Luce attys at Monmouth. I will write Mr Glenn to that effect.

Has Mason been sick except a sore throat? I hope he is now perfectly well.

I shall never be troubled about your "old beau." I am only fearful you will be too much in the habit of staying at home when you might just as well as not see more of society. So do not be afraid of any beau who is "respectable" & not too "old." I shall certainly laugh at you if you get "old maidish" while I am absent. I shall have to "rally" you a little in return for getting me out of a supposititious fit of the "dumps."

Sunday last we were on Picket on Shelbyville Pike, I being in command of the Station guarding the Pike. In the night I had the honor of passing out of our lines "Vallandigham"[1] & his escort. You should have heard some of the remarks of the "boys" when they found out who it was. It would have made his ears tingle. They would have carried him out on the points of their bayonets if they could have had their way.

Since I wrote you I have had Rev Mr Cass & his brother Capt Cass dine with me. They seemed to be pleased with it. By the by, I find that the expense of living in camp is much more when you get acquainted and there are means of procuring a variety for the table. I live pretty well now and follow your desire expressed in a former letter to live in a manner suitable to my "dignity." I hear that we are soon to be paid again probably next week. This is good news for us all.

Saturday last in the afternoon I enjoyed myself "hugely" in the manner following. Soon after Dinner, Rev Mr Cass, Capt Cass, Lt Barstow of Capt Longworths old company, Capt Campbell of the 36 who was taken prisoner at the battle, & myself got horses and rode over to the Battlefield in order that Mr Cass might see the location &c. We first rode to the rebel line which is nearest town & then around through the cedars & out to our line where the 36 & 88th were posted. What is known as "Hardings" house was in the rear of our position and was occupied as a hospital at & after the battle. We alighted there and went in. We found the old man & wife daughter & some young children at home. It looks vastly different now from what it did when I visited it immediately after the battle. Then it was crammed full of our wounded & desolation was all around. The cannonball hole through the side of the home to the left of the door and about six inches above the floor which in its passage through the house had killed four wounded men & broke one of the legs of the piano was still left without being boarded up. One of the wounded men was a member of my company. The old man Harding was present & he grieved a good deal the boy said because his piano's leg was mutilated but not a word of regret for the poor wounded & killed Union soldiers.

We found two majors of Indiana regiments had arrived before us. The old gentleman was very polite when he found that we were of Sheridan's Division & of the 36th and 88th. The old lady was sitting on the porch with a babe in her arms and a little boy about the age of Mason standing near her knee with black eyes & light hair. I entered into conversation with her & the boy. He did not seem inclined to come to me, when I took our your pictures & holding up Masons before him asked him to come and look at it. Up he came instantly & was very much pleased with it. This attracted the old lady's attention & I showed her successively yours & Annies. I was greatly amused at her remarks. She asked among other things if you & Em were my sisters & whether they were married. She seemed to think it strange & odd that you could be so young looking & a wife. On looking at Mason she thought he was a fine little girl. I thought it rather odd that a mother should be so completely at fault. I thought it was quite a compliment to you at least. You may hardly know what a yearning I had for an embrace of my own darling boy as I sat with this little child on my knee.

After this I rose and asked the old lady if the young lady would not favor us with some music on the piano, stating at the same time that I had heard none since I came in the service. She spoke to her daughter who very gracefully complied. I advanced to the piano & she smilingly asked what she should play. I told her "anything you prefer." She played a very fine polka & then one of the Indiana Majors came forward and asked her to sing his "favorite" song. Well, she did and it was the "bonny blue lag" a secesh song. You may imagine how I felt standing on the very spot where one of my boys was torn to pieces. It required all I could do to choke down any exhibition of temper so that no one should discover it. As it was I had invited her to sing & of course I must show my good breeding & gentlemanly behavior at least. She sang with a rich soft melodious voice the piano was in excellent tune & one of "Gilberts" of Boston, & she was a perfect mistress of it. I just wanted to kick that major though! He is from southern Indiana & was quite interested in the young lady as we all "of one accord" afterwards remarked. Well after she had sung every verse of the "Bonny Blue flag" I asked her to sing "Lorena." It was very happily rendered. She had quite a variety of new Chicago music & the other Indiana Major asked her to sing the "Battle Cry of freedom." I accompanied her with this chorus & also "Kingdom Coming." This put us all in good humour with ourselves and then after she played a march & a polka. I was "very much obliged to her" & we bowed ourselves out. Capt Campbell who had just returned from "Dixie" was not over polite in his remarks on that Indiana major. We remounted our horses, rode over to the graves of the 36th & 88th & then along towards the left onto the Nashville Pike then to the fortifications & so home having had a very pleasant trip taking it all together. Mr Cass was very much gratified & when he calls on you will most probably speak of it. The young lady has black eyes black hair an aquiline nose and not more than ordinary features. Still she was agreeable and perfectly at ease. I hope the relation of this visit will not tire you in the reading.

I was down to town the other day & learned that Sarah Stebbins was not well, so I did not see her. At "dress parade" of the 36th Wednesday eve I was introduced to Capt Wood of Dixon of the 34th, & Lt Blodgett of the 73d fellow prisoner with Col Miller. The "ladies" are here yet. Mrs Pierce I see more that the others. She has beset me for my carte de visite. She wants one of all the line officers. I recd a very good letter from Jessie recently. McClurg has returned and has got detailed on McCooks staff. This leaves my 2d Lt in command of his Co leaving me entirely alone. If this remains so all summer it may prevent my coming home. There is another rumor in camp that Govt will send home all the captains of those regiments that have been reduced in numbers as ours have, to remain at home "waiting orders" without pay. This would not be treating us exactly right but there would be a jolly lot of "captains" & no mistake. Don't flatter yourself however that your husband will have any such luck as that. Well! what do you think of the policy of my applying for authority to raise a colored regiment? I could make an efficient one if anybody could. I shall direct this to Chicago expecting you will be there. I want you to make a good long visit there. Give my love to all friends. As ever I am your devoted husband

John A. Bross

1 Clement L. Vallandigham, Ohio congressman, had become a leader of the Peace Democrats in 1863 and was considered a "Copperhead." He was clumsily arrested by General Burnside for denouncing a "wicked, cruel, unnecessary war," convicted by a military commission, and sentenced to indefinite imprisonment. In order to minimize political consequences, Lincoln commuted Vallandigham's sentence from imprisonment to banishment and on May 25, he was escorted under flag of truce to the Confederate troops of General Bragg, who reluctantly received him.

On "out Post duty" Salem Pike.
June 4th 1863

My Dearest!

Yours of May 31st & announcing your arrival in Chicago on Monday has just reached me and truly it causes me sad & mingled emotions of pleasure. Glad very glad to hear from you & yet sad to say that at this time I must tell you not to think of my coming home for the present. The long looked for day has come at last. I am just in the midst of making the final preparations of the Company for the march, divesting ourselves of every thing that will impede our progress and getting all things in readiness to leave tonight or early in the morning. A portion of the army has already gone forward and ere this reaches you we shall probably be far away from this place. Of course I cannot say for certainty whither we are going but we expect to "Stir up" Bragg. Firing has been quite frequent in our front to day & there will be more of it ere many days. I am firm in the conviction that we shall come off "more than conquerors." The army is confident and thoroughly disciplined & happily rid of all "Skulking" officers, at least those that made such a record at "Stone River." - - I feel unpleasant to write you of our expected movement knowing how anxiously you will be looking & watching for news from me. Yet the papers will probably tell you of the movement ere this reaches you. Be strong & of good courage dearest. I have faith that I shall yet see you come what will, and resignation if Providence wills that my life shall be sacrificed for the good of my country. I rejoice to know that I am conscientiously discharging a debt and duty which every man owes to his country. When it calls it is the supreme law. I cheerfully obey it. God grant that I may be spared to return to the bosom of my family after fully discharging that debt & duty. You will need no promise from me that nothing else in this world will ever separate me from your society again. I write with the full recollection of seven years of married life shining in full radiance upon me, the sweetest pleasure that memory sets before me out of her richly laden treasures. This afternoon completes seven years since we vowed before the world to love each other for "better for worse." My beloved I have not words to praise you to express all my feelings & sentiments. Tomorrow is our glorious anniversary & be assured whatever I am about you will be in all my thoughts.

I am pained to hear your report that Mason's health is delicate. I shall be anxious for him all this summer. I sincerely pray that he may grow to maturity.

I suppose we shall be paid as soon as we reach some stopping place. I wrote father in answer to his letter that he sent with your letter next previous to yours of to day that I would forward to him what I shall set apart from my next payment.

I hope you will tell me all particulars of your visit to Chicago & Morris & be sure & make a good long visit to both places. I presume that all the taxes on the Chicago property are properly paid. - - I sent by Chaplain Thomas the other day two pipes made from "Sweet brier" root taken from the battlefield. I had no time to send any word to "Si" to whom they were directed. One is for him & the other for Charley. One had been boiled in oil, the other not. They can select which they prefer.

I shall try & keep a record of events for the next few days & forward by the earliest opportunity. - - I am well as usual. One unpleasant feature of the past few days is a pair of sore eyes. I caught cold in them & they have been slightly troublesome but they are now much better. This is the first instance of the kind since I have been in the service. Then I have read a good deal also. Our regiment is better supplied with reading matter than any other I believe. At least "Moody" who has been here told me so recently. We have regularly the Atlantic, Continental, Harper, Eclectic, The N.Y. Times & Tribune & Post, besides other papers the Chicago Daily Tribune, Cincinnati Gazette & Commerce, Louisville Journal, Nashville Press & Union & also a deal of religious reading matter. Give my love to all my friends. You shall hear from me soon. Hoping the time is not far distant when I may prove my devotion to my darling wife by my personal presence. I close with a heart full of love.

Ever yours
John A. Bross

On out Post duty
Friday June 5, 1863

My Beloved Wife!

I wrote you yesterday in great haste supposing that to day would see us on the march. I am mistaken for this once and I am quietly doing duty along the picket line. What is more, all is silent as the grave. Yesterday we were all on the alert. Our cavalry in our front had a great deal of skirmishing and very heavy cannonading was heard all day towards Franklin, the extreme right of our line, distant about twenty miles. Everything indicated <u>our</u> advance & I so wrote. Well this will satisfy your mind that I am <u>not</u> unerring in my judgment of what <u>is</u> to take place.

To day everything speaks and sings of thee. If I should have a skirmish I know I would go at it with blessings upon your name. Happy in our wedding, happy in seven years of wedded life, I feel a glow of pride and joy and intense devotion that I trust will increase while mortal life shall last, and "spread undivided operate unspent" through the countless ages of eternity. Oh! tongue cannot tell nor pen describe <u>how</u> much I should enjoy being with you to day! How gladly would I comply with your request to come home soon and fold you to my breast my own darling wife! When I think of the long months I have been absent from you I can scarcely realize that I could be away so long. It is certainly no pleasant part of the picture either to think you are in circumstances that prevent your coming. I have no <u>valid</u> reason at all to offer <u>why</u> I should leave at this time, & if I had I do not think that I could get away. The officers are needed with their Companies in all movements & especially where there is only one. I think I have told you that both of my Lieutenants are absent from the Company, Gibson since Nov

30 & Cole since March 2. This is another reason against my coming home though perhaps I could get Rae who is now 2[d] Lieut in Co I to take charge of my company in my absence. I should feel very loth to leave here on the eve of a general movement. A mans reputation would certainly suffer by it. That of itself would not prevent my coming if I had leave. I feel that it would be my duty to stay to see my Co safe through any advance. I do hope that matters will so shape themselves that I can come home in a month or six weeks.

Dearest do enjoy yourself for the next six weeks at least, in Chicago & Morris, if Masons health will permit you to remain, & I know he will have good care in your absence. I will write you soon again. I pray God may spare us to witness in each others society many happy returns of this day & that I may never be absent from you another anniversary of our union. Love to all.

Yours ever
John

On out Post duty
"Salem Pike." June 20, 63

My Beloved Wife!

I find myself writing to you once more from the picket line, feeling very well & yet tempted to exclaim as I read your sweet letter written from Morris & received this P.m., "How long" "Oh Lord! how long" will it yet be before I can see again the idol of my heart! Right here let me say that I shall make an effort and a desperate one too, to come & see you next month or in August rely on that. So if it should fail I know it will not be my fault. Captain Hubbard returned yesterday & called on us in Camp. He does not look in vigorous health. Willie called on me last night he is very well. His burden is now very light indeed. - - I am very happy to know of your being interested in your visit to Morris. I knew Father & Mother would want to see Mason and so you will do well to go down again with him as you have promised. I am very much amused at Capt. Longworth's "Stories." That about my "waiting" upon my servant is "very good." Perhaps you did not see the point of the matter. I have been compelled to wait for him considerably but that I should be a servant to a servant is not in the nature of things. You should just remember that I am in the habit of command and my "nigger" is getting to be quite an adept in looking after all my wants. You correctly judged when you thought he did it for fun. As to "foraging" be sure I shall live well in an enemy's country & no mistake. On our Franklin expedition in March I never lived better in my life & it came out of secesh smoke houses too so far as I am informed & believe. One good "thing" the Capt had on me & that was in carrying such a heavy "pack" through Kentucky. He laughed me out of it & I shall never do it again. If Govt cannot carry my blankets for me I will go without. But it is slightly different now from then. The fact is the 88th have learned some valuable lessons from the 36th in the art of soldiering & we are not far behind them in the knack of helping ourselves at all times when occasion offers. So when you have a good long talk with Capt Longworth just say that the $100 men[1] have about as much horror of stealing and foraging as those who came into the service before them & could not get their $100, & ergo was not worth it. - - I was greatly interested & amused at Jennies[2] remark about your beauty not being equal to mothers expectations. Perhaps mother had formed an extreme ideal but I know I judge correctly if I am your husband with regard to your good looks. I wish I could put on paper the remarks of friends here on seeing your pictures who did not know that you were my wife. I consider that one pretty good test. Another reason I might suggest why Jennie made that remark but no matter. Mother Mason wrote me you looked better now than for several years and I know it must be so from your picture. By the by I hope if this reaches you in Chicago you will not fail to send me a good carte de visite of your self. I want one for myself & Mrs Pierce. She has been married 6 ½ years, has no children & is now in her twenty third year. In comparison with you in appearance & complexion she is nowhere. She is a very agreeable lady however. Yesterday she asked me about Mr Charles Wright of Sterling. She visited him once. Someone presented her sometime since with a very fine horse and she & Mrs Sherman ride a great deal. Col Ducat & Col Hepburn respectively Inspectors Genl of Infantry & Cavalry on Rosecrans' staff call on these ladies very frequently & hence we see them often. Our Regiment gets some very high compliments from these gentry in the matter of drill, discipline, cleanliness & soldierly appearance.

Sabbath morning 21st. I suppose you are preparing for church while I am writing this. I do wish from my inmost heart I could be with you to day and enjoy again your society. I forgot to mention before that I have received those berries in the package you sent me. I had them prepared for use before we came out here and I appreciated them very much, particularly as they came through so many dear channels of love and affection. We are not paid yet and can not say when we shall be. Will let you know of course. I shall not be able to send as much this time owing to my better style of living and the purchase of some shirts and other wearing apparel. However I will do the best I can. I suppose it is as well that you postponed the purchase of a little memento of Cora. I do not like the idea of having the appearance of neglect of our offspring & yet I accord with you fully in the desire of procuring something original if possible. Meanwhile I wish the lot properly taken care of a matter I know that is not necessary to mention to you. I know you would not forget my request relative to the bagnet. I am very glad that you have such faith in my returning to you again. Do not despond in any manner. In this connexion I have thought that you might misconstrue a portion of my last letter which you may have received by this time referring to your going east with Will. It might interfere with my seeing you in Chicago, but it is needless to tell you I would see you in case I had a furlough if you were any where on the round globe outside of "Dixie," & of course I'd fight to get you out of there. I do not remember that I ever told you that Rae is now 2d Lieut of Co I, Capt Spauldings Co. He makes a fine officer. I am writing to you on an ammunition box under the shade of a great Persimmon tree. As to the Black regiments, officers applying have to pass an examination & if approved Govt assigns a district for them to recruit in. I do not fear an examination so far as tactics in the Infantry arm is concerned & I presume that is all that would be required. To day is our 2d day out here. We shall go in to camp Friday next. I shall write again in a few days. The last of this month brings a vast amount of business for a commander. It would be useless to tell you of all the reports & returns & muster rolls that we have to make out. My love to all friends. Accept my heartfelt thanks for this last letter & the one acknowledging the wedding gift & believe me ever your devoted

John

1 Congress authorized a $100 bounty in July of 1861 to men enlisting for three years.

2 Jennie was Jane Ann, John's four-year-younger sister.

In "Bivouac" about 12 miles
South of Murfreesboro
June 23rd 63 7 ½ A.m.

My Beloved Wife,

The march has come at last. I sent you a note on Tuesday eve announcing orders to march and yesterday at 6 ¼ A.m. our Brigade left its position on out post duty on the Salem Pike & took up the line of march southward on the Shelbyville Pike. We arrived at a little church & neighborhood called "Christiana" about noon where skirmishing commenced. A little further southward the pike crosses a range of hills through which is a defile, & along which the road passes to Shelbyville. Here the rebs have a strong position and our generals are maneuvering to turn the position by a flank movement to the right & left. We lay in line of battle at Christiana until 3 ½ P.m. when our Brigade & other troops filed to the left (eastward) along a dirt road and "Bivouacked" for the night. Yesterday we experienced again what "soldiering" is. For a couple of weeks in camp with the exception of an occasional shower it has been very pleasant. Yesterday after we commenced our march it began to rain, & it has rained ever since. We had just such exposure when we left Mill Creek to fight the battle of Stone River and it was colder then. I am writing to you under a couple of rubber blankets laid on top of a gate which is set up one end on the ground & the other raised about 3 ½ feet which makes quite a shed. The mail reached us yesterday P.m. while we were laying in line of battle at the little church. We lay in a wheat field a part of which had been cut & put in shock. I had "gobbled" a shock, laid down the dry sheaves & then rested on them covering myself up with the rubber. I was enjoying myself hugely under my blanket with the rain pouring down in torrents when the mail was announced. Soon my servant handed me your letter & I read it under the blanket. I had some queer sensations of pleasure as in that position I read your words of love & to hear for the first time that Will was interesting himself for me about a colored regiment. I have not received his letter you speak of. Perhaps I shall get it soon as arrangements have been made for the post bags to follow us with the mail from Murfreesboro. I shall be delighted if I can secure such a position and I will write him about it the first opportunity. But it is impossible to speculate about the future now. You must both acquiesce in the fact that this is a general movement of our forces and we know not what a few days may bring forth. So content yourself dearest for the present, because it is absolutely impossible to make any arrangements about it for a few days. If Providence spares my life we shall probably end this campaign before the middle of next month & then I shall make good my word to see you. How dearly I should love to be with you now. It would be rather amusing to see you looking after & presiding over the Dr's big farm & all his bees, cows milk &c &c. It would be more in consonance with my wishes however if you could accompany William on his tour east. I was glad you had a view of [illegible],[1] & I hope you will avail yourself of all opportunities of pleasure. I well know that amid it all your dear heart will beat with love for me. I wish to state one thing that you ought to know. Major Chandler & Capt Smith have applied for a negro regiment one as Col & the other as Lieutenant Col. That might have some effect against me but I trust not. If Major should be mustered out of this regiment still it would give me no chance for promotion as there is an order of the war department against any more officers being mustered where companies & regiments are below the minimum number & of course ours is below it.

This storm is a terrific one. Had it been otherwise I presume we should have left our Bivouac very early. As it is when we do leave it the march will be very disagreeable but of that more hereafter. - - I am happy to hear that Mason is getting along so well. Tell him that "John" will come & see him soon & bring along his sword too, & pa will teach him how to hold a little gun, & how to "present arms." - - We have not heard from Vicksburg & so we do not know whether this is cooperating with him or an independent movement. We know however that our whole army is on the move. I will send a line to you every opportunity.

My eyes are very well now the inflammation having all disappeared. I do not anticipate any further difficulty. I will comply with your request however about reading. There will be but little reading done anyway for the next two weeks to come. - - You speak of going to Egbert's to tea. It reminds me that I found in the 36th relatives of Mrs Weed one of the Hinsdale family. Also one of the Lieutenants in Longworths old Co has a brother married living in Morris to one of the Hinsdales. She was formerly Genevreau. Perhaps you heard of her there.

I am very well indeed and try to be prudent as to my health on the march. Yesterday while it was raining as hard as could be "Bill" started a fire out of the inevitable cedar rails and made me a first rate cup of tea. I was the first one that did it while others were shivering around & longing for a big drink of whiskey. Have no anxieties for me in this respect I shall rub along and come out of it I hope strong & vigorous. I came near breaking my leg this morning at 3 o'clock when I got up to call the men into line. It was as dark as Erebus & in going through the bushes I stumbled against a decayed knotty cedar & fell over it clamping my right leg against it & the ground. It finally slipped out but it was scaled from knee to foot. It is nothing but a good strong scratch. Good Bye love.

John

1 Two words were evidently erased.

"In Bivouac" on march
Saturday morning, June 27, 63

My own Beloved Wife

How vividly your own dear form is in my mind this morning. Perhaps you are anxious about me but I hope not too much. I thought I would try and give you the incidents of this march as we go along. Accordingly I wrote you two days ago. Since then we have made about three miles on our way. The cause is this. The rain I spoke of continued all day of the 25th & yesterday it seemed as if the last & biggest window of Heaven was opened on our devoted heads. We did not leave our Bivouac as I intimated in my last that day. The reason was the state of the dirt road caused by the rain. We have to pass from the Shelbyville pike east to the Manchester pike and the rain made the road horrible. Consider that thousands of wagons have to pass over it and you can form an idea how it would be cut up. Consequently we came at a snails pace yesterday. I should tell you however that our Division was ordered to guard the wagon trains & that left us in the rear. It is a work we do not like to do because we have to "wait for the wagon" & often we do not get into camp until midnight which is always unpleasant to the soldiers. We are crossing from Shelbyville Pike to the Manchester Pike (the first running south the 2^d south east) just north of a range of hills running east & west, the pikes pass through two gaps, the first "Guys" the 2^d "Hoovers." Yesterday we heard a great deal of firing in the direction of "Liberty" gap which is a pass in the range of hills between the first two & directly south of where we lay when I wrote my last letter. It seems the 89th Ill in which is Capt Blake was in the affair. The 89th belongs to Willichs Brigade Johnsons Division of our "corps" and they charged on a battery in that gap. They drove the rebels but I am pained to learn this morning that Capt Blake is mortally wounded being shot through the abdomen near the navel.

In "Hoovers Gap" 9 A.m.

I wrote the foregoing at 5 A.m. We are resting on a side hill while the wagons are filing by. The rain is over & gone but it is awful muddy underfoot. Yesterday in marching three miles I was most of the time in mud & water up to my knees & over; this is no exaggeration but the actual fact. I wear shoes in the summer in preference to boots but boots would have been of no avail unless they had covered all my limbs. So I just waded along, while the rain poured in torrents. It was astonishing how well the men bore up under the difficulties of the situation. They would go along laughing & joking over the matter in great glee. Several of the officers in crossing a deep ditch which was full to overflowing fell in over head to the great delight of the men. We camped last night in a nice forest where I slept as if nothing in the world could disturb me. Yesterday at noon where we rested for dinner my servant had cooked some "shoulder" & a good cup of tea. Just as I sat down one of my men brought me four new potatoes that he had just boiled taken from a secesh garden in the vicinity and a canteen of fresh milk, this with my crackers & sugar made me a capital dinner. I hope it is not sacrilege when I mention the fact that I thought of the 23[d] Psalm "Thou preparest a table before me in the presence of mine enemies" &c. This morning we had a difficult march through the hills and I do wish you could have viewed the scene. It will last long in my memory. We are safely through on the pike and it is a sight to behold the army trove of ammunition, commissary, & pontoon wagons. They are all here and it is exceedingly picturesque to see them in "caricle" [?] and stretched for miles away along the pike that leads through the gap southward. It is an undoubted evidence that the whole army is in motion and that work is ahead of us. I know not how long we shall remain with the wagons, but there is comparatively little danger as long as we are here, it is our duty to protect the train from secesh cavalry that may be lurking in our rear. As we filed into our "resting place" a little while ago, Willie stood waiting to see me pass by, looking as calm & serene as if no danger or hardships had anything in the way of dread for him. He has nothing in the world to do on the march but to ride his horse & sleep when he wishes. - - Such is army life. I am glad for his sake that he has such an easy position. I was much amused at myself this morning. I had eaten my last cracker last night, had a guest for supper & had to beg this morning, taking care however to make provision for the evening. In coming along the road two or three of the commissary wagons had broken down & the cracker boxes of course were thrown out by the side of the road. Along with hundreds of privates & a "right smart" sprinkling of officers, I attacked the boxes & "rationed" as much as I wanted, filling my haversack to repletion. With coffee & crackers I do not dread any march. To be short of rations is a very unpleasant prospect for any soldier.

In camp "Manchester" Coffee county June 28th P.m. Yesterday we left the spot we rested at, the north end of the "gap" on our way south. The gap is two or three miles long. Right in the "pinch" of the gap the rebs had thrown up earthworks for artillery in a first rate position commanding the road to the northward for miles. At the south end of the gap we reached "Roseys" Head Qrs. We stopped a couple of hours & I got no dinner which was very unpleasant in its effects as the sequel will show. It is 13 miles from the south end of the gap in a south east direction to Manchester, but our Division was ordered to take a dirt road south to Fairfield a little town in the eastern part of Bedford Co about six or eight miles from the gap. We reached Fairfield at 5 P.m. where we went into line of battle there being some skirmishing on the road leading south. It lasted some little while & there, we were ordered to report at Manchester last night, a distance from Fairfield of 12 miles east. This was tough. To me the prospect was awful. I had eaten no dinner at all had breakfasted at 4 A.m. & at Fairfield I was very weary. Well I gathered up courage & started off. Our way was up a little creek which the rains had raised & all along were little springs. It was warm & I became heated very much & I drank a great deal of water & the perspiration exuded in streams. Just at sundown we rested and I was almost exhausted and very faint. I tried to eat a cracker but it was as hard and dry so much so in my condition that I could scarcely chew it. One of my men gave me a piece of cold boiled beef & with that I ate a cracker. This helped me some. We started again and I thought of everything to keep me up, & at times I would feel quite buoyant but then again came the depression & I felt like sinking beside the road. It required all my tenacity of purpose, an obstinate will, all my pride to keep along with the Regiment and I succeeded, but I never had such a strain upon my powers of endurance before and all because my contraband fooled away his time at noon of yesterday. I have detailed this fact only to give you an incident of life on the march, & I hope you will not be too anxious about it. Well we did not reach Manchester as ordered. The men "fell out" so much that finally our surgeon told Gen Lytle that if we come through we would lose more than if we should fight a battle, and so he took the responsibility to Bivouac about half way on the route at a secesh home, an old man and a South Carolinian. I lay down on my rubber the moment we stacked arms, borrowed a blanket of the men as the wagon containing the officers blankets did not come up and thanked Heaven that the days work was over. It had been the severest test of strength in all my experience. Well, I had not laid two minutes before one of my boys came in having taken in that time seven chickens, while my servant had taken two. In the meanwhile Barber made me a strong cup of coffee & with that & some good crackers & fresh milk (taken without asking) for my coffee I was very soon in a more pleasant condition. Soon it came on to rain & Barber & I went to the porch of the old mans house & lay down with nothing over us but our rubbers. I never slept more profoundly in my life. Well this morning I was myself again especially after I had eaten very freely of those chickens although I was quite desirous of not having this same experience again. To day we left there at 7 and in carrying a gun of one of my men who was wounded at "Stone River" I lost my rubber blanket where we halted to rest. I think I shall find it again as the 24th was just behind us, who doubtless picked it up. Soon after I lost it, rain commenced pouring down & so continued until we filed into our camp here at Manchester, soon after which the sun came out in pleasant mood. I however got a good wetting for my forgetfulness. We are resting to day, keeping the Sabbath, Rosey's well known habit not being changed in our case. "Duck River" is here & this is the county seat of Coffee county. The scenery is magnificent or rather beautiful. I am reminded of my native home. I would like to describe it all but I can notice but one romantic spot. I have been down to this spot & first of all had a most delightful wash of my person which was needful after five days march such as I have narrated. You remember Minnehaha falls. Well directly below our Camp is a waterfall which is almost precisely like it in shape only this is magnificent & much larger. The height is about fifty feet and the water falls over in broken drops before it reaches the bottom. The shelf of rock is almost a perfect semi circle the chord of which may be 200 feet in length, the ravine below is filled with huge trees. The roof of the shelf is smooth & horizontal and the action of the water has hollowed out underneath the carmel coal & soft slate which underlies the shelf so that there is a beautiful walk clear around behind the little fall & better than at Minnehaha it is perfectly dry. There in this romantic spot I forgot all of yesterday, at least I said it was worth about all I endured to get a sight of this most charming and romantic spot. In puris naturalibus I stood under the fall & such a shower bath formed by nature I never enjoyed so much in all my life. The sun made the rainbows dance in my eyes as I stood taking this tremendous shower very philosophically.

I forgot not the useful in the romantic and putting my stockings under the fall the mud & dirt was literally beat out of them in a minute. I am astonished that some enterprising southern Yankee has not improved this spot, as it is, no spot is more in a state of nature. I am feeling delightfully cool & pleasant. Our shelter tent & blankets & what is better our rations have come up & so I am perfectly at ease. I have said nothing about what we have done because the army is the greatest place in the world for rumors. I learn to day that we hold Shelbyville which is probable as we are across Duck river at this place. There is also a rumor that we have Knoxville which I hope is true. I shall not speculate whither we are bound. We are moving however in the direction of Chattanooga, and I shall try and describe incidents as I go along. The papers in the meantime will give general news as to our whereabouts. I know you will be very anxious about me when you know that the whole army is on the march. But dearest let us both be calm and trustful, knowing that our Heavenly father will do that which is for the best with all his creatures.

We have all been spending the day in making ablutions and in cooking &c. I have a small pocket edition of the book of Psalms that I carry in my haversack. I lay down to rest soon after getting into camp and as I am reading the book in course, I read the 35th, 36th, & 37th. Oh how much comfort to me in these precious words and then to think that you & mother & father and all were at the same time worshiping at home in Gods temple, and remembering me at the throne of grace. Evening. I have been attending to necessary company duties and preparing for the march. It is very pleasant tonight, the moon is shining gloriously while the air is balmy and zephyr like. Troops, troops, wagons, wagons, camp fires all round makes an animated scene. I have just come from making a call on Col Miller 36th, had a pleasant call. While there saw Tribune of 23^{d} & a Nashville Press of the 26. In it is an item speaking of a rumor that our Division had been doing some desperate fighting with great losses on both sides and that we occupied Shelbyville. I was amused at it for myself but very much "put out" as I thought of its being possibly spread broad cast over Illinois to make thousands of females heart sick with anxiety for no possible cause. There are eight regiments of Illinois troops in our Division & so such stories are disgraceful. It is time enough to give information after we do have an engagement. We have just heard to day of Lee's still going to Pa. while Bragg's force or 20,000 of it is garrisoning Richmond. A few days will determine if this is so. I hope my dearest you will not become tired of these wayside notes. It gives me great pleasure to jot them down as I have opportunity knowing that at least you will be glad to hear from me if my letters do not come regularly to hand. Our mail met us here to day and I was somewhat disappointed not to hear from you. Will's letter you spoke of in your last did not come. I rec[d] one from Barbers father in which he paid me a high compliment for being a friend to his son. I will leave a line of this for tomorrow morning. I hope that our next mail will bring a letter from you although I have no expectations that our mail will be regular while on the march. I will close tonight by uttering a blessing on your head. Monday morning. 6 o'clock. The mail is just closing & so I must close this letter I suppose we shall move this morning but I cannot say at what time. Give my love to all at home & with kisses for Mason I am ever your own devoted husband.

John A. Bross

P.S. I send a bill of sale of a slave who had common sense.

On Picket in front of Cowan's Station,
Nashville & Chattanooga R.R.
87 Miles from Nashville. 11th day
of the campaign July 4th 1863

My Dearest,

I wrote you last at a point between Manchester & Tullahoma on the 30th of June. I have carried the letter with me as there was no mail returning. On the first of July (Wednesday last) we left our Bivouac when I last wrote, at 1 P.m. for Tullahoma. We arrived at 5 P.m. The enemy had evacuated in great haste leaving their siege guns, carriages burning as we entered; a vast amount of ammunition, tentage ripped up, camp equipage, kettles, officers mess chests, all indicating great excitement & panic. A great many of the tents were left standing without injury. Our Brigade entered town with the band playing the "Battle Cry of Freedom." We found plenty of papers a couple of which I send you. The defenses of Tullahoma were very strong, & to have stormed them would have been attended with immense loss of life then expending. This is one result of our flank movement to the north east of this town. Since Wednesday we have been pressing them hard & having been taking prisoners every day. - - Thursday the 2ᵈ at 4 A.m. We left Tullahoma for Winchester, which is south of Elk River. When we arrived at the bridge it had been destroyed & on account of the river being high we had to make a long detour in order to reach a ford where we might cross. We reached it in time to get over, before sundown. Shall I tell you how I got over? I stripped off coat, pants drawers stockings tied them up in a bundle rolled my shirts up under my arm pits & then with my haversack & bundle slung on my sword over my shoulder, I went along with the boys who shouted & hurrahed. It was just as much as men could do to keep their feet on account of the swiftness of the water. As I reached the other side I took off shirts & went in for a good swim while the rest of the Brigade was getting over. This was very pleasant after the heat of the day. We camped that evening near by this ford where although the prospect was at first unpromising, I had a good bed of dry grass for my couch in my shelter tent & I had a very refreshing sleep. Yesterday morning 3ᵈ (10ᵗʰ day of our march) we left camp at 4 o'clock, and reached Winchester county seat of Franklin county, one of the southern counties of Tennessee, at 7 A.m. Here I saw the rebel cavalry leave town as ours entered. Several of them were captured belonging to the 7ᵗʰ Alabama. We rested an hour & a half near the eastern skirt of the town & the boys availed themselves of the neighboring gardens to fill their haversacks with nice new potatoes & onions a great treat for them & for your humble servant. While laying at Winchester our cavalry went forward a couple of miles where the road crosses a branch of Elk River: Boiling Creek, & were very nearly ambuscaded by the reb cavalry. One of my men was wounded & two horses killed. The boy was pluck all over. He wanted to go right ahead & kill a lot of rebs. After this the Rebs left but about the same time a sad accident occurred. One of our sharp shooters belonging to 21ˢᵗ Michigan had stationed himself near the ford on a hill & as the rebs retired he saw some one waving his hat and hurrahing on the opposite side. He immediately fired at this man & he fell. Soon afterwards we crossed the creek & found that the sharp shooter had killed the son of a Union man, the boy 14 years old having been hurrahing for the approach of the Union troops. It was a pure accident but we all felt sorry for the poor father. This creek we forded with our "breeches on" in a drenching rain as usual. We reached here about 5 P.m. last night the rebs having gone off in great haste, Bragg being on the last train. I suppose we shall remain here to day as a relief from the 36th if our Brigade is just coming to relieve us from picket. The country just here is beautiful. The spurs of the Aleghanies are just to the south east of us through which the R.R. passes & also our road—over them lies the Tennessee River. It seems as if I could say while viewing these mountains with Rob Roy MacGregor, I am on my "native heath." For several days we have been marching through evidences that remind me of Pennsylvania. The Station here is the first one south east of Dechard which you will probably find on the map. We are waiting again for other Divisions. I do hope we shall destroy Braggs army before the close of this campaign. - - P.m. In camp. 3 citizens came into my picket line this morning who had gone away two days ago fearing a battle at this point. They represent the Tennessee portion of the rebel army as entirely demoralized. We went on Picket last night or rather 7 companies of the Regt. I had command. We had to establish a picket line & I had a hard time running through the wet brush & fields. After 10 o'clock P.m. I came to dry my clothes which had been wet all day. It was after midnight when I got them dry. I then lay down on two rails before a small fire without a blanket or over coat & slept soundly. Sometimes I wonder how I pass through such rough & tumble life but I do not think it injures me in the least. I am perfectly willing to suffer & endure it all if it brings me nearer to the enjoyment of your society. To day two salutes have been fired in honor of the anniversary. It is a Sabbath of rest to us all & I hope tomorrow will be also. We have just had a general read to the companies from Gen Sheridan expressing the thanks of Rosecrans to our Division for the manner in which it has led the advance from Hoovers Gap in pursuit of Bragg. This afternoon I had a very pleasant conversation with Gen Lytle at his Qrs. He is naturally a man of great talent & very social in his disposition.

Sunday morning.

We are ordered off on a scout & to leave our shelter tents & other things behind us. I will close this letter in order that it may be sent by mail if there is one. I send a paper, among those taken at Tullahoma. I rec[d] Wills letter yesterday. Will write him the first opportunity. Love to all the dear ones and kisses for my boy. We will feel the enemy I presume this morning. With much love I am always yours

John A Bross

Note: The following letter is to William and constitutes John's acceptance of his older brother's proposal that he become commander of a colored regiment in Illinois.

"Cowan" Tennessee
July 5, 1863

My Dear Bro

Yours of 27 ult. reached me yesterday. I should be pleased to command a colored Regiment if the opportunity offers. If I come safely out of this campaign I will write you more fully about it. In the mean time if you can make any arrangements for me, all right.

This is the 12th day of our campaign. Our Division led the advance from Manchester to this point which is at the foot of the spurs of the Cumberland mountains on the Nashville & Chattanooga R.R. About 2 miles S.E. of the station there is a tunnel through the mountain 2228 feet long. The 88th & 21st Michigan went on a scout & to the tunnel & top of the mountain to day, to support a reconnaissance of cavalry beyond the mountain. I should like to describe my march but have no time. I feel like M[c]Gregor on my "native heath" the country reminding me of Pennsylvania. We have been awaiting concentration of troops here, the rains having made it physically impossible to move a large army over a few roads. As it is we have been very successful the enemy "limbering" to the rear in great haste as is indicated all the way from Tullahoma to this point. I should like to speak of what we have all endured but it is soldiers life & God has given me health & strength to stand it. The army is in excellent spirits perfectly confident in itself and fully determined to do whatever is required of it. I have no doubt that but for the elements, Bragg would have been driven from his line of retreat and his entire army captured or destroyed. Our flank movement on Hoovers Gap & Manchester was perfectly successful, & we all prayed for clear weather to give Bragg the coup de grace. Tell Jessie I have her letter in my haversack among a chosen few and shall answer it from some point in Dixie. Love to all. Good bye

John A Bross

In Camp Cowan's Station
Tennessee. July 6th 1863

Dearest!

I closed my letter in some haste yesterday as we were ordered off on a scout to the mountains. The 21st Mich & the 88th started about 9 o'clock following the Rail Road until it enters a tunnel under the mountain 2228 feet long. Thence we wound up to the top of the mountain and lay in line of battle for a couple of hours. The object was to support a scout of cavalry beyond the mountain. While on the mountain we had our usual heavy rain storm wetting us all to the skin as no one scarcely thought of taking a rubber blanket. It was decidedly cool up there in the rain. Soon after the rain ceased the cavalry sent in a courier that they had gone as far as ordered & were returning. When we turned our steps homeward down the side we came in mud & slush where recently the rebs went up in great haste leaving evidences of their flight all along the way. I was glad to rest after our return. I am beginning to be anxious to hear from you again though I know I should not expect any for some time on account of the difficulties of mail transportation. To day I have been resting and enjoying the day albeit there are sad recollections of our great loss two years ago. Time has mellowed the anguish of her loss and yet how vivid in our minds is her dear sweet cherubic form. I trust that God will spare our boy.

We may lay here yet several days by reason of the state of the roads & high water. It is gratifying to know that our Division is in the extreme advance of this Corps. I have just dined having for my dessert just as many black berries as I could possibly eat. There are immense quantities all about & they are very good in a sanitary point of view.

There is a correspondent of the Tribune here by the name of Coleman. I have not been introduced to him yet. I have not seen my friend Crissy the other correspondent since we started. I enclose in this a pass countersigned by Ballard which I wish you to preserve for me. I wish to keep his signature. Also I send some poetry taken from an officers memorandum book picked up here by orderly Barber. The officer was of the 10th Mississippi. It shows he was in Kentucky with Bragg last summer & fall. I do not think he could have composed it. Barge Town is Bardstown which we entered Oct 5.

Also I send some of my own composition, the part as far as the star 3d page written May 8th the day that Mason was as old as Cora, the balance written since I commenced this letter. I hardly feel like sending it & yet it may be of interest for yourself to look over. The last part does not suit me. I hope it will not be unpleasant to you.

I have a rumor which may be pleasant to you though do not attach any importance to it until I write you again & that is that we are to camp here for a month. If this is so I shall make a determined effort to come home. I have written to Bro Will in answer to his letter of the 27th. If the campaign stops here I want to turn my attention to that matter, and above all I want to see you. Language is not a vehicle to express my longing hearts desire to see my beloved and friends. I supposed we should push ahead against Chattanooga immediately & it is my opinion that if we could only have gone ahead a few days ago it would have been very disastrous for Bragg. I am getting very well rested, my health is good & the cup of my happiness would be full if I could only see you and enjoy your society again. I suppose William & family will be on their way east about this time. If we stay here we shall have pleasant scenery. The rail road is not much damaged & we expect a train here in a day or so from Murfreesboro. There has been one already to Tullahoma.

Give my best love to father & mother Annie & Em & Zad Kisses many & warm for Mason

Ever yours
John

Dechard. July 11th 1863

My Beloved Wife,

I write in great haste from this point, having heard yesterday that Charley Wheeler was here through one of our officers that came with him as far as Tullahoma. I got on a horse this A.m. also Capt Chickering and came up here to get the package sent by Charley. It was lucky I came as Charley is just going to leave for the North. I do not know how to thank you for your remembrances. I received your letter of 28th two days ago on picket but did not write as there has been no mail. How glad I am to hear from you—I prize your package highly. I am very well indeed. Our Division is at the first station S.E. of this 5 miles at the foot of the mountains & in the extreme advance. There is no enemy near us they having been awfully scared & are not within 40 miles of us across the mountains. We have been waiting here for rations a whole week, & for the roads to dry & bridges to be built &c. The news from Vicksburg & the Potomac makes us all feel like coming home very soon & peace all around. God grant it may soon be. I have written to Will about the colored Regiment. Please act for me in the matter and have him see what can be done. I did not feel like writing to him until I got his letter. I wish I could describe to you things here and the scenery & my own appearance. I am not presentable in a drawing room but I am well if my campaigning does make me look a little rough. I do hope you have received some of my letters by this time. I am in cheerful mode and am anxious to cross the mountains into Georgia & Alabama. How gladly I would be home but I well know the shortest road home is to have this campaign finished. This morning I had a hearty laugh with Bob Demming aid to Gen Sheridan over some incidents of his life in Sterling, which will be of interest to Em & Annie but I have no time to relate them in this letter. I will write you again from Cowan by the next mail. I shall give this copy of myself to Bob Demming. He is the son of the Methodist preacher stationed in Sterling six years since. He remembers E & A. Give my love & thanks to Sister Mary & all friends. I have directed some letters to S—but I hope you will still stay in C. a long while. Oceans of love.

Yours ever
John A Bross

Cowan, Tenn. July 12, 63

My Beloved Wife,

Yours of July 4th & 5th came to hand this evening and I write immediately as the mail will leave in the morning. I was very very glad to get your letter. I wrote by Charley Wheeler from Dechard yesterday which you will get direct I hope as he said he should go right through. Now the first thing I want to say is, accept Toms offer and go with him & Mary. Tell him I am grateful for making so kind an offer. I know you will enjoy it & do not fear if I should need your services here. The telegraph would reach you at the east as well as at the west. So on all accounts if this reaches you in time I wish you to go.

After returning here yesterday I enjoyed the cake hugely, distributing also to friends among others Col Miller, Lt Col Olson & Major Sherman of the 36th with whom I enjoyed a pleasant supper. And now I must tell you how amused I was at your present of dried blackberries. We have been almost surfeited here with fresh ones for the past ten days. Yesterday in going to Dechard & back we ate just as many as we could, while hundreds of soldiers from Dechard and Cowan were going with all sorts of kettles & pails full. At tea last night with Col Miller & I had some delicious blackberry pie, so you see we are not without some luxuries after all. In fact this is the greatest country for this fruit I ever saw. Today I have eaten just as many as was prudent. I was certainly pleased with your desire to make my campaigning pleasant. I shall preserve the dried berries to use when the fresh ones are gone. The sardines & lemons I shall use some day on picket. We have splendid water here at the foot of the mountains. There is a stream here an affluent[1] of Elk River that is very cold. We bathe in it and it makes us shiver nevertheless we like it.

We are still uncertain when we shall move from here. Bradleys Brigade is 15 miles from here in the mountains. Rations are the chief impediments in our way.

Col Chadbourne is here. He had a furlough because of the approaching event in his family & he is now a happy father of a boy. It was only by special favor that he got his leave & on account of his own feeble health in the bargain.

I shall be ready at any time to come home upon an order of the Governor to raise that Regt. I have thought however that there would be such a rush for it that there would be no possible chance for me. All I have to say is that if I should have the chance I would make it a regt that would be creditable to the State. I am a firm believer in the capabilities of the negro in the matter of soldiering. True it will require discipline—but men of any color require it. My servant now will handle a musket better than some of the white men in the regt & he has frequently told me when I have laughed at him for running at Stone River, "Captn! Capt. Ise shamed myself. Jist give me a gun and see if I ever run agin."

I forgot to mention when speaking of fruit that I have apple sauce from green apples every day. Do not know how long this will be but I intend to have it as long as there are apples around. New potatoes are also quite frequently on my table. So we are not destitute of all the good things of this life.

I do not wish you to imagine an ideal of my present appearance that my presence will dissipate. I think myself I am looking better than when you last saw me, but campaigning has given me several gray hairs which I did not discover before I left home. Console yourself however that several of our officers younger than myself have a great many more. I was thinking of you & your curiosity as I was looking into a large slice of a secesh looking glass to day, and wondering if I could look any older than when I left you. Well, I thought I would just caution you not to let your imagination dress up my countenance that might be disappointed when I come home.

I have really no news to tell you. It is all quiet here. Saw the 19th yesterday.

I do not exactly like a certain air about them. In fact I think they have been petted a little too much.

Mrs. Pierce was married at 15. She & Mrs Sherman were left at Murfreesboro.

I am glad to hear of Capt Wheelers promotion. By the by I was surprised to hear that so many had gone to the war from our church. I wish Mr Swazey would send me a list of them & their regiments, rank & whereabouts. It is a great satisfaction to hear that Mason is well and being so, I hope you will not hesitate to go with Tom. I am only fearful that this will not reach you before he goes. But you ought not to wait for it if he goes after what I wrote in a former letter. I do want you to see the scenes of the East & I think there is no better time than now. If the opportunity offers we can very easily repeat the visit when I am through with this war. As to funds I presume that Father or William will furnish all you need & do take enough to be at ease in any emergency. I shall really be happy to know that you are enjoying yourself in my absence. Monday morning July 13. I have just breakfasted (5 ½ o'clock) with some of your berries for a dessert. How much I enjoyed them. I will speak of when I see you. They will be most agreeable on the march after a fatiguing days travel. And now love don't fail to go east. With my whole heart devoted to you I am now as always yours

John A Bross

1 An archaic meaning of "affluent" was a tributary stream.

Jackson County, Alabama.
Sunday morning July 19, 63

Dearest!

I am in a cotton state par excellence! Every step of the way from Louisville to this point I have footed it. Kentucky & Tennessee will ever be associated in my mind with the march, its fatigues, its dangers & its battles! I am grateful to my maker for sustaining me thus far. Well you will certainly wish that I particularize a little more with reference to my locality. Take an Appletons Guide Book & you will find a little station called "Anderson" 102 miles from Nashville on the N. & Chattanooga R.R. This station is about 200 yards north of the Alabama Line. Yesterday P.m. I did not rest on arriving here until I had gratified my desire of "kicking up a dust" in the state that could hold such a man as Wm L. Yancey.[1] So across the line I went echoing Alabama! Alabama! "Here we rest." I suggested to a brother officer whether it would not be best to put our ears to the ground to see if we could not hear the roll of the waves upon the shore of the gulf. But I am ahead of my story. I must begin at the beginning & tell you of our march from Cowan to this point. Friday I was on picket & yesterday morning our Regt & the 24th Wis was ordered to march to this point at 5 A.m. I came in from picket & marched immediately with my regt being delighted to receive your letter of July 10, which had come the night before. So I read & reread it along the road and I came along joyfully all day. It was a tough march for some of the boys, a few being impaired by sun stroke and drinking too much water. The distance is 15 miles which we marched all along the track. Two miles east of Cowan is the Cumberland Tunnel 2228 feet through the mountain. Soon after passing through the Tunnel the road strikes the sources of a stream called "Crow Creek" down the valley of which it is laid to Stevenson the junction of this road with the Memphis & Charleston 10 miles south east of this. The object of our being here is to patrol the road & act as a sort of guard while the mechanics & pioneers repair a few bridges damaged by the rebs. We expect the cars at Cowan today & perhaps we shall see them here to morrow. This little valley of Crow Creek extending in length about eighteen miles from near the top of the Cumberland to the Tennessee is quite romantic and beautiful. Mr Anderson residing here is a monopolist of land owning eight miles of the valley from this to Tantalon the station S.W. of this, 20,000 acres in all, & $160,000 of stock in the R.R. Of course he is a reb, but his pocket got the better of his secesh sentiments as I am informed he persuaded the rebs not to blow up the Tunnel nor burn some of the most important bridges near here. The bottom lands are filled with the finest crops of corn & all along the track are billions of blackberries. I really enjoyed yesterdays march. I felt that in some aspects I had yourself with me & my heart was light. I carry with me the first picture you sent me of you & Mason. How pleasant it is to look upon that smile of yours. Our camp is on a steep side hill just within the Tennessee line & north of the station house. Barber & I got a door of a house, carried it up in the hill under a clump of trees leveled it up with stones put on the door some wheat straw & then with one blanket over us committed ourselves to the care of the all wise one. This morning I took a bath in the creek which is here about twice as large as the Elkhorn at Uncle Penningtons and am here writing to my beloved. Don't think because I have waited this far along in my letter to speak of it, that I did not appreciate yours. I do believe it gave me strength & vigor for the march that I should not have had without it. I hope you have rec[d] a dispatch from me & several letters by this time, & I trust you will go with Turley. I am thankful that Gov Yates will "look out" for me. I shall wait with patience as long as we are at work here & going ahead. When we stop our campaign then I want to come home instantly to see you & see what can be done for promotion. I shall not be slow to accept anything that comes in an honorable & acceptable manner.

2[d] Sheet

Tantalon, Tenn. Monday
July 20, 1863.

Dearest,

Since I wrote the last sheet I have lived a week almost in a few hours. About a ¼ to eleven A.m. yesterday we heard the scream of the locomotive at Anderson. Down to the Depot I went & there was a locomotive tender & platform car, with Gen Sheridan & a portion of his staff, a guard &c. Capt Whiting invited me to take a ride to Stevenson distant 10 miles which is the junction of this with the Memphis & Charleston. Nothing loth I got aboard & in less than an hour was at Stevenson. I enjoyed it hugely being my first ride since leaving Louisville. After a little while Capt Whiting, Sheridans brother, Lt. Allen & myself were invited over to a Mr Wallace's to dinner. And such a dinner! All sorts of vegetables cooked in style. A half dozen ladies had been invited there to dinner. We came to town entirely unexpected & were just in time for the dinner with the ladies. I shall not recount all we had but will simply mention ripe luscious peaches. And fresh apple pie!

After staying there an hour or so we returned to Anderson. In the meantime our regiment had been ordered back to this station which is 7 miles from Cowan & 8 from Anderson. So I came on here on the locomotive having a rail road ride of 28 miles in all and huge enjoyment all round. It was a day I shall not forget. Our hostess at Stevenson is a large portly woman & was very agreeable & pleasant as also her husband. They are from East Tennessee. I spoke of my friends by that name in the North. They do not know of any relatives by that name in our portion of the Union. The lady told a good story of a woman who saluted the last train of rebels out of Stevenson on the 4th the day they evacuated that point. As the train was leaving the Depot she swung her bonnet over her head and shouted, "The Lord send the yankees, calico, & coffee." To appreciate this you should know that the commonest calico costs in the south $30 for a dress pattern, ladies boots $25, gents boots $100. Coffee not to be had at any price. Tantalon is where we meet the first level ground in coming down the mountain. There are no precipitous steeps but the creek to this point comes down a ravine with here & there a patch of cleared land on the side hills. Here the valley begins to widen and the stream runs more sluggishly. I am reminded here continually of my native state & county. All that is lacking is a little hemlock to make it complete. - - I do not know that I can do any thing at present for Mr. Swazeys cabinet. I thought of sending him something from Perryville & Stone River but there has been no good opportunity. As to keeping anything myself it is almost impossible now. I will send in this a specimen of cotton picked up yesterday at the depot in Stevenson. - - I am perfectly satisfied that Willie has an easy place. It relieves my mind of one anxiety. My position brings with it responsibilities that he does not have, & if I have to endure privations that he does not it is because I had the forethought to relieve him of them. He is grateful for the place & that is sufficient for me. My Darkey has done a great deal better since that day. I was very sorry to hear of Major Medills wound. I hope he will soon recover. As to that bill of Windett I do not propose to pay a cent of it until I see him myself & you can so inform Br. Josiah. I feel that mother & Taft should be paid because I employed them & their bill is reasonable. I am glad the title is settled, & you may now rejoice that you have at least a home of your own. I shall not be slow to give Mason some lessons in tactics when

I come home. I wish I had that bottle that was not drunk to John & Jessie. I shall keep this open until we have a locomotive here, or are ordered back to Cowan where I can mail it. I may send a note of yesterday to the Tribune.

Tuesday July 21, 63

Yesterday after writing the 2^{d} sheet we were ordered back to Cowan where we now are, and will perhaps remain a few days & be paid off as the paymaster is here. I am very well this morning and my trip has been a pleasant one all the circumstances considered. Our camp is being fitted up, bowers built and it looks as if our further forward movement is at an end for the present, certainly for a few days to come. There is no enemy near us and the mountains have a few bush whackers of both sides, some intent on doing a small business in the way of robbing occasionally. I am hoping that I may now have a chance to come home for a few days. How pleasant it would be to sit down to a Thanksgiving dinner as per order of "old Abe" on the 6th of August next. I have not had a letter from home since we left Murfreesboro. I have been hoping to hear from some of them. I hope the Sterling folks enjoyed themselves in Chicago on their excursion. I hope that Mason continues in good health. I shall not perhaps write you again until after I am paid. My love to all. Ever your devoted husband

John A Bross

1 William Lowndes Yancey (1814–1863) was an Alabama politician and leader of the Southern secession movement, appointed by Jefferson Davis to head a diplomatic delegation to Europe in an unsuccessful attempt to secure recognition of the Confederacy.

Bridgeport Jackson Co. Alabama
Thursday August 6, 1863

My Darling Wife!

I was delighted yesterday afternoon to receive your letters from Detroit & N.Y. both coming by the same mail. I avail myself of the opportunity afforded by Mr Scudder who goes north by the first train to write you a short letter hoping it may reach you in New York City. First let me give you a brief note of my movements. On the morning of the 30th July we left Cowan for Stevenson reached there July 31st. August 1, we came here & went into camp. The bridge across the Tennessee at this point is destroyed and it will take a long while to repair it. How long we shall stay here it is impossible to tell. I had made arrangements at Cowan to send up an application for a furlough this month based upon imperative business reasons, had about commenced the day after our arrival here to write it out when I received a note from Capt McLurg on McCooks staff stating that all such applications were returned not granted. As there was a large mass of them disposed of in this manner, McClurg advised me by all means not to present my application now as something was on the tapis. Now it is almost overwhelming us both with bitter disappointment to have our hopes of seeing each other this month broken like a potsherd. I am no more content with the prospect than you can be. We shall have to make a virtue of necessity however, & still cling to hope in the future. I cannot allude to this with any degree of composure & shall dismiss the subject. But what of the future? If this reaches you in New York I do hope you will make your visit out. Stay just as long as you can & do not have any thoughts about the expense. I have sent to father $300 received at Cowan & I hope you will now enjoy your trip east to the fullest extent regardless of expense. I shall only be too happy to furnish it knowing that it will be contributing to the happiness of my best love. If you should need any more funds draw on father. I hope you will have decided ere this to go to Vermont & pay your friends a visit. Remember that now is perhaps as good an opportunity as ever you may have. I certainly look forward to the time when I may pay another visit with you to the East but we know not what accidents may delay it far into the future. Business after I come home may tie me fast to the west. It is just as economical in every respect to make a good long stay. I should dearly love to visit with you some of my early associations in NY. & PA. but that must be when I am out of the army. - - The first day we arrived here I received that good long letter from you & the album with pictures. I should have received it at Cowan but was on picket the day that Major Davis was there. These three letters I highly prize and I need not attempt to tell you how much has been the happiness that they have brought to your husband. I have really enjoyed it as I anticipated, to read from your own hands mention of the new scenes you are now visiting. I am sure it is also pleasant to know that you have found new acquaintances and friendships. Ah! how peculiarly pleasant is it to read your dear little heart all through your letters, and witness the words of affection, gentle as the first pressure that ever answered the grasp of my hand in yours and yet thrilling me to the deepest recesses of my heart. We are very far apart & yet worlds cannot separate our love. How grateful to know that one heart so far away was yearning for its mate. Bless you darling for that word! It will bear me up in hope though years shall yet separate us. - - If there is the remotest chance this month or next to come home believe me I will avail myself of it. I am anxious that this shall reach you in New York and so you must excuse a long letter, I would allude to many things & shall hereafter if I do not get the opportunity to speak of them in person. I wrote to Jessie the other day and shall write to William when I am sure of reaching him. I need scarcely tell you that I am very well. I do not despair of seeing you ere the fall or winter campaign but how is yet a mystery. I am continually revolving it in my mind you see & will try & dismiss it for this letter. - - I have been paid to June 30th receiving $507. I owed $90 to the Quarter Master & sutlers for table articles, shirts, concentrated milk &c. The balance I have retained after sending to father $300 as before stated. I have lived better since we went into camp at Murfreesboro making it however more expensive. Some articles I will not have to purchase again soon as a pair of shirts, some cooking utensils & the like. My clothing a/c with Govt will be settled perhaps next pay day and so I cannot send you as much as I have heretofore. Still I propose to make it $1000 for the first year. There is no great necessity of spending much on the march. It is always more expensive living in camp. I do not owe a dollar here and do not intend to. It may be satisfactory to you to know however that my credit is good with every body so that in any emergency I can always procure what I wish with or without cash. In fact sutlers are only too willing to accommodate at enormous prices. My album is already full with a place reserved for yourself. Fathers & Jennies pictures are very lifelike & natural. I am very glad that father has such a genial expression of countenance. He looks as if he is just about to speak of something that amuses himself hugely.

I shall look with a great deal of interest for yours. I wish very much also that I had father & mother Masons. It will not be complete without them. I have received no letter from home since you left for New York. I hope you have received all that I have sent you. I have not written direct to you for nearly two weeks not knowing where a letter would reach you. - - There is a Brigade of rebels across the river & on the island. There is a great deal of conversation and joking going on between the men, bathing on their respective sides of the river &c. Of course we do not know how long this will continue. We are to have soon I think a board of examination in this department of those who wish commissions in Colored Regiments. Shall I go before the board & ask for a Regt from the U.S. authorities? I suppose regiments will be raised in this department. If I passed a favorable examination, I might get a chance to come home before entering on the business of recruiting. One thing I am convinced of [is] that a large mass of colored troops will be in the service before this year closes. And now dearest I hope this will reach you ere you leave N.Y. With a heart full of love, yours ever

John A Bross

Camp Roberts, Bridgeport
Alabama. Aug 20, 1863

My Beloved Wife!

Yours of 9th inst. postmarked 12th came to hand yesterday. I was of course very glad to hear from you & to know that you felt so well. But I am afraid you will again be sadly disappointed about my coming home. To day we are sending back all our tents, baggage &c to be stored at "Stevenson," and our campaign I presume is about to begin again. I have not the slightest idea of our destination. There has been some talk of our going to "Huntsville" about 60 west of here on the Memphis & Charleston R.R. to garrison that place. A few days will determine. I am very well & shall go cheerfully forward to do my share of what I trust may be the last act in this great drama of rebellion. Have faith that God will give us the blessed opportunity of seeing each other ere long. There are to be some officers sent home after conscripts after this movement is made and I may be so fortunate as to be one of them. There is a rumor to that effect in camp and if it should turn out to be true how happy we shall both be. To come home in that way would be very agreeable to my feelings and would certainly be pleasant in a pecuniary point of view. My wages would be the same and I would have my expenses paid by Government. I know not where to address this letter but will make it sure by sending it home. I received letters from Capt Longworth & Ira this morning. Capt L. has a great desire that you shall make him a visit. He says he will meet you in Chicago at any time. I hope that you will have made a visit to your friends in Vermont before you turn your footsteps homeward. I have no news to send. I am busy in sending off our "traps" by rail and so you will not expect a long letter. Should we move westward, I will write you from Stevenson & wherever we go on the march you will hear from me whenever there is a chance to send a letter back. May Heaven bless my dearest and keep you & your husband safe from all harm. Ever your affectionate husband

John A Bross

Bridgeport, Alabama
August 21st 1863

My Beloved Wife!

"Let us rejoice." I send you good news! It will make your heart glad! I am coming home! I have slept soundly many times in front of the enemy but I could not sleep much last night in view of the prospect that now opens before me. The way home has been apparently blocked up all the time and now it has suddenly been cleared away. I cannot write calmly and I do not care to measure my words. Yet, I must explain how it is. Three officers of every regiment are to be sent home to bring back recruits or rather the conscripts when the draft is made. Day before yesterday Col Sherman sent up my name to Department Hd Qrs as one of the Officers to go from this regiment & last evening he told me of that fact. It was rumored in Camp to the same effect on yesterday when I wrote you but I did not feel like attaching too much importance to it. Now you will be anxious perhaps to know when I will come. I cannot say certainly. It will depend somewhat upon when the draft will take place in Illinois, & also upon our movements here. But the main fact is quite certain that I will be with you as soon as possible. Won't it be happiness for us and all our friends? I have felt a strong degree of faith that I should come home this fall but how to get there I could not see. I would rather that you & friends keep this news to yourselves for the present, except to those who are at work for me in that colored enterprise. I shall send a letter by the mail that takes this, to Br. Josiah, which will be satisfactory to him. It will be pleasant to come home in the manner mentioned. I would be very glad to have this regiment filled to the maximum & the object of our coming or one of the main ones is to induce conscripts to select our regiment as they will have I believe the right to decide which they will join, and in that work I will most cheerfully engage. I will have the opportunity of visiting different sections of the state at the expense of Uncle Sam & I give you an invitation in advance to go with me. Now I have told you about all I can in this letter. I hope to be at home by the 10th of next month and I know that we shall both feel differently from the parting moment on the same day last year. We are here still and the impression is that we shall be here yet several days. Our baggage all left yesterday, and the line officers are stripped to "light marching order." Now dear let us praise the Lord, and thank Col Sherman for one kind act to your husband. With love to all

I am as ever yours
John A Bross

Bridgeport Alabama
August 28th 1863

My Beloved Wife!

I was delighted to receive yours of 28th inst. written at Chicago this morning. I read it again and again and have been happy all day. I hope that by this time you will have received my letter announcing that I shall be at home some time next month. I can scarcely wait for the time to come. Your letter satisfied my mind about your going from Greenport. I received the one from you written at that point the day before you started and although I feel that any lady can travel almost anywhere, I could not repress anxiety for your safety. And so I was extremely happy to get your last letter detailing the incidents of your trip, and to know that you were safe in Chicago. I was sure that a journey east would be beneficial to you & I know we shall never regret that you went. Of course I would have been glad to go with you, but we shall take another together some time in the future. - - You will wish to know when I will be at home. Nothing as yet has turned up to determine the time but I hope to get home by the 10th of next month. Oh! how I shall enjoy the meeting of friends after so long an absence. We are still in the quietude of our camp but preparations are going forward to cross the river. Since we occupied this place the army has been gradually taking up positions on the river from above Chattanooga to below Bellefonte a distance of more than a hundred miles with the bulk of the army at & around Stevenson. One of Burnsides Corps (the 23d Army Corps Gen Hartsuff) is in communication with us at Pikeville at the head of the Sequatchy valley & the 9th a.c. is also expected soon. We have between 60 & 70,000 of our own troops, 15,000 of Burnside with the balance of his force coming up. You may judge from this that there will be a big thing when we do go. Of course what I have just said as to forces and location must be kept private. Mrs Pierce & Sherman are still in camp and will remain until we leave. They seem to be thoroughly domesticated in camp. - - I shall certainly not have another year pass in my military life without having you present with me part of the time. I am glad that Jessie thinks so much of her uncle. McClurg I thought spoke of her with a great deal of interest albeit Jessie said in her letter he was engaged to one of her friends.

I received a good letter from Charley this morning dated the same day yours was written. - - I received yesterday the letter of William written June 15th asking about my wishes in respect to a colored regiment. Long while on the way wasn't it. For the last two days it has been remarkably cool here with wind from the north. I never knew it colder in Illinois this month. The nights here are generally cool & pleasant. - - Deserters are coming across the river daily. Yesterday a squad of twenty came over together. I will write a note of thanks to Tom to day for his kindness in your behalf. And now my love I bid you good bye hoping that I soon may send you word by lighting[1] that I am on the road home.

Ever your own husband
John A Bross

1 This is most likely a reference to the telegraph.

On "Look Out" mountain
Thursday Eve Sept 10, 1863

Dearest!

I am and have been thinking of you all the afternoon and eve. I am on picket writing to you beside a blazing bivouac fire. Our trains are all in the rear not having come up the mountain and as a consequence the officers blankets & shelter tents are behind. But what of that! We are after Bragg once more & we are all full of ardor and cheerful over our success in climbing the second range of mountains on our march, & now the "road to Rome" is open before us. We lay in camp where I wrote you last until this morning. We had a dusty road up the Look Out valley and the heat was very severe so much so that quite a number of soldiers gave out from its effects and two from the 42d died. We have marched sixteen miles to day and are in DeKalb co Alabama, the range of the valley & mountains being to the west of south. We expect to be in Georgia again tomorrow. The night is warm and I do not expect much inconvenience in consequence of having no blankets. We are on and near a little stream that leads off the mountain southeasterly into the Chattanooga an affluent of the Coosa, having left the waters of the Tennessee in our march to day. There is right by the Camp a deep gorge of about 100 feet, down which the creek rushes, the whole forming a most romantic scene. We are about 35 or 40 miles south of the Tennessee line. - - I enjoyed myself in our last camp. I called on a Mr & Mrs Wingfield near by whose permanent home is in Macon but are now living in Look Out valley. They came there to be out of harms way but run right into it. Our troops were the first infantry ever in the valley, and they made desolation reign immediately so far as corn fields

& potato patches are concerned. While at their home yesterday a detail from Col Bradleys Brigade came & took all their bacon which they had nicely hid away in their garret loft. But a soldier is a good man on the scent of most any thing in the eatable line. I felt very sorry for the lady but I told her frankly that it was the true mode to forage. She has a most interesting family of three children two boys and a little girl who is a very bright and fascinating child. The soldiers had stolen three coffee pots from her, every article of the kind she had in the house & I had brought her one that day. She was more than grateful to me for this little act of kindness and I was amply repaid. She is a true lady without the hauteur and contempt which most of the f.f.! display for northern men. We talked of every thing and I was very sorry that I had not my album with me to show her your phiz. Her husband is nearly 13 years her senior. He is a retired merchant. I speak of this family as it is really the first lady with whom I have talked with since I came in the service.

Well Dearest I have nearly filled a sheet and have not said a word of something in my heart! One year ago! Three words, and yet oh how much are crowded in them! Never shall I forget the last look the last kiss and the last pressure of your hand. It thrills me now by the lonely pine knot fire & I see your gentle, sad countenance as I convulsively rush from you to the cars. Through all the dangers, the lengthening absence, the long and fatiguing marches, this form moving further & further from you as each day succeeds to day yet oh yet "My heart untraveled fondly turns to thee." Let us have faith in the Lord who is our fortress, our refuge, and trust in him that he will grant us the happiness of each others society again. I lay down on a few oaken leaves blessing your name.

Ever yours
John

Alpine, Chattooga Co
Georgia, Saturday
September 12, 1863

Dearest!

Yesterday morning before we left our Bivouac the mail from Stevenson arrived bringing your letter of 3[d] & 4th inst. How lightly my heart bounded to get this evidence of your remembrance. The march yesterday although fatiguing and awfully dusty had very little if any draw backs to me. The whole Corps is now concentrated in this valley. The three Divisions have not been together since we left Manchester the last of June. The length of our march yesterday was twelve miles on the mountain, & we are now in the valley on the east side of the Look Out range. It is very fertile and the soldiers "live high." I saw the first capture of cotton yesterday. All Northern Georgia is hilly & mountainous & hence not adapted to cotton but we are getting down where they raise some on the alluvial bottoms. The rich southerners have to suffer wherever we go, and it is right to make them feel the horrors, of what they were the instruments of bringing upon our beloved Country. Alpine is no more than a post office and neighborhood with a few rich men. It is just within the State line & you can doubtless find it on the map. We are resting to day and it is understood that our cavalry will occupy Rome to day which is distant about 24 miles. The rebs obstructed the road a good deal where it comes down the mountain into this valley but the trees were soon removed by our pioneers. The cavalry had a skirmish here three days since with Forrest. We lost several killed & wounded. The rebs left us in full possession of the valley. It looks as if our movement of itself is a great victory. The army is in splendid condition and will make a grand record whenever the opportunity offers. I cannot speak of the movements of the whole army! For the best of reasons that I know nothing about it. One of our chief pleasures on this march has been our daily mail—bringing us Nashville, Cincinnati, Louisville & Chicago Dailies—and above all letters from home. …

I was pleased to hear that father had received the $300. Did he get it in "Green backs"? You say that Mason has entirely recovered! Has he been very sick, I do not remember of your speaking of his being sick. I am glad that he is so well & hearty now. I hope that the friends will have a pleasant trip east. Willie has known ever since we received that butter that part of it came from Mr Dinsmoor. I shall remind him that he should duly acknowledge it when I see him. He gets 40 cents a day extra for being clerk but he spends all his wages I fear & more too. I have already lent him a small amount. I would not mention this to his friends there. The clerks at Division Qrs have a mess of their own, & they spend a good deal on it & that is the reason why they spend their earnings. They live better at all times than company officers. Hence you can easily judge of Willie & his free style of doing things. - - I understand that Capt Whiting has sent in his resignation if this is so and it is accepted, Willie may be sent back to the Company. I received a letter from Si a few days ago in which he spoke of some water rents for which the house was liable. I will send money to pay it when I am again paid which will be I presume soon after we go in camp again. I was greatly pleased in reading a statement by Gov Yates that there would be a draft in Ill. If there is you will surely see me I think by Masons birth day. I should say perhaps that I am very well and have really come along on this march with no difficulty at all. And now dearest again good Bye. How glad I should be to drop in upon you & father & hug my dear boy.

Ever yours
John

In Bivouac Thursday Sept 15

Dearest!

I have time to send you a short note of my whereabouts. Since I wrote you we have made a retrograde movement & our Brigade together with the whole Corps train is back on Look Out Mountain at the point I wrote you from on the eve of the 10th inst. while the other two Brigades & two each from Davis & Johnson's have gone down into Look Out Valley & towards Trenton about 15 miles & up another road on to this same mountain to help Negley to defend that pass over the mountain. It seems that the rebs concentrated at LaFayette, Walker Co between our corps which lay Saturday & Sunday at Alpine & Chattanooga intending to cut us off from the centre & left, but they have found we are too quick for them although it invoked the necessity of our "crawfishing" a little & of course I do not see Rome quite as quick as I desired. Our Gen Lytle commands the 3 Brigades detailed to protect the wagon train and it is a pretty big job but we can do it. I do not know as you can understand all this brings but I guess you can. The fact is our communication with the centre & left was endangered and we had to get out of the valley east of this mountain as quick as we could. It has been accomplished successfully trains & every thing are up the mountain, but it was awful hard work. It seems Johnston is in command & there are reinforcements from Virginia & Rosecrans found out just in time that they were trying to get him into a trap. But he did not step in. A few days will develop something huge in the way of strategy, and it is a "very pretty game as it stands." I do not yet believe we shall have a fight this side the Chattahoochie, still a general engagement may be brought on by the rebs attacking us, & in that they will find us "perfectly at home." We camped here last night being the last Brigade of infantry out of the valley. The cavalry had captured a confed cavalry captain, who marched with me all day. He is a Kentuckian by birth, has lived in Georgia near Savannah since 1856, & was admitted to practice law at Shawneetown in Illinois. He "stood up" with Gen John A Logan when he was married. I had long "talks" with him about all subjects. He ate dinner with me & he enjoyed coffee & crackers very much. Our camp here is a pleasant one. I went down last eve to the "Devils Hole" underneath the waterfall heretofore spoken of, & the view from below is extremely beautiful. Anyone who marched as we did all day yesterday through dust six inches deep & so thick in the air that you could not see three rods ahead of you would gladly seek a mud puddle to rid himself of some of the mixture of dust & sweat that had accumulated during the day upon his person. There is a great basin of water at the foot of the fall & in that hundreds went very quickly. It is another item in my memories of attractive natural scenery. Do not know whether we shall be all day here or not. You must wait in patience to hear from me, as occasion offers. Love to all.

Ever yours.
John

Monday Sept 21st 1863

My own Darling Wife,

Again have we occasion to give thanks to God for preserving my life through another terrible & most awful battle. I have not time to give you particulars now. Suffice it to say I escaped without a scratch, but several of our officers have been wounded. Lt Rae had his leg broken, Capt Sheridan & his two Lts McMurtry & Griffin were all wounded. Capt Chickering is also wounded. Our Brigadier Gen Lytle was killed at the commencement of the battle. There seems to be a fatality in all the Brigade Commanders of this Division. The battle com. on Saturday the 19th in which our Brigade was not engaged being held in reserve to guard a wagon train. Col Bradleys Brigade was in action however that day & they behaved nobly, Col Bradley being severely wounded. Our position is the extreme right of the army. The engagement yesterday commenced in our front about noon, the centre (Thomas Corps) having been engaged for hours & the Heavens & earth literally trembled with the cannonading & crash of infantry fire. At last they came at us. I was with my Co deployed as skirmishers & had the first chance at the Devils. They came up in mass & I held on with a good fire until they came within a few yards before I gave the command to retreat on the main body. It is a miracle almost that we were not all shot down in our tracks. The result of the matter was our Brigade was nearly broken up by a mistaken order in making a tactical evolution the Brigade "going in" nearly by the flank instead of the front. But I presume such things are all Greek to you. I believe I wrote you last from Look Out Mountain. Since then it was a continual effort to get down the Chickamauga valley (southeast side of Look Out Mountain) in order to mass our troops on our own left, in front of Chattanooga. The Battle yesterday was fought about 9 miles from Chattanooga. It will afford me material for the longest tale of battle to tell you that I have yet gathered up in my experience. Our army was badly cut up but I am proud of the pluck shown in the face of superior numbers. This army may be exterminated but it will fight to the last. There is a large force here from Lee's army & it is but just to admire their bravery. It is worthy of a better cause. - - My men say I held them too long before retreating but they stood up to it nobly. The right of my Co rested in an open corn field. I was towards the left in the woods keeping back the fire of my men until they had a good chance to fire. Casting my eyes towards the right I saw the boys giving way. I ran back & ordered them to face about & advance. They did so as if on drill & went up a little in advance of the original line. The fact was they saw more than I did. The rebels were coming through the corn field & the result of my order was to bring us within a few yards of each other. I saw that if there was any virtue in legs now was the time. I told the boys to "go it" just as a whole regiment poured a volley into us tearing up the dirt, cutting off leaves & branches of bushes right where we stood. It was a race about neck & neck but we came out ahead. To tell you all the varying scenes of the day would be impossible. They are treasured up to be told you hereafter. I have only fifteen muskets out of 32 I took into action but I shall gather up most of them. I may attempt to describe the scenes hereafter. It was necessary for us to withdraw our lines nearer to Chattanooga & possibly we shall yet have a 3^d^ trial. If so may God protect us. It seems to me more & more & more that we are fighting the last battles of the Rebellion. Adieu I will write you again. May God bless us both. Love to all.

Yours ever
John

Chattanooga Saturday
Eve September 26th 1863

My Beloved Wife!

Since I wrote you last we have taken up position at this point & have been at work like beavers entrenching ourselves all around the town. We left our barricades near Rossville spoken of in my last letter under cover of the night & took up position here just at daylight. Spades & picks were at a premium & our boys fell to it with a will, the idea of being compelled to evacuate Chattanooga the object of this campaign & fall back across the Tennessee thereby losing all the hard work (and the good name beside, of this army) since we left Bridgeport was intolerable to us. Hence every one was animated with a desire to hold this point to the last extremity & it will be held if any army on this continent can do it. But oh! dearest, how we have been bruised & battered. Men whom I have made friends & do love them for their noble qualities are maimed & shattered for life while others have gone to their long account. Of many can I say as Longfellow in his "Warden of the Cinque Ports" said of Wellington

> Him shall no sunshine from the fields of azure
>   No drum beat from the wall
> No morning gun from the black forts embrazure
>   Awaken with its call.

I am in no condition yet to tell of that terrible Sabbath which swept away 6,000 out of 14,000 in our (McCooks) Corps. And yet my dear let all northern hearts who love their country be proud of the stubborn obstinacy of the Union troops borne down by overwhelming numbers on the field of Chickamauga. It will be impossible for you to correctly understand without a long tale how we came to fight this battle. I recommend you to read the Cincinnati & N.Y. papers if you can get them. The main point to remember is this: our Corps was sent bag & baggage way off towards Rome in order to draw Bragg out of Chattanooga: this was done but in the mean time they concentrated at LaFayette drew reinforcements from Richmond & tried to cut us off from the rest of the army. We just saved ourselves that disagreeable alternative & had to fight them because we could not avoid it. The army feels very much depressed on account of its great losses but its spirit & confidence in self is just as strong as ever. We hold another of the great "key points" and have punished the enemy severely. Rest and reinforcements being had we shall go on conquering these everlasting hills. My faith is as strong as ever in our ability to beat the rascals. We shall certainly hold this place against all comers. The Brigade to which the 75th is attached was not in the fight. I called on the officers a couple of days since, saw Kilgour Bennett & McMoore. Bressler is one of the missing ones yet, in my Co. I am afraid he is captured. My health is very good. Since I wrote last I have procured my over coat & a blanket & can now get along with the cold nights very nicely. This campaign however has made me thin again. The exposure at nights has been extreme and severe, yet there is no apparent ill effects. You will naturally enough ask when I shall be home. I cannot now say anything about it. The killing & wounding of so many officers may prevent my coming. Some of our officers who are very slightly wounded who could just as well be with their regiment as not are hugging the hospital on the other side of the river. Dearest, I do hope when this flurry is over and while the regiment is resting & the army again preparing to move I may have the blessed opportunity of seeing you. I write this having notice that there will be a mail for the north in the morning. I could have written a day or so since but all mails have been stopped for fear of guerillas. Dearest amid all this turmoil & confusion and hellish strife of war your own dear countenance is still before me to cheer me in all my toil. Love to all.

Ever yours
John A. Bross

Chattanooga Thursday
October 1, 1863

My Beloved Wife!

The "Big mail" for which this army has been looking anxiously day after day until the heart was sickened with disappointment, arrived to day bringing yours of the 16th Sept & one from Ira of the 17th together with a half doz tri-weekly Tribunes & a lot of N.Y. weeklies. How gladly I read your letter knowing all the while that the news of our advance would be disheartening to you. I have often imagined that this awful depressing influence that will come over us at the prospect still lengthening out of our separation is worse in its effects upon you than upon myself. To me this campaigning tough though it be has a species of excitement & tends to drive away for the time being home sickness, & yet I cannot tell you how often under the Broad Canopy of Heaven have I gazed upon the stars and wished that I might look upon you as they upon me. Doubtless your heart has agonized over my safety in the past ten or twelve days & I hope that long ere this you have been assured of it. And now as to coming home. It looks darker than ever. Some five line officers of our regiment were wounded & they have all gone or will go home from the hospitals to be absent perhaps for months. This reduces Co officers to almost one to a Co. I am alone again, Cole being first assigned to another Co & now is acting Adjutant. Capt Smith is recognized by Lt. Col Chadbourne as acting major & so it is not pleasant all things considered. I just let things take their course with a sort of blind indifference to my fate having given up anything like a hope for promotion or favors in this regiment. I sometimes think that of all persons in this army after trying to do my duty thoroughly I am the worst off. I do not anticipate a forward movement from here before November or December but for reasons above stated I do not see much chance to come home on furlough. I have thought seriously of tendering my resignation if I cannot get away otherwise. There is another way perhaps that may get over the difficulty. The companies of the regiment might be consolidated & in that event I might get out. I do not hope for anything from that proposed colored regiment, I do not believe it will be raised. I am afraid it was only raising false hopes when my brother wrote me about it. As to getting a command of that description here you might as well try to scoop out Rock River dry with a spoon unless you had the favor of certain army cliques. I cannot write you all I would about these things. If God in his Providence ever permits me to see you again I will have long tales to tell you. - - This is the anniversary of our leaving Louisville on the march through Kentucky. It has been raining hard all day the first since this campaign commenced & I have been within my shelter tent reading & thinking of you. I do not forget that next Sabbath is the birth day of Mason. How I should like to take him in my arms. - - I saw Ed Mills on Look Out Mountain the day you wrote your letter & had a long chat with him about Sterling. I was sorry that the jelly met with such a disaster.

Col Sherman has returned and is in command of the Brigade. McCook & Crittenden are severely censured for their conduct in the late battles and many think a change will be made relieving them of their commands. Sheridan stands high & if there is a change he will most likely take McCooks place. McCook managed very badly on the field if the statements of high officers are to be believed. I know that our position was a remarkable one & no one at a distance without diagrams could well understand it. So far as myself was concerned I was left in my position to be sacrificed without an order from Col Chadbourne or notification of the movements of the regiment, & so I fought as it were on my "own hook," & extricated my command from the skirmish line on my own responsibility at the last moment. Of that battle there are many things to say which I shall not commit to paper. Of my own share in it I shall say no more than if I had it to do over again I would do the same. I am not ashamed of my record. - - Our mail facilities here are by no means regular & you must wait patiently a circuitous route to hear from me. Give my love to all friends.

Ever your affectionate husband
John A Bross

Chattanooga, Oct 4, 63

My Beloved Wife!

Yours of 20th ult. I received Friday P.m. & I thank you sincerely for the motive which prompted it. It did me good & cheered me in a lonely hour. Our Brigade is on picket for four days close to the Look Out Mountain while the rebs are within musket shot of us. However no firing of any extent is heard along the lines. The first day we came out (Friday) our Regiment was on the sentinel line. We are now on the reserve and nothing to do but rest. It is very much like a quiet Sabbath with us. Willie has just come out to see us & we have been talking over matters at home. He tells me that Mills was "gobbled" in the late fight. I should say that Mills told me that he enclosed a note to me containing one from Annie about the jelly, but it has never reached me. We are without any news from the north but rumors plenty as blackberries. In the mean time I have rec^{d} on yesterday Harper, Atlantic & the Continental for October & so have plenty of reading matter wherewith to beguile the time. I shall keep your letter of the 20th written on the day of the battle on account of several sentences it contains as well as the general tone of it. I send by mail along with this letter to father a package of letters & papers I have collected from a house since I came out here on picket. We are near a large rolling mill which was used by the confederates. I thought some of them might be interesting to father & friends. I want you to have him preserve the requisition for the Ram Manassas.[1] It contains the signature of the notorious "Hollins." The vessel you may remember was destroyed in the operations that led to the surrender of New Orleans to Farragut. You will also find inside the "Rebel" a ring made from a muscle shell taken from "Stone River." If Zed will accept of it you may give it to him with my compliments. It is not worth as much as gold but then there is the remembrance to me of associations that can never be forgotten. I am not in the habit of wearing rings but have worn this one and one other since we left Bridgeport on the march & through the terrible engagement two weeks ago. - - You may be sure I have been thinking of you & Mason to day—and of the glad morning to me three years since. Would I could be with you & return my boys kisses thrown from the window. The way seems dark so far as coming home is concerned & yet beyond it all is your own loving countenance and the prattling of my boy to cheer me on with faith & hope that there will be a time when I shall see you both. - - I hope that "fair week" was not too fatiguing to you. Your remark with reference to Em set my imagination at work. Please give her sage advice from me, to be very careful how she stumbles & tumbles down stairs in the future. She has my profound sympathy under such, as well as any other set of circumstances. When Annie gets home I want her to write me an account of her trip. - - Sherman had a sick leave. His being absent from this last battle will prevent his ever getting a star if he ever had any prospects before. I hope you have heard of my safety long ere this. With much love I am always your devoted husband

John A Bross

1 The CSS Manassas, originally the steam icebreaker Enoch Train built in 1855 in Massachusetts, was converted in 1861 in Louisiana to the first ironclad ship built for the Confederacy. Flag officer George N. Hollins, CSN, led it in a surprise attack on the federal blockading squadron on 12 October, 1861, in which action it lost its iron prow. It was sunk in battle on April 24, 1862.

Chattanooga Oct 8th

Dearest,

There has been no mail since I wrote on the 4th & so I will add another note. Monday last the rebs having succeeded in getting some cannon up the side of Look Out Mountain opened on us with shot & shell. They threw their missiles all over & around us but fortunately no one on the picket line were injured. We were yet on picket & was therefore close by say ¾ of a mile. They kept up a well directed fire all the afternoon & it was amusing to see some officers dodge in the rifle pits. I never got in the pits but amused myself in watching the discharge from the battery, counting the seconds before the report came, & judging from the sound of the shell where or on which side it was going. After a little I could tell very well where the ugly customers were bound. I begin to believe that shells have quite a moral effect if they don't hit, for quite a number were most awfully nervous. Perhaps it argues a want of sensibility on my part. Well I'm sure I'd dodge too if I thought the "enlongated"[1] were coming straight at me. So don't think I will unnecessarily expose myself. The next morning was remarkably quiet. Our regiment went again on the sentinel line before the fog lifted relieving the 36th. When it cleared away, one of our sergeants mounted a breastwork & shook a paper. At once it was answered from the reb picket line. One sergt went half way & was met by a reb sergt who exchanged papers, the rebs & our boys in the mean time throwing aside their guns and appearing in great numbers on their respective lines. It was quiet all day. No picket firing no artillery practice. Towards night we began to observe movements on the side of the mountain & finally we saw them gathering their guns down off of the mountain & to hear all sorts of noises in their camp. It was evident they had heard of something. It is now believed they have left our front. Well you have seen that the 20th & 21st Corps are to be consolidated. I am glad of that for various reasons. I am anxious to hear from you about my future course. As soon as things are a little settled I shall make another effort to come home by furlough. If not I am strongly tempted to resign. Have father & Bro Will each write a letter making it just as strong as circumstances will admit of the urgency of my personal presence about business matters. It will have some effect. I can use them to advantage. I may get a chance to come home on recruiting service but it is uncertain and we do not know when the next draft will take place. Willie is here & well. He may be sent back to his Co if he is not wanted at Division Hd Qrs. There has been some Chicago folks here of the Christian Commission,[2] Messrs Hosmer & Tuckhorn. They have gone back however. We are feeling very well over the reinforcements which are coming to us from other departments. I am very well but I would give a great deal for a barrel of potatoes and onions. We have been on half rations for two weeks & it is pretty tough, however we are on the turning point of better times. I should just like to go back to Alpine where we had such capital forage. You see I am yet a soldier. Yesterday Col Lane Raymond was made a citizen & Maj. Davis I understand will also resign. I presume there will be a good many resignations now. I am hoping to hear from you soon. With much love to all I am always your devoted

John

1 An "elongated" was a type of artillery shell used during the Civil War.

2 The United States Christian Commission was an organization that furnished supplies, medical services, and religious literature to Union troops.

CHAPTER 3

Letters from May 1 to July 23, 1864: Virginia, Battle of the Crater

Alexandria, Va Sabbath
Eve May 1, 1864

My Beloved Wife!

I am on the "sacred soil" of Virginia—having arrived here this afternoon about an hour before sundown. My regt is in the "Soldiers rest" and I am here to write first of all to my own beloved. We left the city of Chicago Wednesday afternoon at 3 o'clock. We were somewhat delayed so that we did not reach Pittsburgh until about 9 P.m. of Thursday. We marched to the Soldiers rest in that city where supper was all ready for us. We were treated in good style. I spoke to the rgt, they sung and we gave cheers for the Ladies, Gov. Yates, Curtiss,[1] the old flag &c. &c. after which we marched to the cars and left at 11 ½ P.m. for Harrisburg. We did not stop or change cars there but run on to Baltimore which we reached at 9 P.m. Friday. After taking supper at the Soldiers rest, we were quartered in the Adams house a secesh concern the owners of which have been hunting their rights away down south. I spent part of Saturday in trying to get orders about changing my destination

& finally secured transportation for Washington. We reached there about 8 P.m. last night & was quartered in the Soldiers rest. We stayed there until after dinner today, when we marched down Pennsylvania Avenue in grand style and then to this point. I was pleased with the regt and the occasion. Little did I think three years ago when I sat on the steps of the Treasury building and looked down the Avenue to the Capitol and cried with indignation over the affairs of the country, that I should at this day march a regt of Colored Troops down that same avenue. The whole street was lined with an enormous crowd of whites & colored. I have the vanity to believe that your husband never appeared better or felt more keenly the promptings of a proud and joyous spirit. My charger performed his part of the play in gallant style. He is a noble animal. I shall always feel grateful to Mr Smith for his efforts in procuring it for me.

My regt behaved well on the way—so much so as to provoke comparisons in their favor and to the detriment of white soldiers. This morning I had religious services, a Scotchman of the Christian's Commission officiating. He is from Paisley & his name is Smith. I led the singing & it did me good to hear them sing. Tomorrow I make all arrangements for fitting out & next day I leave here for the Corps which is at present doing guard duty along the R.R. So much for that. Now a word of domestic matters. I gave William a small amount of money that will partly pay the debts I made in fitting out. I will get the balance as soon as I can here, or you may pay a little of it from the rent. Be assured I will send you all I can. I am going out of sight of hotels & will <u>save all</u> I can. I shall be very busy for the next week and may not get time to write to anyone but this to you. So do not be anxious about me. I do not expect we shall be very much <u>exposed</u> for the present. I will try & keep you advised as to my whereabouts if Uncle Sam does not cut off all our mails during the pending operations.

And now dearest it is getting late and I have a heavy days work tomorrow. Say to Will that I want him to pay me a visit when he comes to Washington. Kiss my boy for me and love to all the dear ones. I shall labor to win the respect and esteem of my superiors and I hope soon to show you the <u>eagle</u>.[2] Again love to all.

Ever yours
John A Bross

1 This may refer to Major General Samuel Ryan Curtis.

2 The etching in the *Memorial* from the photograph of John shown in the front of this book was altered to show on his left epaulet an eagle, which he did not yet have.

Head-Quarters, 29th Regiment
United States Colored Troops,

Camp Casey Va
May 4th 1864.

My Beloved Wife

I wrote you at Alexandria and did not send it. I was making out all my requisitions at that point for my outfit when an order came for me to come to this point & report to Major Gen Casey. I am now the Commanding officer of this Camp, & barracks, near fort Albany opposite Washington and not far from the celebrated "Arlington Estate."[1] The barracks are fitted up in sumptuous style almost too good for soldiers—I can see I think already one difference here in the more luxurious style of doing things. I have a splendid "out look" from here. The weather is delightful & I am at work in my profession! Oh that you could be with me a few days. I should be perfectly happy. - - The 28th Colored from Indiana are here. The officers are way below par. I took command yesterday & soon brought order out of chaos. You may be sure I have been very busy and I devote myself to it cheerfully being determined to let every one know with whom I come in contact that I am an "officer." I had a very pleasant call on Major Foster yesterday Chief of Bureau of Col Troops. Every thing is as I wished except the appointment of Barber & Dinsmoor. Perhaps I can accomplish that hereafter. I want several things but I am so busy this morning I can scarcely write what I want to. Give my best love to all at home. Will write you again soon.

Ever yours
John A Bross

Note: In pencil at the bottom of this letter, the following appears to have been written by Belle.

My Ever Dear Parents.

I send you my first letters from John, which I received last Saturday. Knowing you will be anxious to hear from him. Perhaps you saw the allusion to his regiment in the Washington letter of yesterdays Tribune. I am so sorry I did not go with him. Yesterday Annie and I spent at Mrs Nortons and attended the opera last evening. She can tell you of these matters as she expects to return to Sterling tomorrow. Whether to send Mason is still an unsettled question. I hope Aunt Ann will come this week. Goodby in haste with love, affectionately

Belle

Please be sure and preserve these

1 The residence of Robert E. Lee prior to the war, seized by the federal government after the war began; it is now Arlington National Cemetery.

Washington May 11th 64

My Dear Wife

I have just recd your letter of the 8th and am profoundly grateful for it. I am here busily engaged in getting my officers mustered and please say to Mr Aiken that Hector is the ranking Captain beyond the possibility of doubt or cavil. He is mustered to day—the others will be tomorrow—that settles the matter forever without question. So much for that. I wish you would also send word to John V. Farwell that Wm B. Gale is discharged to accept promotion & so is Fred Chapman.[1] Excuse me from answering your letter to day I shall not omit opportunities to speak hereafter. Your approbation is better music to my ears than thousands in a crowd. Send a line to Brown to hurry up that Co—have it mustered & come right along—or send me word when he is ready. He will be mustered as Major just as soon as that Co is raised. I will write you a long letter just as quick as things get in some order. The labor of arming & equipping my regt & of "Comdg a Brigade" is considerable. But I am equal to it. Bro Will & Jessie left me last night—may God bless them for their interest in you & me. You see I am scarcely my very best at "Willards." The town is in huge excitement about the battles now going on.[2] I hope this is the last spring we shall see such rivers of blood. Love to all my friends & kisses for Annie, Jennie & Mason.

Ever your affectionate
& devoted husband
John A Bross

1 Lieutenant Frederick A. Chapman (b. 1843) had worked as an errand boy at William's *Democratic Press*. He served in a Chicago Board of Trade battery and afterwards joined John's regiment at the age of 21.

2 General Grant began his Virginia Campaign on May 5, 1864. On the date of this letter he was engaged in the Battle of Spotsylvania, prior to the Battle of Cold Harbor on June 3.

Hd Qrs 1st Provisional Brigade
Camp Casey Virginia
Sabbath May 15th 1864

My Own Beloved Wife!

Your letter of Wednesday last reached me this afternoon just before tea. How much I enjoyed it I cannot tell you. I thank God daily for such a wife. I hope some day your virtues and devotion to the interests of your husband will be known & read of all men.

I am through the duties of the day. I have just been singing "silently the shades of evening" with my heart in Chicago, for I know you & friends are there and I presume your desire to know about me is now being gratified by William & Jessie. I have worked hard since I have been here but it has been with cheerful, pleasant anticipations of the future. I have felt a proud satisfaction of knowing that I am acting in a position that I could fill if I had the rank shining on my shoulder. I have as many men now under my command as Col Sherman. I fancy I am as strict as he is and yet a good deal more of a gentleman if I do say it myself. I would be glad to have any of my brother officers in that regiment see me on Battalion drill. Friday I made up a full regiment and spent the afternoon in Battalion evolutions. I was pleased with myself and the men. I would give a great deal if I only had my regt full. I am confident I could make a regiment equal to any in the service.

The men improve rapidly in the use of the musket and in their general duties and should I stay here, I shall certainly have you here. I would be glad to show you the capitol from my quarters and more than that show you that I am making myself felt. I think I have already made a good impression at Gen Casey's Hd Qrs. I attend to my business and do not allow anything else to interfere with it, certainly not my own ease or comfort. I shall not be at any trouble to visit Washington for the reason that I do not care to visit it. I should if you were here.

As to "Lt. Col" Wheeler rest easy with reference to him. I have read him as in a glass long since. I am amused and gratified at your "hurrah for the next step." I really did not suppose there was so much enthusiasm in your nature. I have many things to write and will soon send you more remembrances of me. The mail is about to close & I must cut this short. Love to all

Ever yours
John

Hd Qrs 1st Prov Brigade
Camp Casey Va May 18, 1864

My Sweet Wife!

Yours of Sabbath last was recd this P.m. and it delighted me as your letters always do. I have closed up my work for the day it being about 10 P.m. & I thought I would send you a line by tomorrows mail. I rise early & sit up quite late so you may suppose with my "daily duty" I am prepared to sleep. I am happy at the thought of seeing you here & father. I shall be most glad to see you but I hardly know what to advise. We are unable to tell what a day may bring forth. I shall decide however that you shall come and see me. Prudence I think dictates in opposition to affection & inclination that Mason stay at home. Then if you do come I do hope to have you free from any clog. You could not do just as you would like with him along. I should richly enjoy a visit with him. I think with his unfolding mind he would ever remember a visit here although so young. Yet I am fearful of bringing him here where he might be exposed to disease. Why cannot father come this way with you, or at least as far as Harrisburgh. There is no danger but what you can find the way alone however. If you should come with the next Co. you would scarcely have to pay anything. I doubt whether it would be policy for Major Brown to come on with the next Company unless he returns to the recruiting service. He has authority from Gen Rosecrans to recruit in Missouri and it is important for my interests that he remain where he is to superintend the recruiting service. I have no pistols. I am glad you spoke of Lt. Chapman's. I wish William would have it thoroughly cleaned & oiled before Fred gets to Chicago so that he may bring it on. That field glass would be very acceptable but I will not ask you to get it. I cannot tell yet when I am to be paid as I do not expect to get it now until the regt is paid. I will make all the means available that I can to pay off that $500 to Green this summer. I wish William would see Scoville and have him wait for the $100 until I get my pay. I am living as frugal as I can. Capt Aiken & Lt Gosper constitutes my mess. I have just taken also the Lt Col & Adjutant of the 28th. Lt Col Russell (of the 28th which was raised in Indiana) arrived Monday evening & took command of his regt. I was a little anxious to know whether he ranked me but he does not. He is a captain in the regular army. I have witnessed his movements & drill of his Battalion with the natural feeling that a regular should be superior in military to a civilian volunteer officer. I returned to my office entirely changed so far as he was concerned, feeling that I knew more than he did in some things at least, in fact a good many things. This of course for your own ear. - - I have no napkins. Please bring a few for me & your own use when you come also if you can put a couple of sheets & pillow slips in your trunk we can make you a nice couch. I hope you will not think I wish to make a parade of my religious profession when I tell you I commenced my "mess" in saying grace and I shall continue so to do. I did not do this in the 88th. The 5th Mass Cavalry Colored were here some days last week. The first afternoon they came I entertained the officers at supper. They were hungry and pretty well exhausted. As they took their seats, one young officer partly in a half serious half comic mood asked me if I would say grace. I was standing at the head of the table at the time, having been engaged in seating them. I replied gravely that it was always my habit at home and should be pleased to do so here, and said it. There was a hushed set of officers for the time being and very respectful conduct through that meal, though the conversation on military matters towards the last took a lively turn. More & more since I have been here do I feel the weight of responsibility. Since being here the pleasure arising from the consciousness of executing what is just & right towards men & God has been great. I have felt the force of example and shall try and continue it. If I have neglected religious duty heretofore I will try hereafter and not have the terrible words "Ye knew your duty but ye did it not" applied to me.

Thursday morning 19. This is a cool cloudy morning. I greatly wish I could see you and take not one but many many kisses from you. I have had many glimpses of you, not as in a glass darkly but as it were face to face. But that is nothing to the living breathing presence. You have my desires for you to come & see me. - - I felt that Br Will & Jessie would be with you last Sabbath, I am extremely grateful that my conduct met their approbation. It was by sister Marys kindness & forethought that I was enabled to give them good sugar for their tea at my "soldiers table." Please give them the strong love of a brother.

Write me often all the news. Yours ever.

John A Bross

Camp Casey Va May 22d 64

My Dearest!

Your note with that of Major Browns was recd yesterday. He has been written to several times and has doubtless been reading my letters ere this. There are no signs of our moving and yet we may go any day. I have hopes of seeing you this week. If this should reach you before you come I wish you would bring that valise of mine or a larger one. I shall have to store my trunk when I do go and I do not wish to carry much more than a tooth brush. I would also like my slippers, they would be very nice in these barracks. I have only two pairs of boots and sometimes they are hot. I am pretty well fitted out otherwise, my fatigue coat however is getting to be too heavy.

If I ever get paid again I will buy one similar to the first blouse I had. I wish you would remember to call for that old carpet sack at the Tribune office. It is in one of the drawers at the "Counting room." It has in it some old correspondence and that "Musqueto box" I brought home with me from Chattanooga.

I am getting thoroughly "at home" in my position. For your ear I am getting to be called "awful strict" which is pleasing to my military ear. I am proud of its effects upon my own regiment. It is the best by all odds in its discipline. I hold them up to it in every respect. If I can only get a few more officers I will be nicely situated. I do not visit Washington frequently, having been there but three times since coming here. I have quite a Staff in a Brigade Q.M. & acting "assistant Adjutant Genl." Sounds large don't it? I smile frequently at your "hurrah for the next step." Oh that I could have you here while I remain in command of this camp. Two ladies of the 23[d] say I am quite retired & that I work too hard. I tell them I enjoyed society as much as any one but my first duty was in Camp, and to the interests of my men. I have issued some pretty stringent orders since I commenced operations about gambling & licentiousness. The other evening I had the guard house nearly full of soldiers for running into a Contraband Camp hard by. I also arrested one woman, kept her under guard all night & then with three others sent them over to "freedmans village" where they are living on bread and water. That evening there was a good deal of excitement among the men, and I took the precaution to have one of my own companies ready with loaded arms, at their quarters for emergencies. I was determined to stop this bad conduct of wenches at all hazards. I ordered all men to their barracks and enforced it at the point of the bayonet and every man who had slipped through the guards was arrested and clapped in the guard house without mercy. The camp wears a different aspect. I have some officers of other regiments engaged in the same nefarious business as the colored soldiers and as sure as they are caught wo[e] be to them. I am laboring with all my might here to build up a reputation for my own rgt. and to thoroughly familiarize myself to the duties of my position. I am succeeding I think quite to my satisfaction. Do not think I am neglecting other things or my own interests. If I ever felt ambitious to excel and to work for ourselves it is now. I am anxious to hear from Brown about the prospects of recruiting to a full regiment. I might perhaps get filled up by order of the Govt but I don't wish to have it done at the cost of losing the first place.

And now dearest I should like to write an affectionate letter but I presume it might be an old story. Hoping to see you soon I will wait to tell you all over again how much I am your devoted husband. I shall send this to Chicago. Saw Rev D. B. Nichols yesterday; is about ¾ of a mile from me at Freedman's Village. One of his daughters married a Lt in a New York rgt. He has two little red heads here. I am very anxious to see you, more than I can express in a letter to you. Remember me to all friends and especially to Wm, Sister Mary, & Jessie. I wish you would call on Mr & Mrs Joseph Medill and thank them in my name for their interest manifested in raising the rgt. Hoping to hear from you & see you soon.

I am ever yours,
John

Hd Qrs 1st Prov Brigade
Camp Casey Va May 27 1864

Dearest,

It seems an age since I received your last letter. I have been looking for a few days to hear from you again & you must pardon me if I say I am growing impatient to hear from you & also from home. This day one month I left you at Chicago. The rgt & officers have improved greatly in that time & I have become seated for a time as a sort of Brigade Commander. You might just as well as not have been here all the time & enjoyed with me the locality. Why have not any of the friends at home written to me? Major Foster Chief of Colored Bureau is very kind & attentive to all I want at his department. He will aid me in getting the date of my muster as Lt Col altered to April 6th instead of April 24th as it is now. You see I am doing something for my own interests.

Capt Aiken is doing finely as commanding officer of the regt. I could not ask for better conduct on his part. All seem to devote themselves to drill and discipline of their respective companies. Several 100 day regts from Ohio are here & more coming. All the old regts have gone to the front. Yesterday I rode over to Washington & returned by the way of Arlington Mansion. Wednesday I dined with Rev D B Nichols. Mrs Major Hall of the 23^d U.S.C.T. gave me the enclosed leaf of ivy & cedar for you. She took them from the Arlington garden. You are aware that this was Gen Lee's estate. Mrs H. is a modest homely lady of middle life. Since being in camp she has lost a boy of ten years. She had a melodian here for a few days after I came and the first Sabbath after William left I had quite a sing with her. There is also a Mrs Munger, wife of a Lt who is positively homely & has three children with her. There are also a bevy of wives of officers of the 23^d boarding at a private house just across the road from my camp. I do not seek their acquaintance. In fact I have the reputation of being a recluse. Last eve on my return from Washington I found a splendid banquet on my table. I learned it was from Mrs Hall. Now is not that kind? She has a great respect for my conduct here as comdg officer. Oh that you were here. I am sick of waiting to see you.

Love ever so much love to you
John

Hd Qrs 1st Prov Brigade
Camp Casey Va May 30th 1864

My Beloved Wife!

This note is the last I shall write you from this point. We leave this morning for Alexandria where we go aboard transports for the "White House" via York river. I cannot express to you how anxious I have been to see you before I go but it is not to be. I am very well and go to the "peninsula" with high hopes that the campaign will be successful. Of course I expect to do my duty and to "show myself a man." I will write you for the coming month whenever there is an opportunity. I know you will be anxious, yet I am proud to know that your coolness and decision is worthy of me and of a soldiers wife. I am sorry that I cannot hear from you before I leave here. Mr Aiken came yesterday just in time to see us leave. He is pleased with the situation of matters. I am obliged to you for the pistol. I do hope that I may see [you] before the summer ends. I have no matters to speak of at home except to give them all my devoted love. I heartily wish you & Mason & Br Will could see my command move off from here. If you should come to Washington after I leave I hope you will run over to this camp to see the place where I <u>began</u> to be an "acting B.G."

I was full of rejoicing at Br Wills success. I hope you will do all that your womanly tact will suggest to aid him in the canvass. Give my love to Jessie & Mary. I shall always love them for their kindness to you & me. I will now close as I am pressed for time. With hundreds of kisses and embraces I bid you good bye.

Ever your devoted husband
John A Bross
Lt Col &c

Hd Qrs 1st Prov Brigade
Alexandria, Va May 31, 1864

My Beloved Wife!

I will write you a short note from this point. We are here awaiting transportation for the "White House" on the Pamunkey. Port Royal on the Rappahannock has been abandoned as a base of supplies. The weather has been about <u>hot</u> enough to suit us but it is beautifully clear.

Enclosed I send you a note that speaks for itself. I hope you will preserve it as a memento of my conduct at Camp Casey and perhaps the wish expressed therein may at some future time be fulfilled. I have thrown away a dollar this morning on the enclosed ambotype. We expect to leave today and I may send you another note from here.

I am dearest ever yours
John A Bross

Potomac River on board
of the "George Weems" June 1st

My Dear Wife

We embarked on this boat yesterday afternoon at Alexandria. Just as the sun dipped below the horizon the "plank" was drawn in "by order" and we moved away for the front from the secesh city of Alexandria, I write you from near "point look out." All is well with me thus far. The day is breezy & warm. I have an awning made on the hurricane deck and two ladies going to the front are <u>visiting</u> me. I have a fine place for an out look and plenty of air. We have a cabin for officers but I would not stay in it last night. I slept on the hurricane deck with the free air of Heaven circulating about my ears & face. The view of point lookout is very fine. We are just entering Chesapeake Bay, and I may be sea sick. I will report of that in a P.S. to this letter at White House. I doubt if you can read this very well. It is caused by the jarring of the boat. In conversing with one of the ladies I learn she is the wife of one of Williams pupils at Ridgebury. I suppose he will be interested to know that his name was Joseph Kimber. We have been talking of old times in Orange County. Kimber is dead. If I mistake not he was a crony of "Doctor" Peter Bross. The other lady is the wife of a citizen of Alexandria, she is going to the front taking a boy about the age of Mason. She has been with the army before and seems perfectly at home. They are both middle aged & <u>as</u> <u>usual</u> homely. I sometimes feel intensely vexed to meet females navigating towards the front & I can't have the earthly heaven of your society. Sometime I <u>will</u> have you with me anyhow. I am in cheerful hopeful spirit. Your approbation is continually in my mind. Yesterday just as the bugle sounded for the men to fall in to go aboard the boat, Mr C Bentley, lawyer of Chicago, who had come down from Washington to visit hospitals came up and grasped me by the hand. He promised to report to William as having seen my command. He was the last Chicago man I saw or expect to see for some time to come. I am anxious to get letters from you but it will be weeks now I am afraid before I hear from you. - - Pamunkey River June 2d. I was interrupted yesterday as we entered Chesapeake Bay. We had a pleasant ride and reached historical Yorktown as the sun set. Here our Captain wanted a pilot as he had not been up the river before. The boat was lowered and the ladies having a desire to go ashore they got in & we had a pleasant boat ride up the York river about a mile & a half to the north shore to find our pilot. We got him at last & reached our steamer about 10 P.m. Oh if you & Annie & Jessie could have been my companions. We are now approaching White House & I must draw this letter to a close. I feel that I am now in my proper element. Of course I can't tell yet what is to be my destination as I have to report to the Depot Commander at White House for orders. The day is warm and clear. I shall not soon forget this day. With a heart full of love for you I must close.

Ever yours.
John

"White House" Virginia
June 3^d^ 1864

My Beloved Wife

I again write you a line to describe the events of yesterday. You may be anxious and I will keep you advised as long as I can of my whereabouts. We arrived here about 11 A.m. yesterday and as I stepped ashore to report to Gen Abercrombie Depot Commander I had an opportunity to mail my letter of yesterday & day previous. Having reported, I was ordered to march this morning at daylight for the front. This was subsequently countermanded and I await further orders. All day yesterday we heard cannonading and all sorts of rumors came in. These were very natural to me but of course they did not affect me. There has been great loss of life on our part in the last few days but there is no doubt of our success thus far. I presume you know as much of the location of our army & more than I do. Every thing seems to be tending to this point in the way of reinforcements. Even rgts of veterans are coming up to guard these points. I can scarcely realize that I am within twenty five miles of Richmond. I am well as usual. Yesterday I became acquainted with a squad of ladies assigned to the 9th

corps as nurses every one of whom are anxious to go to the front but there is no chance for them beyond this point. If I should meet with an accident, I would be well taken care of. I suppose we shall go forward as soon as we can get some teams. I will write you another note when we are ordered forward. Love to all.

Ever yours
John A Bross

White House Va June 5th 1864

My own Darling Wife!

I know you remember this day. I know that eight years since I never thought of being here in the capacity of commanding officer of three Battalions of Colored troops. Yet it is real fact. How your dear self stands out before me as I write and how fixed in my memory is the day of our union. Time but shows to me the value of your love and devotion, and the happy choice I was so fortunate as to make. I do not feel like referring to the events of the past eight years. While they are indelibly fixed in the store house of my memory I yet from my peculiar position have my thoughts fixed on the present and future.

As I have written before we arrived here on the 2d inst. and immediately went into camp. We were ordered to report to the Army of the Potomac which I supposed meant the front but Gen Abercrombie Depot Commander has kept us here. How long we shall stay I am unable to say. The Genls Qrs are in the house where Washington first saw his wife. The White House where she lived is burnt down. This is a very pretty location almost a level plain but a few feet above the river. Scattered all over the plain are the evidences of McClellans army when they camped here two years since. I have been reading with great interest his report of that campaign and of course everything in the military view is deeply interesting to me. I devour everything that will give me information of the "situation." I have had within the past four days new experiences of army life. The wounded in the battles of the last few days are coming in aggregating a very large number. There are also large numbers of contrabands who have followed the army on its march from the Rapid Ann. Then the perfect forest of shipping—the Christian Commission, the Sanitary Commission—the relief associations of different states, the extensive Corps Hospitals and squads of army nurses, combine to present a new picture to my mind. By the by it is agreeable to be near the Sanitary Commission. I have aided them in detailing some men to help unload their boats & your husband can get any delicacy he wants. This perhaps had better not be mentioned outside the family. I speak of it as that you may be satisfied that I am in a position to get favors if I need them. I am making acquaintances every day which I hope will not be injurious hereafter. Yesterday I sent a line to Gen Sheridan. I wish sometimes I could be on his staff in some of his dashing movements. It would just suit my wishes. I suppose however there is no chance to get off on any such after the "Johnny Rebs." The fighting has been desperate since the first of June but we have whipped them every time. It has been accomplished however at a terrible cost of human life. My heart has ached for the poor wounded soldiers. It is very different to be here and see the results of a hard fought battle. I have not felt the same in the enthusiastic tension of the mind on the field. Yet I also feel that in all history there is no such example as is now shown by our people in its lavish expenditure for the care of the wounded. I am glad that I have been here to witness it. I am also more than ever proud that I am one of the grand army of the union. Whatever be my fate I know I can give to my child this one thing, "His father fought for the union and the 'old flag.'" My beloved wife I pray Heaven to grant me life & health to see the end of this war, that again I may enjoy the sweet influences of your presence in peaceful times. - - I understand the Colored Division of Burnside has not been in action, also that Gen Meade is averse to putting them in because they will not take prisoners, fearing that the enemy will murder our white soldiers captured by them. Wishing that I could embrace & kiss you a thousand times to day and my dear boy I am as eight years since your devoted husband

John

White House V<u>a</u> June 7th 64

My Beloved Wife!

My heart <u>aches</u>. Last night I received the first mail. I have no words to express my vexation at noticing the post mark & your superscription. Before I opened your letter I discovered all. Dearest how bitter was the disappointment to you & none the less to me. Yet I trust you were properly cared for in Washington. I received quite a large mail with yours including a dispatch from William to Horace White & a note of his to me forwarded by mail, also a letter from Jessie dated May 27th. I could go to the front cheerfully feeling perfectly contented were I ignorant of the fact that you had come so far to see me & show your devotion. As it is I know I shall inwardly fret against the freaks of cruel fortune. Dearest, if I had only known I should have brought you here even if I had left an officer to escort you. You could have come thus far without difficulty, and I could have returned you to Washington by any boat. Be calm about my being in the front. I learn the colored Division has not yet been in action & are not likely to be, they are guarding trains in the rear. I presume if Grant coops Lee up in Richmond we shall have our chance at "digging." I will keep you advised by every mail of our movements. My beloved let us hope that we <u>shall</u> meet each other very soon. I would have given my commission to have met you. I cannot write you a long letter this morning as the mail is about to close. With a thousand embraces for my darling wife, I am always

Your loving husband
John

White House V<u>a</u>
June 7th 1864
2 P.m.

My Beloved Wife!

Since I wrote you this morning I have received orders for one Battalion to go [to] the front as escort of a wagon train. I am going with mine. Do not be anxious over much for me. I do not think we shall be put in the "fore front" of the army and therefore rest easy. I am not content to sit here and brood over our mutual disappointment in not seeing each other. A few miles further towards the front will suit me as well and I shall be just as safe. "Onward" is my motto. Let us hope that my career will also be upward. Love to all. God Bless Mason & yourself

Ever yours
John
I march at 3.30

Army of the Potomac
June 8th 1864

My own Beloved,

As I wrote you yesterday afternoon my Command left White House about 3:45 P.m. as escort to a wagon train to "the front." These last two words sound natural enough. I have been assigned to Gen Ferrero's Division of Col Troops, 9th Corps. It was one o'clock this morning before I bivouacked but our march was very successfully made. This forenoon I reported in person to Gen Williams A.A.G.[1] to Gen Meade. My command is now lying in a grove of yellow pines near Gen Meade's Qrs awaiting orders from Gen Burnside to march to our Division, I believe it is the 4th of the 9th. Among my duties of yesterday was to bring forward some eight privates as deserters & a 2d Lt of the 187th PA who had had his straps stripped from him, sword buttons &c. After reporting to Gen Williams I reported in person to Burnsides Qrs. I met the Gen on my way over and knew him instantly. Of course I did not stop him on the road to make myself known. I had a very pleasant interview with Col Lewis Richmond & Major Neill of his Staff. I left for the Gen my letter of introduction from William. Since waiting here near Meades Qrs I staid near the Hd Qr Guards until noon to see the Gen personally as he came out from being closeted with Meade, Wright, Warren & Grant. Getting tired & wishing my men to get their coffee & dinner I came over to dismiss them & as I did so & was drinking a cup of coffee myself he came out & left. I am sorry as I wished to become personally acquainted with him immediately. You see I am not going to be too modest as you have thought. I intend to let all officers know who I am. I shall seek the first opportunity for a personal interview with Gen Sheridan. He left yesterday I understand on a big raid the other side of Richmond. If this be so I presume you will hear of it before I do. My men keep up remarkably well. They have become conversant with the manner of "getting on" in taking care of themselves. Weather does not seem to hurt them. Their spirits seem to raise in proportion to the disagreeable state of the Elements. We left all our baggage at White House in charge of Lt Gosper. As usual I had forethought enough to carry my poncho, mattress, blanket, shelter tent & haversack of provisions & I found it came in good stead for Capt Aiken & myself. We had wagons of four corps & in guarding them to their destination companies were separated. My cook & Captain Aikens waiter with all his blankets got with the first Co & I did not see them till this noon as I had Capt Aiken guard the rear & as I wanted to see the last of the train in I was with that. We took a midnight supper of hard bread and pickled pork & no coffee. Then we lay down on the ground with my poncho over us and slept as if there was no enemy within the bounds of the ocean bound republic. You may associate three things as of yesterday. 1st, Old Abe's renomination I presume, although I have not heard of it. 2d my march from White House Va to the front & 3d a huge vexation to know that you had been in Washington & I could not see you. I am not posted as to positions of the different corps. I am very desirous to become posted on all these matters. I will write often for the next few days & will give you a sort of daily journal account of my experiences. It is a great pleasure thus to make these minor matters of detail well knowing that I have a loving and attentive listener to all my personal experiences of daily life. Kiss Mason for his father & say that papa will write him a letter some of these days.

Ever yours,
John

[Written in left margin] I should say that this army is not across the Chickahominy yet.

1 Major General Seth Williams served as Assistant Adjutant General of the Army of the Potomac.

Hd Qrs 29th U.S.C.T. Camp
in the Field near "Old
Church tavern" June 9th 1864

My Beloved Wife,

To day I marched from Gen Meade's Qrs to the Hd Qrs of Brigadier Gen Ferrero Comdg 4th Division 9th Corps. I have just been assigned to the 2d Brigade & as luck would have it am the junior Lt Col. Well I am content to work & wait. Having become familiar with the workings of a Brigade Organization I shall be all right when it does come my turn. We are about 13 miles from Richmond on the extreme right & rear, there being a white Division of our Corps nearly four miles in advance of us. I write you this from a grove of yellow pines in which our camp is pitched on the extreme left of our Brigade. Gen Ferrero & Col Thomas received me with great cordiality and kindness. I am of the opinion that we shall not be here three days. Every thing looks to a change of base again towards the James. I may be mistaken but I think when this reaches you we shall be miles away from "Old Church." We can make only one more change of base, this will bring us to the south & east of Richmond. It is very warm here now & dusty. I do not think we shall have the chance of entering Richmond from across the Chickahominy in this direction. Last night there was a great deal of picket firing throughout the night near where we lay. It was quite like old times. I met to day Mrs Halls husband. He is a very pleasant man but not so very much refined after all. I am equal to any of them! Don't you think that remark smacks strongly of vanity. The future will tell whether I am right or not. We are going to move (if we go) very light handed. We have not a single team with us and all our baggage is back at White House, & if we change it will go mainly by water. You may just as well expect as I do that I am in for a long campaign. I will however write you at every opportunity. I am now "in the line of duty" and feel that I am in the right place. I expect to endure hardships but that is a soldiers life. I am anxious in these things not to shirk the inevitable consequences connected with the profession. I wish to take matters as lightly and easily as possible and you may be sure I shall not fret at the small inconveniences of soldiers life. I shall not probably allude to this again except in actual occurrences in my "report" to you. I have no news, and our papers are few. The world is a blank to me almost, except my business. I do think it a great misfortune that I could not meet you at Washington. I shall not talk of my feelings towards you. Wait wait until I see you again. After this campaign is over if my life is spared we will be together for life. I do hope it will not be in the far future. I hope you will not be tired in reading my hasty notes from the battle field. Kisses for Mason & love for all

Yours ever
John A. Bross

Near Old Church Tavern Va
Friday June 10, 1864

My Beloved Wife!

I commence another "Bulletin" to you but will hardly send it today. The evidences of a movement from here increase & I have no doubt it will be done before this reaches you. I have met most all the field officers of this Brigade and I have no fault to find with their bearing towards me thus far. I propose to pursue a straight for ward course and one I hope that will be upward. I am not very highly impressed with the Army of the Potomac thus far. Perhaps I am unduly inclined towards my own Army of the Cumberland. I see little ear marks of things that ought not to appear at all. - - I presume you will hear from us somewhere on the "James" before many days. Will get this off before we go.

Saturday morning 11th. Yesterday after dinner we had a genuine alarm caused by a dash of rebel cavalry upon our cavalry pickets in front. They captured a couple of dozen of our cavalry & killed one captain. I was building breast works at the time & as soon as the alarm was given our men "fell in" with a great deal of spirit. The musketry firing was quite brisk for a time and we expected to have our cavalry fall back on us pell mell, but we did not get a chance to see a single "reb." My men behaved admirably, no desire to slink or shirk. They came into line promptly & on the "double quick." Our camp is in a dense growth of yellow pine difficult for cavalry to operate in, yet a field is in front of us. We had no breast works in our front as I said, yet the men took position as calmly as if they were in a fort. I took position in front of the regiment where I could have a good look & also quietly walked along the lines to see that all was right. "Col! we don't want you out dar," broke through several stockades of ivory. I told them I would be with them whatever happened & in the right place at the proper time. After being in line about an hour we stacked arms and went again at our breast works. We did good work in the P.m. at that. All the officers came down to see my men handle the ax and spade & my work was the neatest & best along the whole line & so said by other officers. I occupy the extreme left of our Division. I will give my opinion of some of the officers hereafter. Dont consider me egotistical in what I have said before or will say hereafter. I feel my dearest a perfect consciousness of equality at least, with the best of them & if providence spares my life I shall hew my way among them all. I know you will encourage me in this. We are all on the topmost expectation of a movement. We can be off in ten minutes but are "waiting orders." I enclose you some roses I plucked from a climbing rosebush on the "Old Church Tavern" this morning. They will be withered when this reaches you but they will remind you of my love. I am anxious to hear from you from home, & to know all about friends. I first received the news this morning of the nomination of Lincoln & Johnson. Love to all.

Yours ever
John

Bivouac in the field near Diascon
Bridge, Chickahominy
June 15th 64

My Beloved Wife

I was greatly pleased to hear from you last night in your note of June 7th.

I am very well. Sunday night we left Old Church, marched towards White House, camped at Tunstalls Station. Monday marched to New Kent Court House. Tuesday (yesterday) marched 8 miles towards Williamsburg & then by a by road south to this point where we are guarding most of the Army train. All the baggage has left White House for James River. As to Daggett, his commission was issued April 22, & he is discharged from the V.R.C.[1] I am surprised he has not got his commission. Gov Yates has it. This need not stop him. He can get a copy at Washington. Let him apply to Gov Yates for it immediately & come forward with the company. Let Major Brown go on with recruiting. I am writing in haste to get this in the mail in order that you may know where I am. Don't be anxious about our Division. It looks as if we are to be in the rear all the time. Now dearest if I do get sick who so well qualifies to take care of me as you. I will send for you when I do & after this campaign is over I will try & get you here any how. Love to all & kisses for Mason

Ever yours
John

1 Veteran Reserve Corps.

Sabbath June 19th 1864

My Dear Wife,

We arrived in <u>position</u> in front of Petersburg this morning. I have only time to say I am well. We crossed the Chickahominy at "Cole's Ferry" on Thursday and marched to Charles City Court House. Friday crossed the James at Charles City landing. Yesterday we marched to this point & this morning are in position to the southerly side of Petersburg near the rebels first line of defences. We are <u>not</u> in the very front but expect to be. Capt Brockway joined us at the James River. He was appointed in place of Naylor declined. I expect that Gale & Chapman are at City point. We did not go there on our march. This week will be very full of events I think. From our position the spires of Petersburg are in full view. While I write the gun boats are practicing a little on the Appomattox. I send this in an envelope to Anne which I had addressed some days since in anticipation of writing her a note. She must wait until I have more time. Should we succeed in capturing this place it will make Richmond untenable. Give my best love to all at home. I am anxious to hear from you once more. Good bye dearest and may God bless you all & preserve us to meet again.

Ever your own
John

Camp near Petersburg Va
June 20th 1864

My Beloved Wife

I sent you a note on yesterday after we stacked arms. I send another today. We have not moved from our position since yesterday. I have been resting from the fatigues of the march and picket firing does not disturb me scarcely any. I told you we were in reserve. Both sides are hard at work digging. We are located to the south east of the town, the left of our army resting beyond the rail road leading to Suffolk. I cannot learn whether we are near the great southern line of rail road to Weldon or not. It has been very quiet since yesterday except some cannonading this morning. There will be something done I presume ere this reaches you. I learn this afternoon that it is the intention to hold us in reserve or at least be very careful how we are placed in front. I hope you will not be too anxious about me. I am glad as a soldier that I am in this campaign. I think if we capture this place it gives us Richmond. Dress parade is called & you must excuse short notes as it is also mailtime. We are about ten miles from City Point. Gale & Chapman have not reported yet. I have letters for them. I cannot see where they are. Capt Brockway left Knoxville after they left their Battery. I hope you are all well. I will try & send you frequently an item of myself and all the news though you will get a great deal more than I do in quicker time. I get no letters from you, the last one I had was immediately on your return to Chicago. Others get letters; I presume you write but they do not reach me. I get along quite well here. I am anxious to hear from Major Brown & how recruiting goes on in Ill and Mo. Saw a Chicago journal yesterday with Williams name in it for Lt Gov. I did not tell you I believe that Jessie wrote of Father Mason doing a great deal for his nomination. Love to all. Yours ever. Do write

John A Bross

Prince George Court House Va
June 29th 1864

My Beloved Wife

To day I have been writing to brothers, fathers, & sending them some relics of old times in this county. I thought I would wait until tonight before I wrote to you. This noon our mail came, and it "never rains but pours." I have just now received I presume all your back letters being those of April 29th, May 21st, & 26, June 11th & June 19th; also fathers letters of May 3d & May 28th, also Mr Wetherbees letter of May 28th; also a letter from Annie & Helen, also three large packages from Major T Jeff Brown, a letter from Tom Turley & Srgt Barber & a host of business letters. I am in a maze of bewilderment & yet through it all I will untangle the skein by sending you a short note. Tears my love followed the reading of your letters. May God Bless my darling for her devotion to me. I am not able to answer these letters to day, I wish to send something to you immediately. A great many things have been cleared away by these mails, one thing that of the "commissions." I could not understand why you did not get them. Col Loomis in a letter to Brown which I received to day says they were left for me at Willards Hotel. What a world of trouble and vexation it would have saved if I had only known that fact. I was ignorant of it until to day. We have been in the trenches in front of Petersburg for about a week where the bullets whized around our ears. One of my men was seriously wounded. It has been a good school for the men. In fact they became too careless of their persons. Two days ago we were ordered here, seven miles east of Petersburg to guard the rear from any flank movements of Lee. We are in a pleasant locality and we are enjoying ourselves with but little to do except to keep a good picket line. Lts Gale & Chapman joined us on the 23d & they are doing finely. There was another Lt appointed in place of Strickler who came up the day before Gale & Chapman. We were laying in the trenches. He became "fearfully demoralized" & went back. His name is Van Arman. He wanted to be major of my regt but I refused him. This is the last of him. Last Sunday Burnside sent me word he wanted to see me. I shall take occasion to call on him the earliest opportunity. He was not at Qrs when I reported to him & so I left Williams letter, since which time I have had no opportunity to leave the regt for compliments. Be assured I shall call on him early. - - I will write to the War Dept this afternoon about Wetherbee. Enclosed I send you Photograph of Dr Mackay my surgeon. He was surgeon of the 79th New York Highlanders which was mustered out of service this spring their term having expired. He is a full blooded Scotchman from Glasgow & is a very scientific man. I am fortunate in that appointment. I have omitted writing you for several days hoping that something would occur to send you a line with something interesting. I hope you will excuse this rambling letter. I will write you again very soon. There may be some things omitted but I will write you again. How I would like to be at Uncle Penningtons at the planting of the oak. How much I would enjoy it. Kisses for Mason & love to all.

Yours ever
John A Bross

In trenches July 1, 1864

My Beloved Wife

Yesterday we left Prince Geo Court House and marched to trenches on the extreme left of our lines. We are west of the Norfolk road and not far from the Weldon. Our march yesterday was about eight miles. It has been very quiet to day along this end of the line. Our position is as it were in reverse, that is the left of the line is doubled back more or less on itself, the left of our line fronting Petersburg runs nearly west or certainly south west while we are facing south & are behind a heavy line of breast works. Yesterday forenoon & all day to day I have been very busy in attending to returns pay rolls, & other rgtl business and business correspondence. I have no time as yet to revert to your package of letters, or to answer them in detail. I am getting along as well as you could wish. Among other letters I have just received an order to be mustered back to April 7th the day after I was mustered out of the 88th, this is something if not as much as I ought to have. The delay in mustering me when I was entitled to it makes me junior in rank to the Lt Cols of the 19th and 23d. I rank the Lt Cols of the 28th & 31st. I jokingly tell Col Perkins of the 19th & Col Campbell of the 23d that I shall "command the Brigade" after the first fight. They are very pleasant gentlemen and have both had the advantage of foreign travel. Still for all that your husband is not ashamed to converse with them on any subject or to go into a fight with them at any time

I send you the card photograph of Lt Gosper acting Rgtl Quarter Master. I also send you the last list of "countersigns" I used at camp Casey as commander of the Provisional Brigade. In a letter to Brown to day I have requested him to send you his photograph & also one to me. I send you this short letter to inform you of my whereabouts. Will write you more fully as I have time. Love to all. Where are you going to be in the absence of father & mother? Kisses for Mason.

Ever your affect
John A Bross

Camp near "Wells' House" Norfolk
R.R 7 miles from Petersburg Va
Sunday July 3d 1864

My Beloved Wife!

Yours of 26th June reached me last night. I read it a dozen times also to Capt Aiken, Gale & Chapman. Under the circumstances, while resting after a hard march in a Virginia sun, your "bill of fare" and the description of the ceremonies were peculiarly interesting to us all. But why did you disappoint me so very much in not sending me a copy of the poetry? I was surprised and greatly delighted that you had acted as chairman and "poetess" of the occasion. I have always felt that under your self possession and coolness, was a vein of the purest and richest poetical feeling, and I am proud to know that for once you have drawn upon it. Send me the verses in your next. A thought or so had passed through my mind since your former letter apprised me of the intended ceremony that I would like to contribute the poem & lo & behold my better self did it. I am pleased that at least my absence has drawn you out. You judged rightly in giving me a full description as it did give me a great deal of pleasure. "Oakside" will be as deeply impressed on my memory as on yours. While you were dedicating & planting the oak I was "in the trenches" in front of Petersburgh. I hope that I shall be with you next year as you meet by the tree, & may we all be there.

Let me now give you a short history of our operations since the 19th. Monday night 20th we were ordered into the 2^{d} Line of trenches. Our Division relieved the 6th Corps, which was transferred to the left. There was a good deal of picket firing during our movement but the men acted very well. At early daylight we were moved somewhat to the left, where we lay until night of 23^{d} when we were moved still further to the left and rear. You should understand that this position we occupied was on the easterly side of Petersburg and nearly a mile inside the outer line of rebel fortifications. Our lines at this point & the rebels' are very close. We were in just as much danger from sharpshooters in the 2^{d} as in the first line. All these nights there were attacks on our pickets and on Wednesday night especially the bullets went over my quarters and through the tree tops in a perfect hail storm. They were perfectly harmless however as they all went too high. Wednesday afternoon June 22^{d}. Lt H Van Arman who had been appointed, making an extra Lt, came up and staid with me a couple of hours. During this time cannonading was carried on in our front very briskly & the popping of sharp shooters completely "demoralized" him and he wanted to get back to the rear. He had come up with the expectation that I would appoint him Quarter Master or Adjutant, which I would not do, more particularly as he was unfitted for either position and as he had made such an exhibition of himself I was glad to let him go back. He is a brother-in-law of Capt A. B. Coon of Woodstock, McHenry Co. & is the one that tried so hard last winter to have me appoint him major. He is a regular whiskey drinker & blower.[1] He came to Washington last winter to be examined for a col's commission & passed for a 1st Lt. at the same time he planned the insertion of an item in the Chicago Tribune that he was appointed Col of a North Carolina Colored regiment. Just before I left Washington Major Foster showed me a letter from Van Arman asking him in the name of God to give him an appointment saying that he would fight the devil if called on. Knowing as I did his character I told Major Foster that if it was Farnsworths desire the appointment might be made. The major significantly said that if he did not suit me I could send him before a board for examination. Well on that day he reported thinking that he was to be adjutant and certainly Q.M. In order that you may understand it I had appointed for two extra lieutenants to be detailed as Adjt. and Q.M. That is, with five companies I have 7 1st Lts. either one of which I have the power to select as my Adjt. and Q.M. Well I have selected them and I was not going to change for an inexperienced and as the event proved a man of no courage. He told me there was no use, he could not go into action. Well if he could not go into action in the line he cannot go as a member of my staff. I have been this particular in order that if any stories are told by him and his friends in Illinois you may promptly correct them. The night before he joined me he staid at our Division Hospital in the rear. While the cannonading was going on he begged that he might be permitted to go back so I gave him permission for a day or so on the advice of my Dr. The next morning the surgeons discharged him as fit for duty. But instead of his coming to me he went direct for City Point and being acquainted with Gen Rawlins, Chief of Staff, he told him that I gave him permission to go home and on that Rawlins let him go. Rawlins told Gosper that the best thing I could do was to let him throw up his commission as he was utterly worthless for anything and I am of the same opinion. I have already asked Major Foster to revoke his appointment and to promote Chapman to 1st Lt in his stead. Also to appoint "Willie" Dinsmoor to a 2d Lieutenancy. I have also made recommendation for the Co at Quincy upon the recommendation of Major Brown. But by the by it is singular I never knew until the reception of that large mail the other day at Prince Geo Court House that the package of commissions were left by Col Loomis at Willards for me it explains some allusions in your letters which I never could understand. You may say to Mr Wetherbee that I have directed his son's commission to be sent to me. I wrote to Horace White to get the package, send Browns to him Hatch's to Orin Hatch, Daggetts to Wm & the rest to me. I long wondered at what had become of them & why Gov Yates had not forwarded them. Gale & Chapman have not theirs, & as a consequence cannot be until I get their commissions.

To return to my little record of events. Saturday last, we rested in an open field a little to the left of our trenches. Sunday we changed camp further to the rear in a piece of woods, rested there on Sunday the date of your letter. Towards sundown we had a Division review by Gen Ferrero. This day Gen Burnside sent me word to come & see him. Have not done it yet because we have been on the march most of the time since then. Monday 27th was Division "Officer of the day." At noon the Division marched for Prince Geo Court House, arrived there about 6 P.m. As Div Officer of the day I had to go the picket rounds which compelled me to ride a good many miles, taking me far into the night before I got through. Tuesday 27th [sic] my regt is one of the advance rgts of the line. I have a good place, near an ice house which I guard for officers use. To day Col Russells rgt (28th) joined the command. They were left at White House when I moved to the front. He has had a much harder time than I. The officers told me that they thought when I left White House that I made a great mistake & that they had a very soft place. Now they say I was the luckiest of all. I told them I was quite sure the result would justify my action at White House, & it is a pleasure to have my conduct praised at this day by them. They were very anxious to remain behind. It was in my power to send them instead of going with my own regt. As commander of the Provisional Brigade all the orders for wagon escorts come through me. I was sure that we would all be moved from there soon & so I decided to go & let Col Russell come up when he wanted to. I did not like their conduct in wriggling to stay behind and I think they have got enough of it. I think you will now say I did right. True I would like to remain in the command of a Brigade but I was well aware that the one I commanded was only temporary. I know dearest I have lost nothing in the estimation of others in promptly going to the front when the opportunity offered. All my officers now congratulate me on doing it. True I would like to have had the éclat of being in command of a Brigade at White House when the attack was made, but as it was if I had staid I should have had only my own rgt. Then when the 28th did leave, their marching & work was much harder than ours. Now they would gladly exchange positions, so far as our history since being at White House is concerned. Wednesday 29th. The mail came. Spent this day in writing letters. One from Tom Turley offered to do any thing for me if I would only ask it as he is nearer than you. I am grateful for his kindness. This eve Gen Sheridan with the 1st & 2d Divisions of Cavalry arrived at our camp from Powhatten landing James River. Thursday 30th called on Gen Sheridan who was glad to see me, also his brother Capt Sheridan on his staff, also Major Forsyth 8th Ill Cavalry who was delighted to see me, Aiken, Gale & Chapman. He is a dashing soldier & enquired particularly for Jessie and seemed anxious to know whether she was really engaged to Charley Scannon son of Hon J.Y. I assured him she was not engaged to anyone. Jessie could do much worse in selecting others instead of him. In P.m. the Brigade moved from Prince Geo Court House to our trenches as I told you in another letter. Yesterday July 2 we moved here which is about six or seven miles directly south east of Petersburg. We have been enjoying since yesterday, the shade of a grove of oaks & yellow pines trying to keep cool but it is awful hot nevertheless. We have found another ice house & while I am writing one of my Lts is making me a good lemonade. So you see we are not perfectly destitute. Yet our march yesterday was terribly severe upon some of the soldiers. In the afternoon a soldier of the first Brigade was found near my quarters in the woods dead. He had stood up to his duty, kept up with the rgt and died without anyone knowing it where he lay down to rest. It is one of the features of the service. It affects me more than the excitement & loss upon the battle field. I have thus given you an epitome of occurrences for the past two weeks. I will try and give you a weekly record or oftener if I can hereafter. I run over in my mind the past & I do not forget my marching of one year ago and our arrival at Cowan, Tenn and of the severe campaigning I was then engaged in. I am very thankful I am so much better situated away from the jurisdiction of a man who never appreciated me and was afraid of me as well. I do not forget also that some of my then friends are now in the grave, Lane, Brigham, Rae a trio of noble young men whose patriotism was pure & noble as their lives were pure &

virtuous. Peace to their ashes. - - I am glad Gen White comes to our corps. I hope he will command our Brigade or Division. I will then be in a better position to ask favors if I wish to. It will be every way better for me if he gets our Division to command. In any event I am glad he is to come to us. While I think of it you may send me a dollars worth of stamps. I will write to Mr Osborn as you suggest. I cannot tell when the paymaster will be around but I will send you my "pile" to use a vulgar expression, when I get it. I am sorry that you have to think of these old matters while I am so far away. My horse is in good order & the admiration of all. My valise has come up with Col Russells baggage. Fred opened it at White House & the apples were all rotten. The col's cook got hold of the crabs & cooked them all for him. I found one solitary small one on opening it [at] old church. Such is army life. Keep that letter of Mr Swazey. I don't wonder you liked it. It was a source of great pleasure to me for days after I received it. I am very sorry Em's health is so poor, I hope she will soon have strong vigorous health.

I have been looking over again with great interest your letters from April 29th received at Prince Geo Court House. That of 29th alluding to the reception of the address &c I shall remember as long as I live. Connected as it [was] with that event and that you were proud of me is worth all my toil. I only wish that I might be successful in promotion on your account. I do know that you may & would honor any high position. Then your letter of June 5th. How it is calculated to draw out all my affections for you and Jessie. If I ever get it home I shall keep it as a relic of my campaign life and of your love. In your letter of June 19th you speak of John M Warmsley[2] he is a sergt in the Co left at Quincy. Father was quite cute in his reply to Rev McRoy. In any little notices you may see of myself and rgt in the papers I wish you would cut them out and send them by letter. I will comply with your request about sending you card photographs. Gen Ferrero has promised to give me his. I wish you would send me a few of yours also some of the best pictures of myself. The letter of Rev McMiller I have read. I am glad his son is in another regt I shall not promote him to a captaincy in mine. I suppose father has gone to Maine by this time. I will write him there as I have opportunity. I have another captain here in place of Naylor declined. His name is James W. Brockway formerly of the Elgin Battery. I have now four officers who have been in the artillery service. I send you an item of him from the "army mail bag." Captain Aiken is getting along first rate. He makes a good officer. He likes to live well though. He is passionately fond of butter and mourns for it when we are <u>out</u>. I laugh at his rueful countenance when "our mess" is out. We live better here as a general thing however than one could ever do in the army of the Cumberland. This is because our line of operations and <u>base</u> of supplies is so short. City Point is only a few miles from here & the rail road is already complete to our lines. Then again the Sanitary goods come here more freely. I had more of <u>their</u> articles in one week than I ever had altogether in the army of the Cumberland. You need not fear but what I will do pretty well in the way of living here. True I can get along with a frugal meal, hard tack & coffee & not think anything of it. But as long as everything is so close by I shall not want more than a day or so. I think most of our operations now are in the nature of a <u>siege</u>. Our Division for the last two weeks has acted in the capacity of <u>supports</u> & to guard the <u>rear</u>. It looks as if that will be our duty. Yet in emergencies we may be put in the front. I don't think there is to be much more charging of breast works except upon some urgent necessity. We are now located on the left & rear facing to the south west to protect our left flank from cavalry. Sheridan is some where to the south of us on the <u>Blackwater</u>. That stream heads near Petersburg and we are not far from some of its springs. The country here is completely level, covered with oak & yellow pines where it is not cultivated. These woods were cleared fields 70 or 100 years since. The corn or tobacco ridges are distinctly traceable. They have been worn out and left to grow up the crop of which is yellow pine. The soil is <u>sandy</u>. All the people have fled at the approach of the "Yanks" except here & there one. - - I am thinking this long rambling letter will be too much for you at one sitting. I have been doing nothing but thinking and writing to you to day. Since writing the above the mail has come with letters from Jessie & William. He sends me bad news from mother Bross. I am fearful I shall never see her alive again. - - All the officers who have seen you speak in great praise of you Brown in his last letter speaks of your devotion in coming to Washington. Wills & Jessies letters were written the same eve that yours was. Yet yours came a day sooner. I have just had <u>dinner</u>, and in addition to our coffee & hard tack, we had fresh <u>roast</u> <u>pig</u>, new onions dried apple sauce, and a large dish of nice ripe blackberries. It reminds me of your package of blackberries a year ago. These things with ice for lemonade and we are thankful for what we have. It is not often that we fare so well. You may think me forgetful of Mason, my heart is bound up in him. I am almost always fearful to read about him in your letters. I hope & pray he may be preserved. Yet I cannot become so much tied to him as to Cora. May God keep him & leave him with us. Kiss him daily for me. With much love to all friends, I am always your devoted husband

John A Bross

1 A "blower" meant a braggart.

2 This is probably Sargeant John Walmslee of Dixon, Illinois.

Monday P.m. July 5th 1864
Camp near Norfolk R.R.

Dearest

Yours post marked June 30 reached me to day. We have remained here since the 2d. I presume you will receive my long letter of Sunday last before long & others which will explain about the long lost mails. To day I received a letter from Col Loomis written April 26 informing me that the commissions were at Willards. It had been sent to camp Delaware Ohio & there remained until 30th June. Also one from Major Brown again asking for his commission. I have sent him a note of a similar purport to the one I wrote a few days since. My letters properly addressed will now come quite regularly. Be sure & put on the Brigade Division & Corps & Army of the Potomac. There is a 29th Connecticut Colored Rgt & I do not wish to have any of my letters go way down the Atlantic Coast to Hilton Head & all along shore. I cannot now recall that $100 in Uncle P's account. Perhaps I may hereafter when I will write you about it. It has been remarkably quiet for the past few days. Yesterday was more like a northern Sabbath it was so quiet. The fact is that neither party I think dare make a direct assault on the others breast works. They are almost impregnable on both sides. We shall dig them out or Grant will play some game on them. As to our ultimate success I have no manner of doubt. We ought to have an increase of force as soon as the Govt can get them up & send them to the field. We have rested pretty well in our present camp. How long it will continue is impossible to say. We commenced our usual camp drills to day which looks like a stay here of some little time though of course we may be switched into a fight or off on some expedition to the rear. Sheridan is now massed on the left, our right is protected by the James. Our base of supplies is at City Point & the Rail Road trains come clear up to our lines. We are in a position where all the rebels this side of the "bottomless pit" cannot drive us out. Perhaps this is a pretty strong expression but it is quite true I think. I do not know whether you would like specimens of old records I got at Prince Geo Court House. I sent a lot to various friends but none as yet to you. I have quite a pile saved in my book desk at City Point. If you want any I will send you some. How do you like Dr Mackay's picture? He is a good surgeon. Do you expect to stay with Bro Zed? I am unconcerned of course but that you will have friends everywhere yet I am a little anxious to know what arrangements you make for a home during the absence of father & mother. I have painful news about mother Bross & am afraid every mail will bring tidings of her loss to us. - - I live pretty well. Yesterday I received some tomatoes & canned milk from the Sanitary Com.[1] It is a slight return for the contributions my friends here made to that institution & truly it is a grand work. I have again to say that I am much better off than I was in the Army of the Cumberland. Give my kindest love & regards to Em & Zed with kisses for Mason & remembering our loss of the dear one whose anniversary occurs to morrow. I am dearest

Ever yours
John A Bross

P.S. I know not when we are to be paid. I have spent all my money after economizing all I could. If you can send me ten dollars I will be obliged also some postage stamps. I will be obliged. I can get along but I dislike to be entirely out.

John

1 The United States Sanitary Commission (USSC) was a private relief agency created by federal legislation in 1861 to support wounded and sick Union soldiers.

Camp in the field Norfolk RR
Thursday July 7th 1864

My Beloved Wife,

I write you a short note on order "45" showing what I have to do sometimes. I am very well to day. We are still in camp we occupied on the 2d. We have been drilling, but it is awful hot and dirty. It seems as if it would never rain here. Report has it that our Division is to make a change soon but that has been the word every day since we reached the front. One thing I can say to you that when we do make it our Brigade is to act as support & not make the charge. I do not say this to allay any anxiety you may have as there is danger, but I know you will be a brave good wife. I wish you to act as you have done heretofore. I will certainly send you word immediately if anything should happen to me. I am looking forward to the time when I shall have another of your grand letters. I will say that I am still luxuriating on ice, fresh veal, mutton new potatoes occasionally, and occasionally some Sanitary goods. - - I enclose a few lines written last eve and finished today. They may be the substance of what I may have heretofore written. My tent door faces directly towards the setting sun and last eve was strikingly like three years ago. I hope you are well and that Mason is getting robust and strong. I hope you will watch closely for similar indications as was too late remarked in Cora. - - I am most sorry I sent for money the other day. I learn we are to be paid towards the end of the month. Love to Annie, Em Zed & all friends.

Ever Yours
John A Bross

Camp in the Field near Petersburg Va
Norfolk R.R. Saturday July 9th 64

Dearest

Yours written one week ago has just been received. By the time you will receive this providing you receive all my other letters you will certainly call me a good correspondent. I have taken a great deal of pleasure in writing to you and in thinking of you and all of you at home. We are still located along the Norfolk RR where we camped one week ago to day. Our march from the entrenchments (the day you wrote your letter) to this point was terribly severe upon men & line officers. It almost overcame Capt Aiken & Lt Gale. Capt Aiken has been sick since but is now nearly well again. - - When I first learned the state of the case about the "commissions" in seeing that "big mail" June 29th I was very much nettled & vexed at being kept in ignorance of the fact so long on account of the trouble it gave me in getting duplicates for the officers with me when all the time I might have laid my hands right on them at Willards. I know you & Major Brown will acquit me at once of negligence on learning the facts. No one could have more regrets about it than myself. When I came to look at it quietly it has an air of ludicrousness about it were it not for the delay that has occurred to all the officers by reason of the letter of Col Loomis being sent off to Camp Delaware Ohio & remaining there until June 30th. I have been amused at your allusions to the matter & also in letters of Major Brown received since I received the "big mail." I hope that all is explained by this time in my recent letters. You must have received my letters written a week or more since in answer to my first knowledge of the affair. - - On reading your letter I sent an orderly to Col Russells Qrs (28th USCT) to learn of the whereabouts of the 14th U.S. Infty. Col Russell is a capt in the 11th Infty. He informs me that the 14th is near Gen Warrens Qrs 5th Corps. I had never thought of Lt Warren until your suggestion at the instance of Sister Annie. I shall take the first opportunity to learn of the whereabouts of the Lt & send for him or call on him as opportunity offers.

I am happy to inform you that I am making my way along in this Brigade. I am acquainted with all the "field officers" and I don't think I am too modest or carry too high a head. I only know I am not afraid to "pit myself" against any of them either in a knowledge of the military art or that other necessary quality of the officer & soldier "courage." This I could write to none other but yourself. I will make a further remark for your ear alone which I would not repeat. It seems to me that the colored troops has been made an asylum for some of the "poorest sticks" in the service. We have one capt in the regular service, who is a col commanding a Brigade, another capt in the regular service who is now a Lt Col comdg a rgt. They were both appointed from civil life in 1861. One of them has never "smelt powder" & yet the lives of thousands are dependent upon the orders he shall give. I did have a profound admiration for the "regulars," but I must confess I have been sadly shocked in that respect for the past two months. I have sometimes felt in the last three years that the "Tribune" was too bitter in its attacks upon a certain class of regular army officers. Recently I have felt that their apparently caustic articles were drawn entirely too mild. Still what noble examples we have of a military education being the prelude to a splendid career as in the cases of Grant Rosecrans Sherman Sheridan and others. I have spoken of these things because I could not shut my eyes to them. I hope you will not be anxious for me in this respect, & I think you had better not allude to it. Just consider I am pretty generally cool & collected & shall know what to do under certain contingencies. In this connexion I heartily wish that Gen White could take command of our Brigade. I would then be all right, & in a situation for procuring little favors that otherwise I would not have. Gen Ferrero Division Commander is a very pleasant man. I expect to send you his photograph soon as he gets one for me.

You allude again to Wetherbee. My former letters will tell you all about that matter. I asked Major Foster to telegraph him. I have not yet heard from Washington. I shall be thankful when this vexed matter about commissions is ended. It has been a great "wear & tear" upon the patience but we shall get over it soon I hope. In this connection I will say that I have been remustered to date from the 7th of April, which takes me back to the time of my being mustered out as Captain. This is part justice but I could not have succeeded in doing better. You will see that I have not gone to sleep and let that matter remain fixed. I will thus save at least $100 & two thirds of a month in rank but it will not make me out rank the two Lt Cols of the Brigade who are my ranking officers. I was determined not to be a citizen without pay & working for the Govt & fund myself if I could help it. - - I wish you could step into my "arbor" just now. I am located in the edge of a yellow pine and oak grove fronting on an oat field through which runs the Norfolk R.R. to the south east. Our Brigade is camped in line diagonally across the road. "Head

Quarters" (my own) are as I said in the edge of the grove fronting towards the west. My bed is made up by one of my "shades" and on it for one thing is a nice babys quilt, one of the old style made up of stars & squares just such as one as I helped sew when "I was a boy." It is not quite long enough at one end, but then it is capital to lay under me. I presume it is one of unused articles that some excited rebel left when he started off post haste for Richmond. If I do not wear it out & ever come home I will bring it home as part of the "spolia opima" [sic] of this civil war. I must again give thanks for secesh ice & our Sanitary Commission, mixing the two together & they are not bad in using the small things. I don't wish you & Jessie to expend too much sympathy on us poor mortals in "these Hd Qrs" & thereabouts for the past week. After tonight you may let it flow again. Pardon dearest if I speak lightly, but we have had so many good things that I wonder how I have been so fortunate. When I think of the privations I have undergone and those I may have yet to undergo I feel like being jubilant over the present. Sometimes I think a soldiers life has a tendency to make him adopt the latin motto for his guide, "Dum vivimus, vivamus," and certainly "in campaign" so far as subsistence and sanitary supplies goes I generally act upon the principle use the best you have and enjoy it while you may whenever you can get them.

Lt Gale & Chapman take hold of their work like good soldiers. They are willing and ready at all times for any duty. It is a pleasure to associate with these three young Chicago officers. I have also an acting Adjutant for my rgt who belongs to the 31st. His name is Downing. The rest of my officers are good men but they have not the education or refinement as the officers I have just mentioned. It is a pleasure to have a battalion drill with these officers. I always explain the evolution to be performed and then go through it with animation. Gale & Chapman although "green" in infantry catch everything instantly and I have no doubt they will be a couple of the best officers in my command. It is a source of great pleasure (all the more so by contrast) to think as I gallop over the field & around my battalion as it goes through its evolutions molding it to my own will without any clap trap, noise, or loud swearing, how I could have done the very same in the 88th and how much better I know I stand in the eyes of my men. If I ever feel a pride and desire to excel, relishing the excitement it is when I mount "Dick" for Battalion Drill. I well know dearest I could do the very same in "Brigade Evolutions." The day may not be distant when that event shall again happen. There! Do you not laugh at this afternoon's scribbling? I cannot do otherwise this P.m. I just wish I could give you a downright old fashioned hug to use a Saxon phrase & so sisters Em & Annie too with lots of kisses for Mason. I intend to write to father Mason soon. And also to Annie. I think if nothing occurs I shall try & see Burnside tomorrow & also Lt Vernon if he is with the regiment. I send you the card of Mrs Capt Brockway. His brother is Postmaster at Belvidere. Should you visit Chicago you might call on her if the opportunity offers. She is a niece of Myrick who used to keep a public house near Cottage Grove. Now dearest I shall not promise to write you another letter tomorrow. We shall see however what occurs. Have you read "Lucile" by Owen Meredith?[1] If not get it & read it. I have really enjoyed it the past week. "With heart to heart & soul to soul" I am yours ever

John

1 *Lucile*, whose glamorous and romantic heroine saves a marriage and goes on to devote her life to caring for the sick, was a popular novel in verse.

Tuesday July 12, 1864. Camp along Norfolk R.R. about 4 miles from Petersburg

Dearest,

Yours of 6th inst. has just been received for which I am much obliged. Since I last wrote you we have changed positions twice. I wrote you last Saturday. On that evening immediately after dark we had orders to be ready to march at a moments notice. At twelve midnight our Division left its position and marched west & north westerly across & west of the Norfolk R.R. to the same position we occupied on the first of July when I wrote you near the house of a Mr Williams just west of the Jerusalem Plank Road. We staid there Sunday & yesterday, our Brigade in the mean time being on fatigue duty building a huge fort towards the right of our then location about a couple of miles. Last night we were ordered to march at 3 A.m. this morning which was delayed until daylight, when we marched to this point being about 4 miles from town & two miles nearer Petersburg than where we were located on Saturday last. The Brigade is now working on a new redoubt and I am in a little copse of bushes resting & writing to you. After having written the above I have given you all the news that I can tell you in this army, save that long ere this reaches you the 6th corps which has been with us since we have been here will be much nearer you & Washington. We have just got news of the movement of the enemy north. If it shall rouse the north to more patriotic action instead of gaseous noise I shall be glad. We hear this morning of the defeat of Wallace & his retreat to Baltimore. The 6th must be there by this time & I hope the rebs there will be "gobbled." I do not feel like letting go our hold on this place even if Baltimore, Harrisburg or Philadelphia should be burned. Let the North do its duty now and we shall soon have no more occasion to fight battles.

I have been looking anxiously for the reports of casualties since the battle at Kenesaw Mountain as I had seen in the reports that Newtons Division of Howards Corps had been engaged & were repulsed. I felt that there would be casualties in the 88th & somehow was not disappointed at the news you send me of the death of Col Chandler. He was a brave officer, and after a year of service began to treat me as though he appreciated me. This advances Major Smith one step. I do not think any major can be appointed otherwise Captain Holden would be the man. This is not the place to speak of the merits of my comrade in arms. I would do him justice as I would mete out the same to Col Sherman. I cannot however in all my associations with my former brother officers forget the months of cool neglect and jealous fear with which some of them seemed to regard me. I have too much good sense to cherish up unpleasant feelings against a single one of them. It was but nature perhaps. My position here dearest only brings out in the strongest contrast some of the harder features of my captains life. Even the hard lot itself was not so hard to bear as false statements that went home, one of which Sherman put into Williams ear himself which caused him (Will) to write me so long a letter about my conduct, duties, &c. If I was ever provoked it was then. No one ever can appreciate my situation then.

Too proud and independent to bow to the [illegible] set against me I could but show them all how little I cared for any of their sordid envy. Out of it all came good, for it stimulated me to be a good soldier if nothing else could.

Here I have nothing of the sort to contend with, all the officers treat me with the greatest consideration and while I do not let down the least in my "military" I am much happier, much better situated in every respect, and to tell you the truth do not have to do half the hard work as formerly. I do not rejoice over having so much lighter work except that it may be of some satisfaction to you. Still the anxiety that my rgt shall do well is of course in greater proportion than when I was a co. commander. Still how much greater is the ease with which I can manage a Battalion than I could my company formerly. Lt Col Chandler deserved the unqualified admiration of his friends for his cool determined bravery. He saved the rgt at Chickamauga. I admired his conduct when I joined it after I had been driven from the picket line of which I have said so much to you. If I could speak to the young men of Chicago over his dead body I would dwell upon his good deeds. It is no time to cherish unpleasant feelings when men of such coolness and daring as he possessed are stricken down in the midst of their usefulness.

2d Lt T. M. Conant appointed in place of Strickler joined me for duty on Sunday eve. He was formerly in the 57th Ill. James Lang of Chicago & Samuel Hoard are his uncles. He gives promise of being a good officer.

I am still amused at your ignorance of the commissions' whereabouts. It seems to me the next letter I get will tell me that you have recd mine of July 1 explaining the matter. Lt Conant reports that while he was at Camp Casey an Aid-De-Camp of the Gen told him that Major Brown was ordered to Camp Casey with what men he had. Conant thought Brown would reach there before he left, but a detacht. for the 23d was ordered to join the rgt & Lt Conant was ordered to accompany it & so I got another officer all of which is satisfactory to me. Conant also came down on the boat with Quarter Master Galt but could not recollect the Division to which he belonged. If you know his location give it me in your next as it might take a year to find it here. I do not desire to show any anxiety to find him out yet I would like to know where he is. - - I saw a Captain in the regulars yesterday comdg the 11th. He says he knows Lt Vernon but that he is not with his regt now, nor does he know where he is. I have not succeeded in paying a visit to the 5th Corps yet, nor of calling on Burnside, I got ready on yesterday washed up, brushed up, put on a "collar" and rode up to Brigade Qrs to see to a matter of business & get permission to go. While there, orders came for the Brigade to get ready to move at a moments notice. So my visit was necessarily postponed. I shall go the earliest opportunity however. Do not have any fear about that. Perhaps I shall learn to be <u>too</u> bold some of these days what do you think of it?

In this connection I was pleased with your allusion to Wards 2 ½ hour speech. It was flattering to my vanity. It must have been a "<u>bore</u>." Twenty minutes or one half hour is long enough for 4th July speeches. He could not have kept a corporals guard of <u>soldiers</u> together during his speech. - - I think a great deal of <u>your</u> proceedings at <u>Oakside</u> and anticipate a great deal of pleasure in reading your poetry when I get it. I hope you will send it as I have heretofore requested. Perhaps I will <u>match</u> you with one more stanza or so although I shall not succeed as well as you. I can <u>see</u> you all seated by the fountain just as if I were present with you. - - I am extremely glad to hear of Masons health being so very good. I have been anxious about him for several weeks. - - We left White House June 7th on the eve of the 6th we had a shower there. It was the last until we got a slight sprinkling last night not enough to lay the dust however. You can imagine what dust there must be with the constant movement of an army such as this. - - My health continues good and I trust it will remain so with the blessing of Heaven. - - The chief difficulty I have met with this far is in getting some wagons for "transportation," which I hope to remedy soon. Capt Aiken has not been well for a week but is improving. He is too great an eater when he has anything good. You see I keep an eye on all my "military family." I have not seen a great deal of Dr Mackay as he is at Division hospital & not with the rgt. I hope you have received his photograph. I hope this letter will not be seized by the "Johnny rebs" on its way through Pennsylvania. Hoping to get another letter from you tomorrow & with love to all friends I am dearest your affectionate husband

John A Bross

Camp in the field
Norfolk RR
July 13th 1864

Dearest,

I write you a note about the commissions. I told you in a former letter that I wrote to Horace White to send Brown's to Quincy, Daggetts to William, & Hatch's to Springfield. To day I received the package with them all including Browns, Daggetts & Hatch's. It seems by a note I recd from Washington that White was sick. He got another man to get the package from Willards & he sent it unopened to me, not complying with my request to forward Browns to him. I have mailed Browns & Daggetts to Gen Casey with a request that if they have not reported to him to send them forward as directed. I write you all this in order that you may understand the facts. There seems to be a fatality about these commissions. I trust the end of the difficulty is near at hand.

I received a letter from William of July 7th in which he speaks of receiving one from me of June 29th. I presume you will have received one from me of the same date & of the 1st July. I am making myself as comfortable as possible. I wrote you yesterday & hope you will receive it soon. I wish I could write all I wanted to.

Major Forsyth called again to day. We have no rain yet. Our men are working like beavers on the fort I spoke of yesterday. I have not much to write now except to say that I am anxious to get some letters from you. July 6th is the last one I recd from you. Love to all my friends in & around Sterling. With much love I am your affect. husband

John A Bross

In Camp Norfolk R.R.
Tuesday July 19, 1864

My Beloved Wife!

Yours of July 10 reached me last night. Also letters from father & mother Mason of the 13th & one from lra of the 15th. I suppose Brown arrived in

Washington just in time for the scare.[1] I have heard nothing of him. I presume he is yet in Washington and will remain there until transportation can be provided. I am very well. I came off duty yesterday as Division field off. of the day. Calling at Gen Ferrero's Hd Qrs as etiquette requires, he received me more cordially then usual. He soon mentioned that Gen White had called on him the day before and had spoken about me. Of course I did not ask what was said but presume it must have been favorable. Gen White & he were with Burnside in East Tennessee both commanding Divisions. You see I am "getting on" in making acquaintances and showing that I deserve the good opinion of those who are in positions of influence. I am unable to fawn and blow my own penny whistle. Still I am pleased when my superiors take some interest in me. It is a greater satisfaction however to know and feel in my own heart that I am capable of occupying a higher position than at present. I am conscious of it, shall do what I can honorably to attain it, nothing more. - - I wish in my heart I could see you and tell you all I know of things here. I keep my "eyes & ears open" and a prudent tongue. Sometime when the opportunity offers there will be changes in the Brigade. If the result does not help me any it will perhaps be beneficial for the service. - - Brown will probably stay here when he reports. I shall apply to the Secy. of War to be filled up. I am done spending money for recruiting. Govt claims to appoint all the officers even if we spend our money in enlisting the men. I have no doubt if friends in Ill will help me I shall get the four companies. I have already written to Will to make application for me. I shall do it myself through the regular military channel. William can back it up especially if the state authorities and members of congress will aid me. Gen Burnside cannot do anything for me unless I should apply for a position on his staff which I do not wish to do. Everything you know goes by rank. I was assigned to this Division there being no other and was put in this Brigade which in fact is the best that could be done for me. Two officers rank me & I rank two. By the by Lt Col Ross of the 31st is a pleasant gentleman. Remember the similarity of our names if there should be an engagement. We laugh at each other frequently about orderlies making mistakes in bringing orders to the wrong one & perhaps one of us may wake up some fine morning & find ourselves famous and our names spelt wrong in the papers. Gen Ferrero gave me yesterday three photographs which I shall dispose of to you Annie & Jessie. I will not send them in this letter as I wish to get his autograph on them. It is raining very hard to day having the appearance of a settled storm & so I am keeping close in my "fly." You should see however how comfortably I can live under it. The rain is most grateful to the parched earth and it will be a grand thing in supplying the army with water. If it rains ten days I shall not regret it greatly.

I shall take that trip with you someday down the St. Lawrence, possibly when I wear the "star." Give my compliments to Sarah Stebbins, she might have plenty of work about City Point. I have written to William about Merrills matter asking him to settle according to his best judgment. You [were] in error about Wilson's contrabands. He had over a thousand but the rebels recaptured them all & all his artillery. He got pretty roundly thrashed though he did immense damage to the rail roads. In my allusion to taking command of a Brigade with Col Campbell I was jesting with them about receiving some honorable <u>scratches</u> which would thus put me in command that was all. Now don't consider me "wicked" for doing it.

I am glad Mr Erskine preached one patriotic sermon. I do <u>not</u> fare "all this time" on soldiers rations. I have been fortunate enough to get a few things from the Sanitary Commission. This army is better fed than I ever knew the Army of the Cumberland to be. All kinds of vegetables are issued daily or at least some kinds daily. The Sanitary Com are engaged in this work. They also issue to officers & so in this way I am living quite well. Anything you can reasonably do for the "Sanitary" is well laid out. It will help some poor officer or soldier. I am grateful for what has already fallen to me. It has made me feel very well during the burning heats of the past month. We have now been exactly one month before Petersburg. I feel that I have been doing my duty here while it is the greatest sacrifice I can make to be away from you. I think after you have made all the visits you wish about Sterling, if you can as well as not I would prefer you go to William's. I would like to have you be there in October & November & then be in Springfield with him during the session of the legislature. This of course if he is elected which I hope is beyond doubt. I am sorry you did not take Mason & go with father & mother. What is the expense compared with your health & Mason's. If I am ever located so that I can send for you I would have you fly to see me. I wrote you letters on the 3d, 7th, & 9th, also the 12th. Some of them I am fearful may have been burned by the rebs as on that western mail that was burned. I hope however they will reach you. I shall close this letter now with the intention of writing to father & mother Mason. I hope Mason will be better when I hear from you again. Love to all.

Ever yours
John

1 15,000 rebel soldiers under Jubal Early marched unopposed down the Shenandoah Valley towards Washington, appearing in front of the Washington defenses 5 miles north of the White House on July 11th. Grant quickly sent the 6th Corps to a panicked Washington. The Union forces arrived just in time to man the fortifications, and Early returned to Virginia without serious injury from pursuing Union forces.

Note: The following undated letter appears to belong here.

In camp Norfolk R.R.

Dearest

Yours containing the poetry reached me last night. I had been expecting it for several days and was sure I would get it last night. I was not disappointed. Of course I am proud of it. I have been reading it to Fred Chapman. I think you have exhausted the subject and shall not try to match you with any stanzas of my own. I am not going to write you a long letter to day as I am just going to Battalion drill & it will take about all the afternoon. The mail now leaves about sundown. We are still in the same camp as when last I wrote you. Last night I received five letters for Major Brown and some letters for the enlisted men of "Co F" but no Major Brown. I presume they will keep him at Washington for some time. I have no news to tell you at all. For a couple of days we have been resting from fatigue duty. Since the rain the weather has been delightful. I am in good health as usual. I wrote to father & mother Mason on yesterday. Your statement of money matters was certainly explicit. You know dearest I do not desire you to make them for well I know that you are better in taking care of the "dimes" than I am. I really wish you could be at the sea side with father & mother. Mother spoke of Mason being there & I really wish you could spend some time with them. I will do as you request about sending all my money to the Deacon to liquidate that note, in the mean time I am as economical as possible. I spend nothing & will have only my mess account to settle for when l am paid. I hope to send enough to pay William up but I may not accomplish it. As yet we know nothing about our being paid that is as to how soon. - - Capts Aiken Gale & Chapman are well. They are superior in every respect to the great majority of those who have "passed" boards. They are not quite so well posted in "military" but they will become so in due time. They are about the only ones I care to associate with in my own rgt. although there are some others who are worthy. I say this of course in confidence. You say well of Dr Mackay. He has not been with the rgt much, he having been at the Division Hospital which is a couple of miles from us for nearly a month. He is considered the best operating surgeon in the Division. He is a "genuine Scot." By the by I wish you to get "Lucile" by Owen Meredith and read it. I was much interested in it having obtained it from Col Thomas comdg our Brigade. I would send you Gen Ferrero's picture with this but he has gone to Washington for a few days & I wish to obtain his autograph. I presume this scribbling will be not very satisfactory.

Kisses for Mason & one at least for Em & Annie & with love for yourself

I am always yours

John

In camp near Petersburg Va

July 23d 1864

My Beloved Wife

Your letter of 17th inst. came duly to hand last night enclosing five dollars which was very acceptable indeed. We left the Norfolk R.R. yesterday where we had been in camp on the extreme left and are now near Corps Head Qrs on the same ground occupied by us on the 19th of June last when we first arrived in front of Petersburg. We have had a great deal said of our Division being about to make a "charge." Some of the Quid nuncs would have it that last night we were "going in" sure but I slept all night without being disturbed at all. I enclose you Capt Aikens picture also one of Gen Ferrero. He has been relieved of his command by Gen Burnside, the senate having failed to confirm his nomination. He has gone to Washington to look after it. I wanted to get his signature but now not knowing when he will return if ever I forward it to you. I think he is a good looking man. He has always treated me with a great deal of cordiality. Brig Gen White succeeds him which is just "good enough for me." He took command on yesterday. I have not seen him since he took command. Will try & call on him to day. Burnside can not help me towards recruiting my regt except to endorse my application to have four companies assigned to my regt. There are two Cols now in the Brigade, Col Thomas (19th) who commands the Brigade & Col Campbell (23^{d}) whose regt has been filled since I came into the field. Both of these regts were recruited in Maryland. I am anxious as you are to fill up my regt. It does seem that the more a man works for the Govt & spends his means the less it cares for him. I could have had one of these same regts I presume if I had consented to "figure" at Washington. I did not & am only a "Lt Col" in consequence. Still however you must not think me dissatisfied with my position. I have the consciousness of working for my position & do feel that I have earned it, and what is more can fill it. I am now in good relations at Corps & Division H^{d}Qrs and I presume I shall always be. - - Now a word of "home" matters. I am glad you give me details of Mason. I am rather amused as well as pleased that he has "temper." He would not be a Bross if he hadn't. I know that you will exhibit all the firmness necessary to direct that temper in the proper channel. As to Zed accomplishing what you say, I am not alarmed. I am pleased that Mason thinks so much of him. My Dr says that fresh air, the country, & exercise will be a preventive of Leucogthermia. Naturally I think of that whenever you write of his being ill. Tell him that papa will write him a letter some of these days, when he is not very busy. As to your being with Em & Zed this summer, I have only to thank them for their kindness, which was natural to them. I agree with you about Em's resemblance to mother in her disposition.

I am somewhat surprised about Jessie's opinion of Major Forsyth. I should think less of him myself if he has been guilty of treating Miss D in the manner you speak of. It only confirms my opinion that he is very ambitious. I can appreciate his desire not to be "entangled" with any one until he is out of the service or the war closes. He has his eye on one star at least and perhaps two, and my word for it if he lives and the war lasts he will deserve promotion if he does not get it. I speak thus of his soldierly qualities because I know his real determination to excel, and I honor it.

John Warmsley is with Major Brown who has not yet reported here. Neither do I know where he is as Aiken rec^d a letter from Naylor from Washington of July 17th saying that Brown had not yet got there. I presume it was occasioned however by the breaking of bridges north of Washington. I hope you will preserve all the notices of my rgt. in the papers. I do not see them and they will be extremely interesting when I have an opportunity to read them. I am obliged for the stamps you sent me. Say to Annie that I am keeping a letter in my mind for her which will be drawn out some time. And now with much love to all my friends and with one more good bye I am ever your affectionate husband

John

EPILOGUE

After John's death, **Belle** and Mason continued to live with her parents in Sterling, Illinois. Belle evidently took Mason to Europe, as there are photographs of them taken in Dresden, Germany, in the early 1870s, judging from the age of Mason in the photographs; perhaps they were traveling with her parents. She moved back to Chicago, probably still living with her parents, in 1874. In 1875 she was married for a second time to Azariah T. Galt, a Chicago attorney who was the older brother of her sister Emily's husband, Zadok (Zad) Galt, and who, like Zad and John, had come to Chicago from Pennsylvania. Azariah was the lawyer for William Bross and his family, so Belle must have known him through that connection as well. After their marriage, Belle and Azariah lived in Chicago and had one child, a son, Mason's 16-year-younger half-brother, Arthur T. Galt, born in 1876. Belle had remained a member of Third Presbyterian Church but moved her membership to Fourth Presbyterian Church, closer to their residence, probably when her parents moved their membership to that church in 1887. She continued her interest in writing and was an early member of The Fortnightly of Chicago, a ladies' literary and intellectual club formed by a few leading Chicago women, including Jessie Bross, in 1873 while the city was being rebuilt after the fire. She was probably the author of the *Memorial* about John, and there is a printed memorial article about a deceased member of the Fortnightly written and read by Belle in 1902. There is also a 17-page printed lecture she wrote and delivered entitled "The Case of the Indian," which states that it was read before the Missionary Society of the Fourth Presbyterian Church, probably in 1905; it discusses the difficult situation of American Indians, pushed from their land and culture by the white man, reflecting the same progressive concern for an oppressed minority group that she and John had earlier directed to enslaved blacks. On September 22, 1909, the *Tribune* reported:

> Mrs. Isabelle A. Galt, wife of Attorney Azariah T. Galt, was found dead in bed in her residence, 1432 Dearborn avenue, yesterday morning. She was in apparently good health when she retired Monday evening. When Mr. Galt failed to arouse her yesterday morning he called a physician, who, after an examination, said Mrs. Galt had died during the night of heart disease.

Belle was 72 years old when she died; her husband Azariah died in 1922 at the age of 87. They are buried at Graceland, another cemetery in Chicago.

Belle, later in life; by this time she was married to her second husband, Azariah T. Galt (Private Collection).

Belle's parents, **Nelson** and **Desire Mason**, remained in Sterling for several years after the war, Belle and Mason living with them. Nelson served for three terms as Mayor of Sterling, in 1860, 1862, and 1865, one two-year term and two one-year terms.[1] He gave the city of Sterling the land now known as Central Park.[2] In 1874 the Masons moved back to Chicago, Belle and Mason probably with them, and remained there for the rest of their lives. They rejoined Third Presbyterian Church but moved to Fourth Presbyterian Church in 1887, probably because at about that time they all moved to a new residential neighborhood a mile or so further north, in the area now called the "Gold Coast," where they were closer to Fourth Presbyterian, which had been founded in 1871. Nelson died on May 7, 1893, at his house at 530 Dearborn Avenue (now 1404 North Dearborn Street) a few doors down from the house of Belle and Azariah, who lived at 550 Dearborn Avenue (which became 1432 North Dearborn Street when the Chicago streets were renumbered in 1909). Desire then moved in with the Galts and died at their house on January 26, 1897. A Sterling obituary said, "She was of a gentle and quiet disposition, and by all who knew her she was sincerely loved."[3] They are buried at Rose Hill Cemetery, not far from the memorial to their son-in-law John.

Mason grew up in Chicago with his mother, attending the Babcock Preparatory School and graduating from the Union College of Law in the class of 1884. At the memorial meeting of the Chicago Bar for his father held in August 1864, attorney George Herbert, in his speech introducing the resolutions, had said, "I too at the age of four years, was the orphan son; my mother, now eighty years of age, was the widowed mother. I can well remember these long years of orphanage, in which there was no father's hand between me and the cold charities of an unfeeling world." The psychological world of a boy growing up as an only child with no father, under the guidance of a strong-minded and wealthy mother, must have been very different from that of his father, who grew up in a rural setting as one of 11 children in a family that encouraged education but was not wealthy. Mason was well known in Chicago society but would not have been described as professionally ambitious. An obituary article about him in the *Chicago Legal News* said:

Mason, probably aged eight (Private Collection).

> Mr. Bross was a member of the Chicago Bar Association, of the University, Saddle and Cycle, Onwentsia and Chicago Literary Clubs. He was of a quiet, unostentatious manner and temperament, genial and a universal favorite among his friends and acquaintances. Never known as very active in the actual practice of law at the bar, he was yet known by a few appreciative clients as a good lawyer, sound and conservative in his views, and safe in counsel and advice.[4]

He was an outdoorsman who liked sailing, camping, and exploring. He had a keen interest in botany; some of the specimens he collected are now in the collection of the Field Museum of Natural History in Chicago.

Mason did not marry until 1906, at the age of 46, when he wed another

Mason Bross as an adult (Private Collection).

Isabel, this the sixteen-year-younger daughter of George E. Adams, a prominent Chicago lawyer who had moved to Chicago as a boy from Keene, New Hampshire, and was the first Harvard graduate from Chicago. Adams served as a Republican member of Congress from Chicago from 1883 to 1891, was a founder of The Chicago Symphony Orchestra and of the Art Institute of Chicago, and served as the first Overseer of Harvard College from west of the Alleghenies. Isabel's mother, Adele Foster Adams, was the daughter of Dr. John H. Foster, who had with his wife, Nancy, moved to Chicago from New Hampshire in the late 1830s, taking over several lots of Chicago real estate that had been purchased by his deceased brother Amos, an army officer who had served at Fort Dearborn in 1829. Both Mason and Isabel were, therefore, the descendants of ambitious, able, and well-educated Chicago settlers from the Mid-Atlantic and New England states who had contributed significantly to the commercial and cultural growth of the city. Isabel was active in Chicago cultural institutions, including the Chicago Symphony Orchestra and the Civic Opera of Chicago, being herself an accomplished pianist. On November 20, 1906, the *Tribune* reported:

> Mrs. A.T. Galt's reception yesterday afternoon for her son and his bride, Mr. and Mrs. Mason Bross, was given in the Fortnightly rooms, Fine Arts building, instead of at the Galt residence in Dearborn Avenue. It was one of the largest affairs yet given this season, the guests numbering several hundred. Mrs. Bross' mother, Mrs. George E. Adams, assisted in receiving, and there were a number of young matrons and maids assisting in entertaining.

Mason died of heart failure at the age of 57 on October 27, 1917, in Cambridge, Ohio, while he and his wife were returning from a motor trip to West Virginia. Like his father, Mason left a young son and only child, John Adams Bross, born in Chicago in 1911, to be brought up by a strong-willed mother named Isabel who made sure he had a good education and took him on trips to Europe. John graduated from Harvard College, like his grandfather Adams, and from Harvard Law School, lived for most of his life in Washington, D.C., and died in 1990 after a distinguished career in the Central Intelligence Agency, having served in its predecessor agency, the OSS, during the Second World War. He was married twice, first to Priscilla Prince from Boston and then to Joanne Bass Field, also her second marriage; Joanne, too, was a descendant of Dr. Foster through her grandmother, but her father, Robert Bass, had returned to New Hampshire and become its prominent progressive Republican governor. John was the father of three children by his first marriage—Wendy Bross Frazier, John Adams Bross, Jr.,

Mason Bross with his son, John (Private Collection).

and Justine Bross Yildiz, the last two of whom are the editors of this volume—and one child by his second marriage, Dr. Peter Foster Bross.

William Bross was elected Lieutenant Governor of Illinois in late 1864 and was always proud of the role he played in making Illinois the first state in the Union to ratify the Thirteenth Amendment to the United States Constitution, which abolished slavery in the United States, signing the ratification as the presiding officer of the Illinois Senate.[5] He was almost equally proud of his role in securing the repeal of the notorious "black laws" of Illinois, which had made it a crime for blacks to live in the state. In 1865, together with Schuyler Colfax and others, he made a celebrated trip to California to observe the landscape and the progress of civilization in the West. At that time, in Colorado, Mount Bross was named for him. He was in Chicago when most of the city was destroyed by fire on October 10, 1871, and his account of the conflagration, published in his *History of Chicago*, is among the most vivid. He played a leading role in the rebuilding of the city: while the ashes of the ruined city were still warm he was on a train to the East Coast, where he made a persuasive address to the relief committee of the New York Chamber of Commerce and other speeches, successfully assuring East Coast investors of the essentially sound physical and social foundations and bright future of Chicago and encouraging the investments, which were forthcoming and were vital for rebuilding the city. He continued to live in Chicago, active in cultural events and serving as president of the Chicago Tribune Company until his death at the age of 77. His *History of Chicago*, published in 1876, is a collection of earlier articles on commercial and financial statistics rather than a conventional history; it also includes personal reminiscences of life in the city after 1848 and his account of the Chicago Fire. In 1889, the year before he died, he wrote a letter to the *Tribune* that charmingly illustrates his love of nature, his pride in the city, and his unflagging belief in the power of the press and of commanding rhetoric to promote the public well-being. The letter praises the commissioners of Lincoln Park for planting water lilies:

> They could not have done a more acceptable thing for the pleasure of their visitors. They are fragrant and beautiful plants. Several years ago there was a large patch of that beautiful plant—the Egyptian lotus—growing on the Grand Calumet. ... As it is a native and has a fine, showy flower, it is hoped the Park Commissioners will take measures to transplant it to their waters. It would be a great calamity to have it die out.

William died on January 27, 1890. His attorney Azariah Galt, now married

Moses Bross with his son William, his granddaughter Jessie Bross Lloyd, and his great-grandson William Bross Lloyd (Chicago History Museum).

to his brother John's widow, Belle, was named the trustee of his estate, and Mason, his nephew, was named as the successor trustee. His beloved wife, Jane, lived on until 1908, surviving William by 18 years and dying at the age of 93. They are buried at Rose Hill Cemetery.

William's only surviving child, **Jessie**, often mentioned in John's letters, married Henry Demarest Lloyd in 1873 at the age of 29, by which time she had established herself as a person of consequence in Chicago, being one of the two first "lady members" of the Chicago Historical Society (now the

Chicago History Museum) in 1870 and one of the charter members of The Fortnightly in 1873. Later she and her well-known muckraking journalist husband became identified with the civic life and philanthropy of the Chicago suburb of Winnetka, but they remained active in charitable and cultural affairs as well as progressive politics in Chicago. When Jessie died in 1904, Lydia Ward, another charter member of The Fortnightly, said of her, "She was like a great, beautiful jewel, splendidly scintillating, catching light from every direction, only to give it back to all of us in passing."[6] At a memorial gathering, Jane Addams said that Jessie was the only person she ever knew who led an entirely sheltered life of wealth but cared for the downtrodden as if they were her own.[7] The Lloyds' oldest child, their son William Bross Lloyd, was perhaps the original model for a "limousine liberal," being a Harvard-educated lawyer who continued and extended the family tradition of progressive reform politics by becoming one of the original members of the Communist Labor Party in 1919 and was prosecuted for conspiring to overthrow the United States government in a celebrated Chicago trial in 1920, the defense attorney being Clarence Darrow. He and his co-defendants were convicted but after an appeal, his sentence was commuted.

Moses and **Jane Bross**, the parents of John and William and their nine surviving brothers and sisters, moved to Morris, Illinois, in 1863, all but one of their children having gone west. They may have chosen to live in Morris because Jane's youngest sister, Mrs. Thomas Alford, was living there. William bought five lots and built a house for their use near the center of Morris, which was situated on the Illinois and Michigan Canal that was so important for the economic growth of Chicago, as chronicled by William in the *Democratic Press* and subsequently in the *Tribune*. When Jane died on February 24, 1868, a memorial article in the *Tribune* described her as "a mother, contriving in her labors to make home the chief attraction to her children and to rear them to lives of usefulness." Moses continued to live in Morris for another 14 years, dying there on August 19, 1882. His obituary in the *Tribune*, probably written by William, recounted his early life in the Delaware Valley and his founding, with two others, of the Presbyterian Church in Milford:

> Deacon Bross was a very genial, pleasant gentleman, with a kind, cheerful word for all by whom he was surrounded, always a close student of the Bible, a constant, careful reader of religious and political history, an enthusiastic, unswerving patriot, giving the life of his son, Col. John, one of the bravest and noblest of men, to his country, and always an earnest supporter of whatever could promote the intellectual and the religious welfare of his fellow-men; through his long life he commanded the confidence and the respect of all who knew him.[8]

On December 8, 1866, the *Morris Herald* reported on a family Thanksgiving gathering at the home of Deacon Moses Bross, who "came to Morris three and a half years ago from the Delaware Valley, in Pike County, Pa., to live here the remaining years of his well-spent life," giving an account of all twelve of the Bross children, the five who were present and the seven who were not. The five who were there included William; Josiah, by now living at Oglesby, Illinois; Edward, working at the Northwestern Railway; Ira, working at the Rock Island Railway; and Jennie, "the only remaining sister, one of the efficient teachers of our graded school." This was Jane Ann, the ninth child, who lived in Morris with her parents, working as a teacher; she died in Chicago in 1912 at the age of 82. The article reports that another of their three daughters had died in infancy and the third had died in 1856; this was Margaret, the older sister to whom John had written about his failed romance, who had married Chauncy Thomas of Shohola, Pennsylvania, and lived there until her death at the age of 35. The article reported that two of the other five sons had been there three years before: Charles, now the manager of a business at Madison, Wisconsin, and John, who would have visited his parents in late 1863, when he returned to Illinois to raise the new regiment. Of the remaining three sons, the article reports that Phineas had died in 1857, and "one is a physician in California and the other is engaged in mining operations in Colorado." The physician would have been Peter, who died in Auburn, California, in 1892, and the one engaged in mining operations would have been Stephen. By 1866, therefore, the entire surviving Bross family had moved west.

The story of **Stephen Decatur Bross**, the family's second child, retold in an obituary article about William, illustrates one relatively unsung facet of the settlement of the American West. Stephen, two years younger than William, had also attended Williams College, doubtless at considerable financial sacrifice to the family and in hopes that he too would become a Presbyterian minister, but unlike William, he did not graduate. At some point he went to New York City and was never again heard of by his family. When William toured the mining district of Colorado during his 1865 voyage to the West, several people told him he closely resembled a mining engineer whose name, he was surprised to hear, was Stephen Decatur, known as "the Commodore." Later William returned to Colorado to investigate and found his way to the mountain ranch where Decatur lived with his Native American wife. He was not home, so William waited. When the man approached, William immediately recognized him and said, "Stephen, my brother, my long-lost brother!" Decatur stood still for a minute and then gruffly said, "Who are you? I never saw you before in my life." In spite of scars on his body that William recognized, Stephen insisted that his name was Decatur and that he had never heard the name Bross before. Stephen had left New Jersey around 1840, abandoning a wife and two children, and arrived in Nebraska in 1841, founding the town of Decatur in 1856. In 1859 he moved to Colorado, leaving behind another wife and child. He became prominent in Colorado, representing Summit County in the territorial legislature. In 1876 he represented Colorado at the Centennial Exposition in Philadelphia and visited William for some days in Chicago, but he never acknowledged a relationship and never talked about anything before 1859, when he moved to Colorado. The western verdict was "domestic troubles," for "in those days many a man out west 'knew how it was himself.' " Stephen died in 1888, two years before William.[9]

The 1866 Thanksgiving article from the *Morris Herald*, in naming the two sons who had been there three years before, mentioned Charles:

> [A]nd the other was the gallant Colonel John A. Bross who fell bravely fighting at the head of the only colored regiment raised in this state, at Petersburg, Va., on the 30th of July, 1864. He was one of the purest and the best of men as well as a lawyer of superior ability, for many years in

Chicago. His name is forever identified with one of the most causeless and bloody disasters of the war; but no man ever fought more bravely or died more nobly for his country than Colonel John A. Bross.

NOTES

1. Charles Bent, ed., *History of Whiteside County, Illinois* (Clinton, Iowa: L. P. Allen, 1877), 410.
2. *Sterling Standard* (Sterling, Ill: Sterling Standard Print) May 11, 1893.
3. Sterling Evening Gazette (Sterling, Ill: C., H.L., & M.D. John) January 27, 1897.
4. *Chicago Legal News*, Vol.10, Chicago: Chicago Legal News Co. (August 2, 1917 to July 25, 1918): 117.
5. Charles A. Yount, *William Bross 1813–1890* (Lake Forest, Ill: Lake Forest College), 1940, 9.
6. Muriel Beadle, *The Fortnightly of Chicago; The City and its Women: 1873–1973* (Chicago: University Printing, 1973), 14.
7. Heavner, "A Wayside Winnetka Woman," The Winnetka Current 4–24–2013.
8. *Chicago Tribune* (Chicago: Chicago Press and Tribune) August 21, 1882.
9. Newspaper article by J.H. Beadle (1840–1897), possibly printed in Milford, PA, January 1890, copy in *William Bross Papers*, Chicago History Museum, Box 1, folder: Letters 1889.

ACKNOWLEDGMENTS

We have many people to thank. Indeed, we have come to see that a book such as this is really a team effort, the authors being as much referees and compilers as independent writers; such a book is actually the product of many hands and scholarly minds.

Without being able to mention every person whose help has been gratefully received, we especially wish to thank the following:

David Spadafora, President and Librarian of the Newberry Library in Chicago, who offered friendly and helpful advice on available experts and research resources. Also at the Newberry Library: Martha Briggs, Lloyd Lewis Curator of Modern Manuscripts; John Powell, Digital Imaging Services Manager; and Patrick Morris, Map Cataloguer and Reference, for their generous donation of time and attention to the research needs of an amateur scholar.

Susan M. Bielstein, Executive Editor for Art, Architecture, and Ancient Studies at the University of Chicago Press, who kindly read the manuscript of Part One and suggested our approach for framing its narrative. Also, Timothy Mennel, Executive Editor for American History and Regional Studies at the University of Chicago Press, who gave us useful advice on reference material and on publication alternatives.

James M. McPherson, George Henry Davis '86 Professor Emeritus of United States History at Princeton University, who reviewed the letters in 1996 and more recently gave us advice and made introductions for us as we considered various possibilities for publication. More generally, we wish to thank him for his entire career, which has provided a definitive narrative of the Civil War and has made clear for all of us what the war meant, and still means, for America.

Tom Lingner, Customer Service Manager at Imaging Services of Harvard Library, his colleague Yuhua Li, and their helpful staff at Widener Library, Harvard University. They accomplished with patience and skill the considerable task of scanning all the letters and envelopes in chronological order, without which it would have been extremely difficult to produce correct transcriptions.

William Tyre, Executuve Director and Curator, Glessner House Museum, and a director of Friends of Historic Second Church in Chicago, for valuable assistance over several years from his deep knowledge of Chicago family histories and the general history of Chicago during the period covered by this volume.

Gary T. Johnson, Edgar D. and Deborah R. Janotta President, Chicago History Museum, for general support of this project. Leslie Martin, Research Librarian at the Research Center of the Chicago History Museum, and other members of the staff at the Center, always friendly, helpful, and willing to provide expert assistance in accessing the Museum's rich resources, including original documents, rare books, and items from their digital archives.

Paul W. Grasmehr, Reference Coordinator at the Pritzker Military Museum and Library, for his thorough and helpful guidance. Also, Theresa A. R. Embrey, Chief Librarian, and Kat Latham, Director of Collections at the Library, for their valuable advice.

Terence Buckaloo, Director & Curator, the Sterling-Rock Falls Historical Society, for friendly assistance in making his wide knowledge of the history of Sterling available to us for details of Belle's early life and family history.

James M. Cornelius, Curator, the Abraham Lincoln Presidential Library, for assistance with research there and for advice on other sources. Also, Debbie S. Hamm, Library Associate in the Manuscripts section of the library.

Ann M. Shumard, Senior Curator of Photographs of the Smithsonian's National Portrait Gallery, for her kind assistance with photographs, especially those from the remarkable exhibition "Bound for Freedom's Light: African Americans and the Civil War," which she organized.

Lori Strelecki, Director, Pike County Historical Society at the Columns, in Milford, Pennsylvania, for her skillful assistance with research on Milford during the period of John's childhood.

The helpful staff of the Presbyterian Historical Society in Philadelphia, who furnished records of the Third Presbyterian Church, John and Belle's church in Chicago.

Professor Dorothy L. Drinkard, Director of Africana Studies at East Tennessee State University, distinguished scholar, friend, and author of *Illinois Freedom Fighters: A Civil War Saga of the 29th Infantry, United States Colored Troops* (1998), an invaluable source of information about John's regiment. Dorothy attended the installation of a memorial plaque for John at Lake Forest College in April 2003 and on that occasion gave a lecture in the college chapel about the soldiers and officers of the 29th Infantry, USCT, which was enthusiastically received.

Noah Andre Trudeau, who kindly gave permission for the use of a map published in his outstanding book, *Like Men of War* (1998).

Matthew S. Witkovsky, Ellen Sandor Chair and Curator, Department of Photography, Art Institute of Chicago, for his interest and support; James Iska, Assistant Conservator, Department of Photography, and Anna Kaspar, Associate, who were able to furnish us with high resolution copies of the framed, and only, photograph we have of John.

Arthur Miller, Archivist, now retired, of Lake Forest College, for his kind assistance with research material on the William Bross family in the Lake Forest College library.

Celia S. Hilliard, social historian, author, and friend, for her sound advice as we began our research.

Thomas E. Campbell, distinguished Chicago attorney, scholar, friend, and author of *Fighting Slavery in Chicago*, a groundbreaking study of Chicago's own leadership in the abolition movement.

Cleaver White, genealogist and family friend, who resides on the Hudson River in Cold Spring, New York, and has done extensive research on the New Netherlands ancestors of John. She guided us to Milford, Pennsylvania, where John spent his childhood.

Kathleen Heyworth, author of *Private Lewis Martin and African-American Civil War Soldiers in Springfield, Illinois* (2015), who gave us a copy of her interesting book, and from whom we learned of the existence of the John Bross Post 578 of the Grand Army of the Republic, in Springfield,

Illinois. She also supplied us with the photographs of Lewis Martin and William Freeman.

Dorothy Ramm, Volunteer Research Assistant at the Chicago History Museum and a family friend, who is herself a second-generation Chicagoan and who supplied information on, among other things, the renumbering of Chicago streets in the early twentieth century.

Katharine Galt Allen, along with the authors of this volume a great-granddaughter of Belle, who kindly assisted us in contacting members of the Galt family for information about family papers relating to Belle.

Joan Marie Hammarstedt, adopted daughter of Arthur Galt, Jr., who graciously provided us with background information about the distinguished history of Belle's Galt descendants through her second son, Arthur Galt.

Diane Gonzalez, scholar, neighbor, and friend, who gave us information about Lt. Frederick A. Chapman.

Lola Moonfrog and her cousin John B. Lloyd, Jr., friends of ours and descendants of William Bross, who led us to resources for research on William and the heritage of his distinguished descendants.

Professor Linda Landis Andrews at the University of Illinois at Chicago, who put us in touch with several faculty members and staff of the University and generally gave us valuable advice and support in the preparation of this volume.

Nick McCormick, PhD, for his assistance in scanning the original transcripts of the letters and for his advice and work in proofreading the transcripts.

Margaux Brown, a PhD student at the University of Illinois at Chicago, for her painstaking work in organizing and compiling endnotes for Part One.

Libby M. Goldrick, a recent graduate of the University of Illinois at Chicago, for valuable assistance with proofreading the transcripts and researching publishable photographs and maps.

Alice York, John's stepdaughter, whose skill in editing and proofreading is invisibly reflected throughout the text of this book. She also played a lead role in the acquisition of, and securing permissions for, the maps, photographs, and illustrations included in this volume.

Our brother, Dr. Peter F. Bross, who furnished the military books that John studied in 1862 and who owns John's sword, and our sister, Wendy Frazier.

Our children, who have given ongoing support for this project, including Justine's children, Leyla F. Yildiz, who suggested the title of this volume, Ayse Yildiz Wilson, and Timur T. Yildiz; John's children, Suzette Bross Bulley, Jonathan Mason Bross, Lisette J. Bross, and Medora Smith Bross; our sister Wendy B. Frazier's children, Wendy A. Frazier, Gillian T. Frazier, and Caleb R. M. Frazier, who has supplied relevant family documents; and Judy Carmack Bross's children, George E. C. York, Charlotte York Matthews, and Alice Mercer York.

Our grandchildren, whose lives we hope will be inspired by a Civil War ancestor who gave his life to defend the American Republic, a beacon of hope to the world: Callum and Duncan, the children of Ayse Yildiz Wilson; Lucy (whose request for a class talk about John started the ball rolling for Part One of this volume), Daphne, and Allan, the children of Suzette Bross Bulley; Parker (who helped with the identification of maps) and Avery (who found several photographs for the project), the children of Jonathan Bross; Addison Louise Caccioli, the child of Lisette Bross; Eloise and Hilary, the children of Medora Bross Geary; Alex and Mason, the children of Caleb Frazier: Oliver and Henry, the children of George York; and Colin and Clara, the children of Charlotte York Matthews.

Last of all, but most important of all, John's wife, Judy Carmack Bross, journalist, author, and magazine editor, without whose constant support and advice this book would not have been written.

BIBLIOGRAPHY

Adelman, Garry E. "Civil War Military Organization". *Essential Civil War Curriculum.* last modified 2014, http://www.essentialcivilwarcurriculum.com/assets/ files/pdf/ECWCTOPICOrganizationEssay.pdf.

Aldrich, C. Knight. *Quest for a Star; The Civil War Letters and Diaries of Colonel Francis T. Sherman for the 88th Illinois.* Univ. of Tennessee Press, 1999.

Altschuler, Glenn C., and Stuart M. Blumin. *Rude Republic: Americans and Their Politics in the Nineteenth Century.* Princeton University Press, 2001.

Andreas, A. T. *History of Chicago from the Earliest Period to the Present Time.* 2 Vols. Chicago: A. T. Andreas, 1884.

Arnold, James. *Chickamauga 1863; the River of Death.* Westport, Connecticut: Praeger, 1992.

Battles and Leaders of the Civil War. Edited by Robert Underwood Johnson and Clarence Clough Buel. Vol. 4. New York: The Century Company, 1884.

Beadle, Muriel. *The Fortnightly of Chicago; The City and its Women: 1873–1973.* Chicago: University Printing, 1973.

Bent, Charles, ed., *History of Whiteside County, Illinois*, Clinton, Iowa: L. P. Allen, 1877.

Biographical Sketches of the Leading Men of Chicago; Written by the Best Talent of the Northwest. Chicago: Wilson & St. Clair, 1868.

Brands, H.W. *The Man Who Saved the Union.* New York: Doubleday, 2012.

Bross, John A. "Historical Sketch". *Danenhower's Chicago City Directory for 1851.* Chicago: W.W. Danenhower 1851.

Bross, William. *Legend of the Delaware: An Historical Sketch of Tom Quick. To which is Added the Winfield Family*. Chicago, 1893. Nabu Public Domain Reprints.

____, *History of Chicago; Historical and Commercial Statistics, Sketches, Facts and Figures, Republished from the "Daily Democratic Press."; What I Remember of Early Chicago; A Lecture, Delivered in McCormick's Hall, January 23, 1876*. Chicago: Jansen, McClurg & Co., 1876.

____, *William Bross Papers*. Chicago History Museum, Chicago.

Burlingame, Michael. *Abraham Lincoln, A Life*. 2 Vols. Baltimore: Johns Hopkins University Press, 2008.

Burley, Augustus Harris. "The Cairo Expedition." *Reminiscences of Chicago During the Civil War*. Chicago: Lakeside Press, 1914.

Campbell, Tom. *Fighting Slavery in Chicago; Abolitionists, the Law of Slavery, and Lincoln*. Chicago: Ampersand, Inc., 2009.

Cannan, John. *The Crater; Burnside's Assault on the Confederate Trenches July 30, 1864*. Cambridge: Da Cao Press, 2002.

Castro, Selena. "the mountains! the mountains!: Slavery in Williamstown, MA." Undergraduate Paper for Dr. Dorothy Wang, Williams College, Fall 2015.

Chernow, Ron. *Grant*. New York: Penguin Press, 2017.

____. *Washington: A Life*. New York: Penguin, 2010.

Chicago Tribune, Chicago: Chicago Daily Tribune.

Chicago City Directories:

Cooke, D.B. & Co. *D. B. Cooke & Co.'s Chicago City Directory for the Year 1860–61*. Chicago: D. B. Cooke & Co., 1860.

Danenhower's Chicago City Directory, for 1851; Containing an Alphabetical List of the Mechanics and Business Men with their several places of Residence; Also, Brief Notice of the Religious, Literary and Benevolent Associations of the City, Military, Fire Department, Etc., Etc., Etc., Etc. Chicago: W.W. Danenhower, 1851.

D. B. Cooke & Co.'s City Directory for the Year 1858. Chicago: D. B. Cooke & Co, 1858.

Directory of the City of Chicago Illinois for 1843. Compiled by Robert Fergus. Chicago: Fergus Printing Company, 1896.

Fergus, Robert. *Fergus' Directory of City of Chicago, 1839*. Chicago: Fergus Print. Co., 1839.

Gager, John. *Gager's Chicago City Directory for the Year Ending June 1st, 1857*. Compiled by John Gager. Chicago: J. Gager, 1856.

General Directory and Business Advertiser of the City of Chicago for the Year 1844: Together With a Historical Sketch and Statistical Account to the Present Time by J.W. Norris. Chicago: Ellis & Fergus Printers, Saloon Buildings, 1844.

Hall & Co.'s Chicago City Directory, and Business Advertiser: For 1854–55. Chicago: R. Fergus, 1854.

Hall, Edward. *The Chicago City Directory and Business Advertiser, 1855–6*. Chicago: R. Fergus, 1855.

Halpin & Bailey's Chicago City Directory for the Year 1862–63. Compiled by T.M. Halpin. Chicago: Halpin & Bailey, 1862.

Halpin & Bailey's Chicago City Directory for the Year 1863–64. Compiled by T.M. Halpin. Chicago: Halpin & Bailey, 1863.

Hatheway, O.P., and J.H. Taylor. *Chicago City Directory and Annual Advertiser for 1849–50*. Chicago: Jas. J. Langdon, 1849.

Kennedy & Co., R.V. *D. B. Cooke & Co.'s City Directory for the Year 1859–1860*. Chicago: D. B. Cooke, 1859.

Norris, J.W. & Gardiner. *Norris' Chicago Directory 1846 & 7*. Chicago: Geer & Wilson, 1846.

_____. *Norris' Chicago Directory for 1843*. Chicago: Norris & Taylor, 1843.

_____. *Norris' Chicago Directory for 1847 & 8*. Chicago: J.H. Kedzie, 1847.

_____. *Norris' Chicago Directory for 1848 & 9*. Chicago: Norris & Taylor, 1848.

Smith & DuMoulin's Chicago City Directory for the Year Ending May 1, 1860. Chicago: Smith & DuMoulin, 1859.

Udall & Hopkins Chicago City Directory For 1852 & 1853: Comprising an Alphabetical Directory of the City, Census of the Various Societies, Associations, and Institutions, Military and Fire Departments, Etc. Chicago: Udall & Hopkins, 1852.

Commager, Henry Steele, ed. *Documents of American History*. New York: Appleton-Century-Crofts, Inc., 1958.

Cornish, Dudley Taylor. *The Sable Arm: Black Troops in the Union Army, 1861–1865*. Lawrence, Kansas: University Press of Kansas, 1987.

Cozzens, Peter. *This Terrible Sound; The Battle of Chickamauga*. Chicago: University of Illinois Press, 1994.

Craighill, William Price. *The Army Officer's Pocket Companion: Principally Designed for Staff Officers in the Field*. New York: D. Van Nostrand, 1862.

Cronon, William. *Nature's Metropolis; Chicago and the Great West*. New York: W. W. Norton & Company, 1991.

Cullum, George Washington. *Systems of Military Bridges in Use by the United States Army: Those Adopted by the Great European Powers, and Such as are Employed in British India. With Directions for the Preservation, Destruction, and Re-establishment of Bridges*. New York: D. Van Nostrand, 1863.

Democratic Press. Chicago: Scripps & Bross, 1852–1858.

Dickey, Christopher. *Our Man in Charleston: Britain's Secret Agent in the Civil War South*. New York: Broadway Books, 2015.

Dreyfus, Benjamin W. *The City Transformed; Railroads and Their Influence on the Growth of Chicago in the 1850s*. 1995. http://www.hcs.harvard.edu/~dreyfus/history.html

Drinkard, Dorothy L. *Illinois Freedom Fighters: A Civil War Saga of the 29th Infantry, United States Colored Troops*. New York: Simon & Schuster Custom Publishing, 1998.

Duane, Capt. J.C.. *Manual for Engineer Troops*. New York: D. Van Nostrand, 1862.

Duncan, Russell, ed. *Blue-Eyed Child of Fortune; The Civil War letters of Colonel Robert Gould Shaw*. Athens: University of Georgia Press, 1992.

Duparcq, Edouard La Barre and Nicolas Édouard Delabarre-Duparcq. *Elements of Military Art and History: Comprising the History and Tactics of the Separate Arms; the Combination of the Arms; and the Minor Operations of War*. Translated by Brig. Gen. George W. Cullum, Chief of Staff of the General-in-Chief of the Armies of the United States. New York: D. Van Nostrand, 1863.

Egerton, Douglas R. *Thunder at the Gates: The Black Civil War Regiments That Redeemed America*. New York: Basic Books, 2016.

First Presbyterian Church, Milford, Pennsylvania; One Hundred and Fiftieth Anniversary, Commemorative Booklet. First Presbyterian Church. Milford, PA: 1975.

Gale, Edwin O. *Reminiscences of Early Chicago and Vicinity*. Chicago: Fleming H. Revell Company, 1902.

Glatthaar, Joseph T. *Forged in Battle: The Civil War Alliance of Black Soldiers and White Officers*. Baton Rouge: Louisiana State University Press, 1990.

Goodheart, Adam. *1861; The Civil War Awakening*. New York: Alfred A. Knopf, 2011.

Grossman, James R, Ann Durkin Keating, and Janice L. Reiff. *The Encyclopedia of Chicago*. Chicago: University of Chicago Press, 2004.

Grant, Ulysses S. *The Complete Personal Memoirs of Ulysses S. Grant*. Seven Treasures Publications, 2009.

Grinspan, Jon. " "Young Men for War": The Wide Awakes and Lincoln's 1860 Presidential Campaign." *The Journal of American History* 96, no. 2 (2009): 357–378.

Guelzo, Allen C. *Fateful Lightning; A New History of the the Civil War & Reconstruction*. New York: Oxford University Press, 2012.

Hafendorfer, Kenneth A. *Perryville: Battle for Kentucky*. Louisville, Kentucky: K H Press, 1991.

Halleck, Henry Wager. *Elements of Military Art and Science; Or, Course of Instruction in Strategy, Fortification, Tactics of Battles, &c., Embracing the Duties of Staff, Infantry, Cavalry, Artillery, and Engineers*. New York: D. Appleton & Company, 1859.

Heyworth, Kathleen. *Private Lewis Martin and African-American Civil War Soldiers in Springfield, Illinois*. Springfield, IL: Bluelily Press, 2015.

Hicken, Victor. *Illinois in the Civil War*. Chicago: University of Illinois Press, 1991.

Holzer, Harold. *Lincoln and the Power of the Press*. New York: Simon & Schuster, 2014.

____. *Lincoln, President Elect; Abraham Lincoln and the Great Secession Winter*. New York: Simon & Schuster, 2009.

In Memoriam; Jessie Bross Lloyd, September 27, 1844 – December 29, 1904. Chicago: Press of the H. G. Adair Printing Co.

Irving, Washington. *A History of New York*. New York: Penguin Books, 2014.

Kennedy, Frances H. *The Civil War Battlefield Guide*. Boston: Houghton Mifflin Company, 1990.

Kinsley, Philip. *The Chicago Tribune; Its First Hundred Years*. 2 Vols. New York: Alfred A. Knopf, 1943.

Kirkland, Joseph and Caroline Kirkland. *The Story of Chicago*. 2 Vols. Chicago: Dibble Publishing Company, 1894.

Lincoln, Abraham, *Speeches and Writings 1859–1865*, New York: The Library of America 1980.

Lindquist, Charles A. "The Origin and Development of the United States Commissioner System." *The American Journal of Legal History* 14, no. 1 (1970): 1–16.

Lloyd, Jessie Bross. *Jessie Bross Lloyd Papers*. Chicago History Museum, Chicago.

Mason, Nelson. Obituary: "A Pioneer Gone". *Sterling Gazette*. Sterling, Illinois: May 10, 1892.

"Mason, Nelson". *History of Ryegate, Vermont Biographical Sketches and Family Records*. The Electric Scotland Classified Directory. *electricscotland.com*. n.p. n.d. 14 June 2017.

Mayer, Harold M. and Richard C. Wade. *Chicago: Growth of a Metropolis*. Chicago: University of Chicago Press, 1969.

McClellan, George Brinton. *Manual of Bayonet Exercise: Prepared for the Use of the Army of the United States*. Philadelphia: JB Lippincott, 1862.

McDonough, James Lee. *Stones River, Bloody Winter in Tennessee*. Knoxville: University of Tennessee Press, 1980.

McKinney, Megan. *The Magnificent Medills; America's Royal Family of Journalism During a Century of Turbulent Splendor*. New York: Harper, 2011.

McPherson, James M. *Abraham Lincoln and the Second American Revolution*. New York: Oxford University Press, 1990.

_____. *Abraham Lincoln*. New York: Oxford University Press, 2009.
_____. *The Negro's Civil War: How American Blacks Felt and Acted During the War for the Union*. New York: Vintage Books, 1993.
_____. *Battle Cry of Freedom*. New York: Oxford University Press, 1988.
_____. *For Cause and Comrades: Why Men Fought in the Civil War*. New York: Oxford University Press, 1997.
_____. *This Mighty Scourge: Perspectives on the Civil War*. New York: Oxford University Press, 2007.
_____. *Tried by War: Abraham Lincoln as Commander in Chief*. New York: Penguin Books, 2008.
_____. *The War that Forged a Nation: Why the Civil War Still Matters*. New York: Oxford University Press, 2015.
Memorial of Colonel John A. Bross, Twenty-Ninth U. S. Colored Troops, By A Friend. Chicago: Tribune Book and Job Office, 1865.
Miller, Edward A. *The Black Civil War Soldiers of Illinois; The Story of the Twenty-ninth U. S. Colored Infantry*. Columbia, South Carolina: University of South Carolina Press, 1998.
Moses, John and Joseph Kirkland. *History of Chicago, Illinois*. Chicago and New York: Munsell & Co., 1895.
Palmer, William Pitt. "POEM," delivered to the Anti-Slavery Society of Williams College, 1828.
Political Debates Between Hon. Abraham Lincoln and Hon. Stephen A. Douglas, in the Celebrated Campaign of 1858, in Illinois. Columbus: Follett, Foster and Company, 1860.
Powell, David A. and David A. Friedrichs. *The Maps of Chickamauga; An Atlas of the Chickamauga Campaign, Including the Tullahoma Operations, June 22-September 23, 1863*. California: Savas Beatie, 2009.
Proceedings of the Republican National Convention Held At Chicago, May 16, 17, and 18, 1860. Republican Party National Convention. Albany: Weed, Parson, & Co. Printers, 1860.
Report of the Adjutant General of the State of Illinois, Volume V; Containing Reports for the Years 1861–1866. Springfield, IL: H. W. Rokker, State Printer and Binder, 1886.

Revised Regulations for the Army of the United States, 1861, By authority of the War Department. Philadelphia: J. B. Lippincott & Co., 1862.

Rosecrans, Major Gen. W. S., U. S. A. *Report on the Battle of Murfreesboro, Tenn*. Washington: Government Printing Office, 1863.

Schmutz, John F. *The Battle of the Crater; A Complete History*. Jefferson, NC: McFarland & Company, Inc., 2009.

Shorto, Russell. *The Island at the Center of the World: The Epic Story of Dutch Manhattan and the Forgotten Colony That Shaped America*. New York: Vintage Books, 2005

Slotkin, Richard. *No Quarter; The Battle of the Crater, 1864*. New York: Random House, 2009.

South, Fred S. *It Never Recoiled: A History of the Seventy-fifth Illinois Volunteer Infantry*. Prophetstown, Illinois, 1995.

The American Heritage Picture History of The Civil War. New York: American Heritage Publishing Co., Inc., 1960.

"The Battle of Stones River: A Hard Earned Victory for Lincoln by Jim Lewis, Ranger, Stones River National Battlefield," *Blue & Gray Magazine*, 28, no. 6 (2012): 14–15.

The Second Presbyterian Church of Chicago, June 1st, 1842 to June 1st, 1892. Chicago: Knight, Leonard & Co., 1892.

Thomas, Benjamin P. *Abraham Lincoln; A Biography*. New York: Alfred A. Knopf, 1952.

Trudeau, Noah Andre. *Like Men of War: Black Troops in the Civil War*. Boston: Little, Brown and Company, 1998.

_____. *The Last Citadel; Petersburg June 1864 - April 1865*. El Dorado Hills, CA: Savas Beatie LLC, 2014.

Tucker, Glenn. *Chickamauga; Bloody Battle in the West*. Dayton, Ohio: Morningside Bookshop, 1984.

U. S. Congress. Joint Committee on the Conduct of the War. *Report of the Joint Committee on the Conduct of the War on the Attack on Petersburg, on the 30th Day of July, 1864*. Washington: Government Print Office, 1865.

Waugh, Joan. *U. S. Grant; American Hero, American Myth*. Chapel Hill: University of North Carolina Press, 2009.

Wayland, Francis. *The Elements of Moral Science*. University of Michigan, The Michigan Historical Reprint Series, Boston: Gould and Lincoln, 1856.

White, William Lee. *Bushwacking on a Grand Scale; The Battle of Chickamauga, September 18–20. 1863*. California: Savas Beatie LLC, 2013.

Wills, Brian Steel. *George Henry Thomas; As True As Steel*. University Press of Kansas, 2012.

Wood, Gordon S. *Empire of Liberty: A History of the Early Republic, 1789–1815*. Oxford University Press, 2009.

Worthington, Sarah. "Retrospective." *Evening Gazette*. Sterling, Illinois: December 2, 1893. Sterling-Rock Falls Historical Society, 2006.

Yount, Charles A. *William Bross 1813–1890*. Lake Forest, Ill: Lake Forest College, 1940.

INDEX

Note: Page numbers in *italics* refer to illustrations.

Facing page: Last page of letter dated July 23, 1864, his last letter to Belle.

the war lasts he will deserve
a promotion if he does not
get it. I speak thus of his
soldierly qualities because
I know his real determination
to excel. and I honor it

John Wormley is with Major
Brown who has not yet reported
here Neither do I know where
he is as Aiken rec'd a letter from
Naylor from Rocky Mount N.C. 17th
saying that Brown had not yet
got there, I presume it was
occasioned however by the breaking
of bridges north of Washington. I
hope you will preserve all the
notices of my Regt in the papers, I
do not see them and they will
be extremely interesting when
I have an opportunity to read
them. I am obliged for the stamps you
sent me. say to Annie that I am
keeping a letter in my mind for her
which will be drawn out some
time. And now with much love
to all my friends and with one
more good bye I am Ever

Your affectionate husband

John

Made in the USA
Lexington, KY
27 September 2018